OVERCOMING TRUMPISM

OVERCOMING TRUMPISM

HOW TO SAVE AMERICAN DEMOCRACY

Larry N. Gerston

BLOOMSBURY ACADEMIC
NEW YORK • LONDON • OXFORD • NEW DELHI • SYDNEY

BLOOMSBURY ACADEMIC

Bloomsbury Publishing Inc, 1385 Broadway, New York, NY 10018, USA
Bloomsbury Publishing Plc, 50 Bedford Square, London, WC1B 3DP, UK
Bloomsbury Publishing Ireland, 29 Earlsfort Terrace, Dublin 2, D02 AY28, Ireland

BLOOMSBURY, BLOOMSBURY ACADEMIC and the Diana logo are trademarks of
Bloomsbury Publishing Plc

First published in the United States of America 2026

Copyright © Larry N. Gerston, 2026

For legal purposes the Acknowledgments on p. viii constitute an extension of this
copyright page.

Cover design: Eleanor Rose
Cover image © DOMINIC GWINN /getty Images

All rights reserved. No part of this publication may be: i) reproduced or transmitted in any form, electronic or mechanical, including photocopying, recording or by means of any information storage or retrieval system without prior permission in writing from the publishers; or ii) used or reproduced in any way for the training, development or operation of artificial intelligence (AI) technologies, including generative AI technologies. The rights holders expressly reserve this publication from the text and data mining exception as per Article 4(3) of the Digital Single Market Directive (EU) 2019/790.

Bloomsbury Publishing Inc does not have any control over, or responsibility for, any third-party websites referred to or in this book. All internet addresses given in this book were correct at the time of going to press. The author and publisher regret any inconvenience caused if addresses have changed or sites have ceased to exist, but can accept no responsibility for any such changes.

Library of Congress Cataloging-in-Publication Data

ISBN: HB: 979-8-7651-2818-3
PB: 979-8-7651-2817-6
ePDF: 979-8-7651-2819-0
eBook: 979-8-7651-2820-6

Typeset by Newgen KnowledgeWorks Pvt. Ltd., Chennai, India
Printed and bound in the United States of America

For product safety related questions contact productsafety@bloomsbury.com.

To find out more about our authors and books visit www.bloomsbury.com
and sign up for our newsletters.

*For those fighting to protect American democracy.
We must press on; we have no choice.*

CONTENTS

Acknowledgments	viii
Introduction	1
1. Understanding American Democracy	5
2. The Rise of Trumpism	27
3. The Explosion of Bigotry	55
4. Disrespect, Destruction, and Disenfranchisement	77
5. Undermined Institutions	105
6. Weakened Sociopolitical Fabric	131
7. Destabilizing Public Education	153
8. 2024: Donald Trump Returns to the Presidency	177
9. Trumpism 2.0	205
10. Restoring the Power of the Vote in a Democracy	245
11. Assuring Media Integrity	275
12. Educating for Democracy	307
13. Reinforcing Democracy for the People and by the People	333
About the Author	357
Index	359

ACKNOWLEDGMENTS

In the movies, just after the names of the leading actors appear, a list follows of valued supporting artists who round out the cast. And so it is with books and similar enterprises.

Over the period when this book was researched, written, and prepared for publication, several individuals contributed to the process. At San Jose State University, Professor Lawrence Quill was generous with his time and guidance. Ted McConnell, highly regarded authority on civic engagement, weighed in on the invaluable connection between that topic and democracy. John Blanchard, Bruce Galler, and Barbara Richley read and gave their thoughts on several chapters. Lee Gerston read every page of the manuscript and offered editorial advice that was of great value.

At Bloomsbury, Senior Editor Katherine de Chant shepherded the preliminary review process and acceptance of the project. She was succeeded by Lilith Dorko who guided the effort through the final steps, assisted by Saville Bloxham. Others who contributed to the development and production of the project include Dharani Padmajothi, Project Manager and Sugirtha Loren, Copy Editor.

All of this valuable support notwithstanding, I alone am responsible for the project's preparation and final product.

INTRODUCTION

In the English language, an antonym is a word whose meaning is the opposite of another. Bearing that definition in mind, we begin this discussion with a brief example: Trumpism is an antonym for democracy. Is that too harsh of a comparison? Not if you understand the meanings of these two words.

Trumpism is an elaboration of all matters and political behaviors related to Donald Trump. That's because America's forty-fifth and forty-seventh president has spawned a political movement of sorts. More than a candidate and office holder, Trump has put forth a loose set of ideas intended for governing the United States and its people. Those who believe in Trump's thoughts are known as Trumpists, while Trump's overall approach to politics is referred to as Trumpism. Many Trumpists display alienation, feel left behind, harbor anger toward immigrants for disrupting their lives, fear that the country has been hijacked by the "deep state," and want someone who will rid us of these problems now! Donald Trump has presented himself as that person, and his followers are loyal to the core.

Rather than embodying America's most noble values, Trumpism treads on some of the country's darkest themes. His public personality reveals intolerance, bigotry, anger, revenge, and contempt for anyone who challenges what he sees as unquestioned authority. As president, he and his followers have rejiggered many of this country's treasured institutions and norms in such a way so as to render them virtually impotent. In short, Trump seeks to "govern" the United States on his terms without challenge. "Direct" might be a better word.

All of this has produced the Great American Tragedy. If he isn't one already, Trump has embraced the tools and objectives of an authoritarian, a person who demands strict obedience, has the tools to enforce it, and is unhesitating in punishing anyone who dares to interfere with his rule. His followers have worked hard to assure Trump's reorganization of American politics and institutions. They stand not only ready to serve Trump but also to fight for him, as we witnessed on January 6, 2021, with the violent insurrection against the US Capitol. But how could this malevolent behavior come to be in what was not so long ago described as one of the world's greatest democracies?

Overcoming Trumpism

The answer begins with the regrettable disclosure that too many Americans have gone soft on democracy largely because they don't even understand it. Oh, they hear about the term and throw out the word "democracy" in a sentence now and again as if to show others the extent to which they are attuned to society's political issues. But too much of the time such discussion is puffery and little more. Most Americans couldn't define democracy if their lives depended on it. Oh, they'll show up to vote now and again, but that's only the most obvious part of the ingenious framework that has sustained America for 250 years.

To be sure, the larger portion of American society doesn't dismiss democracy per se; rather, it views democracy as a given, almost a self-regulating political process that seems to roll along on its own, or it has until now. Most Americans see the nation's political system as a teeter-totter of sorts where things balance out over time. This view is wrong, very wrong. Inattentiveness to the concept, norms, and workings of democracy in some ways may even be more harmful to democracy's future than those determined to end it.

Against a rather blasé approach to democracy are millions of Trumpists ready to replace historic principles and values with a repressive form of governance that controls our lives while erasing pluralism, diversity, and tolerance. These disrupters are unhappy with many of democracy's attributes. They rage against what they see as unconstrained deliberations over controversial issues, the watering down of our Western Christian White "heritage," and policies all too concerned with attention to equality, due process, freewheeling speech, and several forms of freedom they see as impediments to the right life.

Trumpists want a more simple, less disruptive society free from people of color and non-Christians whose existence dilutes the "true" American creed. They have no room for exchange of ideas. These true believers will do whatever it takes to assure success of their vision from deporting those who don't fit to forcing conformity among those who remain. Most of all, Trumpists count on Americans being complacent, rather than incensed about anti-democrats who espouse authoritarian management of American society. Sadly, for much of the past decade, too many Americans have done just that.

There will be some readers who view this discussion as overly dramatic and not worth the time to even consider the argument. Surely there are built-in constitutional checks to prevent an authoritarian takeover of the United States, they would say. Trumpism works from within by way of

Introduction

legitimate elections that put would-be authoritarians in power. That's what happened in 2016 when the voters put Trump into the presidency. Once in power, Trump nearly succeeded in illegally keeping power with his support of the January 6, 2021, insurrection, despite losing reelection in 2020. Only a handful of people in key positions of authority somehow prevented him from unconstitutionally remaining in office. Yet, it turns out that Trump was just warming up.

Having learned from his early years in office, Trump's second act makes his first term look like amateurism, and perhaps it was comparatively. Now, accompanied by hundreds of zealous fellow autocrats who have been placed into key Executive Branch positions, Trump and his allies are moving at lightning speed to finish the job. Between incredibly cooperative Republican majorities in both chambers of the US Congress and a US Supreme Court majority all too willing to cede vast amounts of power to the presidency, Donald Trump is quickly remaking American government and society.

In addition to overtaking the other two constitutionally designated centers of power, Trump has also seized control of the Republican Party, intimidated much of the Press, browbeaten major elements of the private sector, terrified election officials, taken major strides to rid the country of "undesirables," and attempted to remake American public education. Turning away from traditional concerns about norms and ethics, he has obliterated the line between right and wrong. For Trump, making money off the presidency is just another perk of the job that he has enjoyed immensely.

Many observers now look at Trump's capture of American institutions and wonder how there will possibly be a fair presidential election in 2028. Some wonder if there even will be any election at all.

There are some Trump devotees who support him for reasons of less government, reduced taxes, and his dedication to turning over some federal policies to the states. These are legitimate debates about the role of government in modern American society. But the merits of these debateworthy issues are subsumed into the larger Trumpist framework where Trumpism is more than what government should do; it's about perverting the reins of government in such a way so as to deny democracy in American society. Under Trumpism, basic American freedoms now hang by a thread.

Overcoming Trumpism: How to Save American Democracy may be one of the last warnings to keep our democracy from permanent destruction. To that end, the following pages call out Trumpism for what it is—a bareknuckled political attempt to strip the United States of democracy and replace it with authoritarian rule while tens of millions of Americans freeze in reaction much like the deer blinded by headlights. The discussion is replete with evidence of Trumpist efforts to divide American society and wield brute power as we fight each other.

But there is hope in the form of actions we can take to preserve our democracy, and they are included in the book. As Americans struggle to keep our democratic footing on an increasingly dangerous political landscape, we must remember one fact: Trumpism didn't happen overnight; it has been building for years, largely aided by the neglect and distraction of otherwise well-intentioned Americans.

Given our present circumstances, we must realize that defeating Trumpism will not come with the positive result from a single election, or even the passing of Donald Trump or other Trumpist leaders. Our vulnerabilities have grown over at least two generations, and it may take as long or more to reverse them. If we resolve now, we just may be able to preserve American democracy for our children and grandchildren. They may not know it, but their futures are in our hands. We have to seize it before we lose the opportunity altogether.

CHAPTER 1
UNDERSTANDING AMERICAN DEMOCRACY

Have you ever tried to have a serious conversation with someone about democracy? Chances are that if you have, most people would rather change the subject to just about anything else. One reason might be because so few people actually understand the term "democracy." Another might be because some people equate democracy with election outcomes, such as democracy exists when my candidate wins and yours loses. Others are just plain sketchy about the meaning and value of the concept. In fact, it turns out that a sizable chunk of American society knows little about what democracy is and how American democracy works.

Here's some data on the aspects of the topic. A recent national poll found that only 39 percent of Americans could name all three branches of American government; even more revealing, 22 percent couldn't name any![1] At the same time, recent national data show that most Americans overwhelmingly support core democratic values such as protecting the right to vote (91 percent), no one is above the law (89 percent), and each of us should have an equal chance to be successful (86 percent).[2]

Positive values notwithstanding, most Americans seem to doubt everyone else. Nearly six out of ten have little faith in the political wisdom of the American public.[3] Moreover, Americans aren't happy about our democracy. A 2024 national Gallup poll found that only 28 percent of Americans (38 percent of Democrats and 17 percent of Republicans) are satisfied about the state of democracy in the United States—the lowest percentage since Gallup began asking the question in 1984.[4] While slightly more than three-fourths of Americans favor democracy over authoritarianism, 21 percent either don't care or would actually prefer a dictatorship.[5] To that we add the results from a 2024 poll, where 41 percent agreed with the statement that "having a strong leader who does not have to bother with parliament or elections" is a good or fairly good way to run a country.[6]

What's going on here?

These data tell us a lot about America—a nation where substantial numbers barely know how democracy works, have little trust in their fellow citizens, wouldn't be particularly fazed by a dictatorship, but if so, might almost be relieved from having to worry about the "Big Picture." This is the troublesome condition of our American democracy, which until recently was viewed around the world as the role model of freedoms found in few other countries.[7]

The politically adrift condition of our existence reveals something compelling, namely that America is hardly on solid ground when it comes to defending democracy. After all, how can we support a political belief system if we can't explain it? Sadly, our ignorance has left us vulnerable to being captured by those with less than admirable political objectives.

The fact is, for democracy to exist, people must understand it, want it, and be willing to defend it, no matter what as we witnessed millions of Americans do during the Second World War. Nearly one hundred years ago, Joseph Schumpeter wrote that "democracy cannot be expected to function satisfactorily unless the vast majority of the people in all classes are resolved to abide by the rules . . . and are substantially agreed on the fundamentals of their institutional structure."[8] Today, however, the critical combination of political ignorance, lack of support, and openness to tyrannical rule have provided the perfect conditions for an autocrat to fill the leadership gap, while providing hope and assurance for a confused public along the way.

In the midst of our collective self-doubt, Donald Trump and his minions have worked to take advantage of the sorrowful gap in democratic commitment and stand ready to replace American democracy with a streamlined form of authoritarianism. There's a decade-long string of history here. Trump began his pursuit of power with a narrow victory in the presidential election of 2016, after which he commenced an imperial style of rule by circumventing the democratic corners of governance in the name of expediency, but more accurately to do as he wished, irrespective of legality. When Trump lost his bid for reelection in 2020, he attempted to remain in power via a failed coup culminating with the January 6, 2021, insurrection on the Capitol as legislators set about to confirm the 2020 presidential election results.

Ingrained with the notion that there is nothing worse than being a "loser," a more politically sophisticated Trump charted a course to regain the presidency in 2024, where he openly promised to resume aspects of undemocratic rule upon an election victory. During the campaign, Trump called for "termination" of parts of the Constitution, lest the document

Understanding American Democracy

impede his efforts to govern;[9] declared that some leaders of the military during his previous presidency should be executed;[10] pledged to prosecute political opponents for election interference and journalists for failing to reveal confidential sources;[11] and promised upon reelection to "carry out the largest domestic deportation operation in American history" of undocumented immigrants irrespective of their residential status.[12] He was so self-righteous about his approach to governance that Trump publicly vowed to be a dictator upon taking office, a pledge he quickly amended to the first day only upon receiving massive criticism.[13]

Regardless of the 2024 election outcome, Trump said he would accept the result only if it was "fair," then adding that his 2020 election loss was not fair.[14] In other words, a fair election would only be one where Trump wins! From these recent accounts, we are reminded that there is little democracy in Trumpism.

Against these dark pictures, we begin our discussion of democracy, Trumpism, and the prescription for American society to overcome the most serious threat of home-bred authoritarianism to our democracy in modern history. We do so with no illusions about the daunting challenge, but with the hope that a refresher course on democracy along with enlightenment on the perils of authoritarianism may persuade Americans to reconsider the path that Trumpists would take us—a path that would lead us far from the values we have worked so hard to preserve and improve over the past 250 years.

The Essentials of American Democracy

Every nation is built on its own unique political foundation, guideposts of sorts that help to form the framework of its governance. Different frameworks will produce different forms of authority and the use of power. A theocratic nation such as Iran functions in a framework dependent on the strict religious leadership of the Ayatollah, or Supreme Leader, who serves for life without objection and directs all outcomes from the other government institutions. An autocratic nation such as Russia functions in a similar top-down manner, although in this case, the president defines policy objectives that are symbolically rubber-stamped by legislative and judicial institutions without any meaningful challenge. In both cases, their Constitutions imply a democratic framework that is replete with colorful symbolism, but nothing more.

Overcoming Trumpism

Historically, the United States has been characterized as a democracy, but with fundamental differences compared to non-democratic societies. In the American setting, the government depends on the guidance and periodic approval of the people who play a central role in confirming its legitimacy. Specifically, Thomas Dye and Harmon Zeigler write, "The underlying value of democracy is individual dignity."[15] Those in governmental positions of power are obligated to consider and perhaps act on the demands of the people, although responses may not satisfy all because of many views on the same topic. This is the unique covenant that distinguishes democracies from other political arrangements.

Beyond that distinction, the American governmental apparatus includes several guarantees specific to our democracy. They include law-based governance, a set of rules that outlast the rulers, representation through regularly scheduled elections, separation of powers, federalism, free expression, and the guarantee that ultimate power lies with the people. In other words, power is designed to flow from the bottom up, not from the top down. To those who feel isolated from government, such a description may feel illusory, if not disingenuous. But relative to other forms of government, American democracy presents a real connection between those who govern and the constituents who keep or remove them from power.

Law-Based Governance

Laws are rules laid down by policymakers selected by the people to keep order and continuity in society. Order is critical, for without it we have chaos. Imagine if there weren't stop signs on streets, no regulations for what goes into pharmaceutical drugs, or voluntary taxation where we just paid what we wanted, or not at all? Society would break down rather quickly under such conditions. Laws bind us to the greater good. The more we adhere to them, the easier it is for society to thrive.

In a democracy, laws are supposed to apply to everyone the same way regardless of position or influence, but most of us know, and sometimes see, wiggle room in their application. For example, an individual may hear about someone of financial or other means receiving more generous treatment from a judge in a case before a court than another person with a similar case but without the same pedigree. Under such circumstances, the person with fewer attributes might become justifiably disgusted with what could be viewed as favoritism. The good news is that in most cases, such abuses of the rules are pointed out and dealt with by those in higher positions of authority.

Understanding American Democracy

Even then, a law-based government is not perfect. Laws and regulations are sometimes tilted in favor of some groups when compared to others. If we find a law repugnant to our values, we try to persuade those we have put in power to change it. And if the lawmakers refuse, we may choose to vote for someone else in the next election. In many states, voters can themselves change the rules through initiatives or referenda, otherwise known as the components of direct democracy. The point is that laws are permanent only until they're changed, and they're often changed with the evolution of society.

Another point about laws: they provide predictability. By adhering to the laws, usually we have a good idea how things will turn out. We expect that regardless of our feelings, if we honor the rules, they will be carried out as written or intended. We expect that if we pay our taxes, governments will provide the services connected to the revenues garnered from those monies. With respect to governance, we count on those we put in power to solve public problems within their areas of responsibility.

By honoring law-based governance, we understand our role in the system as well as the problems that come from those who act otherwise. Moreover, our laws and rules don't appear from thin air; rather they are results of attempts by lawmakers to meet society's needs. Nor do laws transform with those who hold office. On the contrary, those elected to office must operate within the framework of laws that were in place before them and will continue to be in place after their departure.

Regularly Scheduled Elections

Our democracy is more correctly referred to as a "representative democracy," where a few are chosen to rule on behalf of the many. This system is utilized because the population is too large for us all to cast votes on the issues at hand. Imagine all or most of the 340 million people in the United States attempting to participate in deliberations of the myriad issues impacting American society. Even with modern technology, it could take days to tabulate answers to determine the outcome of public opinion. Representation is the middle ground between someone deciding on their own for the common good and the chaos associated with mass participation.

Having the ability to choose people to act on our behalf in regularly scheduled elections connects the polity with the leaders, or at least intended as such. As a general rule of thumb, the more controversial the questions before the voters, the more likely the elected official is to listen closely to the constituents. Most of the time, we tend to pay little attention to matters of little consequence, leaving policymakers the ability to enact laws with minimal input from their constituents because of lack of voter interest. On other occasions with contentious topics or issues, policymakers are more likely to consider the wishes of their constituents, assuming the voters agree on a point of view. Some leaders see themselves as much more knowledgeable about issues than those who put them in power; as such, they act in terms of their own values and little more. Others, a few to be sure, view the public's views as irrelevant to their goals and act accordingly. Such circumstances can be problematic for democracy but may be resolved through replacement of inattentive representatives at subsequent elections.

To be sure, there is nothing precise nor automatic about these varied conditions. These examples of wayward leaders who abuse the laws can be disconcerting. But in a democracy, the more that leaders separate themselves without regard for the rules, those who put them in power or, for that matter the collective good, the more that there is the risk of irresponsible governance. Our system depends on a connection between leaders and the public, or at least on the recognition of that connection.

Whatever our differences, elections are meant to settle them in a nonviolent, orderly way with losers accepting the results. Losers can take consolation, knowing that they will have an opportunity to gain control possibly as soon as the next election. Along with that reality, winners must understand that their triumph is guaranteed only until the next election when they will have the opportunity to appeal for continued service in office. Democracies count on this kind of predictability.

Separation of Powers

The United States came into being with a sizable distrust of arbitrary rule by those in power. Decades of increasingly sour experience with the British king and his laws left many of the then-colonists believing that their rulers were increasingly disinclined to honor the interests of the new Americans. It was not surprising that after endless attempts to negotiate less onerous living conditions with their rulers, on July 4, 1776, several prominent colonial leaders signed a Declaration of Independence that promoted liberty in the name of natural rights, a government dependent upon consent of the governed, and the right to revolt against repressive and unjust rule.[16] Those roots became the starting point of the successful American Revolution. We mention this historic moment as a reminder of this nation's philosophical roots steeped in individualism and liberty.

Understanding American Democracy

Given a foundation of great suspicion against uncontrolled arbitrary rule, in 1787, the founders of the Constitution, soon the nation's principal governing document, created a system that simultaneously created a central government with power limitations. Under the new governing organization, power would be distributed to three co-equal branches: the executive, the legislative, and the judicial, with any one branch able to keep the others from acting irresponsibly. Thus, the thinking went: that governance would be restrained and depend largely upon the cooperation and coordination of all three branches. A Congress divided into two chambers might even further minimize the possibility of an excessive central government running roughshod over individual liberties. With the expectation that agreement would come about only through consensus, the founders believed the "Separation of Powers" doctrine would assure limited government by creating a system of what became known as "checks and balances."[17]

The Separation of Powers doctrine has gone through at least two fundamental transformations. First, barely defined in the Constitution, the responsibilities of the judiciary in the policymaking process seemed minimal at best. Yes, there would be a Supreme Court, but its responsibilities as well as the lower rungs in the federal court system weren't created until the Judiciary Act of 1789. Operating in a rather vague political environment, the most important power of the judiciary emerged not through the Constitution, but rather with the *Marbury v. Madison* case in 1803. In its decision, the Supreme Court justices asserted that the courts could declare laws (and later regulations) unconstitutional if they were at odds with the nation's guiding document. Through this incredible development, the courts—at the federal and eventually the state level—assumed power that greatly added to the heft of the judiciary.[18]

The second major change to the Separation of Powers doctrine emerged with the growing power of the president and the executive branch. For the first hundred years or so of the nation's existence, presidential power was relatively limited along with national government authority in general. During the last three decades of the nineteenth century, however, economic industrialization created serious discontinuities throughout the nation, often generating waves of protests. The power of the chief executive, early in the twentieth century as President Theodore Roosevelt, used the "bully pulpit" to pressure Congress into passing a series of laws on economic and social conditions. Change came next during the Great Depression when President Franklin Roosevelt (ironically a third cousin of Theodore) issued a series of rarely used executive orders to shut down the nation's banking system, and another executive order to call Congress back into special session to consider various proposals by the president. Under Roosevelt's New Deal, the president took charge of the nation's economy. A series of agencies within the executive branch was established to develop programs designed to guide the nation out of the Great Depression, the most serious economic deterioration in the nation's history. From that time on, the presidency has clearly emerged as a clear first among equals in the national government. Those unequalled powers exist today for anyone who sits in the Oval Office.

Changes in the Separation of Powers doctrine notwithstanding, the concept provides a layer of accountability for the federal government. Its design is such that government action can't move forward without widespread agreement from the various sources of power, including the Congress and courts. Without this creation, a single individual or branch might find it easier to rule with little counterbalance.

In theory, the Separation of Powers doctrine discourages any one person or branch of government from governing without the cooperation of the others. In theory. Discussion of the concept's violation by then-President Trump at the end of his first term of office, and even more so during his second term, follows later in this narrative.

Federalism

Some democracies operate with the national government assuming responsibility for everything from defense to local roads. This is known as a unitary system of authority. Romania, Ireland, and Japan are examples of democracies with unitary governments. Another group of countries relies upon federalism, a system where power is distributed to various levels of government. Canada, Germany, and India incorporate federalism, along with the United States. Note that federalism doesn't necessarily distinguish democracies from nondemocratic countries. However, it is commonplace in most large democracies.

As with the Separation of Powers, the idea behind federalism is to distribute power and responsibilities among more than one governmental unit operating within the same geographical setting. The United States was an early adopter of the concept, courtesy of the Tenth Amendment to the US Constitution, which reads "The powers not delegated to the United States by the Constitution, nor prohibited by it to the States, are reserved to the States respectively, or to the people." Beyond distribution, federalism frames the way that various governments simultaneously influence, depend upon, and push away from each other. In a sense, it's a vertical version of the Separation of Powers doctrine we find horizontally within national, state, and even local governments.[19]

Under federalism, each level of government assumes control of various issues. In the United States, the distribution of power assignments originates with Article I, Section 8 of the Constitution where the preponderance of major responsibilities rests with the federal government. These range from defense to creation of a national currency to even the establishment and operation of a postal system. Much of what's not mentioned in Article I, Section 8 and a few other parts of the Constitution falls under control of the states, courtesy of the Tenth Amendment. Such areas as public education and policing clearly exist under state jurisdiction. A few areas such as taxation are not exclusive to either level of government.

Over time, with the growth of the national government, some of the lines of responsibility have become a bit blurred. Federal aid to education, national health programs, and grants-in-aid, in particular, state policy areas of interest to national leaders, have led to cooperation in some instances and accusations of interference in others. These days, disputes of exactly which roles should be left to each level often land in the federal courts. As a general rule, Democrats tend to desire more federal help for the states and cities, while Republicans tend to want states to be free of what they describe as unnecessary federal intervention. These differences aside, federalism does divide power between the two basic levels of governance.

Freedom of Expression

In a democracy, few rights are more important than the right to free expression. So important is this concept that it is the heart of the First Amendment to the Bill of Rights, added to the Constitution soon after its completion to provide an additional level of protection for the people from excessive national government meddling. Its need stems from the colonial days when people who expressed increasingly angry opposition to British rule through speech or the written word were often punished. The contents of the First Amendment include guarantees of free expression with respect to speech, the press, assembly, and religion. A free press is essential to democracy because it provides independent platforms for publishing criticism and concern. The First Amendment also explicitly provides the right for people to petition the government with their grievances.

Overcoming Trumpism

In recent years, the courts have equated political campaign financial contributions as a form of speech. In that vein, the Supreme Court has removed virtually all contribution limits and disclosure requirements. As a result, it has become very difficult for interested parties such as public interest groups to ascertain the origins of donations. Critics have described this situation as an unfair way of tilting the outcome of elections in the direction that the most untraced funds have come from.

Congress has also weighed in on speech with the passage of the Telecommunications Act (1996). In Section 230 of the law, Internet companies were exempt from any responsibility as to the truth in "information" posted on their websites. Critics believe that over time the section may have led unwittingly to "free speech" abuses because of the lack of accountability for those using social media.[20]

It's worthwhile to note that as with other parts of the Bill of Rights, the various guarantees are not absolute. In the case of the First Amendment, freedom of speech is not protected if it incites a riot. Similarly, if an individual knowingly falsely says or writes that another individual has committed a crime, he or she may find themselves at the other end of a civil suit, or perhaps even a criminal charge. Our First Amendment rights are broad and generous, but not without boundaries. Still, freedom of speech in all its forms is a prominent staple of democracy in the United States and elsewhere.

Power from the People to the Government

Lastly, we turn to the wellspring of the democratic experience. It goes without saying that government is an essential component of any modern society. As noted earlier in this chapter, a major responsibility of government is to provide order for the people. In a democracy, the ability of government to maintain tranquility and other necessities for the population stems from permission from the people. It's a subtle, tacit agreement in that there are no occasional conventions or public declarations that endorse the government's existence. Rather, the connection between those who govern and those who are the recipients of the government's applications exists as an understood element of the democratic arrangement. This linkage is also critical to our system of representation.

Democracies function with the firm agreement that elected leaders remain in office as long as the voters support them. If previously elected leaders are replaced as a result of the will of the people via elections, it's

Understanding American Democracy

expected that they leave without any attempt to resist the will of the those who put them there. That trust is paramount to understanding that the power confirmed to the officeholder is temporary. Consent by the people may be implied, but it's consent, nonetheless. Consent is a boilerplate-like assumption that is part of the democratic arrangement. With that unstated authorization, leaders in a democracy go about their affairs protecting society from harm, hunger, and other problems that might prevent the people from leading their lives. Periodic elections provide approval or disapproval by the people of the government's activities.

Authoritarian regimes operate on an entirely different basis than democracies. There, rulers don't depend on public approval for their actions because they don't consider the public part of the governmental equation; it is simply on the receiving end of government activity. The "legitimacy" of authoritarian rulers is artificial in that it is determined by their physical power, intimidation, and other tyrannical means totally exclusive of public input. Most of the time, the rulers remain in control until they are replaced either by chosen successors or even more powerful authoritarians. Only on rare occasions revolutionaries with democratic mindsets overpower dictatorial regimes, such as the American Revolution commencing in 1776 and the Egyptian Revolution in 2011 that ended the thirty-year reign of Hosni Mubarak.

A caveat: no system of governance is perfect, and that includes democracy. The linkage between the people and those who govern sometimes may be strained, weak, or temporarily absent altogether. That said, opportunity and accountability exist much more in a democratic setting than any other form of government. If you think that claim is a stretch, just ask immigrants from troubled heavy-handed authoritarian nations who risk their lives through adverse weather conditions, threats by thieves, and hostile border agents upon their arrival here. For the most part, all they want is a chance to be part of an open society where they can be free from oppression and have a say in their own welfare as well as the political goings on in their new country. Historically, at least, as recently as 2024, a solid 75 percent of Americans agreed that undocumented immigrants play an important role in American society by filling jobs that citizens don't want, particularly in construction and agriculture.[21] Yet, judging from the issues dominating the 2024 election and Trump's victory, America's open hand may be more of a clenched fist these days, perhaps showing a current critical tension point in American society.

Values, Beliefs, and Political Culture

Beyond institutional arrangements, societies are often understood by their overall values and attitudes of the public toward life's attributes, including feelings about governance. Whether democracies or other forms of governance, a sizable portion of those values are subsumed in political culture, described by one expert as "the set of attitudes, beliefs, and sentiments that give order and meaning to a political process . . . including the underlying rules and assumptions and rules that govern behavior in the political system."[22] With respect to democracies, there are two major elements that help explain the extent of commitments to democratic values: inclusivity and clashing principles. Bear in mind that these qualities are not necessarily inculcated in every member of the society, but the more that they predominate, the more that the population in general tends to support democratic values.

Inclusivity

Democracies are characterized in part by the willingness of the population to accept different values and individual life experiences within the same overarching political environment. Where there are racial, ethnic, and religious differences within the same nation, the population is challenged to acknowledge each person as valuable and worthy as the others. That can be a chore with a dramatic upward tick in immigration, but the transformational conditions present opportunities for a more vibrant society. To be sure, however, those opportunities are anything but automatic.[23]

In democracies, education about and exposure to different groups go a long way toward instilling familiarity, thereby overcoming suspicion and distrust. Failure to utilize this antidote to xenophobia can place a democracy at risk, for fear or even ignorance about the unknown can go a long way toward causing political and social havoc. On the contrary, to the extent that inclusivity permeates a multifaceted culture, democracy is less threatened because there are fewer cracks in the foundation of the social structure.

As a nation that has witnessed streams of immigrants almost since its inception, the United States has experienced mixed results in being racially and ethnically inclusive. Strangers from other lands have been more welcomed at some points in American history than others. During those periods when immigration is resented by some of those already here, that intolerance spills over to the political realm and can become a key issue in forthcoming elections. Here, an irony of sorts exists in that virtually all Americans are immigrants, albeit perhaps one, two, three, or more generations removed from the time when our forebearers first arrived. The point is, outside of the Indigenous people, we're all immigrants, some more recently than others.

Support for Clashing Principles

American democracy is unique because of the conflicting principles that came with its birth. Egalitarianism and individualism are concepts that often intrude upon one another, yet they appeared early in the struggle for American independence. Regarding the former, the colonists, fearing a possible tyrant along the lines of a king, upon independence, wanted each man to have a voice equal to the others. Thus, we note the "all men are created equal" pronouncement in the Declaration of Independence, surely a pointed jab at their rulers.

At the other extreme, the colonists railed against the various layers of economic, social, and political barriers that often defined the British at birth, with little opportunity to move upward. Upon securing victory in the revolution, the Americans wanted assurances that their paths to mobility would be without predetermined constraints. Those guarantees would be sown into the Bill of Rights, the first ten Amendments to the Constitution. Pointedly, as discussed earlier, the Tenth Amendment provides that "The powers not delegated to the United States [federal government] . . . are reserved to the States respectively, or to the people." This ability has become the basis for states pursuing different, and often contradictory, directions in their management of basic national issues. Gun rights and abortion are two current examples.

These two concepts are major pieces in America's political collage, seemingly at odds with one another, yet somehow supportive—to a point. At times, they have managed to coexist, albeit awkwardly, but coexist, nonetheless. At other times, one strand has almost run over the other. For example, in the United States, utilization of federal welfare state policies has addressed economic inequality, particularly during times of great economic stress, at least to the extent of providing minimum economic floors. Meanwhile, through the Thirteenth, Fourteenth, Fifteenth, and Nineteenth Amendments, federal courts have addressed political inequality for minorities and women, at least with respect to the right to vote. At other times, the impact of individualism and states' rights have blunted the federal government's efforts to clearly establish socioeconomic and political guarantees for all members of the polity, especially those who have been left behind through various forms of discrimination. For example, inconsistencies have emerged with varying state responses to issues such as public education, vaccination requirements, and voting requirements.

Left unresolved in the struggle between equality and individualism are the conditions of political participation by racial minorities, women, and sexual orientation. The concept of "all men are created equal" first mentioned in the Declaration of Independence addressed neither women nor people of color, leaving those large blocks of society caught between the two political tectonic plates. Just as earthquakes release kinetic energy on occasion, so the causes of true racial, gender, and religious equality have upon occasion encountered political jolts such as *Brown v. Education* and *Roe v. Wade*. Subsequently, the demands of individualism have roared back to minimize or do away with the same guarantees for all.

As a result, sometimes "one step forward" actually boomerangs to "two steps backward." Consider that seventy years after the *Brown* decision, school desegregation has been less than a complete success. A report issued by the US Government Accountability Office in 2022 found that more than a third of public education students attended schools where 75 percent or more of the students were the same race or ethnicity. One out of seven students were present at schools where 90 percent of the students were of the same race or ethnicity.[24] These examples don't bode well for the concept of desegregation.

A similar outcome through a different process has impacted control of women's reproductive health. In 1973, relying on the Right to Privacy in the Fourteenth Amendment, the US Supreme Court declared in *Roe* that a woman has the right to choose an abortion until a fetus became viable, considered at between 24 and 28 weeks of the pregnancy. In 2022, nearly fifty years later in *Dobbs v. Jackson Women's Health Organization*, the Court handed that "right" to the states. That decision has yielded incredible state to state differences. By 2023, twenty-one states banned abortion earlier than the time limit established in *Roe*, with fourteen of them banning abortion in almost all circumstances.[25] However, during the same year, six states adopted a woman's right to choose as a constitutional right, followed by six more in 2024.

Still unresolved are issues related to sexuality. While *Obergefell v. Hodges* offered constitutional support for gay marriage in 2015, vestiges of discrimination remain. Beyond that, equality for transexuals and nonbinary gender identities remain in the frontiers of constitutional resolution.

Understanding American Democracy

Out of this ebb and flow comes the need for members of a democratic society to find ways to straddle the differences between the belief in equality and support for individuals and states doing as they please. On one hand, excessive equality in public policymaking puts a damper on individualism. On the other hand, extreme individualism surely intrudes on those with the long-overdue quest for equality. Finding the sweet spot between these two themes is a never-ending goal in American democracy.

Toward a More Perfect Union?

Democracies represent a unique partnership between the governed and their leaders, placing great burdens on each side: for those holding the reins of power, honoring election outcomes that may result in replacement, and for citizens, using their power as potential change agents wisely and judiciously. With so much on the line, it's easy to see how things can go wrong, either from leaders who may reject public decisions by deciding not to leave their posts after losing an election or the voters who fail to do their homework on the issues before them as well as the best officials to carry out the voters' choices. For these reasons, virtually every democracy is a work in progress.

There is reason to worry. Across the globe, a number of democracies have succumbed to authoritarian strains in recent years. According to one account, Brazil, Hungary, India, Mexico, the Philippines, Turkey, and Venezuela have shown "decidedly undemocratic proclivities" in recent years, with freely elected leaders assaulting constitutions, the courts, the free press, and various laws designed to check their official power.[26] Larry Diamond, founder of a journal dedicated to democracy, believes that since the early years of the twenty-first century, democracies have gone into recession due to factors such as growing economic inequality, widespread job losses, globalization and technological change, cultural diversity, and expanding immigration.[27] Other assessments add proof to Diamond's concern.[28]

Which takes us to the current condition of the United States. To be blunt, we have seen better times. Over the past few years, American democracy has taken a hit. Much of the country's problems have centered on sizable numbers of the population forgoing key values such as tolerance and mutual respect, while embracing hate, intolerance, and erratic governance directed by a few instead of rational, deliberate, and inclusive decision-making processed by the many. These harsh behaviors have only increased with the politics of Donald Trump and his minions.

Overcoming Trumpism

We leave this chapter with two inescapable conclusions: First, American democracy is much more fragile than that which meets the eye and vulnerable to political implosion. Second, in recent years, the battle to keep democracy in the United States has suffered more losses than gains. Together, these are unmistakable threats to our well-being.

Democracy Is Fragile

Think about the various components that combine to form the essentials of democracy. When the parts work well, they are mutually reinforcing, and democracy thrives as a result. But if too many parts become dysfunctional, the system sputters and could even fail altogether. That is the dilemma we face today.

Consider the Separation of Powers doctrine. There, each of the three federal branches has its own responsibilities, but they must be exercised in such a manner so as to protect the integrity of the Constitution. If the members of one branch of government no longer abide to the extent of checking possible wrongdoing of the others, democracy is at risk. Thus, when Donald Trump refused to use his presidential authority to stop the insurrection against Congress on January 6, 2021, his inaction placed the other institutions in jeopardy of falling to anarchy as the first step to dictatorship. On the same topic, had Congress failed in its January 6, 2021, gathering to comply with its obligation to confirm the 2020 election results, its inaction would have placed the nation in a precarious position because of a breakdown in moral presidential leadership.

Various combinations of potential threats to our democracy occur on a regular basis, but thankfully, almost all people in appropriate positions of authority either do the right thing or face consequences if they don't. An earlier danger to our democracy occurred with what became known as Watergate, the name of an office complex, where burglars working for the then-president Richard Nixon's reelection campaign broke in and stole information from Democratic Party headquarters. In 1973, after congressional investigators learned of tape recordings confirming a series of illegalities by Nixon and other bad actors, the Special Counsel assigned to the case subpoenaed the material.[29] Nixon resisted complying with the order, and the subpoena ultimately landed at the US Supreme Court. After the Justices agreed with the Special Counsel by an 8-to-0 vote, the nation waited three days before Nixon agreed to the demand and eventually resigned from office. Had Nixon resisted, a major constitutional crisis would have emerged.

Other recent crises in American society have placed us one step away from political chaos, if not disaster. Consider a couple of recent examples. After he claimed victory in the 2020 presidential election that he obviously lost, Donald Trump insisted to confidents that he would not leave the White House. For days, many Americans held their breath about his intentions. Trump ultimately departed office, although he has claimed victimhood of a stolen election ever since.[30]

A more recent instance of a potential constitutional crisis occurred during Trump's second term in 2025. In response to a protest in Los Angeles over questionable arrests of undocumented immigrants, Trump ordered seven hundred marines to be available for quelling the disturbance. While marines have been utilized six times in American history, the circumstances have always been extraordinarily compelling.[31] If deployed, many local officials believed the very presence of marines on the scene would precipitate violent responses.[32] Fortunately, two hundred marines stayed near federal buildings and left crowd control to the local police and the National Guard also ordered by Trump. Incidentally, the alleged riot resulted in 575 arrests in a six square mile in a city of 500+ square miles over four days, hardly a situation requiring massive response.

As noted above, the very nature of democracy leaves it vulnerable to threats and possible failure. Often when considering that potential event, some people tend to point fingers at our foreign enemies as the sources of our dilemmas. These days, China and Russia come to mind for their military might and technical prowess with cyber penetration of communications or other systems. True, these threats occur in an existential sense and should not be dismissed, but the more problematic concerns for American democracy come from within. Cracks in our political pavement, most notably demonstrated with the January 6, 2021, insurrection against the Capitol remind us that our system of government is more exposed to political disaster than some of us would like to think. And tragically, the most serious threats now come from within our nation, not from outside.

American Democracy on the Wane?

Which takes us to our current condition. Over the past decade or so, distrust of our institutions, violence against government, and political alienation have inundated American society. These feelings have replaced values such as respect for election outcomes, tolerance of different opinions and values, and a sense of collective belonging. Not all Americans find themselves in such an unenviable position, but a sizable percentage do. The disaffected spew hatred and advocate—and in some cases actually participate in—violence toward others, often directed toward racial, ethnic, religious, and gender minorities. They blame immigrants for much of the nation's problems, view government leaders as crooked and self-absorbed, and would rather have a strong leader manage political problems than endure the often-lengthy democratic process of governance. These are the people who look to Donald Trump and his allies as their saviors, as leaders who will rescue them from their doldrums and disappointments in life. The problem is that support for a "leader" with the characteristics of a demagogue places our democracy at risk.

All this comes at a cost. Recent studies show that the United States is losing its position as the beacon of democracy. The well-regarded *Economist Democracy Index* is a case in point. Annually, the magazine uses five criteria to determine the political conditions of a nation, ranging from "full democracies" to "authoritarian" governments. The criteria are electoral process and pluralism, the functioning of government, political participation, political culture, and civil liberties. Out of 167 countries researched between 2006 and 2015, the United States was considered among the world's leading democracies, ranking twentieth in 2015 with a score of 8.05. Norway, New Zealand, and Finland had perfect scores of 10.00. By 2022, the United States was downgraded to a "flawed democracy," with a score of 7.85 and was ranked thirtieth.[33]

Another longitudinal study by Freedom House had similar observations about the decline of American democracy. Using a hundred-point scale, the think tank focused largely on Civil Liberties and Political Rights practices and included the political conditions in 210 countries. In 2024, the United States was tied for fifty-seventh place with 84 points along with Mongolia and Samoa, and was down 9 points over the previous decade. The Freedom House findings attributed much of the decline to the many questionable policies and practices during and immediately after the first Trump administration. The causes of the decline included undemocratic treatment of people of color, police violence against Black Americans, public distrust in government, Trump's behavior after the 2020 election, and distorted political and civic discourse.[34]

Viewed in totality, American democracy is in trouble. The contention here is that while it may be difficult to point out a single cause of our contemporary national malaise, the rancor of Donald Trump and his supporters appears to have played a major role in the downward slide. It's a deterioration of our democracy that we can ill afford. The discussion of the extent of our problems and possibilities for renewal begins in the next chapter.

NOTES

1. "Americans' Civics Knowledge Increases but Still Has a Long Way to Go," Annenberg Public Policy Center, September 12, 2019, https://www.annenbergpublicpolicycenter.org/americans-civics-knowledge-increases-2019-survey/.
2. "Americans, Deeply Divided, yet Share Core Values of Equality, Liberty, & Progress," Sienna College Research Institute, October 25, 2021, https://scri.siena.edu/2021/10/25/americans-deeply-divided-yet-share-core-values-of-equality-liberty-progress/.
3. "How Americans View Trust, Facts, and Democracy Today," Pew Research Center, February 19, 2020, https://www.pewtrusts.org/en/trust/archive/winter-2020/how-americans-view-trust-facts-and-democracy-today.
4. "Record Low in U.S. Satisfied with Way Democracy Is Working," Gallup Poll, January 4, 2024, https://news.gallup.com/poll/548120/record-low-satisfied-democracy-working.aspx.
5. "Poll: A Strong Majority of Americans Endorse Democracy, but Some—Especially among Younger Generations—Are Skeptical," NPR News, January 18, 2023, https://www.mprnews.org/story/2023/01/18/poll-majority-of-americans-endorse-democracy-younger-generations-skeptical.
6. "Democracy at Risk: 41% of Americans Open to a More Authoritarian Approach," Earth4All, August 1, 2024, https://earth4all.life/views/democracy-at-risk-41-of-americans-open-to-a-more-authoritarian-approach/.
7. "U.S. Image Drops to Record Lows in Many Countries," USC Center on Public Diplomacy, November 5, 2020, https://uscpublicdiplomacy.org/printpdf/91701, and "U.S. Image Declines in Many Nations amid Low Confidence in Trump," Pew Research Center, June 11, 2025, https://www.pewresearch.org/global/2025/06/11/views-of-the-united-states/
8. Joseph A. Schumpeter, *Capitalism, Socialism and Democracy*, 3rd edition (New York: Harper & Row, 1950), p. 301.
9. "Trump's Call for 'Termination' of Constitution Draws Rebukes," *The New York Times*, December 4, 2022, https://www.nytimes.com/2022/12/04/us/politics/trump-constitution-republicans.html.
10. "Trump Floats the Idea of Executing Joint Chiefs Chairman Milley," *The Atlantic*, September 25, 2023, https://www.theatlantic.com/ideas/archive/2023/09/trump-milley-execution-incitement-violence/675435/
11. "Trump Makes More Than 100 Threats to Prosecute or Punish Perceived Enemies," NPR, October 22, 2024, https://www.npr.org/2024/10/22/nx-s1-5155032/trump-makes-more-than-100-threats-to-prosecute-or-punish-perceived-enemies.

12 Quoted in "Sweeping Raids, Giant Camps and Mass Deportations: Inside Trump's 2025 Immigration Plans," *The New York Times*, November 11, 2023, https://www.nytimes.com/2023/11/11/us/politics/trump-2025-immigration-agenda.html.

13 "Donald Trump Repeats Comment He Would Be a Dictator 'for One Day' If Reelected in 2024," *USA Today*, December 11, 2023, https://www.usatoday.com/story/news/politics/elections/2023/12/11/donald-trump-dictator-one-day-reelected/71880010007/.

14 "How Trump Is Laying the Groundwork to Possibly Challenge the 2024 Election Results," ABC News, October 8, 2024, https://abcnews.go.com/Politics/trump-laying-groundwork-possibly-challenge-2024-election-results/story?id=114569420.

15 Thomas Dye and Harmon Zeigler, *The Irony of Democracy*, 12th edition (Belmont, CA: Thomson/Wadsworth, 2003), p. 5.

16 Noble E. Cunningham, Jr., *The Life of Thomas Jefferson* (New York: Ballentine Press, 1987), pp. 49–51.

17 For a robust discussion of the Separation of Powers concept, see William E. Hudson, *American Democracy in Peril*, 9th edition (Thousand Oaks, CA: CQ Press, 2021), pp. 29–68.

18 See Henry J. Abraham, *The Judicial Process*, 6th edition (New York: Oxford University Press, 1993), pp. 270–2.

19 For a full discussion of this topic, see Larry N. Gerston, *American Federalism: A Concise Introduction* (Armonk, NY: M.E. Sharpe, 2007).

20 See Doris A. Graber, *Mass Media and American Politics*, 8th edition (Washington, DC: CQ Press, 2010), pp. 342–4.

21 "Most U.S. Voters Say Immigrants—No Matter Their Legal Status—Mostly Take Jobs Citizens Don't Want," Pew Research Center, October 21, 2024, https://www.pewresearch.org/short-reads/2024/10/21/most-us-voters-say-immigrants-no-matter-their-legal-status-mostly-take-jobs-citizens-dont-want/.

22 Lucien W. Pye, *Aspects of Political Development* (New York: Little, Brown, 1966), p. 104.

23 See Marisa Abrajano and Zoltam L. Hajnal, *White Backlash: Immigration, Race, and American Politics* (Princeton, NJ: University of Princeton Press, 2015), pp. 211–16.

24 "K-12 Education: Student Population Has Significantly Diversified, but Many Schools Remain Divided along Racial, Ethnic, and Economic Lines," U.S. Government Accountability Office, July 14, 2022, https://www.gao.gov/products/gao-22-104737.

25 "Tracking Abortion Bans across the Country," *The New York Times*, December 8, 2023, https://www.nytimes.com/interactive/2022/us/abortion-laws-roe-v-wade.html.

26 Moises Naim, "The Dictator's New Playbook: Why Democracy Is Losing the Fight," *Foreign Affairs*, March/April 2022, pp. 144–54, https://www.foreignaffairs.com/articles/world/2022-02-22/dictators-new-playbook.

27 Larry Diamond, "We Have Entered a New Historical Era," Speech at the Freeman Spogli Institute for International Studies, April 11, 2022, https://fsi.

stanford.edu/news/we-have-entered-new-historic-era-larry-diamond-addresses-future-democracy.
28. For example, see "Democracies in Decline Worldwide, New Report Says," Politico, November 2, 2023, https://www.politico.eu/article/democracy-decline-worldwide-new-report-says/.
29. For a detailed account of the Watergate scandal, see Carl Bernstein and Bob Woodward, *All the President's Men* (New York: Simon & Schuster, 1974).
30. "Donald Trump Almost Didn't Leave the White House. Because, Of Course," CNN, September 12, 2022, https://www.cnn.com/2022/09/12/politics/trump-white-house-lost-election.
31. "6 Times the Military Was Used for Riot Control in the US," *Military Life*, June 10, 2025, https://www.military.com/military-life/6-times-military-was-used-suppress-civilian-uprisings-us.html.
32. "Some Los Angeles Officials Fear Marines' 'Rules of Force,'" NBC News, June 11, 2025, https://www.nbcnews.com/politics/national-security/los-angeles-officials-fear-marines-rules-force-rcna212143.
33. "The Economist Intelligence Unit's Democracy Index 2016," https://www.eiu.com/Handlers/WhitepaperHandler.ashx?fi=Democracy-Index-2016.pdf&mode=wp&campaignid=DemocracyIndex2016, and "The Economist Intelligence Unit's Democracy Index 2022," https://www.scribd.com/document/701938944/Democracy-Index-2022-Frontline-democracy-and-the-battle-for-Ukraine-The-Economist-Intelligence-Unit-Z-Library-63-64.
34. See "Freedom in the World 2024—the United States," Freedom House, https://freedomhouse.org/country/united-states/freedom-world/2024 and "Countries and Territories," Freedom House, 2024, https://freedomhouse.org/country/scores.

CHAPTER 2
THE RISE OF TRUMPISM

In today's politics, many people view Trumpism as a temporary phenomenon. Now, more than a decade after Donald Trump's unhurried descent down the long escalator at Trump Tower, "temporary" clearly is not appropriate. Donald Trump's supporters praise him as a welcome relief to what they consider failed politics and policies long overdue for serious redirection. Trump opponents see him as narrow minded, intemperate, and disrespectful of American institutions. But there's more. In a December 2023 national poll, 51 percent of the respondents agreed that Trump would be "a threat to democracy if he is elected president." Yet, in the same poll asking about preference in the November 2024 presidential election, the respondents favored Trump over Democratic incumbent Joe Biden 47 to 42 percent.[1] That preference carried through the 2024 election, where Trump narrowly defeated Biden replacement Kamala Harris. Come to think of it, "Trump" and "controversy" are two words commonly expressed in the same conversation. And both are not likely to go away soon.

So, what is it that makes Trump so appealing, given that so many believe he will hurt democracy as president? We learn something of an answer in diagnosing Trumpism, the movement that has catapulted Donald Trump to the presidency twice, intertwined in an authoritarian crusade that threatens to continue after Trump leaves office.

In the United States, Trumpism is the latest example of an undemocratic movement dedicated to doing away with fundamental democratic values which, Trump supporters argue, have become corrupted or twisted over time. Trumpism is not entirely novel. Trumpism-like movements elsewhere in American history have presented themselves, at least for brief periods. The Great Awakening Christian faith movement (1740s), the White Separatist movement (1880s), and McCarthyism (1950s) each brought about upheavals in America. On every occasion, the unsettling force promoted antidemocratic principles in one form or another, posing a threat to the relative stability of society, only to subside before reappearing years later in slightly amended forms. Which takes us to the appeal and power of Trumpism.

Overcoming Trumpism

To begin with, Trumpism, like its predecessors, offers a simplistic design for attending to society's complex problems, washing away political demons (and enemies) in the process. In essence, followers view Trumpism as a political cleansing agent that promises permanent change. Without it, promoters argue, the political order as we know it is doomed.

Significantly, Trumpism goes well beyond Donald Trump. For example, large numbers of elected officials agreed with Trump that the 2020 election was rigged. Some expressed anguish through words, others challenged election results unsuccessfully through the courts, and yet others still turned to violence in the name of Trumpism and its values. To that end, it's worth remembering that on January 6, 2021, a day when Congress voted to confirm the outcome of the 2020 presidential election, 147 Republican members decided to disregard the results of an election where Joe Biden won 7 million more votes than Trump along with a decisive Electoral College victory of 306 to 232. Election results are "rigged" according to Trumpists unless their candidate wins.

An Antidemocratic Combination

Trumpism is orchestrated through the interaction of four central ideologies: Populism, racism, isolationism, and authoritarianism. Combined, these four elements have become the latest powerful sociopolitical mechanism for undermining American democracy and pushing society into chaos.

Populism

Populism is an approach to politics where its adherents believe they are the true voice of the people because of the abuse and uncaring policies of those in power. Populism has been invoked by voices seeking power in countries throughout the world. Activists have been particularly successful in mobilizing voters with populist grievances against elites for out-of-control immigration, high minority birth rates, economic abuse of the working class, and other demographic changes taking place because the elites in power don't care enough to do anything about it.[2] In the United States, Populism emerged as a political force after the Civil War and was particularly pronounced through the end of the nineteenth century, although some accounts actually trace the movement as far back as the founding of the

United States, where the anti-Federalists expressed serious concerns about the overreach of political elites.[3]

At its root, the American Populist movement was a reaction to a country that was fast moving toward industrialization and urbanization, with the common person experiencing a sense of abandonment. Many small-town residents and members of the agricultural sector particularly felt ignored and left behind from the rest of society.[4] Racism, anti-Semitism, and a general fear of immigrants were the mainstays in Populism inasmuch as all of these components were perceived as threatening the core traditions of life as Populists knew it. They also resented the growing dominance of government as well as corporations for their excessive profits, all of which contributed to an unnatural reordering of society.

Waxing nostalgia, American Populists yearned for someone to lead them to "a simpler and gentler past."[5] Still, their distrust of authority in both the private and public sectors of life led Populists to pursue the initiative, referendum, and recall election tools as tactics for returning power to the people, described by one observer of the era as "the politics of redemption."[6] All of these elements contributed to a strong anti-Establishment orientation. Briefly a small political party, the Populist movement wilted away by the late 1890s, replaced in part by the Progressive Party which carried on several Populist themes through the 1920s. While the movement and political party disappeared, the citizen redemption changes remained, particularly in the West and Midwest, where Populism was most prevalent.

By itself, Populism is not necessarily antidemocratic; in fact, Populists have appealed for support through democratic elections. Merged with other political ideologies, however, Populism can be dangerous.

In recent years, Populism has reemerged in American society. Growing resentment of "bigness" whether by Big Government, large corporations, outsized interest groups, the persistent economic chasm between the "haves" and the "have nots," or massive immigration have led some Americans to look for a leader who is able to regain control of the American dream. Some observers attribute the need for more control to an increasing disconnect between Americans and these institutions and their leaders.[7] Regardless, Populist activists gain their power on the backs of lost citizens.

At various times, contemporary political candidates have embraced Populism as their road to election. During his 2016 campaign for the presidential nomination, Democrat Bernie Sanders embraced a touch of Populism when he complained about a "class divide" and billionaires who were running American politics, which he called grounds for a peaceful political revolution at the ballot box.[8] Sanders went on to lose the Democratic nomination to Hillary Clinton.

Few modern politicians have seized Populism as a tool for power better than Donald Trump. Repeatedly, he has pinpointed grievances against immigrants and minorities, who are "stealing our culture," exhorting his supporters to "take our country back." Trump would ask rhetorically: And how can such devastating developments be overcome? "I am your voice," Trump declared during the 2016 Republican National Convention. And with respect to repairing all of the problems emerging from the deterioration of American greatness, Trump pronounced, "I alone can fix it." The convention delegates roared with approval.[9] Indeed, Trump's continuous references to an "us versus them" condition in American society have been a hallmark of his political success.

Racism

When Trump urges his rally attendees to join him in the fight to "take our country back," the obvious question is, from whom? The answer is from groups robbing us of "our culture." For those who may still be confused, Trump quickly boils down the discussion to an unacceptable "us" versus "them" situation. The "us" represents largely White Christians, guardians of the American dream, and preservationists of a culture molded by White Christian forebearers. The "them" are found mostly with Black, Brown, Indigenous, and Asian Americans, immigrants of color, and members of non-Christian religions. Trump relied on this division en route to his four years of the presidency. He has continued expressing various versions of the theme ever since, including his second presidential election victory in 2024. Coated with a healthy dose of fear, this approach has also served as a powerful force for supporting the "us" versus "them" concept, leaving a major wedge between Americans.

All this is couched in an approach where Trump presents himself as just a good American speaking the truth about the regrettable condition of the nation. In fact, Trump has repeated on many occasions that he is not a racist. He typically has defined himself to reporters as "the least racist person that you've ever interviewed."[10] Then again, his actions and words indicate otherwise.

Trump's racist attitudes extend back to his earliest days in business, when he uttered one racist epithet after another. His racist comments continued once Trump entered politics. "Birtherism," the baseless belief that a candidate for national office is born outside the United States, has been a favorite tool for Donald Trump. Between 2012 and 2016, he frequently wondered aloud whether then-president Barack Obama, an African American, was from Kenya (his father's place of birth). Eventually, Obama provided a state-issued document affirming Honolulu as his place of birth. Undeterred, Trump continued to "wonder" aloud whether Obama was foreign-born, which would have made him ineligible to run for president. During his 2016 presidential campaign, Trump referred to Obama as "Barack HUSSEIN Obama," slowly emphasizing his middle name as if to point to the former president as one of "them." Trump did not stop questioning Obama's birthplace until shortly before the 2016 presidential election. Going a step further, Trump accused Obama as the founder of ISIS, an international terrorist organization.[11]

Throughout his 2016 presidential campaign, Trump made racism a centerpiece of his candidacy. He accused Mexico and other Latin American countries of sending rapists, crime, and drugs to the United States.[12] He charged American Muslims with harboring Muslim terrorists, and as such unworthy of American citizenship.[13] Upon his election in 2016, Trump pledged to deport every one of the nation's undocumented immigrants, even though government reports showed that close to half of the "illegal" immigrants in the United States were guilty of nothing other than entering legally and overstaying their visas.[14] He repeated that promise during the 2024 election campaign.

An early presidential test of Trump and bigotry occurred in 2017 when a peaceful group in Charlottesville, Virginia, gathered to support the removal of a Confederate monument and were viciously attacked by a group of torch-carrying men displaying Nazi symbols and chanting "Jews will not replace us." At the end of a melee where one person died and dozens of nonviolent demonstrators were injured, Trump complained that "the press has treated [the neo-Nazis] unfairly.... . You had some very fine people on both sides."[15]

But there was so much more. During his presidency, Trump attacked supporters of the nonviolent Black Lives Matter movement for disseminating "toxic propaganda," tried to ban all Muslims from entering the United States, and referred to undocumented immigrants entering the United States from Latin American countries as "animals."[16] And who can forget Trump's reference to COVID-19 as the Kung Flu, his attempt to blame China for causing the virus and subsequent pandemic?[17]

Four years later, during the 2020 presidential campaign, Trump used the birtherism tactic on then-Democratic vice-presidential candidate, Kamala

Harris, the child of Jamaican and Indian immigrants born in Oakland, California. Referring to a column by a conservative law professor later discredited in Trump's effort to overturn the 2020 election, Trump said at a press conference, "I just heard it today that she [Harris] . . . doesn't qualify because she wasn't born in this country."[18] As with the first claim against Obama, conspiracy theorists spread the false claim like wildfire.

Variations of the racist theme continued throughout Trump's presidency and through his bid to return to office via the 2024 presidency. He amped up his anti-immigrant rhetoric, accusing them and other adversaries of being "vermin," a term used by Adolf Hitler against Jews and other enemies. In another echo of Hitler, Trump accused undocumented immigrants of "poisoning the blood of our country" and called for rounding them up, storing them in camps, and deporting them en masse to their countries of origin. Taking a swipe at Republican challenger Nikki Haley, an Indian American, Trump referred to his opponent as "Nimarata" Nikki Haley and that she was ineligible to run for president because her parents weren't born in the United States.[19] Again, the idea was that Haley was one of "them." In fact, Haley's parents were given US citizenship, and Nikki Haley was born in South Carolina and, hence, a US citizen. Nimarata was her given first name, but she has gone by her middle name for most of her life.

Once Harris had been determined as the Democratic presidential nominee, Trump amped up his attacks. Calling her Kam-MAL-ah instead of KAM-al-ah, he made her name rhyme with Allah, the Arab word for God—another not-so-subtle foreign portrayal. Trump also went to work on Harris's biracial background, saying that she flip-flopped on her race depending on the audience she addressed and as such was more devious than authentic. Wherever possible, Trump reminded Whites that Harris was non-White and therefore undeserving of the presidency.[20]

Whether running for office or during his stay in office, Trump repeatedly verbalized racist taunts as if they were a normal part of everyday language. Without a doubt, such insults were a cornerstone of his character that remains with him to this day.

Isolationism

Isolationism refers to the practice of a nation behaving inwardly with respect to interaction with other nations. For more than two hundred years, American isolation was physically guaranteed by large bodies of water to our east and west. True, the United States purchased the Louisiana Territory from France in 1803, and Alaska from Russia in 1867. But these were business transactions, not battles for territory or our way of life. Beyond that, the Mexican American War over the American annexation of territory to the southwest occurred between 1846 and 1848, but that ended soon enough. There was also the Spanish American War in 1898 over Cuba's demand for independence from Spain, but this too was more about ensuring American security than anything else. Simply put, the United States was not in the business of fighting wars abroad.

US isolation ended briefly with late participation in the First World War, from April 1917 until the war's end in November 1918. With the war seemingly over, Americans resumed an inward attitude, with only a distant interest as Europe once again fell into war in the late 1930s. At about the same time, Japan began tangling with China and other nearby nations. Again, not our concern, most American leaders concluded. That remoteness ended in theory with the attack on Pearl Harbor by Japan on December 7, 1941.

Economically, militarily, and politically the international role of the United States changed markedly after the Second World War. The other principal combatants—Great Britain, Germany, Japan, and the Soviet Union—had suffered terribly. Comparatively, the losses of life in the United States were mild next to the other participants. From that point on, the United States became the most powerful nation in the world, and with it came responsibilities not necessarily universally accepted by Americans.

After the Second World War, the United States and eleven nations created the North American Treaty Organization (NATO), where an attack on any one member would be considered an attack on all with a commensurate response. The only time that concept (Article 5 of the NATO treaty) has been invoked occurred after members of al-Qaeda, a terrorist group, hijacked passenger planes and slammed into two buildings at the New York World Trade Center and the Pentagon in Washington, DC. Then, all members offered assistance to the United States in hunting down the terrorists.

Over time, the collection of NATO nations has grown to thirty-two members. These days, along with NATO, the United States has fifty-two collective military arrangements with various groups of nations all over the world, with the most recent being coordination with NATO partners for aid to Ukraine against a Russian invasion in 2022. Combined, these changes have led some Americans to wonder about the extent of American investments— military and political—abroad. If carried out, American isolation would end these relationships.

Overcoming Trumpism

As president, during his first administration, Trump scuttled a several-nation nuclear agreement with Iran, withdrew the United States from the Paris Climate Accord, and renounced American participation in the Trans-Pacific Partnership designed to contain China's influence in Asia. Toward the end of his first presidency, Trump openly expressed the desire to leave NATO and openly told European leaders that as long as he was president, the United States would never help Europe if a member country came under attack.[21] Toward the end of his administration in 2020, Trump even withdrew the United States from the World Health Organization because of disagreement in the best way to manage COVID-19.[22] In isolating the United States from its allies, Trump left European and Asian allies on their own to deal with threats from Russia and China. As part of the process, he also labored to seal off the nation from others. Joe Biden worked to restore several of those discontinued arrangements during his presidency, but Trump's second presidency began the way his first ended.

But isolationism goes beyond severing relationships with other countries. Charles Kupchan offers six elements of the concept. They include capitalizing on national security, serving as a redeemer nation, advancing liberty and prosperity at home, preserving freedom of action abroad, protecting social homogeneity, and promoting pacifism.[23] For Donald Trump, redeeming America and protecting social homogeneity are part of his effort to not only separate the United States from other countries, but to keep the United States from accepting the "thems" from other countries. He has embraced isolationism as the basis for its "America First" theme, which became part of Trump's "Make America Great Again" slogan. If the phrase sounds familiar, it's because it was the call of American Nazi sympathizers during the 1930s who wanted the United States to stay away from the fighting in Europe that prefaced the Second World War.[24]

When discussing American assistance to US allies during his campaign for the presidency in 2024, Trump argued against it. The various military agreements between the United States and allies, he said, had been prohibitively costly to the United States and not worth the investment.[25] The easiest way to deal with such problems, he said, was to withdraw from them.

Authoritarianism

In political life, authoritarianism is an approach to rule resting on intolerance of differences and forced group conformity. Under authoritarianism, there is only one accepted form of behavior: the one declared by the leader and supported by his sycophants. Deviation from an artificially established value system is not permitted. If necessary, authoritarians will rely on force to compel acceptance of their rule. Authoritarians don't control every aspect of political life, only those of importance. Political scientists Steven Levitsky and Daniel Ziblatt offer four criteria for authoritarian behavior: rejection of democratic rules of the game; denial of the legitimacy of political opponents; tolerance or encouragement of violence; and readiness to curtail civil liberties of opponents, including the media.[26] These elements are clearly key elements of Trumpism.

Donald Trump is a believer in authoritarianism. He has been clear about declaring that only he knows what's best for the United States. Recall Trump's statements at the 2016 Republican convention, where he spoke of being the delegates' "voice" and that only he could fix the nation's problems. From Trump's perspective, it was more important for the nation to follow him than interact with him. He was the *only* person to correct the ills in America.

His four years as president between 2017 and 2021 provided ample evidence that Trump was fully committed to authoritarianism. Some examples:

- Early on in his administration, Trump fired the Federal Bureau of Investigation (FBI) director James Comey for his unwillingness to give Trump total loyalty; Comey's loyalty was to the Constitution.[27]
- During the investigation of possible collaboration between Russian agents and Trump during the 2016 presidential election by a Trump administration–appointed special council, Trump blocked all cooperation through the questionable use of executive privilege.
- In 2018, Trump issued a series of executive orders making it easier for the heads of executive departments and agencies to fire civil servants.
- Throughout his presidency, Trump derided the press for presenting "fake news," which was information Trump didn't like.
- Rather than accept the 2020 presidential election results, Trump demanded that the attorney general and secretary of homeland security seize the voting machines in several states that went for Biden, and supported the January 6, 2021, insurrection against the Capitol as members of Congress gathered to officially confirm the election results.
- Upon losing the 2020 election, Trump posted on Truth Social, his social media platform, that the best way to fix the wrongs associated with his defeat would come from terminating the Constitution.[28]

Overcoming Trumpism

All told, Donald Trump used his presidency to maximize his power and prevent anyone from interfering with his activities.

Trump has felt particularly comfortable with fellow autocrats. Rather than associate with prominent democratic leaders, he expressed undying admiration for despots. Often, he voiced effusive praise on China's Xi Jinping, Russia's Vladimir Putin, North Korea's Kim Jong Un, Hungary's Viktor Orban, Turkey's Recep Erdogan, and Egypt's Abdel Fattah el-Sisi—all dictators. In Trump's words, "the tougher and meaner they [autocrats] are, the better I get along with them, [which] is not a bad thing."[29] On another occasion, when assessing the leadership of Xi Jinping, Trump said of the Chinese leader, "President for life! That's pretty good."[30]

Sadly, Trump has not been alone in embracing authoritarian values. As noted in Chapter 1, a substantial chunk of American society is disposed to supporting authoritarianism. The point is, in some respects, Trump has presented himself as a leader responding to those willing to accept his kind of "leadership."

Losing his reelection in 2020 only emboldened Trump for his next calling in 2024. Shortly after he declared for the presidential nomination in 2023, in his first rally, Trump recited his grievances about the "rigged results," and told his followers at a rally, "I am your retribution."[31] Translation: once in office, Trump would get even with his tormentors on his terms. He later spoke of executing at least one opponent from his administration who interfered with Trump's efforts.[32]

Trumpism: More Than an Idea

Combined, Populism, racism, isolationism, and authoritarianism became the essential ingredients of Trumpism. Each element has the potential of being a threat to democracy in its own right. As interactive components, they make Trumpism a commanding antidemocratic force in American politics, perhaps the most powerful antidemocratic threat in the nation's history.

A Divided America

Trumpism has thrived in chaos, much of which exists because of major fissures in contemporary America ripe for exploitation. Many of the issues that divide us today fit well with Trump's "us" versus "them" approach to pitting some Americans against others. Rather than attempt to heal society's ruptures, Trump has used them to pitch his solutions for the "us" part of the nation's politically broken condition. Some of the largest chasms are found with distrust of government, suspicion of elites, and a renewed controversy over immigration. These issues are not necessarily new to Americans; however, the ability of Donald Trump to seize upon them as examples of government dysfunction has added to a feeling of general despair that he has been all too willing to rescue, as in "only I can fix it." Moreover, Trump acolytes have been only too eager to emulate his grievances, indicating that Trumpism goes well beyond its creator.

Distrust of Government

Accompanied by dozens of members elected to Congress, Trump has dedicated considerable energy to faulting those in key positions of power. He and allies, many of whom "serve" in government have sown doubt over the behavior of the military, the FBI, and the CDC (Centers for Disease Control and Prevention). Despite their different responsibilities, the "problems" in these agencies were all part of the "deep state," an alleged clandestine network of government units working with prominent people outside government to pursue their own self-serving agenda. Their conspiratorial claim was soon embraced by many Americans, more than one-third of the nation according to at least one poll.[33] As a result, many in American society no longer have as much faith in cornerstone American institutions, including presidential elections. The weakening of public support for key government bodies has paved the way for people to accept someone with a different approach to solving society's most pressing problems. That "someone" has presented himself in the name of Donald Trump.

The Military—

We begin with reduced public support for the military, long valued by the public as an asset. Trump has described members of the military as "some of the dumbest people" he has ever known.[34] His sentiments have been the most critical when discussing wounded soldiers and those who have been captured during wars, who he referred to as "losers." For example, about US senator John McCain, a badly wounded Navy pilot held by the North Vietnamese for more than five years during the Vietnam War, Trump said, "He's not a war hero. He was a war hero because he was captured. I like people who weren't captured."[35] Trump developed a broad disdain for the military's leaders, at one point saying that the top brass "want to do nothing but fight wars so that all of those wonderful companies that make the bombs and make the planes and make everything else stay happy."[36]

Such statements became mainstays in Trump's presidential campaign repertoire, and they have had an impact. He wasn't alone. Referring to an Army recruiting ad focusing on women and racial minorities, Republican US senator Ted Cruz accused the military and media of turning the military into "pansies."[37] Such talk has taken a toll. American confidence in the military fell to 60 percent in 2023, the lowest since 1997 when it hovered near 80 percent.[38]

Federal Law Enforcement—

Regarding law enforcement, for decades, the FBI, America's most important domestic law enforcement entity, had incredibly high public support for its no-nonsense, nonpolitical work. During the 2016 campaign, the FBI began looking into possible connections between the Trump campaign and Russian agents, fearing that the Russians might try to compromise Trump. Despite the bureau's intentions to save Trump from being coerced, Trump viewed the investigation as a misuse of federal law enforcement.

From that time on, Trump discussed the FBI in negative terms. Then, upon leaving office in 2021, private citizen Donald Trump possessed hundreds of highly sensitive government documents in his Mar-a-Lago residence that belonged in the National Archives. After Trump failed to comply with several requests from the archives, in 2022, the FBI secured a court-authorized search that allowed agents to return the documents to its rightful home. Trump accused the Department of Justice of weaponizing the FBI, a falsehood that was soon repeated by then-House minority leader Kevin McCarthy and several Republican members of Congress as well as other national Republican leaders.[39] Meanwhile, public support of the FBI tanked from 68 percent in 2016 to 37 percent in 2023.[40] Worse yet, in a national poll taken in early January 2024, 25 percent of Americans believed that FBI operatives actually organized and encouraged the January 6, 2021, insurrection against the Capitol.[41]

Disease Prevention—

Lastly, we turn to the CDC. Concerned with protection of the public's health, the CDC was held in the highest esteem by the international medical community and long revered for its value to American society. Disease prevention, environmental health, and protection against health threats have been core responsibilities of this renowned institution, housing the best scientists in the world.

Then came COVID-19, a new deadly virus that threatened the lives of millions of Americans. From the beginning, President Trump minimized the deadly potential of the virus. Shortly after the number of deaths began to grow in February 2020, Trump said the virus would be gone by Easter. He was wrong, very wrong. Dr. Anthony Fauci, the chief medical officer in charge of dealing with the virus, disagreed with Trump's optimism. Within a short time, the virus took its toll on millions of Americans.

Deaths from COVID-19 climbed and Trump began to criticize the CDC for not doing its job. As the 2020 election neared and Trump's popularity waned, the president accused Dr. Fauci and his colleagues of being idiots incapable of managing the disease.[42] Other Republicans followed suit, with several making Fauci a villain in campaign ads, including the message of one Republican US candidate, that said "let's fire Fauci and take back our freedoms."[43] Meanwhile, support of the agency plummeted. Whereas early in the pandemic 79 percent of the public expressed favorable views of the agency in April 2020, within two years, support had dropped to 50 percent.[44]

These examples represent the top of a long list of government agencies facing elimination or serious cutbacks. Some of the others include the Internal Revenue Service (IRS) for abusing taxpayers; the Department of Education for funding controversial programs dealing with gender and race; and the Bureau of Alcohol, Firearms, and Explosives for interfering with gun ownership. Like the other examples, Trumpists see these agencies as embodiments of the "deep state," the enemy of the people. Those agencies plus several others felt the wrath of Trump's retribution after his election in 2024.

What have we learned here? Traditionally, in difficult times, presidents and other great leaders use their positions of authority and respect to manage issues, especially those filled with conflict. As leaders, they use their positions to rally behind public institutions dedicated to overcoming adversity. When a crisis occurs, such empathetic talents are all the more necessary for calming those on edge. But Donald Trump is not interested in healing or reassuring the public; rather, he seeks to rule by division and chaos.[45] Other than building his border wall, he and his allies seek to tear down major portions of the federal government because they are described as unnecessary, expensive, and intrusive. It all fits in with Trump's penchant for chaos. From his perspective, the more frenzied the society, the more he can step in with little opposition to do as he wishes. Others of his ilk have been quick to join the fracas, leaving society all the more concerned.

Distrust of Elites

Elites have always been a group of interest in the United States. To begin with, few people self-identify as elites. Why? Because to be an elite means you are superior to the rest, often in a higher socioeconomic position or status than most, other times with an abundance of knowledge, and yet other times still holding important positions of power. With that rather broad definition, it's easy to see why people may differ on who is or is not an elite. Differences also emerge as to whether elites are helpful or harmful to American society, including politics.[46] The point is, they are controversial.

The ambiguity notwithstanding, some elites are plainly obvious. Donald Trump is one such person. Growing up in privilege, attending a leading university, possessing extraordinary wealth, and prominent on the New York social scene, Trump clearly meets the qualifications in virtually any definition of "elite."

We labor on this point because of its irony: Trump, an elitist, has spent much of his political career bashing elites—people like him! As the populist-in-chief, Trump has made a career of vilifying leaders in industry and labor alike, major politicians, foreign dignitaries, scientists, academics, the media profession, and key bureaucrats. About academics, for example, Trump, the Wharton graduate, has denigrated them and their specializations as the enemy of common sense. In his words, "I don't know of another kind of arrogance worse than academic arrogance . . . coming from reading books, sitting at a desk and learning from reading, versus people out there building the roads."[47] With each assault, he has positioned his comments in the "us" versus "them" mindset, reminding audiences that he is on their side, and that Trump will hold elites to account for self-centered policy objectives far removed from the national mood.

His efforts notwithstanding, Trump has convinced few people that he's like them, but he's convinced many that he's *for* them, particularly as trust relates to the "deep state" in government. Consider the result of a longitudinal public opinion poll conducted by Pew Research Center of trust in government between 1958 and 2023, which found that confidence in the federal government has greatly diminished over time. In 1964, the high point, 79 percent agreed that the federal government does what is right "just about always" or "most of the time;" by 2023, only 16 percent trusted the government "just about always" or "most of the time." When examined by political party, the data revealed trust of the federal government by 25 percent of Democrats and 8 percent of Republicans.[48]

Social scientists cite several reasons for growing distrust of government, among them, scandals, inattention by elected officials, inequitable policies, intentionally withheld information from the public, too little activity for the poor and middle class (most Democrats) and too much activity for the poor and middle class (most Republicans).[49]

Trump can't take credit (or blame) for growing distrust in the government, but he has managed to fuse distrust for government and contempt for elites into one political package. Nowhere has Trump done that better than in his condemnation of judges. Facing four major court cases laced with ninety-one criminal charges, he blasted the judges overseeing his circumstances as racist, partisan, and corrupt. In the process, he reframed prosecutions into persecutions and, more importantly, argued judicial collusion to prevent him from running for and winning the 2024 presidential election. And his efforts worked in some quarters. A national poll on July 23, 2023, found that only 11 percent of Republicans believed that Trump committed any crime related to the now-infamous January 6, 2021, insurrection against the Capitol. With respect to a second set of charges, attempting to overturn the 2020 presidential election, 13 percent of Republicans agreed that Trump was responsible. Meanwhile, only 40 percent of Independents believed that Trump tried to overturn the 2020 presidential election, and 34 percent agreed that he was responsible for events on January 6, 2021. Among Democrats, the numbers were at 82 and 83 percent, respectively.[50]

There's an important takeaway here. Trump's rewrite of the circumstances surrounding the 2020 presidential election have served him well. Think about it: charged and convicted criminals, in Trump's assessment, were patriots and hostages! Between his grievances against the courts and his ability to galvanize a solid portion of Independents, Trump turned the arguments against elites to his advantage. And by pushing the idea of an unresponsive, corrupt government, Trump utilized a key concept in the authoritarian playbook.

Renewed Controversy over Immigration

Throughout American history, immigration has been a contentious tipping point of sorts. Oddly, this country was built on the backs, minds, and hearts of people coming here for a new life free of oppression, discrimination, and artificial limits to success in their countries of origin. At times, Congress passed legislation making it difficult, if not impossible for various groups to take root here. Immigration quotas were often put into place as well as outright blocks against Eastern Europeans, Chinese, Japanese, and Mexican populations, to cite a few examples. On other occasions, such as the post–Second World War era and at the end of the Vietnam War, the United States has been much more generous about accepting refugees. But the current national discussion about immigration is an ugly refrain from previous periods where people were denied entry because of their race, ethnicity, or religion.

The resurging debate over immigration is a thinly veiled attempt by Trumpists at limiting immigration to the types of people who would be "acceptable," which means White Christians. We know this to be the case because Donald Trump, himself, has stated as much in rather blunt terms. In 2018, during a meeting with congressional leaders about an immigration reform package, then-president Trump revealed his true sentiments. Trump seethed over a portion of the proposal that would have protected some immigrants from Haiti, El Salvador, and African countries who had come to the United States for political asylum. To that suggestion he bristled, "Why are we having all these people from shithole countries come here?" He then went on to add that the United States should be admitting people from countries such as Norway.[51] It's pretty hard to find a more racist statement than Trump's blunt comment.

Over the course of his four years in office, Trump was relentless in his effort to minimize immigration to the United States from "shithole" countries. According to one report, Trump used his executive power to make 472 changes in the federal immigration system. The areas of activity included reducing immigrant admissions during the COVID-19 pandemic; border enforcement; streamlining the immigration court system; prior to COVID-19, limiting admission of refugees, asylum seekers, and requests on humanitarian grounds; and tougher vetting on visa requests.[52] On this issue, the Trump record is crystal clear.

As a consequence of Trump's efforts, the numbers of immigrants entering the United States were the lowest in decades during his presidency, but at a cost to American society. Critics expressed concern on two counts. First, the new approach turned away people who were subject to abuse because of criminal activity in their home countries, and second, fear expressed by economists that the new rules have made it harder for the United States to accept skilled foreign workers, which hurt the United States and helped competing nations where foreign workers were welcomed.[53]

The current debate about immigration has a distinctly partisan twist compared to the days before the Trump presidency. Trump's persistent description of immigrants as murderers, rapists, drug dealers, and other criminal degenerates has exacerbated the division between pro-immigration and anti-immigration contingents. When asked in a 2023 national poll whether increasing diversity of races, nationalities, and ethnic groups make the United States a better place to live, 73 percent of Democrats and only 30 percent of Republicans replied "yes." That's a stark 43 percent difference from a 2015 poll, shortly before the 2016 presidential year, when 65 percent of Democrats and 52 percent of Republicans answered "yes" to a similar question.[54] So, what happened between 2015 and 2023? Trumpism and the constant beat from immigrant bashing. As with the growing distrust of government and increasing suspicion of elites and a penchant for aggregating already sensitive issues, Trumpism has turned less politicized questions into hot-button issues, creating new, or at least increased, division in an American society already burdened with contentiousness.

The Restructuring of American Values

Trumpism is a powerful political force, especially for those living in fear—fear of surrendering their place in society to others, fear of government-imposed constraints on their lives, fear of losing their way of life. These examples show how Trumpism thrives on the "us" versus "them" classification of society and the results that follow. That very chaos is the source of strength for Donald Trump and his allies.

It's important to note that in America, divisions are not new. There have always been tensions between Whites and non-Whites, Christians and non-Christians, anchored citizens and newcomers. The very multicultural nature of American society virtually guarantees such tensions; they are endemic to a pluralistic society. By far, the Civil War was the greatest challenge to keeping the United States whole. But for the most part, throughout the nation's history, there have been constraints on what those in power could do to the powerless, whether from competing government entities or the voters. It's an equilibrium of sorts, although rarely justly balanced. Simply put, the United States has always been full of winners and losers, but for many there has been a desire and effort to make it better.

Overcoming Trumpism

Increasingly, the voices of those seeking fairness have been overcome by Trumpists who have no such interest or care. The power of Trumpism has impacted our lives to the extent of promoting hate over tolerance, order at any price, and institutionalized discrimination over informal prejudice. As a result, today we live in an environment that threatens to alter American cultural values.

Hate over Tolerance

In a democracy, tolerance is not only a virtue but a necessity for accepting different views in a pluralistic society.[55] We don't have to agree with others; rather, we need to acknowledge that others may not see things as we do and respect their points of view. From there, good governance comes from those with differing opinions who, on the same issue, seek common ground. This is the essence of tolerance.

Hate, however, interferes with democracy to the extent that it is a key component of authoritarianism.[56] It doesn't have to be that way. Studies show that tolerance in America on issues related to race grew substantially between the 1960s and 1990s.[57] But that seems to be a bygone era. With Trumpism, tolerance has given way to hate and intolerance, especially with respect to racial, ethnic, and religious minorities.

We can assess the extent of growing intolerance in America through the examination of FBI data before Donald Trump ascended to the presidency in 2016 and after. The differences are dramatic. In 2015, the FBI recorded 6,885 offenses against race, ethnicity, religion, sexual orientation, disability, gender, and gender identity. Fast forward to 2022. With Trump out of office but seeking reelection, the FBI recorded 11,634 incidents in the same categories, an increase of 69 percent.[58] Meanwhile, during the same time period, the US population grew by 4 percent.

Given the above, the question remains, is there a direct connection between Trumpism and hate? Authors Griffin Edwards and Stephen Rushin answer the question with a study of the demographic sources of hate crimes during the 2016 presidential campaign. They found that "counties that voted for President Trump in the presidential election [of 2016] experienced the largest increases in hate crimes."[59] That would be problematic enough if hate ended with the election, but it has continued to become a permanent fixture in American society, at least for now. Nationwide research by ABC on the relationship between Trump and violence found at least 54 instances between 2015 and 2020, where Trump supporters physically attacked anti-Trump supporters, sometimes during or after rallies and other times where they cited Trump's name as the source of their anger. Most of the attackers were White young men, similar to the profile at the infamous January 6, 2021, insurrection against the Capitol. Also, most of the assaults were against minorities including African Americans, Latinos, Muslims, and gay men.[60]

The surge of Trumpism-inspired hate in the United States has lessened the commitment to democracy. Moreover, the acts fit with Trump's own remarks during the 2024 presidential campaign where he promised that after resuming the presidency, he would remove undocumented immigrants who were "poisoning the blood of our country," language frequently used by Nazi leaders during their effort to exterminate Jews.[61] For Trump, spewing hate is as natural as drinking water.

Order at Any Price

At one point during his 2024 presidential campaign, Donald Trump almost cavalierly pronounced that upon returning to the presidency, he would be a "dictator," at least on the first day. This was not a slip of the tongue. Through his 2024 campaign, Trump praised authoritarians who rule with an "iron fist."[62] In fact, his declaration to rule on his terms irrespective of the law paralleled Trump's effort to avoid ending his presidency. In those final days, he sought to order the secretary of Homeland Security to seize "corrupt" voting machines from key states where he had lost even though any such move would be patently illegal.[63] That effort failed, yet it offered insight into Trump's thinking about maintaining order regardless of any election outcome.

Trump has plenty of authoritarian followers, which makes his behavior all the more frightening for those concerned with losing our democracy. All we have to do is remember the 147 Republican members of Congress (139 in the House of Representatives and 8 in the US Senate) who on January 6, 2021, *after* the insurrection against the Capitol, voted to overturn the results of the 2020 election despite the absence of any evidence. In fact, some members rejected the description of the assault as an "insurrection" altogether, suggesting that the riot was little more than a rowdy tour of the Capitol. Republican representative Paul Gosar (AZ) went so far as to categorize the insurrectionists as "peaceful patriots" and called then-president-elect Biden an "illegitimate usurper" of power.[64] As for the insurrection, the rioters were simply doing what Trump exhorted them to do: "take back our country."[65] If the mob succeeded in storming the Capitol to restore order, then so be it!

Overcoming Trumpism

The threat of violence from Trump took a huge leap on March 16, 2024, at an Ohio rally. After lambasting immigrants, the failed insurrection on January 6, 2021, the "rigged" 2020 presidential election, and numerous other wrongs in America, Trump made his most direct threat of violence yet: "If I don't get elected, it's going to be a bloodbath . . . for the country."[66] Trump all but promised violence if he lost the 2024 presidential election. Such speech is not only unbecoming of a presidential candidate's rhetoric, but it is also antithetical to the basic tenets of democracy.

The growing comfort with order at any price has seeped into large swaths of American society. A 2023 national poll asked whether "we need a leader who is willing to break some rules if that's what it takes to set things right." Thirty-eight percent of the respondents agreed with the idea, including 48 percent of Republicans.[67] That survey is not an outlier. In a 2022 national survey of Americans, 42 percent agreed that "having a strong leader is more important than having a democracy."[68] Simply put, Donald Trump had considerable support in and out of government for restoring order in an election gone amok. He, and he alone, would restore order.

Lost Faith in Democracy

The restructuring of American culture to include hate and violence coincides with the beliefs of many that American democracy is on the wane. In a 2022 national survey of Americans, 52 percent were "very concerned" with the future of American democracy.[69] Another national poll taken by NPR/Ipsos the same year offers an even more dour assessment, with 64 percent agreeing that "American democracy is in crisis and at risk of failing."[70] Disturbing as this data may be, it shouldn't come as a surprise. Earlier we discussed growing distrust of the bureaucracy, but the loss of public confidence has also turned on the presidency, Congress, and the courts; the media; the police; and even public schools. The decline in institutional faith does not appear to be transitory. In fact, regarding the averages of nine core institutions in the public and private sectors measured by Gallup since 1979, public confidence has reached a record low.[71] To the extent that the presidency, Congress, and the federal courts are the collective center as guardrails of democracy, public support in the Gallup survey is abysmal: 27 percent for the Supreme Court, 26 percent for the presidency, and 8 percent for Congress.[72]

How do we explain the loss of support for American democracy? The NPR/Ipsos poll found political, economic, and cultural concerns. More than

60 percent of the respondents agreed that "traditional parties and politicians don't care about people like me" and that "the American economy is rigged to advantage the rich and powerful." Nearly half agreed that "when jobs are scarce, employers should prioritize hiring people of this country over immigrants" and that "these days I feel like a stranger in my own country." Translated into everyday terms, according to the survey, people have concerns about economic equality and immigration.

But is there more to lost faith in democracy than these criticisms? Public concerns may have something to do with superficial support for the concept to begin with. Thomas Dye and Harmon Zeigler have written that whatever people say or think about democracy, people "have surprisingly weak commitments to the principles of individual liberty, toleration of diversity, and freedom of expression." In contrast, they say, we count on leaders to promote democratic values from the top down to the people.[73] If that's the case, Trumpists have failed us as leaders, for their grievances focus on the "thems"—immigrants and the economic elites ripping off the rest of us. Trumpists would rather exploit differences than heal them, for the discontent, particularly in White Christians with high school–level educations, serves as the wellspring of much of their power. Instead, they should be focusing on political ways to expand the economic pie and the benefits of diversity in democracy. So, the divided society goes on, and no one deserves more blame for that than Donald Trump.

Trumpism on the Ascent

Trumpism may be the latest reactionary political movement to come and eventually go in American society, but its roots are real and deep. Populism, racism, isolationism, and authoritarianism—four powerfully interconnected links—serve as a potentially long-term threat to overturning a 250-year slow, but steady march toward achieving an inclusive democracy. Trumpism has widened fissures into huge chasms, pitting various segments of society against one another.

Trumpism has found a way to not only exploit the political, economic, and social anguish of many Americans, but also to benefit Trump and his adherents from the distress. In fact, the angrier Americans react to Trump's abusive insults, the more that Trumpists seem to thrive from seeing their targets suffer.[74] Yet, the costs are real. Particularly important is that unlike most of the other political movements that have come and gone, Trumpism has infected a substantial segment of American society large enough to become the base of two presidential election victories. Defeating it will require an even larger swath of American society to comprehend the damage and repel it.

NOTES

1. Harvard Caps Harris Poll, December 13–14, 2023, https://harvardharrispoll.com/wp-content/uploads/2023/12/HHP_Dec23_KeyResults.pdf.
2. Cinthia Miller-Idriss, *Hate in the Homeland* (Princeton, NJ: Princeton University Press, 2020), p. 49.
3. See Michael J. Diamond, *Ruptures in the American Psyche* (Oxfordshire, England: Phoenix, 2022), p. 14.
4. Charles Postel, *The Populist Vision* (New York: Oxford University Press, 2007), pp. 4–6.
5. Anthony King, *The Founding Fathers v. The People: Paradoxes of American Democracy* (Cambridge, MA: Harvard University Press, 2012), p. 162.
6. Lawrence Quill, *Nostalgia and Political Theory* (New York: Routledge, 2024), p. 160.
7. See William E. Hudson, *American Democracy in Peril*, 9th edition (Thousand Oaks, CA: SAGE, 2021).
8. Duncan Espenshade, "Populism in American Elections: Bernie Sanders and Donald Trump," Foreign Policy Research Institute, June 10, 2020, https://www.fpri.org/article/2020/06/populism-in-american-elections-bernie-sanders-and-donald-trump/.
9. Yoni Applebaum, "I Alone Can Fix It," *The Atlantic*, July 21, 2016, https://www.theatlantic.com/politics/archive/2016/07/trump-rnc-speech-alone-fix-it/492557/.
10. "Six Times President Trump Said He Is the Least Racist Person," *The Washington Post*, January 17, 2018, https://www.washingtonpost.com/news/the-fix/wp/2018/01/17/six-times-president-trump-said-he-is-the-least-racist-person/.
11. "Donald Trump Calls Obama the 'founder' of ISIS," *The Guardian*, August 11, 2016, https://www.theguardian.com/us-news/2016/aug/11/donald-trump-calls-barack-obama-the-founder-of-isis.
12. "Donald Trump Announces Presidential Bid by Trashing Mexico," NBC News, June 16, 2015, https://www.nbcnews.com/news/latino/donald-trump-announces-presidential-bid-trashing-mexico-mexicans-n376521.
13. "Blaming Muslims after Attack, Donald Trump Tosses Pluralism Aside," *The New York Times*, June 13, 2016, https://www.nytimes.com/2016/06/14/us/politics/donald-trump-hillary-clinton-speeches.html.
14. "Almost Half of Illegal Immigrants Entered U.S. Legally but Stayed after Visa Expired," Washington, DC: Office of Homeland Security, May 3, 2011, https://www.hsgac.senate.gov/media/reps/almost-half-of-illegal-immigrants-entered-u-s-legally-but-stayed-after-visa-expired/.

15 Quoted in "Trump Defends White-Nationalist Protesters: 'Some Very Fine People on Both Sides,'" *The Atlantic*, August 15, 2017, https://www.theatlantic.com/politics/archive/2017/08/trump-defends-white-nationalist-protesters-some-very-fine-people-on-both-sides/537012/.
16 "Trump Calls Some Unauthorized Immigrants 'Animals' in Rant," *The New York Times*, May 16, 2018, https://www.nytimes.com/2018/05/16/us/politics/trump-undocumented-immigrants-animals.html.
17 For a partial list of Trump's racist rants, see "Donald Trump's Long History of Racism, from the 1970s to 2020," Vox, August 13, 2020, https://www.vox.com/2016/7/25/12270880/donald-trump-racist-racism-history.
18 "Trump Stokes 'Birther' Conspiracy Theory about Kamala Harris," BBC, August 14, 2020, https://www.bbc.com/news/world-us-canada-53774289.
19 "Trump's Unsubtle Crusade to Cast Foes as Less American Comes for Haley," *The Washington Post*, January 17, 2024, https://www.washingtonpost.com/politics/2024/01/17/trump-playbook-foes-haley/.
20 "Trump Elevates False, Fringe Attacks to Center of His Campaign," *The New York Times*, August 2, 2024, https://www.nytimes.com/2024/08/01/us/politics/trump-harris-race.html.
21 See "Trump Discussed Pulling U.S. from NATO, Aides Say amid New Concerns over Russia," *The New York Times*, January 14, 2019, https://www.nytimes.com/2019/01/14/us/politics/nato-president-trump.html and "Trump Told E.U. That U.S. Would Never Help Europe under Attack, Senior Official Says," Reuters, January 11, 2024, https://www.nbcnews.com/news/world/donald-trump-us-europe-attack-nato-davos-ursula-von-der-leyen-rcna133396.
22 "Trump Sets Date to End WHO Membership over Its Handling of Virus," NPR, July 7, 2020, https://www.npr.org/sections/goatsandsoda/2020/07/07/888186158/trump-sets-date-to-end-who-membership-over-its-handling-of-virus.
23 Charles A. Kupchan, *Isolationism: A History of America's Efforts to Shield Itself from the World* (New York: Oxford University Press, 2020), pp. 34–58.
24 "President Trump's 'America First' Slogan Was Popularized by Nazi Sympathizers," *The Washington Post*, January 20, 2017, https://www.washingtonpost.com/posteverything/wp/2017/01/20/president-trumps-america-first-slogan-was-popularized-by-nazi-sympathizers/.
25 Donald Trump interview with Maggie Haberman and David Sanger, "Transcript: Donald Trump Expounds on His Foreign Policy Views," *The New York Times*, March 26, 2016, https://www.nytimes.com/2016/03/27/us/politics/donald-trump-transcript.html?smid=tw-nytpolitics&smtyp=cur.
26 Steven Levitsky and Daniel Ziblatt, *How Democracies Die* (New York: Penguin Random House, 2019), pp. 65–7.
27 For his account of the event, see James Comey, *A Higher Loyalty* (New York: Flatworld, 2018), pp. 228–44.
28 "Trump's Call for 'Termination' of Constitution Draws Rebukes," *The New York Times*, December 4, 2022, https://www.nytimes.com/2022/12/04/us/politics/trump-constitution-republicans.html.

29 "Bob Woodward Reveals New Trump Audio Saying He Gets Along with 'Tougher, Meaner' Leaders," *Today*, September 14, 2020, https://www.today.com/news/bob-woodward-reveals-new-trump-tape-saying-he-gets-along-t191592.
30 "Trump Voices Admiration and Envy of Kim Jong Un, Underscoring His Respect for Autocrats," *Los Angeles Times*, June 15, 2018, https://www.latimes.com/politics/la-na-pol-trump-kim-values-20180615-story.html.
31 "Trump, Vowing 'Retribution,' Foretells a Second Term of Spite," *The New York Times*, March 7, 2023, https://www.nytimes.com/2023/03/07/us/politics/trump-2024-president.html.
32 "Trump Floats the Idea of Executing Joint Chiefs Chairman Milley," *The Atlantic*, September 23, 2023, https://www.nytimes.com/2023/03/07/us/politics/trump-2024-president.html.
33 "More Than 1 in 3 Americans Believe a 'Deep State' Is Working to Undermine Trump," NPR/Ipsos Poll, December 30, 2020, https://www.ipsos.com/en-us/news-polls/npr-misinformation-123020.
34 "Trump Stoops to New Low with Comments about Military Officials," *The New Republic*, October 17, 2023, https://newrepublic.com/post/176285/trump-trash-military-officials-dumbest-people.
35 "Trump Attacks McCain: 'I Like People Who Weren't Captured," Politico, July 19, 2015, https://www.politico.com/story/2015/07/trump-attacks-mccain-i-like-people-who-werent-captured-120317.
36 "Trump Launches Unprecedented Attack on Military Leadership He Appointed," CNN, September 8, 2020,
37 "Conservatives Lash Out at the Military over 'Woke' Policies," Politico, May 5, 2021, https://www.politico.com/news/2021/05/21/conservative-critics-military-policies-490197.
38 "Confidence in U.S. Military Lowest in over Two Decades," Gallup Poll, July 31, 2023, https://www.cnn.com/2020/09/07/politics/trump-attack-military-leadership/index.html. https://news.gallup.com/poll/509189/confidence-military-lowest-two-decades.aspx.
39 "Republicans Demand Answers from DOJ and FBI over Trump Search Raid," NPR, August 9, 2022, https://www.npr.org/2022/08/09/1116529783/republicans-react-fbi-trump-search-mar-a-lago.
40 See "Growing Partisan Differences in Views of the FBI; Stark Divide over ICE," Pew Research Center, July 24, 2018, https://www.pewresearch.org/politics/2018/07/24/growing-partisan-differences-in-views-of-the-fbi-stark-divide-over-ice/, and "Americans Sour on the FBI and DOJ amid Trump Investigations," NBC News, July 23, 2023, https://www.nbcnews.com/meet-the-press/meetthepressblog/americans-sour-fbi-doj-trump-investigations-rcna91814.
41 "A Quarter of Americans Believe FBI Instigated Jan. 6, Post-UMD Poll Finds," *The Washington Post*, January 4, 2024, https://www.washingtonpost.com/dc-md-va/2024/01/04/fbi-conspiracy-jan-6-attack-misinformation/.
42 "Trump Attacks 'Fauci and All These Idiots,' Says Public Is Tired of Pandemic, Public Health Restrictions as Infection Rates Rise," *The Washington Post*,

October 19, 2020, https://www.washingtonpost.com/politics/trump-fauci-campaign-biden/2020/10/19/30b2fe58-1226-11eb-82af-864652063d61_story.html.

43 "Fauci Is the Villain in New GOP Campaign Ads," Politico, February 4, 2022, https://www.politico.com/news/2022/02/04/fauci-villain-new-gop-campaign-ads-00005430.

44 See "Public Holds Broadly Favorable Views of Many Federal Agencies, Including CDC and HHS," Pew Research Center, April 9, 2020, https://www.pewresearch.org/politics/2020/04/09/public-holds-broadly-favorable-views-of-many-federal-agencies-including-cdc-and-hhs/, and "Increasing Public Criticism, Confusion over COVID-19 Response in U.S.," Pew Research Center, February 9, 2022, https://www.pewresearch.org/science/2022/02/09/increasing-public-criticism-confusion-over-covid-19-response-in-u-s/.

45 See "Inside the Next Republican Revolution," Politico, September 19, 2023, https://www.politico.com/news/magazine/2023/09/19/project-2025-trump-reagan-00115811.

46 For two different definitions of elitism, see Peter Bachrach, *The Theory of Democratic Elitism* (Boston, MA: Little Brown, 1967), and Thomas R. Dye and Harmon Zeigler, *The Irony of Democracy*, 12th edition (Belmont, CA: Wadsworth/Thomson Learning, 2003).

47 Quoted in "Analysis: Trump's War against Elites and Expertise," *Los Angeles Times*, July 27, 2017, https://www.latimes.com/politics/la-na-pol-trump-elites-20170725-story.html.

48 "Public Trust in Government: 1958–2023," Pew Research Center, September 19, 2023, https://www.pewresearch.org/politics/2023/09/19/public-trust-in-government-1958-2023/.

49 "Americans' Views of Government: Decades of Distrust, Enduring Support for Its Role," Pew Research Center, June 7, 2022, https://www.pewresearch.org/politics/2022/06/06/americans-views-of-government-decades-of-distrust-enduring-support-for-its-role/.

50 "Uncharted Territory: The Aftermath of Presidential Indictments," Bright Line Watch, June/July 2023 surveys, https://brightlinewatch.org/uncharted-territory-the-aftermath-of-presidential-indictments/.

51 "Trump Derides Protections for Immigrants from 'Shithole' Countries," *The Washington Post*, January 12, 2018, https://www.washingtonpost.com/politics/trump-attacks-protections-for-immigrants-from-shithole-countries-in-oval-office-meeting/2018/01/11/bfc0725c-f711-11e7-91af-31ac729add94_story.html.

52 Jessica Bolter, Emma Israel, and Sarah Pierce, *Four Years of Profound Change: Immigration Policy during the Trump Presidency* (Washington, DC: Migration Policy Institute), 2022.

53 See Paul Waldman, "Opinion: The Trump Administration's Immigration Policies Are Impossibly Cruel. That's the Whole Point," *The Washington Post*, May 28, 2018, https://www.washingtonpost.com/blogs/plum-line/wp/2018/05/28/the-trump-administrations-immigration-policies-are-impossibly-cruel-thats-the-whole-point/, and "Trump Immigration Restrictions Expected to Impact

Economy Long after He Leaves White House," *Los Angeles Times*, October 9, 2020, https://www.latimes.com/politics/story/2020-10-09/trump-immigration-restrictions-will-impact-economy-long-after-he-leaves-white-house-experts-say.

54 "Half of Americans Say Diversity Benefits the United States," The Chicago Council on Global Affairs, December 2023, https://globalaffairs.org/sites/default/files/2023-12/2023%20CCS%20Immigration.pdf, and "Beyond Distrust: How Americans View Their Government," Pew Research Center, November 23, 2015, file:///Users/gerstondocs/Downloads/11-23-2015-Governance-release.pdf.

55 Sidney Verba, Key Lehman Schlozman, and Henry E. Brady, *Voice and Equality: Civic Virtue in American Politics* (Cambridge, MA: Harvard University Press, 1995), p. 501.

56 Marc J. Hetherington and Jonathan D. Weiler, *Authoritarianism and Polarization in American Politics* (New York: Cambridge University Press, 2009) pp. 46–8.

57 See Robert D. Putnam, *Bowling Alone: The Collapse and Revival of American Community* (New York: Simon & Schuster, 2000), pp. 352–5.

58 "Latest Hate Crime Statistics Released, 2015," FBI, November 2016, https://www.fbi.gov/news/stories/2015-hate-crime-statistics-released, and "F.B.I. Releases 2023 Hate Crime Statistics, 2023," U.S. Department of Justice, https://www.justice.gov/crs/news/2023-hate-crime-statistics.

59 Griffin Edwards and Stephen Rushkin, "The Effect of President Trump's Election on Hate Crimes," Social Science Research Network, January 14, 2018, https://papers.ssrn.com/sol3/papers.cfm?abstract_id=3102652.

60 "'No Blame?' ABC News Finds 54 Cases Invoking 'Trump' in Connection with Violence, Threats, Alleged Assaults," ABC News, May 30, 2020, https://abcnews.go.com/Politics/blame-abc-news-finds-17-cases-invoking-trump/story?id=58912889.

61 "Trump Repeats 'Poisoning the Blood' Anti-Immigrant Remark," *The Washington Post*, December 16, 2023, https://www.reuters.com/world/us/trump-repeats-poisoning-blood-anti-immigrant-remark-2023-12-16/.

62 "Trump Adopts Strong-Arm Approach to a Second Term," *The Wall Street Journal*, September 15, 2024, https://www.wsj.com/politics/policy/trump-strong-arm-presidency-approach-b39f0f61.

63 "Trump Involved in Proposals to Seize Voting Machines: Report," The Hill, February 1, 2022, https://thehill.com/homenews/administration/592210-trump-involved-in-proposals-to-seize-voting-machines-report/.

64 Quoted on "Republican Lawmakers Claim January 6 Rioters Were Just Friendly Guys and Gals Taking a Tourist Trip through the Capitol," *Vanity Fair*, May 12, 2021, https://www.vanityfair.com/news/2021/05/capitol-attack-tourist-visit?redirectURL=%2Fnews%2F2021%2F05%2Fcapitol-attack-tourist-visit.

65 "Trump Told Crowd 'You Will Never Take Back Our Country with Weakness,'" *The New York Times*, January 6, 2024, https://www.nytimes.com/2021/01/06/us/politics/trump-speech-capitol.html.

66. "Trump Says Some Migrants Are 'Not People' and Predicts a 'Blood Bath' If He Loses," *The New York Times*, March 18, 2024, https://www.nytimes.com/2024/03/16/us/politics/trump-speech-ohio.html.
67. "Threats to American Democracy Ahead of an Unprecedented Presidential Election," PRRI Values Survey, 2023, https://www.prri.org/wp-content/uploads/2023/10/PRRI-Oct-2023-AVS.pdf.
68. "Views of American Democracy and Society and Support for Political Violence: First Report from a Nationwide Population-Representative Survey," medRxiv, July 19, 2022, https://www.medrxiv.org/content/10.1101/2022.07.15.22277693v1.full.
69. "How Concerned Are You about the Future of American Democracy?" YouGov, June 13, 2022, https://today.yougov.com/topics/politics/survey-results/daily/2022/06/13/ba2e1/3.
70. "Seven in Ten Americans Say the Country Is in Cirsis, at Risk of Failing," NPR/Ipsos, January 3, 2022, https://www.ipsos.com/en-us/seven-ten-americans-say-country-crisis-risk-failing.
71. "Historically Low Faith in U.S. Institutions Continues," Gallup, July 16, 2023, https://news.gallup.com/poll/508169/historically-low-faith-institutions-continues.aspx. The nine institutions are church/organized religion, the military, the Supreme Court, banks, public schools, newspapers, Congress, organized labor, and big business.
72. Ibid.
73. Dye and Zeigler, *The Irony of Democracy*, p. 17.
74. "Vulgarities, Insults, Baseless Attacks: Trump Backers Follow His Lead," *The Washington Post*, November 19, 2023, https://www.washingtonpost.com/elections/2023/11/19/donald-trump-insults-vulgarities-republicans/.

CHAPTER 3
THE EXPLOSION OF BIGOTRY

Bigotry is a powerful catalyst for hate. With bigotry, someone focuses on a group they see as beneath them, unworthy of respect or even kindness, as well as a threat to a way of life, core values, or even society. These days, we hear a lot about racism, but bigotry is a step beyond on the hate index. Racism typically denotes one's animus toward racial or ethnic groups. Bigotry includes contempt for those categories as well as animosity toward others such as religious groups, sects, and gender nonconformity. That definition is far more suitable here inasmuch as many Trumpists, in addition to abhorrence of racial and ethnic groups, have a long record of anti-Semitism (Jews), Islamophobia (Muslims), and animus toward those who are gay or transgender.

Bigotry is hardly new to American society. Depending upon one's reference point, a casual examination of the history of bigotry in the United States might begin with reaction to the civil rights movement, the Civil War, or most historically, slavery. In fact, American bigotry actually precedes the creation of our nation. In the earliest days of British colonization of what would become the United States, King Charles II dispatched representatives to the Massachusetts Colony to stop "fanatical" Puritans from abusing Quakers. That both groups were Christian didn't stop one from attempting to persecute the other. Lest anyone believe that this situation represented a departure from more "civilized" behavior in the mother country, the British had the same problem.[1] In a nutshell, prejudicial behavior had been passed from one generation to another and from the Old World to the New.

The United States and Great Britain are hardly alone in exhibiting bigotry; in fact, it is an international affliction. Whether they are democracies, autocracies, monarchies, or theocracies, most societies house elements of bigotry as part of their political culture. In some cases, majorities persecute minorities; in other cases, minorities are actually able to tyrannize majorities.[2] Whatever the situation, by virtue of its resistance to tolerance and equality, bigotry exists as an enemy of democracy. That includes present-day America, the primary focus of our discussion.

Bigotry is foundational to Trumpism. As a means to obtaining and keeping political power, Trumpists exploit bigotry as a forceful wedge for pitting evangelical Christian Whites against others. Of course, not all evangelical Christian Whites are bigots, nor is bigotry restricted to only evangelical Christian Whites or Trumpists for that matter. Nevertheless, in the United States, Trumpism draws upon bigotry for much of its political strength, and its source stems disproportionately from evangelical Christian Whites, also described as Christian nationalists. One post-2024 presidential election national survey found that 85 percent of evangelical White Protestants voted for Donald Trump.[3] In a separate 2024 national survey, nearly two-thirds of evangelical White Protestants scored high on an authoritarian index, higher than any other religious group.[4] The connection between Trumpists, authoritarianism, and evangelicals is real.

Nowhere has Trump's bigotry been more obvious than his zeal for protecting Whites over non-Whites. We're reminded of Trump's comments in January 2018 when he had a frank immigration discussion with some members of Congress. After excoriating the presence of Haitians, Salvadorians, and Africans, he mused, "we should have more people from Norway."[5] In 2025, while pursuing a national campaign to deport millions of undocumented immigrants of color and ending Temporary Sanctuary Status for others, Trump saved room for White South Africans. In this instance, the South African government enacted legislation seizing unused Afrikaner (White South Africans) farmland to address lingering effects of apartheid. In response, Trump signed an executive order that ceased all American aid to South Africa and offered refugee status to White South Africans.[6] The hypocrisy was palpable.

Trumpism has increased the penetration of bigotry into society through reliance on the far-right (sometimes called alt-right) conspiracy theories that add victimhood and grievances to the hate formula that simply pits "us" against "them." And it works. Anne Applebaum, an expert on the decline of democracies, writes that conspiracy theories rely on simplicity for explaining away complicated situations, offering the believer "the satisfying sense of having special, privileged access to the truth."[7] With these tools, Trumpists streamline the American condition into an unacceptable situation where "True Americans" are victimized by those who don't belong among us. Thus, the never-ending grievances by those who deserve better against racial, religious, and sexual interlopers whose very presence threatens our lives. Their anger fuels their hate, and that's where we begin this chapter.

The Normalization of Hate as "Acceptable" Conversation and Behavior

We know that hate has always been part of the culture in the United States, as it has been in most societies. The issue is the extent to which Donald Trump and his acolytes have used their influence to legitimize and elevate bigoted discussions from mostly passive mumbles of disgust to justified outbursts of anger. Understanding this metamorphosis is critical because unlike relatively subdued bigotry-related complaints, anger precedes violence, and violence paves the way to disruption of society.

As noted in Chapter 2, Donald Trump has a history of enflaming large swaths of public opinion, extending all the way back to his earliest days in business.[8] Whatever Trump's personal background, his use of anger-fueled bigotry as a politician lifted the discussion to a new level of anger, given the public whereabouts of his statements and the audiences that received them. From his questioning of Barack Obama's place of birth to his promise to deport 12 million undocumented immigrants, Trump has spewed racial contempt as a political calling card of sorts.

His arsenal of hatred has included non-Christians as well as non-Whites. Recalling the September 11, 2001, Islamist terrorist attacks by al-Qaeda on the World Trade Center Twin Towers in New York City, Trump vowed that upon election to the presidency, he would prevent all Muslims from entering the United States.[9] During the 2024 presidential campaign, Trump asserted that Democratic presidential nominee Kamala Harris "dislikes Jewish people (Harris's husband, Doug Emhoff, is Jewish!)" and that any Jew who votes for Harris "should have their head examined."[10]

Adding to his list of racial, ethnic, and religious undesirables, during his presidential campaign, Trump mocked Asians, speaking in broken English for emphasis at campaign rallies.[11] He referred to the nonviolent Black Lives Matter movement as un-American, criticizing Blacks for "dividing America" and stirring racial hate.[12]

And the list goes on. Over time, Trump expanded his contempt list to the media, people with disabilities, and elites allegedly in positions of power. Perhaps, it would be less concerning if these comments by Trump were rare or flippant or simply poorly tailored jokes, but they were standard elements in his political rallies, usually evoking approval from his large crowds whose racial compositions were almost all White.

Trump's race baiting has been a key source for arousing like-minded supporters at his rallies. At virtually every meeting he would spew bigoted epithets about alleged foreign and domestic enemies of the United States. It was standard fare. Depending upon the moment, Trump's rants could be related to race, immigrants, non-Christian believers, or combinations. Regardless, these outsiders were, he would say, enemies of "the people," otherwise known as Christian Whites. The essence of his message was that "we have to get them (the undesirables) before they get us."

Trump's bigotry has drawn its energy from the far right of American politics, which has long been the primary depository of prejudice in the United States. However, there have been occasional racial bursts from the left. One example, anti-Semitism, draws derisive comments and threats from the left as well as the right. Most notable of these have been the comments by Democratic House of Representatives member Ilhan Omar (MN) who has argued that pro-Israel supporters have a special allegiance to Israel and that American Jews have "dual loyalties" to the United States and Israel. Implied in her statements are that Jews and those sympathetic to Israel are not totally loyal to the United States, and that their dual loyalties render them less than good Americans. Omar's comments surely fit into the definition of racism, but what separates her outrageous claims from those of the Trumpists has been the avalanche of condemnations from members of her own political party and their willingness to publicly criticize the representative from Minnesota.[13]

Few members of his political party have openly challenged Trump for his bigotry. Instead, those who dare to slam the "party line" laid out by Trump are politically excommunicated from the movement. They are quickly designated as part of the "them" and if they are elected officials, they are targeted for removal at the next party primary. More times than not, they are purged and effectively drummed out of politics. Thus, many traditional Republicans who know better work within the guidelines of Trumpism, relinquishing their own values in the name of intra-party harmony.

As part of the "us" versus "them" division, Trump has often singled out members of the press at his rallies, and later his press conferences, as illegitimate distributors of "fake news," which was any report that portrayed Trump or his followers in ways he considered unfair. Neutralizing the press has been critical to Trump's effort to portray himself as the only acceptable deliverer of the truth, thus removing consideration of other explanations for Trump's claims. Bearing in mind a historic difference of opinion on various issues between Democrats and Republicans, Trump has driven an even wider wedge between the parties about the value of the press. Between 2016 and 2022, Democratic trust and confidence in the mass media increased from 60 to 75 percent. Among independents, trust and confidence in the media remained fairly constant, moving from 30 percent to 27. But with Republicans, trust and confidence remained at 14 percent.[14] Why? Because Trump consistently belittled the press as "fake news." With Trumpists disgusted by the mainstream press, they have come to rely on Trump-approved conservative media, far-right blogs, and selected social media platforms as their only reliable sources, adding further to Trump's hold.

Rallies with thousands of followers in attendance have been the mainstays of Trump's success with the masses. There, Trump has been verbally vicious about his enemies, with his supporters eagerly consuming his message with zeal. The mainstream media representatives there have often been called out for writing or showing "fake news;" some have been roughed up by Trump supporters.[15] At other times, fights have broken out between supporters and a few protesters with anti-Trump signs, with the former easily overcoming the latter. Typically, Trump has exhorted his supporters to teach a lesson to the protesters. On some occasions, he would actually mimic the posture of a bully looking to punish anyone challenging his message. At a 2016 rally, regretting his distance from a protester being forced out from the gathering, Trump mused wistfully to the crowd "I'd like to punch him in the face, I tell 'ya."[16] They cheered wildly. In their minds, with their help Trump would save the country from people who didn't belong or deserve to be here.

The COVID-19 pandemic kept Trump from holding rallies during the 2020 election year, taking much of the energy from his campaign. Whereas Trump held 323 rallies in 2016 at a rate of almost one per day, attendance restrictions during the pandemic limited his ability to holding fifty-two events in all of 2020. Things would be different for the 2024 presidential campaign. Shortly after declaring his candidacy for a second term in November 2022, Trump held his first rally in Waco, Texas, where he focused on what he called the "weaponization of government" against him. He also ratchetted up his value as the savior for all those who had been victimized by government oppression. Whereas in 2016 Trump said to his supporters "I am your voice," at Waco he went a step beyond, exclaiming, "I am your warrior. I am your justice.... For those who have been betrayed, I am your retribution."[17] The voice of autocracy had spoken and would continue to do so in that manner throughout the 2024 campaign. His followers loved it.

The symbolism of Waco, Texas, as the first meeting place of Trump's 2024 campaign could hardly be ignored. The date of the rally, March 25, 2023, was exactly thirty years after the federal government's siege of the Branch Davidians, a Waco-based separatist religious group thought to be in possession of a cache of illegal arms. After a fifty-one-day standoff, federal agents moved in, a fire broke out, and seventy-six people died. Ever since, right-wing extremists point to Waco as a prime example of government overreach. Trump campaign officials described the meeting place and date as "coincidental" to any commemoration of the 1993 tragedy. Nevertheless, in the words of one political extremism expert, Waco was the ideal site to "tap into these deep veins of anti-government hate—Christian nationalist skepticism of the government—and I find it hard to believe that Trump doesn't know that Waco represents all these things."[18] Coincidental or not, Waco and all its symbolism served as the official launch of the 2024 Trump presidential candidacy.

Trump may have been the architect for normalizing bigotry as part of the nation's lexicon, but he soon found himself with many others in his political circles employing the same language. During the 2024 Trump presidential campaign rallies, US Senator Tommy Tuberville (R-AL) used anti-Asian racist rhetoric against Elaine Chao, former Trump Transportation Department secretary and spouse of Senate Republican minority leader Mitch McConnell. On another occasion, US Representative Marjorie Taylor Greene (R-GA) warned a Trump audience that "five million illegal aliens are on the verge of replacing you," referring to criticism of the "Great Replacement Theory" which, promoted by White nationalists, contends that racial and religious minorities are secretly attempting to assume the "place" of Whites in the United States.[19]

Republican presidential contenders for the 2024 nomination were particularly careful in their efforts to toe the Trumpism line. Republican presidential candidate Vivek Ramaswamy, an Indian American, compared House of Representatives member Ayanna Pressley (Dem-MA), an African American, to "modern grand wizards" of the Ku Klux Klan;[20] Republican Florida governor and presidential candidate Ron DeSantis claimed that some African American slaves benefitted from their bondage by learning a trade such as "being a blacksmith into things later in life;"[21] and former Republican governor and presidential candidate Nikki Haley excluded mention of slavery as a cause of the Civil War, adding that "America has never been a racist country."[22] These kinds of claims and assessments of America by Republican candidates were not careless statements; rather, they were carefully manicured messages conferring loyalty to Trumpism even as Republican challengers pursued their own campaigns.

Of course, Trump was the master when it came to outrageous racist statements. With one parent being Indian and the other Jamaican, Democrat presidential candidate Kamala Harris proudly claimed identification with both backgrounds. For Trump, this was an opportunity to remind his largely White supporters that Harris was anything but White. In other words, she was part of the "thems." Throughout the 2024 presidential campaign, he accused Harris of changing racial identities in order to gain voter support from both communities.

Trump and his vice-presidential running mate JD Vance dug into racial vilification even more (if that's possible) when they repeated a debunked claim via social media that falsely accused "illegal" Haitian immigrants in Springfield, Ohio, of stealing and eating dogs and cats. The not-so-subtle reference from the claim was that immigrants were less than human. Trump also repeated the lie in his nationally televised debate with Harris, after which he and Vance restated it several more times. It didn't matter that the Springfield mayor, police chief, and the Ohio governor all denied the baseless claim. In the meantime, Springfield residents endured more than thirty bomb threats as well as other forms of intimidation and harassment. Schools were closed, churches were threatened, and city events were cancelled. For all of this, Trump and Vance never apologized. Shortly after the debacle, Vance admitted to CNN anchor Dana Bash that he "created" the story based on what he had heard from his Ohio constituents to draw attention to "the suffering of the American people" from the presence of illegal immigrants.[23] While the entire event may have been offensive to those opposed to racism, Trump and Vance succeeded in controlling the media for the better part of a week, reinforcing their concerns about immigrants inserting themselves into American culture.

In Congress, Republican members closely aligned with Trump have made it an ugly habit to describe opponents with racist language. Some examples: Representative Marjorie Taylor Greene (GA) called Somali-born Congressmember Ilhan Omar "the Representative of Somalia—I mean Minnesota." Republican Representative Troy Nehls (TX) described the Black husband of African American and Democratic House of Representatives member Cori Bush as a "thug." Republican Representative Chip Roy (TX) in a slightly more veiled approach accused Democrats as "colonizers" who wanted to open borders as a way to end Western civilization.[24] Discussing the loyalty of a Democratic member of the House of Representatives, Republican member Lance Gooden (TX) questioned whether American-born Democratic Representative Judy Chu, of Chinese American heritage, should be entitled to a security clearance.[25]

In the Senate, allegedly the congressional chamber with more decorum, Republican US Senator Tom Cotton (AR) asked Shou Chew, the Singapore-born CEO of social media company TikTok, whether he was a member of the Chinese Communist Party, referring to allegations of Chinese interference with social media companies.[26] In another instance, US Senator Tommy Tuberville before an overwhelmingly White audience compared the descendants of Black slaves to criminals.[27] Given Trump's endless racial taunts and a political voting base that is 85 percent White, it's not exactly a surprise that his supporters in Congress would rely on the same outlook on race. Between Republican presidential contenders and so many members of Congress espousing the approach to life, two of the three branches of the national government show little sign of changing course on the topic.

Some Trumpists in Congress have been incredibly open about their relationships with far-right groups. In perhaps the most transparent circumstance revealing the connection between election deniers and racist groups, Republican House member Andy Biggs (AZ) spoke at a rally sponsored by University of Arizona College Republicans and the Proud Boys, known for promoting virulent anti-Semitic, Islamophobic, and racist rants.[28]

Hate as the Fuel for Violence

It would be sheer folly to not expect repercussions from hateful rhetoric beyond the arenas where Trump stirred the emotions of his followers. In fact, the anger there often spilled into the communities where the rallies occurred. According to one analysis, at Trump rallies during the 2016 presidential campaign year, the cities where they took place experienced 2.3 times more violent assaults on their residents than on other days.[29] Another review by the Southern Poverty Law Center found that during the first month after the 2016 presidential election, 1,094 bigotry-related incidents occurred throughout the nation. Of those, 37 percent "directly referenced either President-elect Trump, his campaign slogans, or his controversial Access Hollywood remarks about sexual assault."[30] The list goes on. In the wake of the infamous January 6, 2021, insurrection against the Capitol inspired by Trump, Reuters identified at least 232 violent incidents "fueled by political motives since the storming of the Capitol . . .," including forty-four deaths.[31] The evidence is unmistakable: Trumpism language exhortations yield intended brutal results again and again. The message was equally clear: Enemies of Trumpism must be done away with.

The Explosion of Bigotry

Racial violence is a major part of Trumpist hate, but not the only part. During the Trump presidency, he latched on to suspicion of the "deep state," allegedly a mysterious underground network of high-level government bureaucrats secretly running the United States by working in tandem with financial and industrial leaders of privilege. With this conspiracy theory as an explanation, supporters would now believe that any failures to succeed with their aspirations would be due to the "deep state," not the failure of their ideas.

As president, Trump began accusing various government units of power, particularly the Department of Justice, of weaponizing their power illegally against him. This wasn't the first time Trump relied on a conspiracy theory. As far as he was concerned, any election loss would be the result of "rigged ballots," an argument he put forth after the 2020 election without any proof. Oddly enough, if anyone conspired to weaponize the government, it was Trump. Throughout his presidency, Trump at various times attempted to induce the Department of Justice, the Internal Revenue Service, the Department of Homeland Security, and other government offices to investigate and/or prosecute his enemies.[32] Most attempts were not successful, but that didn't keep Trump from trying.

Trump supporters have bought the "weaponization" theory lock, stock, and barrel. In 2023, the new Republican majority in the House of Representatives created the Select Subcommittee on the Weaponization of the Federal Government as a subcommittee of the Judiciary Committee. For Trump conspiracy theorists, the Select Subcommittee on the Weaponization offered a kind of legitimacy to the notion that such illegal behavior occurred. The subcommittee was tasked to find examples of people victimized by the federal government. To date, the subcommittee hasn't found a single case of wrongdoing. Meanwhile, without a shred of evidence, Elise Stefanik, the fourth ranking Republican in the House and member of the Weaponization Subcommittee, declared that weaponization had occurred by federal authorities in the Department of Justice taking "hostages" at the January 6, 2021, insurrection against the Capitol.[33] The "hostages" she referred to were the same "patriots" singled out by Trump—better known as the more than 1,200 people arrested for storming the Capitol with threats to hang then-Vice President Mike Pence and kill then-House Speaker Nancy Pelosi.

With the swelling of Trumpist anger over time, supporters have taken out their hate against anyone remotely involved with the government who in some way could be responsible for keeping Trump from power. For evidence, all we have to do is begin with the Capitol, where the United States

Capitol Police (USCP) keep data on threats to personnel, including elected officials. In 2018, the first year of such records, there were 5,206 recorded incidents. The number of threats swelled to 9,625 in 2021, the year of the insurrection. In 2024, a total of 9,474 recorded threat incidents occurred, a number nearly identical to the year of the insurrection.[34] Clearly, the Capitol remains unsafe.

Trump loyalists have also focused on racial minorities, Jews and Muslims, and in some cases, women. A study by ABC News in 2020 found no fewer than fifty-four acts of violence against minorities by White males during the year, each of whom declared their allegiance to Donald Trump as the motivation for their actions. In these instances, the victims were not in attendance at Trump rallies, where they might have been viewed as provocateurs. Rather, they were innocent people simply living their daily lives until suddenly attacked, and in many cases killed.[35]

In some instances, bigoted attackers have left tangible evidence of their feelings about Trump. In 2019, a manifesto acknowledging Trump written by a 21-year-old White killer of twenty people in San Antonio, Texas, described the "Hispanic invasion of Texas" as the motivation for his action.[36] At Charlottesville in 2017, Virginia, an innocent supporter of a group peacefully seeking removal of a Confederate statue from the University of Virginia campus was killed by a participant in a "Unite the Right" protest march that brought together several hate groups for the tragedy. Months earlier, Richard Spencer, the lead organizer of "Unite the Right," had chaired a celebration in Washington, DC, after Trump's 2016 presidential election victory, where the members in attendance cheered the election outcome with Nazi-like salutes and shouts of "Hail Trump."[37] Then there were the murders of eleven parishioners of a Pittsburgh, Pennsylvania, synagogue in 2018 by an anti-Semite who actually blamed Trump for not being hateful enough of Jews![38] In 2020, the FBI arrested fourteen members from various Michigan domestic groups for organizing a plot to kidnap the state's governor, Gretchen Whitmer. Their reason? The governor's disagreement with then-president Trump on the best way to manage the COVID-19 pandemic. Ultimately, nine were convicted or admitted guilt to various crimes including providing material for a terrorist act, possessing a firearm during a felony, and conspiracy to kidnap.[39]

The connection between Trump, his rhetoric, and vicious hate-filled attackers has been clearly palpable to anyone with open eyes. Yet, when asked about any role in these atrocities, Trump routinely assigned blame for violence to mental illness, video games, and social media, accompanied by

The Explosion of Bigotry

weak condemnation—then followed by more hateful rhetoric at subsequent rallies and other political events. Clearly, his supporters in and out of government have felt free to express and act out their own bigoted actions.

After the first Trump presidency, hate continued to spread to anyone or institution potentially interfering with Trumpism. With the horror of the January 6, 2021, insurrection at the Capitol as a violent backdrop, candidates running for the US Senate and House of Representatives in 2022 increased spending on their security by more than 500 percent from 2020. Most of the money came from their campaign funds inasmuch as only the leaders of each chamber have full-time security. Meanwhile, House members who had been allotted $675,000 for office security in 2020 received an increase to $1.2 million per member in 2022. Nonincumbents had no office funding and, as such, were essentially left on their own for protection against would-be assailants during their campaigns—not exactly a gold star for a democracy.

In other policymaking arenas, vengeful attacks and threats have taken place against state and local government officials as well as judges and election workers. These contentious and frightening conditions have been taking a toll on public officials at virtually all levels of governance. Regarding elected officeholders, a Brennan Center for Justice survey of 354 responses of state legislators throughout the nation in fall 2023 found that 43 percent had suffered intimidation "implying imminent risk to [their] wellbeing and safety" over the past three years. With respect to elected officials at the local levels of government, 36 percent had suffered threats during their tenure in office. Of these groups, sizable percentages were discouraged from remaining in office or seeking reelection.[40] Who could blame them? Laboring in this kind of environment is not without cost. No one knows how many would-be candidates have been discouraged from seeking elected office because of the potential violence that comes with the effort.

Hate inspired by Trumpism has infested institutions as much or more than people. No institution has been attacked more than the nation's justice system. Chief among the recipients of threatening activities have been the nation's judges. Donald Trump has a rich history of attacking judges extending all the way from his first years in business to his most recent spate of interactions with state and federal members of the judiciary. In 2016, just prior to his election, Trump attacked a federal judge presiding in a case against Trump's real estate school as a "Mexican hater" because Trump was White and intended to build a wall between the United States and Mexico.[41] (The judge was actually born in Indiana.) After assuming the presidency, Trump continued to attack judges for interfering with him. In

Overcoming Trumpism

Trump's words, "As the leader of the free world, I should be able to do what I choose. The court shouldn't be involved."[42] That outburst led a Trump-appointed member of the US Supreme Court to describe Trump's remarks as "disheartening" and "demoralizing" to independent federal courts.[43]

New Hate-Filled Allies

Like a tropical depression that becomes a hurricane as it moves through warm water, Trump's grievances-laden messages have gained punishing strength over time. In the decade or so since his arrival on the political stage, Trump has gathered support from dozens of hate groups throughout the nation. Many describe themselves proudly as members of White Nationalist and neo-Nazi organizations. They share his racist, anti-Christian, and in some cases misogynistic attitudes and have often carried out hostile physical abuse in Trump's name. On more than one occasion, Trump has referred to these groups as "my people." The results of this cozy relationship have been alarming. One study found that during Trump's four years in the presidency between 2017 and 2021, the number of White nationalist hate groups swelled by 55 percent.[44] At a 2020 presidential debate with then-Democratic candidate Joe Biden, Trump was blatant about signaling his intimate connection with White racist hate groups. When asked to condemn the Proud Boys hate group, Trump replied by saying, "Proud Boys, stand back and stand by." Taking Trump's response as a welcome embrace, the Proud Boys and similar groups boastfully spread word of the connection through social media.[45]

Until Trump's overtures, groups like the Proud Boys, Three Percenters, Oath Keepers, and the Patriot Front were small, mostly loosely organized, and generally out of the public eye. But with his own actions, Trump validated White supremacist groups and gave them reason to go public with their bigotry. After all, they had a partner in the most powerful person in the world, and they wanted allies and enemies alike to know about their special connection in the highest place of political power.

One might reflect on the incredible hate-driven attacks during and after Trump's presidency and view them as symptoms of an anxious society. After all, political violence has always been part of American society. From the days of John Wilkes Booth murdering Abraham Lincoln to the pre-Trump era assassination of President John F. Kennedy to the attack on Democratic Congressmember Gabby Giffords in 2011 and Republican Congressmember

The Explosion of Bigotry

Steve Scalise in 2018, there have been spates of political hate manifesting in violence. These occasional attacks were shocking, but far less in frequency than they are today. Trump himself was subjected to two attacks on his life during the 2024 presidential campaigns, which he cleverly turned into fundraising opportunities.[46]

Political intimidation has become commonplace in America's cities, candidate rallies, and even unsuspecting meeting places, and Trump loyalists have been in the thick of it. A study by the Carnegie Endowment for International Peace found that armed people were four times as likely to be found at Trump-sponsored "Stop the Steal" demonstrations than other rallies; a twelve-fold increase in openly White supremacist activity between 2017 and 2020; and support from one out of five Republican men shortly after the 2020 election for violence "right now."[47] Clearly violence, particularly from far-right, White supremacy–based groups has become virtually mainstreamed in America.

Prominent Trumpist political leaders other than Trump have embraced hate groups, showing the extent to which the bigotry exhibited by Trump has penetrated American society. The hate goes deep, including future "leaders" of the United States. In 2022, an examination of 7,383 lawmakers in all 50 states found that 875 Republican state legislators, nearly 22 percent of the 4,011 Republicans studied, had joined at least one far-right Facebook group. The list of groups included White nationalist, paramilitary, QAnon, anti-immigrant, "Stop the Steal," or similar organizations intimately connected with the far right.[48] Only three of their Democratic counterparts had joined far-right Facebook groups. But there's more. Some state legislators have been more than joiners. An analysis of participants at or near the Capitol in the January 6, 2021, insurrection determined that at least ten were candidates for statewide or federal office in 2022.[49] Clearly, these leaders weren't discouraged either by the negative press or several hundred convictions of the insurrectionists. In addition, some Republican state electors who conspired to overturn the 2020 presidential election outcome had the same positions as electors in the 2024 presidential election.[50]

Looking back at recent events, the evidence is clear that Trumpists have a record of spreading hatred and violence particularly against minority and non-Christian religious groups. The hate didn't go away with Trump's 2020 presidential defeat; if anything, it became much more widespread, even supercharged, in the years that followed, further poisoning the 2024 presidential election environment. Moreover, violent acts have been directed at vital institutions as well as groups, undermining them wherever possible.

Overcoming Trumpism

In the halls of government, organized hate is routinely found at the national and state levels, and shows no sign of abating.[51] Simply put, the foundation from which hate and violence are propagated in American society is both wide and deep, which makes ridding ourselves of this disease is likely to be far more difficult than abolitionists might have expected. The next generation of the nation's leaders has a sizable portion of bigots ready to rule.

The Growth of Public Hate

Up to this point, we have focused on prominent political leaders and far-right groups as the sources of expanding hate and violence through Trumpism in the United States. But what about elements of the public as believers and propagators of these anti-democratic operators? To answer this question, we turn first to the explosion of racial and religious bigotry in the United States in recent years. Next, we will examine public opinion on Trumpism-related topics. Specifically, we focus on public attitudes beginning before the 2016 presidential campaign through the 2020 presidential election outcome.

Bigotry, as we have noted, is at odds with democracy for the simple reason that the definition of bigotry includes intolerance and prejudice, which are incompatible with equality, which is a mainstay of democracy. It's worthwhile to review this linkage as we examine the rapid escalation of bigotry since Donald Trump has joined the national political stage. It's also worth noting the dramatic impact Trump has had on public opinion with respect to race over time. For example, in a national study of six hundred non-Hispanic Whites before and after the 2016 presidential campaign, Trump supporters became "more willing to report dehumanizing attitudes about Black people" after the election. Meanwhile, over the same period, Trump's opponents in the sample became less likely to support dehumanizing comments about Black people.[52]

With respect to racist incidents in the United States, in what appears to be the "new normal," deeply alarming data are reported every year. Between 2015 and 2020, the year before the Trump administration and the last year of the Trump administration, respectively, reported hate crimes soared from 5,850 to 11,129, an increase of 90 percent. Of interest is that in 2021, the year after Trump's departure from the presidency, the number of reported hate crimes dropped to 10,530, a decrease of 5 percent, and the first drop since Trump took office.[53] However, as the 2024 campaign approached, the number of hate crimes increased. In 2023, the number of recorded hate crimes reached a new high of 11,862.[54] Clearly, the relationship between Trumpism and public bigotry has become normalized.

We've documented a massive upward swing in hate crimes, but what about public opinion on race? As expected, the differences were substantial prior to Trump's election in 2016. Recall Trump's conflation of Muslims with "terrorists." In July 2016, a Reuters Poll asked respondents how they felt about banning Muslims from entering the United States; Republicans favored the idea over Democrats 48 to 13 percent.[55] Then there was Trump's classification of Mexicans as drug dealers and rapists. In a September 2016 CNN Poll, 73 percent of Republicans favored building a wall at the United States-Mexico border, compared with 13 percent of Democrats.[56] During the 2016 campaign, Trump referred to African Americans as living in "war zones." A Reuters Poll in June 2016 queried voters' opinions on African Americans, with twice as many Trump supporters than Clinton supporters viewing African Americans as "violent" and "criminal" members of society.[57] Finally, in a September 2016 Quinnipiac University Poll, respondents were probed on whether Trump appealed to bigotry; 61 percent answered "yes." Viewed by partisan divisions, 27 percent of Republicans agreed that Trump appealed to bigotry, compared with 61 percent of Independents and 91 percent of Democrats.[58]

What's the bottomline here? Voters knew what they were getting with Donald Trump. Rather than being a Republican "outlier" as so many Republican leaders suggested during the 2016 presidential campaign, Trump and a majority of the voters were on the same page, at least on the subject of race.

These data have only solidified over time, especially when viewing the opinions of Democrats and Republicans. In 2022, when an Ipsos poll asked whether immigrants were more likely to commit crimes or to be incarcerated than the US population, 39 percent of Republicans answered "yes" compared to 17 percent of Democrats. In the same poll, when asked whether the large number of immigrants apprehended at the southern border represented a major problem, 71 percent of Republicans said "yes" compared to 31 percent of Democrats.[59] In 2023, an NBC poll asked which party does a better job of dealing with immigration. Respondents sided with Republicans over Democrats 45 to 27 percent.[60]

Ironically, real data points in a direction far different from what people believe. A study over a 140-year period found that first-generation immigrants in the United States are 30 percent less likely to be incarcerated than US-born citizens.[61] The simple fact is that perception and reality are not aligned.

Nevertheless, Trump has seized on the immigration question. During the 2024 campaign rally, he went so far as to claim that then-Democratic President Joe Biden was intentionally allowing large numbers of immigrants into the United States as part of "a conspiracy to overthrow the United States of America."[62]

It may have been that these attitudes were present before Trump's ascendance, but the data here at minimum implies Trump's presence has encouraged his followers to be more forthright about as well as act out their opinions. And while it might be an overstatement to attribute these changes solely to Donald Trump, it's difficult to deny the impact of Trump, more frequent instances of public bigotry and increasing incidents of hate as factors for frightening and dividing American society.

Which Came First: The Chicken or the Egg?

Until Donald Trump and his allies became prominent in American politics, hate was considerably less of a mainstream issue than it is today. Yes, it existed but with articulated disdain from official centers of public power and authority that served as a kind of restraint. Today, in many quarters of American society, hate is boldly employed as a weapon of intimidation and discouragement from participation in politics. Large segments of American society feel threatened along with government leaders, racial and religious minorities, and members of the press. As the United States exits the first quarter of the twenty-first century, growing numbers of society feel alienated and removed from it.

Polling data shows that hate has a partisan bent. Many of today's Republicans are largely isolationists, inward-looking anti-globalists, and, to a significant degree, supporters of racist dogma. Most are now Trumpists who dominate a political party that is much different than a generation ago. Those Republicans who have been politically excommunicated or left on their own accord have nowhere to go. This begs the question: Has Trump's collection of bigoted values attracted Republicans, or have Republicans served as a political magnet for attracting Trump?

In fact, it really doesn't matter.[63] Trumpism and a sizable portion of American culture share racist histories, and the combination has become explosive for contemporary society. Add to that Donald Trump's domination of the Republican party assures us that Trumpism and hate are not about to go away in the near term. Hateful discussions and violence that were once viewed as abnormal events have in fact become normalized. To that end, as long as Trumpism prevails in American society, democracy is likely to continue under stress and remain vulnerable to failure. Either way, the hatred within the new Republican party spells trouble for American democracy.

NOTES

1. Gustavus Myers, *History of Bigotry in the United States* (New York: Capricorn Books, 1943), pp. 4–8.
2. For some contemporary examples, see Larry N. Gerston, *Trumpism, Bigotry, and the Threat to American Democracy* (Lanham, MD: Lexington Books, 2024), pp. 45–57.
3. "New Post-Election Survey Reveals Stark Religious Divides in Presidential Vote Choice," PRRI, December 12, 2024, https://www.prri.org/press-release/new-post-election-survey-reveals-stark-religious-divides-in-presidential-vote-choice/.
4. "One Leader under God: The Connection between Authoritarianism and Christian Nationalism in America," PRRI, September 10, 2024, https://www.prri.org/research/one-leader-under-god-the-connection-between-authoritarianism-and-christian-nationalism-in-america/.
5. "Trump Wishes We Had More Immigrants from Norway. Turns Out We Once Did," NPR, January 12, 2018, https://www.npr.org/sections/goatsandsoda/2018/01/12/577673191/trump-wishes-we-had-more-immigrants-from-norway-turns-out-we-once-did.
6. "The Roots of Donald Trump's Fixation with South Africa," Vox, February 15, 2025, https://www.vox.com/politics/399855/south-africa-donald-trump-elon-musk.
7. Anne Applebaum, *Twilight of Democracy* (New York: Anchor Books, 2020), p. 45.
8. For a quick review of Trump's bigoted history, see "Donald Trump's Long History of Racism, from the 1970s to 2019," Vox, July 15, 2019, https://www.vox.com/2016/7/25/12270880/donald-trump-racist-racism-history.
9. "Donald Trump: Ban All Muslims Entering US," *The Guardian*, December 15, 2015, https://www.theguardian.com/us-news/2015/dec/07/donald-trump-ban-all-muslims-entering-us-san-bernardino-shooting.
10. "'You're a Fool': Trump Ramps up Attacks on Jewish Democrats," Politico, July 30, 2024, https://www.politico.com/news/2024/07/30/trump-harris-emhoff-jewish-democrats-00171923.
11. "Donald Trump Mocks Asians Using Broken English during Iowa Campaign Rally," E! News, August 28, 2015, https://www.eonline.com/ca/news/690894/donald-trump-mocks-asians-using-broken-english-during-iowa-campaign-rally.

12. "Donald Trump Strikes Muddled Note on 'Divisive' Black Lives Matter," *The Guardian*, July 13, 2016, https://www.theguardian.com/us-news/2016/jul/13/donald-trump-strikes-muddled-note-on-divisive-black-lives-matter.

13. "House Democrats Roiled by Ilhan Omar Comments on Israel, Hamas," Roll Call, June 10, 2021, https://rollcall.com/2021/06/10/house-democrats-roiled-by-ilhan-omar-comments-on-israel-hamas/.

14. "Americans' Trust in Media Remains Near Record Low," Gallup Poll, October 18, 2022, https://news.gallup.com/poll/403166/americans-trust-media-remains-near-record-low.aspx.

15. "Donald Trump Celebrates Violence against Journalists," *The New Yorker*, October 18, 2018, https://www.vice.com/en/article/why-its-no-surprise-a-journalist-got-choked-at-a-donald-trump-rally/.

16. "Race and Racism in the 2016 Campaign," CNN, September 1, 2016, https://www.cnn.com/2016/08/31/politics/2016-election-donald-trump-hillary-clinton-race/index.html.

17. Quoted in "Trump Begins the 'Retribution' Tour," *The Atlantic*, March 26, 2023, https://www.theatlantic.com/politics/archive/2023/03/donald-trump-rally-waco-2024-campaign/673526/.

18. Quoted in "Trump Holding His Next Rally in Waco, Texas, Sends a Message to the Far Right, Experts Say," *USA Today*, March 24, 2023, https://www.usatoday.com/story/news/nation/2023/03/21/trump-rally-waco-texas-history-raid-on-branch-davidian-compound/11510179002/.

19. "Tuberville, Greene Slammed for Racist Rhetoric at Trump Rallies," Spectrum News NY 1, October 10, 2022, https://ny1.com/nyc/all-boroughs/politics/2022/10/10/tommy-tuberville--marjorie-taylor-greene-push-racist-rhetoric-at-trump-rallies.

20. "Ramaswamy Sparks Furor with Comments on Race," The Hill, September 21, 2023, https://thehill.com/homenews/campaign/4214596-ramaswamy-sparks-furor-with-comments-on-race/.

21. "DeSantis Doubles Down on Claim That Some Blacks Benefited from Slavery," *The Washington Post*, July 22, 2023, https://www.washingtonpost.com/politics/2023/07/22/desantis-slavery-curriculum/.

22. "Nikki Haley, Asked about Cause of U.S. Civil War, Declines to Mention Slavery," Reuters, December 28, 2023, https://www.reuters.com/world/us/nikki-haley-asked-about-cause-us-civil-war-declines-mention-slavery-2023-12-28/.

23. "JD Vance Defends Baseless Rumor about Haitian Immigrants Eating Pets," CNN, September 15, 2024, https://www.cnn.com/2024/09/15/politics/vance-immigrants-pets-springfield-ohio-cnntv/index.html.

24. "GOP Congressman Spews Racist Screed on Fall of 'Western Civilization,'" *The New Republic*, February 13, 2024, https://newrepublic.com/post/178981/republican-congressman-chip-roy-western-civilization-migrants.

25. "Texas Lawmaker Denounced over 'Racist' Remarks Questioning Rep. Judy Chu's Loyalty to US," Yahoo News, February 24, 2023, https://news.yahoo.com/texas-lawmaker-denounced-over-racist-212422256.html.

26. "On Capitol Hill, Republicans Use Bigoted Attacks against Political Foes," *The New York Times*, February 13, 2024, https://www.nytimes.com/2024/02/13/us/politics/republicans-racist-language.html.

The Explosion of Bigotry

27 "Alabama Sen. Tuberville Equates Descendants of Enslaved People to Criminals," NPR, October 10, 2022, https://www.npr.org/2022/10/10/1127872936/senator-tuberville-racist-reparations-stereotype.
28 "Rep. Andy Biggs Spoke at Rally by Far-Right Radicals," The Daily Beast, February 21, 2024, https://www.thedailybeast.com/rep-andy-biggs-spoke-at-phoenix-rally-by-proud-boys-college-republicans-united.
29 "Assaults Spiked on Trump Rally Days during 2016 Election," Penn Medicine News, March 16, 2018, https://www.pennmedicine.org/news/news-releases/2018/march/assaults-spiked-on-trump-rally-days-during-2016-election.
30 "The Trump Effect: The Campaign Language of the Man Who Would Become President Sparks Hate Violence, Bullying, Before and After the Election," Intelligence Report, Southern Poverty Law Center, February 15, 2017, https://www.splcenter.org/fighting-hate/intelligence-report/2017/trump-effect.
31 "U.S. Political Violence Driven by New Breed of 'Grab-Bag' Extremists," Reuters, November 15, 2023, https://www.reuters.com/investigates/special-report/usa-politics-violence-far-right/.
32 For a litany of examples, see "All the Ways Trump, Not His Foes, Sought to 'Weaponize' the Government," The Washington Post, July 10, 2023, https://www.washingtonpost.com/politics/2023/07/10/all-ways-trump-not-his-foes-sought-weaponize-government/.
33 Quoted in "Elise Stefanik Refuses to Commit to Certify 2024 Results, Calls January 6 Prisoners 'Hostages,'" Vanity Fair, January 7, 2024, https://www.vanityfair.com/news/elise-stefanik-2024-election-certification-january-6.
34 "USCP Threat Assessment Cases for 2024," United States Capitol Police, Washington, DC, February 3, 2025, https://www.uscp.gov/media-center/press-releases/uscp-threat-assessment-cases-2024.
35 "'No Blame?' ABC News Finds 54 Cases Invoking 'Trump' in Connection with Violence, Threats, Alleged Assaults," ABC News, May 30, 2020, https://abcnews.go.com/Politics/blame-abc-news-finds-17-cases-invoking-trump/story?id=58912889.
36 "El Paso Shooting Suspect's Manifesto Echoes Trump's Language," The New York Times, August 4, 2019, https://www.nytimes.com/2019/08/04/us/politics/trump-mass-shootings.html.
37 "'Hail Trump!': White Nationalists Salute the President-Elect," The Atlantic, November 21, 2016, https://www.theatlantic.com/politics/archive/2016/11/richard-spencer-speech-npi/508379/.
38 "The Nature of Trump's Culpability in the Pittsburgh Synagogue Massacre," Slate, October 27, 2018, https://slate.com/news-and-politics/2018/10/pittsburgh-synagogue-shooting-trump-rhetoric-antisemitism-civility.html.
39 "3 Years after Plot to Kidnap Gov. Gretchen Whitmer, Here Are the Trial Outcomes, Verdicts," Detroit Free Press, September 18, 2023, https://www.freep.com/story/news/local/michigan/2023/09/18/whitmer-kidnapping-trial-verdict-guilty-acquitted/70889492007/.
40 "Intimidation of State and Local Officeholders," The Brennan Center for Justice, New York, January 25, 2024, file:///Users/gerstondocs/Downloads/Intimidation%20of%20Officeholders%20Report%20Jan%202024%20(5).pdf.

41 "Who Is Judge Gonzalo Curiel, the Man Trump Attacked for His Mexican Ancestry," NPR, June 7, 2016, https://www.npr.org/2016/06/07/481140881/who-is-judge-gonzalo-curiel-the-man-trump-attacked-for-his-mexican-ancestry.
42 "All the Times Trump Personally Attacked Judges—and Why His Tirades Are 'Worse Than Wrong,'" *The Washington Post*, April 26, 2017, https://www.washingtonpost.com/news/the-fix/wp/2017/04/26/all-the-times-trump-personally-attacked-judges-and-why-his-tirades-are-worse-than-wrong/.
43 Ibid.
44 "White Nationalist Hate Groups Have Grown 55% in Trump Era, Report Finds," *The Guardian*, March 18, 2020, https://www.theguardian.com/world/2020/mar/18/white-nationalist-hate-groups-southern-poverty-law-center.
45 "Trump's Debate Callout Bolsters Far-Right Proud Boys," CNN, October 1, 2020, https://www.cnn.com/2020/09/30/politics/proud-boys-trump-debate-trnd/index.html.
46 "Trump Asks for Cash after Second Assassination Bid," The Daily Beast, September 15, 2024, https://www.thedailybeast.com/trump-rushes-to-fundraise-off-apparent-assassination-attempt/.
47 Rachel Kleinfeld, "The Rise in Political Violence in the United States and Damage to Our Democracy," Testimony before the Select Committee to Investigate the January 6th Attack on the United States Capitol, March 31, 2022, https://carnegieendowment.org/2022/03/31/rise-in-political-violence-in-united-states-and-damage-to-our-democracy-pub-87584.
48 "Breaching the Mainstream: A National Survey of Far-Right Membership in State Legislatures," Institute for Research and Education on Human Rights, 2022, https://www.irehr.org/reports/breaching-the-mainstream/.
49 "10 Republicans on the Ballot Who Were at or Near the Capitol on Jan. 6, 2021," CBS News, November 4, 2022, https://www.cbsnews.com/news/jan-6-assault-republicans-running-for-office-capitol/.
50 "14 Pro-Trump Electors Linked to Efforts to Reverse His 2020 Loss Are Back for 2024," NPR, September 12, 2024, https://www.npr.org/2024/09/12/nx-s1-5100909/fake-electors-trump-electoral-college-vote.
51 "10 Numbers That Reveal the Real State of Hate in 2024," Life after Hate, https://www.lifeafterhate.org/blog/2025/1/31/10-numbers-that-reveal-the-real-state-of-hate-in-2024/.
52 Ashley Jardina and Spencer Piston, "Trickle-Down Racism: Trump's Effect on Whites' Racist Dehumanizing Attitudes," *Current Research in Ecological and Social Psychology*, September 28, 2023, https://www.sciencedirect.com/science/article/pii/S2666622723000710.
53 See "Latest Hate Crime Statistics Released," Department of Justice, Washington, DC, November 14, 2016, https://www.fbi.gov/news/stories/2015-hate-crime-statistics-released, "FBI Releases Updated 2020 Hate Crime Statistics," Department of Justice, Washington, DC, October 25, 2021, https://www.fbi.gov/news/press-releases/fbi-releases-updated-2020-hate-crime-statistics, and "2021 Hate Crime Statistics," Department of Justice, Washington, DC, October 30, 2023, https://www.justice.gov/hatecrimes/2021-hate-crime-statistics.

54 "FBI Releases 2023 Hate Crimes Statistics," Department of Justice, Washington, DC, August 11, 2025, https://www.justice.gov/hatecrimes/2023-hate-crime-statistics.

55 "Republicans, Democrats Sharply Divided over Muslims in America: Reuters/Ipsos Poll," Reuters, July 15, 2016, https://www.reuters.com/article/idUSKCN0ZV20B/.

56 "Poll: Most Oppose Trump's Wall, Split on Who Is Best on Immigration," CNN, September 7, 2016, https://www.cnn.com/2016/09/07/politics/2016-election-presidential-poll-immigration-donald-trump-hillary-clinton/index.html.

57 "Exclusive: Trump Supporters More Likely to View Blacks Negatively—Reuters/Ipsos Poll," Reuters, June 28, 2016, https://www.reuters.com/article/idUSKCN0ZE2SV/.

58 "7 Percent of Donald Trump Supporters Think He's Racist," *The Washington Post*, September 1, 2016, https://www.washingtonpost.com/news/the-fix/wp/2016/09/01/7-percent-of-donald-trump-supporters-think-hes-racist/.

59 "On Immigration, Most Buying into Idea of 'Invasion' at Southern Border," Ipsos, August 18, 2022, https://www.ipsos.com/en-us/news-polls/npr-immigration-perceptions-august-2022.

60 "Poll Finds Democrats' Handing of Immigration at All-Time Low," MNV News, October 8, 2023, https://www.nbcnews.com/meet-the-press/first-read/poll-finds-democrats-handling-immigration-time-low-rcna118957.

61 See Ran Abramitsky and Leah Boustan, *Streets of Gold: America's Untold Story of Immigrant Success* (New York: Public Affairs Press, 2022).

62 "Trump Escalates His Immigration Rhetoric with Baseless Claim about Biden Trying to Overthrow the US," Associated Press, March 2, 2024, https://apnews.com/article/trump-immigration-biden-gop-voters-border-migrants-1fc6624188f540f495e1087bee64318e.

63 The larger discussion of this question is found with the concept of "critical elections," which are turning points in the organization of political parties and their voters. For more on this topic, see Walter Dean Burnham, *Critical Elections and the Mainsprings of Politics* (New York: W.W. Norton, 1970).

CHAPTER 4
DISRESPECT, DESTRUCTION, AND DISENFRANCHISEMENT

"Election Interference!"

If you were given a dollar for every time Donald Trump uttered that claim, you'd probably have enough money to buy Trump Tower! Those two words or a version thereof have been inextricably linked in every election involving Trump. In 2016, he was convinced the presidential election was rigged. Of course, he won, which would have embarrassed anyone else, but not Trump. Cries of election interference continued through the Joe Biden presidency, with predictions of more such chicanery in 2024. Of course, after Trump won the 2024 presidential election, he declared the event "free and fair!"

Trump has a history of protesting what he has called unfair treatment. During his several court appearances in 2023 and 2024 for charges including bank fraud, sexual assault, and falsifying business records, Trump's mantra on fairness persisted. And so it went with political events. Whether he was speaking outside a courtroom or inside a campaign rally venue, his message was the same again, and again, and (you guessed it!) again: his Democratic enemies would do anything to keep Trump from winning an election and to prevent him from serving the people. His message caught on with allies, where allegations of election interference came from a wide swath of Republican leaders who were only too happy to join Trump's election denier bandwagon after the 2020 presidential election.

Meanwhile, Trump's problems beyond the disputed 2020 election outcome mounted. He found himself on the short end of a long legal stick beginning in 2023 and extending right through the 2024 presidential election campaign. In 2023, he lost the first of two civil lawsuits against E. Jean Carroll, one for sexual abuse and defamation, and the other in 2024 just for defamation (again, of Carroll). Together, they led to $88 million in penalty assessments against the former president. Also in 2023, Trump was charged by Manhattan District Attorney Alvin Bragg with illegally disguising company funds to pay off porn star Stormy Daniels for a sexual dalliance (that he denied) to prevent the information about his association from becoming public before the 2016 election. He was found guilty in that case and appealed.

During the same year, New York Attorney General Letitia James charged Trump with fraudulently lying about his wealth when applying for business loans and then lowering the value of the same properties for purposes of reducing his property taxes. Upon conviction of the charge, the judge assessed a $354 million fine plus $100 million in interest climbing by just over $100,000 per day until the bill was paid. He was found guilty in that case and also appealed.

But Trump's legal problems swelled beyond money. He found himself embroiled in charges on matters particularly serious for someone seeking the presidency. In 2023, Trump was indicted with eighteen others in Georgia for violating the state's Racketeer Influenced and Corruption Organizations Act for conspiring to overturn the state's 2020 election results. Along with Trump, core members of his campaign team were indicted for their participation in attempting to replace the state's electors associated with Biden's victory with a set of electors loyal to the soon to be former president. Trump caught a break there as Fulton County officials dropped the case against him (not the others) after a Georgia Court ordered District Attorney Fani Willis off the case because of a conflict of interest.

And there was more. Along with state charges, in 2023, Trump was hit with the most serious allegations of all. In June that year, Trump was indicted at the federal level by a Miami, Florida, grand jury for knowingly withholding and refusing to return sensitive government documents to the National Archives. Then in August of 2023, Trump was indicted by a Washington, DC, grand jury for obstructing the outcome of the 2020 presidential election before and after the vote. And what were Trump's responses to the total of ninety-one charges in the four jurisdictions? "Election interference" ginned up by the Democrats and validated by the federal courts. "They" were always out to get him, Trump argued bitterly and repeatedly.

But Trump couldn't fight the charges with words alone. Between 2021 and mid-2024, he spent a whopping $100 million on legal fees to fight the various charges. Repeatedly, Trump's well-funded lawyers appealed various charges, delaying trials in some cases and final decisions in others, leading nearly all of the issues to go away after Trump won the presidential election in 2024.[1] It also helped that in the case regarding withheld documents, a Trump-appointed federal judge dismissed the case before any trial could occur. And where did his defense funds come from? Not from the multibillionaire's personal resources, but from the $250 million he received in campaign contributions.[2]

Trump presented himself to supporters as a selfless protector of the people under assault from a web of state and federal authorities. He was the sole human barrier between the evildoers in government and the American people. "They're [the Department of Justice] not coming after me. They're coming after you—and I'm just standing in their way," Trump proclaimed in a rally following the federal indictment alleging illegally withholding sensitive government documents after he left office.[3] It was the latest iteration of his populist "only I can fix it" theme, once again illustrating his indispensability to his supporters. At the same time, Trump and the "us" crowd were bonded against the "thems." Neither would let the other down in the fight for justice.

The "fight," of course, was a sham. In the post-Trump presidency era, Trump was actually accusing his enemies of what he had orchestrated or endorsed through various attempts to undo a legitimately conducted 2020 presidential election with an indisputable defeat—a result that would remove him from power, and worse yet, publicly bruise a huge ego. Trump's victimization claim was a classic political example of "the pot calling the kettle black," a mirror-like reflection of his own behavior that brought the onslaught of charges from federal and state authorities. Such conduct is commonplace with would-be dictators who charge their enemies with the very crimes that they themselves undertake.[4] In fact, if anyone was victimized by criminality, it was the American people and their government—assuming the charges would hold up in court.

It's important to explain the legitimacy of the 2020 presidential election and its outcome. Countless investigations inside and outside state and federal government bodies confirmed that the 2020 election was without anything close to widespread fraud or election interference of any kind.[5] Of course, there were rare random incidents of a "dead" person voting and, in other situations, an individual voting in more than one state. Just as infrequently, there were the scarce examples of people who were registered to vote in more than one location, technically defined as voter fraud. Extraordinarily few voters ever followed through.

Oddly enough, Mark Meadows, Donald Trump's last chief of staff, registered in his home state of North Carolina; South Carolina, a state where he moved; and Washington, DC. He only voted once in the 2020 presidential election, however. Still, there was a rich irony to the extent that Meadows, himself a believer in rampant existence of voter fraud,[6] would be among those who technically broke an election law. Whether from

Overcoming Trumpism

Trump-appointed US Attorney General Bill Barr, judges and justices in sixty-plus state and federal court cases, or the results of numerous impartial postelection audits, management of the 2020 presidential election was given a clean bill of political health, period.

Donald Trump may have been the loudest voice, but he wasn't alone in his claim of election fraud. Numerous Republican leaders in and out of government—soon known as "election deniers"—rejected the outcome. That there were so many allies in otherwise respected positions of power who corroborated Trump's baseless claims attempted to offer a level of respectability to it all, baseless as they were. It remains a mystery whether their support for Trump was out of fear from political retribution, the desire to simply be on what they perceived as the right side of political history, or both. Whatever their motivations, a closer examination would show election denier assessments as outlandish as the former president's. With respect to claims of election illegitimacy, they all fell well below any level of credibility. Despite the foolhardiness of it all, as the 2024 presidential election neared, the numbers of leaders and mainstream Republicans alike moved to Trump's side grew exponentially. For defenders of democracy, the growing synergy between Trump and so many national and state Republican stewards presented its own special peril.

This chapter begins with a review of Donald Trump's litany of ill-founded 2020 presidential election accusations peddled by Trump and his allies—accusations that had the effect of fueling otherwise unfounded suspicions of a corrupt federal government. From there, it points to the real election interference efforts by Trump and his allies who refused to concede the obvious—that Trump lost fair and square. The discussion continues with a review of state-level actions to control the franchise. Finally, we focus on the damning indictments against Trump, meaningful charges that melted away for a variety of reasons. If there's any condemnation of the political process to be found, it lies with Trump and those allies who willingly joined him in an unconscionable effort of attempting to undermine the authenticity of American institutions and threaten our democracy.

2020 Election Grievances

Claims of "rigged elections" have long been a core component of Donald Trump's repertoire of election grievances. They have been foundational in his attempts to persuade the voters that "the system" is riddled with corruption.

In 2016, Trump stated flat out that should he lose the presidential election, it would be only because the media, Hillary Clinton, and other enemies had conspired to keep him from winning.[7] Even when he won unexpectedly, Trump blamed confusion over the surprise victory on "phony" election polls.[8] That's Trump's *modus operandi*: there's always someone conspiring against him.

Thus, it was no surprise to Trump watchers that as the 2020 election approached, he would forewarn that the outcome would present "the greatest Rigged Election in history."[9] With that underpinning firmly planted in advance of the event, Trump established a low bar for the outcome. Yet, the question remained, how would the election be "rigged"? Trump focused on several factors: missing ballots, stuffed boxes with fraudulent ballots, mysteriously appearing late ballots, and corrupt voting machines. Together, these elements comprised the great election conspiracy that would deny the public will. But was there merit to the claims?

The Missing Ballots Accusation

Let's first turn to the missing ballots claim. Trump had asserted that hundreds of thousands of ballots had been intentionally withheld from the polling destinations where they would be counted. In virtually every case, the claim was false, quickly addressed because of human error, or greatly exaggerated. The lies were incessant. Research by *The New York Times* found that Trump made more than eight hundred false claims by November 3, and two thousand by the end of his presidency less than three months later![10] Lost ballots were one of Trump's specialties. In one example, Trump accused the Chicago Board of Commissioners of mysteriously "finding" ten thousand missing ballots with results that were overwhelming for Biden. In fact, the ballots were on hand and had been mistakenly left out in an initial count.[11]

At one point, Trump accused the US Postal Service of collaborating with anti-Trump forces to keep hundreds of thousands of votes from being delivered. In fact, the US Postal Service acknowledged two days after the election that out of 155 million votes in the 2020 election, about three hundred thousand ballots had not been counted, and that they would be in due course. The missing ballots were due to their slow travel through the "postal stream," Post Office representatives said. While they were mailed by the election day deadline, the ballots had not yet arrived at their intended destination, but would in due course. Further, data provided by the US Postal Service showed that in no state did the missing ballots come anywhere close to impacting the outcome of the election.[12] As an aside, it's hard to imagine that Trump had too much difficulty with the legitimacy of mailed-in ballots since he was among the millions who voted by mail from his Florida residence in the 2020 presidential primary![13]

Stuffed Ballot Boxes

In addition to claims of missing ballots, Trump complained of stuffed ballot boxes in Georgia, Wisconsin, Arizona, and Pennsylvania, totaling millions of votes—all swing states, and among the states he eventually lost to Joe Biden. The accusations came from anecdotal but unproven observations of Trump election watchers who "witnessed" ballots in places removed from the others.

Independent postelection investigations in each of these states found no credible evidence of such claims.[14] At least on one occasion, a ballot review numerically harmed Trump's claim. In Arizona, a Trump-friendly auditing company hired by state Senate Republicans found that their review of 2.1 million votes closely corresponded with official numbers with the caveat that the revised count actually found additional votes for Biden.

More than a year after the 2020 presidential election, the stuffed ballot claim was given new life in "2000 Mules," an alleged documentary asserting without any evidence that two thousand people had been paid to illegally collect ballots and transfer them to election drop boxes in critical swing states.[15] Examinations by authorities found no proof of the accusations, with the film's producer ultimately apologizing for using false data.[16] But that didn't stop Trumpists from citing the "evidence" all the way through the 2024 election campaign.

Late Tallies

The most dominant claim by Trump centered on late ballots that weren't counted until well after the official close of the election. When Trump went to sleep on election night, he was comfortably ahead in the battleground states of Pennsylvania, Wisconsin, and Michigan. These states were referred to as part of "the blue wall" for their historical significance in providing electoral votes for successful Democratic presidential victories. By the next morning, the tabulations in each of these states shifted over to Biden, greatly increasing the likelihood of a national Biden victory. Those "extra ballots,"

Trump claimed, gave Biden an illegitimate victory riddled with fraud. Once again, there was a perfectly reasonable explanation for the situation, even if not accepted by the Trump campaign. In the three states, election officials were prohibited by law from counting "day of" votes until they counted mailed-in absentee votes, which came in first. Only after counting the early arrivals could officials turn to the late batches. As it turned out, the most recent votes were sufficiently different in candidate choices than the earlier ones to change the overall election outcomes.[17] Once again, there was no hanky-panky. The bottom line is that Trump's election observers were either woefully untrained or simply looking for a reason to question the 2020 outcome.

Someone perhaps unaware of the idiosyncratic elements associated with election law might have reason to ponder, and even accept, the veracity of any of the charges cited above. However, the greatest unnecessary confusion connected with the 2020 presidential election came not from any vote counting or procedure challenges, but rather the deceit put forth by Donald Trump, himself.[18] The simple, undisputed fact is that Trump knew he lost immediately after the votes were announced, yet he pursued a variety of false claims questioning its legitimacy. We know this from several sources. Liz Cheney, a lifelong conservative Republican and co-chair of the House Select Committee to Investigate the January 6th (2021) Attack on the US Capitol, writes in her memoir that she was told directly by Kevin McCarthy, then-House Republican Minority Leader and close Trump ally, that Trump was well aware of the outcome. In real time.[19]

Second, during the Committee hearings, Cassidy Hutchinson, aide to Trump Chief of Staff Mark Meadows, testified that Meadows told her of Trump's election outcome awareness at the election's end.[20] Finally, in the indictment of Donald Trump by a Washington, DC, federal grand jury for conspiracy to obstruct the 2020 presidential election, a half dozen instances were cited where Trump had conversations with key personnel where he acknowledged his loss.[21] In sum, any claims by Trump and his backers of tainted election results were misleading political fishing expeditions and nothing more.

The truth notwithstanding, the Trump team argued election interference before, during, and after the 2020 vote. Their persistent claims reinforced the resolve of angry Republican officials and Trump voters alike. A post-2020 presidential election review of Republican legislators in the nine states with the closest election defeats found that 44 percent of them attempted to discredit or overturn the outcome in their states despite the lack of any concrete evidence.²² And their feelings of betrayal were deep, although one wonders whether they weren't akin to a lost flock of sheep in search of their herder.

The repeated claims of foul by Trump and his minions took hold of Trump voters. Shortly after the 2020 election conclusion, an astounding 70 percent of Republicans believed that the presidential election was unfair with widespread voter fraud that cost Trump the election.²³ But that was only the beginning of Republican contempt. Nearly three years after the 2020 election, a national poll found that 69 percent of Republicans believed that Biden's win was not legitimate—this despite the January 6, 2021, insurrection, *The January 6th Report*, and the litany of federal and state conspiracy, obstruction, and voter fraud charges against Trump and many of his allies.²⁴ Nothing would shake their collective conviction.

From the 2020 outcome through the 2024 presidential campaign, endless rigged election accusations by Trumpists continued to persist throughout American society, bolstering the unfounded conspiratorial beliefs of millions of Trump voters. Even investigations of voter fraud allegations sponsored by the conservative Heritage Foundation contradicted Trump's contentions again and again. Some examples: An audit of more than 100 million votes in Texas between 2005 and 2022 found only 107 instances of voter fraud. Another Heritage Foundation-supported inquiry into 9 million votes in Georgia between 2020 and 2022 found one instance of voter fraud, while a similar investigation of 6 million votes in Arizona between 2020 and 2022 couldn't find any instances of election tinkering at all.²⁵

The ultimate clarification of the 2020 presidential results came with the work of Ken Block, a Republican voting expert, who was hired by the Trump campaign team to examine state election outcomes for voter fraud. Three-quarters of a million dollars later, Block presented findings from his investigations in Arizona, Georgia, Nevada, Michigan, Pennsylvania, and Wisconsin—all critical swing states. Block's overall conclusion: "Every voter fraud claim presented to me by the Trump campaign was disproven."²⁶ But there was more. Postelection data compiled by government security experts described the national event as "the most secure in American history."²⁷ Resistant to the truth and its many sources, the anger within Trump supporters only swelled over time, setting up an increasingly hostile political environment for the 2024 presidential election campaign, its outcome, and more importantly the struggle for the continuity of American democracy.

Election Interference, Trumpism Style

We've learned repeatedly from the Trump camp about the bogus assertions of election interference that denied him a second term of the presidency. Indeed, this false contention has been foundational to his postelection behavior rejecting the outcome. Now it's time to learn about the real election interference actually conducted before and after the 2020 presidential election by the very parties that professed victimhood. The next few paragraphs focus on hush-money payments, falsifying election data, creating illegitimate electors, and inspiring the January 6, 2021, insurrection.

Hush-Money Payments to Conceal Information from the Voters

We begin with an odd event that actually preceded the 2016 election between Trump and Democratic opponent Hillary Clinton. Although well before the illegalities surrounding the 2020 election, the incident served as a precursor of the various types of Trump-orchestrated transgressions to come.

In October 2016, weeks before the November presidential vote, then-Trump attorney Michael Cohen paid $130,000 in hush money to porn star Stormy Daniels. The money was put forward in exchange for Daniels not discussing a sexual encounter she claimed between her and then-citizen Trump. In 2018, Cohen explained that he was simply the middleman between Trump and Daniels. Nevertheless, Cohen was charged, convicted, and sentenced to prison for violating campaign finance rules. Later that year, when asked about the transaction, Trump described Cohen's payment to Daniels as "a simple private transaction" and nothing more.[28]

After several years of investigation, in March 2023, a Manhattan grand jury indicted Trump on thirty-four felony counts for "falsifying New York business records to conceal damaging information and unlawful activity from American voters before and after the 2016 election."[29] Trump denied the accusations. If true, such a "simple private transaction" denying voters access to potentially damaging information about Trump's character could certainly be construed as election interference.

In April 2024, the hush-money case went to trial with all of its sordid details. After five weeks of detailed testimony that bounced back and forth between a titillating exposé and sketchy financial records, a jury found Trump guilty of all thirty-four counts of intentionally using company funds to hide the relationship with Daniels from the public.

At first, it seemed that the conviction might thwart Trump's 2024 presidential candidacy. In an Ipsos public opinion poll conducted after the conclusion of the trial, 49 percent believed that Trump should suspend his campaign, compared with 39 percent who said he should not.[30] However, a Monmouth University poll found that 57 percent agreed that the charges against Trump were politically motivated, compared with 41 percent who thought otherwise.[31] For Trump, the Monmouth poll provided all the vindication he needed. However, the matter didn't end there.

As is typical with Trump court cases where he is on the losing end, the former president vowed to appeal what he described as grievous abuse of the judicial process by a corrupt judge and tainted jury. Due to Trump's victory in the 2024 presidential election, the outcome of his appeal as well as possible sentencing would not be known until after Trump's election victory. Given those circumstances, on January 10, 2025, the judge sentenced Trump to an "unconditional discharge," which yielded no punishment but left intact the verdict. As a result, Trump became the first convicted felon ever to assume the presidency.[32]

Attempt to Falsify the Georgia Presidential Vote

Among the many accusations about Donald Trump's interference with the 2020 presidential election, some could not be resolved until after long delays, and might well be dismissed altogether if Trump prevailed in 2024. One issue with little question about the basic facts emerged on January 2, 2021, in a recorded phone call from Trump to Georgia Republican Secretary of State Brad Raffensperger. Georgia, like most states, places responsibility for managing the election process and vote tabulation with the Secretary of State. Georgia was also one of the states with a vote outcome that swung from Trump in the 2016 election to Biden in 2020 by the slim margin of 11,779 votes. Trump's thinking was that if he could somehow secure a changed vote in Georgia, he would have a model for replicating the altered result in several other states where he also lost by close margins.

In the sixty-seven-minute conversation recorded by Raffensperger, Trump explained to the Secretary of State that the then-president's Republican poll watchers had discovered hundreds of thousands of Georgia voters who had been denied the right to vote in the 2020 election. Moreover, Trump added, tens of thousands of others had illegally jammed Georgia voting machines and tallying equipment with illegal votes for Biden. Trump asserted, he had actually won Georgia by several hundred thousand votes. Given the "true facts," there was only one way to correct the various errors and illegalities. Trump's very words as recorded were as follows: "So look, all I want to do is this. I just want to find 11,780 votes, which is one more than we have [lost by] because we won the state."[33]

After listening to Trump's litany of allegations, Raffensperger calmly responded that the Georgia election tallies had been counted and audited on three separate occasions without any significant change in the totals. Thus, the Georgia Secretary of State concluded that the presidential vote remained as originally tabulated. Denied any adjustment of vote totals, Trump upped the ante. He warned Raffensperger that he was ignoring election illegalities and that such behavior by the Secretary of State constituted a criminal offense. Undaunted, Raffensperger countered, "Mr. President, you have people that submit information, and we have our people that submit information. And then it comes before the court, and the court has to make a determination. We have to stand by our numbers. We believe our numbers are right."[34] Clearly, if anyone had committed a criminal offense, it was Trump for his effort to change the vote. For his part, Trump later defended his conversation with Raffensperger as merely containing an exchange of ideas, with nothing inappropriate.

Fulton County, Georgia, District Attorney Fani Willis thought otherwise. On August 14, 2023, a county grand jury convened by Willis charged Trump with thirteen felony counts, alleging that he conspired with eighteen others to "unlawfully change the outcome of the election in favor of Trump." With the information gathered from Trump's conversation with Raffensperger, the grand jury levied charges against the individuals conspiring with Trump to change the outcome of the election.[35] Several members of the group entered into plea bargains with the District Attorney to resolve the charges rather than face a trial. For their part, Trump and a few others chose to face a judge and jury.

While Trump awaited his day in court, one fact was crystal clear from the January 2, 2021, recorded conversation with Brad Raffensperger: Trump pointedly demanded that the Secretary of State manipulate the Georgia presidential vote in such a way that Trump would gain more popular votes than Biden, and thereby win its sixteen electors. Fortunately, Raffensperger honored the collective will of the Georgia electorate rather than the illegal pressure applied by the president. Still, it's hard to believe that any elected official, even Trump, would be so brazen as to attempt to illegally change an election result.

Overcoming Trumpism

Once again, Trump caught a break, this time because of Trump lawyers complaining that Fulton County District Attorney Fani Willis had acted improperly in the case because of a romantic relationship she had with a special assistant she had hired. A Georgia Court of Appeals agreed with Trump's argument, essentially shelving the case for the foreseeable future.[36] Nevertheless, the facts of the case courtesy of the infamous phone call could not be disputed. Trump lobbied the Georgia Secretary of State to alter the election outcome.

Phony State Electors

To understand the problem of phony Trump electors in the 2020 election, we must begin with a brief review of the circuitous way we choose our presidents. In American presidential elections, voters do not cast their ballots directly for the president. Rather, they vote for electors who cast all of their presidential ballots on behalf of the candidate receiving the most votes in the election, such as the sixteen electors mentioned in the section above. The number of electoral votes for each state equals the number of seats each state has in the Congress. So, for example, Georgia has fourteen members of the House of Representatives and two US senators, which equals a total of sixteen presidential electors. This formula exists for every state with the exception of Nebraska and Maine, where electors determine their electoral votes based on the returns in each congressional district. One other note: the number of electors allocated to each state may change with each census because the number of congressional districts allocated to each state may change as states gain or lose populations relative to the others.

In all, 100 US senators, 435 members of the House of Representatives, and 3 electors for the District of Columbia, courtesy of the Twenty-Third Amendment to the US Constitution, add up to 538 electoral votes for an esoteric body known as the Electoral College. The candidate emerging with a majority of electoral votes, 270, wins the presidency. At the end of the 2020 campaign, Biden beat Trump by more than 7 million popular votes. More significantly, Biden defeated Trump in electoral votes by the margin of 306 to 232. The outcome was ratified by the Electoral College on December 14, 2020. End of discussion? Not quite.

When the dust settled from the election, a stunned Donald Trump exhorted his supporters to "Stop the Steal," claiming without a shred of evidence that Biden had won through dishonest means. In fact, Trump and his allies were the only ones trying to steal the outcome by organizing a devious plot to illegally replace the Democratic electors won by Biden with Republican electors loyal to Trump.[37] They met with Republican legislative leaders from seven states with a total of eighty-four electoral votes and contrived sets of "alternate" electors who would assert Trump's victory at the Capitol on January 6, 2021, the day when the 2020 election outcome would be officially confirmed by Congress.[38] The idea was for the alternate electors to produce their "credentials" to Vice President Mike Pence in advance of the event, with the claim that the official electors had been determined by election fraud. Then presented with both official and alternate elector lists, Pence would have the grounds to send the election back to the states for clarification and new votes, if necessary. That's exactly what happened. With so many electoral votes now in play, elected officials in Republican-controlled state legislatures might have the opportunity to reverse the election outcome.

It didn't work. Trump besieged his Vice President to "do the right thing" and accept the alternate electors. At first, the Vice President said little. Finally, on January 5, the day before a massive January 6 rally near the Capitol, Pence told Trump that the 2020 presidential election results had been ratified by the Electoral College on December 14, 2020, as expected. Further, Pence said, after consulting constitutional experts on the topic, the Vice President had no power to reject electors chosen by the voters. As for the largely ceremonial confirmation vote on January 6, 2021, Pence added, he would preside over the symbolic vote and acknowledge the outcome from the November 3rd election.

Pence's refusal was cited by an angry Trump at the infamous "Stop the Steal" rally held on the morning of January 6, 2021. So incensed were the Trump insurrectionists who stormed the Capitol at the rally's end that some of them actually constructed gallows with the intention of hanging the Vice President. The insurrectionists forced closure of the Capitol for hours as hundreds of members of the Congress who gathered for the ceremony fled for their lives. To his credit, Pence remained on the premises in a secret room in the Capitol. When order was restored hours later, Pence performed his duty as intended.

In the months following the alternate delegate scam, criminal indictments took place in Georgia, Michigan, and Nevada. In other alternate delegates states, some groups apologized or attorneys general elected not to press charges because of ambiguities connected with the efforts of the participants. But once again, one fact was abundantly clear: the only people attempting to steal the election outcome were Trump and his loyalists.

Overcoming Trumpism

Insurrection against the Capitol

That leads us to a discussion of the insurrection against the Capitol, the purpose of the participants, and the outcome of their efforts. Even though Trump knew he lost the 2020 election, he continued to claim that he won at a series of postelection events and rallies. And he wasn't about to give up. As early as a month before the January 6, 2021, congressional election confirmation meeting, Trump and his allies began planning a rally on the National Mall not far from the White House. A memo written by Trump campaign attorney Kenneth Chesebro on December 6, 2020, had set up the outline of a plan to create the false electors. In a second memo, Chesebro argued that the January 6 certification date would be far more important than the Electoral College meeting on December 14, 2020.

Meanwhile, Trump pumped up the January 6 rally, tweeting announcements about the gathering seven times between December 19, 2020, and January 6, 2021. He predicted in one tweet that the rally "will be wild." The plan was for supporters to attend the event in hopes of convincing Congress not to confirm the 2020 election result, even though exactly that had occurred when the Electoral College announced the official outcome at its scheduled meeting.

On January 6, at least ten thousand supporters descended on the rally site, hundreds of whom were members of several right-wing extremist hate groups that had become immersed in the effort to keep Trump in office. The leaders of at least two extremist groups, the Oath Keepers and the Proud Boys, met on January 5 to coordinate efforts.[39] Many had weapons including guns, Molotov cocktails, and pipe bombs.[40] This would not be a run-of-the-mill political rally even by Trump standards.

At the meeting prior to the insurrection, Trump spoke for seventy minutes and worked the assemblage into a frenzy. After telling the crowd that "our country has had enough," that "the states had been defrauded," and that "we won [the presidential election] by a landslide," he exhorted the soon-to-be-mob to "fight like hell. And if you don't fight like hell, you don't have a country anymore ... . So we're going to walk down Pennsylvania Avenue . . . and we're going to the Capitol." And with that encouragement, the crowd did just that, although Trump did not join them due to the Secret Service's inability to control the highly unstable environment. More than two thousand rioters violently overpowered the contingent of Capitol police and penetrated the Capitol in a bloody confrontation lasting three hours.

Disrespect, Destruction, Disenfranchisement

Although he was not physically present at the insurrection, Trump's hands were all over the tragedy. Plainly stated, the riot came at his urging not only on January 6, but in response to a series of tweets written by Trump weeks before where he implored supports to gather in Washington on January 6. In other words, the event was carefully choreographed well in advance. The results were dramatic and costly. Over 140 Capitol police officers were injured, and five lives were lost. More than 1,600 rioters were arrested for various crimes, and nearly all were convicted or pleaded guilty to charges ranging from trespassing to seditious conspiracy, with more trials yet to come.[41]

As the insurrection went on, Trump watched the melee at the Capitol from the White House, ignoring urgent requests from members of Congress and some of his own staff to provide more police personnel. Finally, more than three hours after the insurrection began, he called on the menacing crowd to disperse, while telling them at the end of his meekly worded video that "we love you." The incitement inspired by Trump was the worst assault on the US Capitol since the British burned the Capitol down in the War of 1812. And how did Trump view the insurrectionists, the rowdies who sought to overturn the 2020 presidential election? He called them "great people," "hostages," and "patriots." Republican members inside the Capitol during the insurrection agreed with the former president. One member called the riot the action of "peaceful patriots." Another doubted that the insurrectionists were Trump people. A third Republican member said any reference to the event as an "insurrection" was a "a bold-faced lie."[42] Perhaps the most astonishing statement came from newly elected Republican representative Andrew Clyde, also present inside the Capitol that day, who described the riot as "just a normal tourist visit." Oddly enough, photographs later showed Clyde barring the door to his office during the insurrection![43] There's something incredible about denying the undeniable.

But the story doesn't end there. On January 6, 2024, the three-year anniversary of the greatest threat to American democracy since the Civil War, Trump pledged to consider pardons for most of the insurrectionists if the voters sent him back to the White House.[44] After all, for in Trump's words, they were patriots who had been taken hostage for no legitimate reason by the Capitol police.

Fast forward to the first few months of the second Trump administration and we see another example of revisionist history. Upon his inauguration, Trump pardoned virtually all of the 1,600 insurrectionists. Shortly thereafter, in May 2025, Trump's Department of Justice agreed on a $5 million payment to the family of Ashli Babbitt, an armed Air Force veteran and rioter who was shot to death by a Capitol police officer as she tried to climb through a smashed window into the Speaker's office.[45] That payment seemed to open up a Pandora's box of future lawsuits by other insurrectionists. In June 2025, five leaders of the Proud Boys, an armed far-right group with sixty members who had been convicted of several crimes associated with storming the US Capitol on January 6, sued the federal government for $100 million on the grounds that their constitutional rights had been violated.[46] Let's remember that during the unprecedented assault, more than 140 officers were hurt protecting the Capitol, but for Trump, their service apparently seemed inconsequential. The same president who signed an Executive Order offering federal support for state and local law enforcement "to relentlessly pursue criminals and protect American communities"[47] apparently didn't feel the same way about the Capitol police.

With Donald Trump and his allies, rhetoric and reality are often two worlds apart. Despite raging, unfounded accusations about a stolen election, the Trump-inspired illegal effort to prevent confirmation of the 2020 presidential election was the only "steal" to be stopped. Likewise, the Trump-led attempts to change vote outcomes, falsify election results, and replace legitimate state electors with imposters were the only actual conspiratorial endeavors to "rig" the outcome of the election. For all these machinations, the American public paid a dear price in the forms of suddenly vulnerable institutions and malevolent ambition from a would-be authoritarian president. Nevertheless, baseless doubts sown by Trumpists took hold on a sizable element of American society, creating a kind of pollution that would be tough to separate from truth in the political atmosphere.

From Federal Indictments to Dismissals

A centuries-old saying holds that "the wheels of justice turn slowly but grind exceedingly fine." Implied in the quote is that sooner or later a wrongdoing will receive the appropriate punishment. In the case of the federal allegations against Donald Trump, the saying is only half-right. The wheels moved slowly enough, but the appropriate result did not occur as many expected.

The Investigation and Federal Charges against Trump

On January 13, 2021, shortly after the January 6 insurrection, the House of Representatives quickly issued its second impeachment hearing against

Trump, making him the only US president ever to be impeached twice. Trump was charged with incitement of an insurrection against the US Capitol. Although Trump was no longer president, the trial was held in the US Senate between February 9 and 13, 2021, after which the Senate acquitted Trump by virtue of a 57-to-43 vote to convict, short of the required two-thirds vote. Still, seven Republicans joined fifty Democrats in the vote.

Meanwhile, on July 1, 2021, the Democrat-controlled House of Representatives voted to create a Select Committee for investigation of the January 6, 2021, insurrection. The inquiry lasted eighteen months and included interviews with more than one thousand witnesses. On December 23, 2022, the committee, and later the full House, voted to recommend that the Department of Justice charge Trump with the following federal allegations: obstruction of an official proceeding; conspiracy to defraud the United States; conspiracy to knowingly make a false statement; and assisting, aiding, or comforting an insurrection.[48]

Not until November 18, 2022—nearly a year later—did Attorney General Merrick Garland announce the appointment of Jack Smith as Special Counsel to investigate efforts to overturn the 2020 presidential election. In June 2023, per Smith's request, a federal grand jury in Florida indicted Trump for intentionally withholding more than one hundred classified documents that belonged to the National Archives. Two months later, in August 2023, a Washington, DC–based federal grand jury indicted Trump for conspiring to overturn the November 3, 2020, presidential election. On both indictments, Trump pleaded not guilty to all charges.

Trump's Defense

The Trump legal team based their defense against prosecution on the belief that presidents are shielded from liability especially during official conduct in office, and the courts couldn't really decide what was and was not "official." On this issue, the Supreme Court had offered conflicting decisions in the past, leaving everyone a bit uncertain about what the justices would say.[49]

With such uncertainty, Trump needed a backup plan. Beyond the legal arguments, Trump's defense had three planks: delay, delay, and delay. He had good reason. Had Trump been reelected without a favorable Supreme Court decision, per federal tradition, he wouldn't be tried until after exiting the presidency on January 20, 2029. A multitude of things could happen during such a long period, maybe even a favorable decision or a new law during the interim. Thus, delay was clearly Trump's best option, his pleas of innocence notwithstanding. On this, a well-known defense attorney said admiringly, "Trump's legal team has done a masterful job delaying and going on the offense—litigating and appealing everything. His delay is his best defense."[50] Endless challenges on various legal issues before judges along a circuitous route to trial, the benefit of a multitiered federal court system, and deep financial pockets to fund it all worked to advantage the Trump legal team.

By far, the biggest break for Trump came with a Supreme Court decision on June 30, 2024. In *Trump v. United States*, the justices ruled in a 6-to-3 majority (including all three Trump appointees) that presidents and former presidents have broad immunity from prosecution for official acts conducted while in office. The justices weren't specific in drawing a line between official and unofficial acts, and ordered a lower court to decide the differences, with future cases no doubt coming from any disagreements on the definitions of official and unofficial acts. Critics howled over the court's interpretation, which seemed to establish an incredibly broad umbrella protecting presidential power.[51]

Sometimes, Being Right Is Not Enough

That was enough. In the Florida case on classified documents, almost immediately, District Court Judge Aileen Cannon, a Trump appointee overseeing the allegation and who had already ruled favorably on several Trump requests, dismissed the case.[52] The case in Washington, DC, languished until after the November 3, 2024, presidential election. Weeks later, Special Counsel Jack Smith asked District Court Judge Tanya Chutkan for and received dismissal of the charges against Trump for his role in the January 6 insurrection.

Clearly, the circumstances, not the facts of the case, dictated Smith's withdrawal. He wrote in his final report to the attorney general, "Indeed, but for Mr. Trump's election and imminent return to the presidency, the office [of the special counsel] assessed that the admissible evidence was sufficient to obtain and sustain a conviction at trial."[53] Between the evidence cited in Smith's final report and *The January 6th Report* issued by the House Select Committee is almost impossible to conclude otherwise. Smith had the goods on Trump, but an unusual set of circumstances dictated otherwise.

Biased State Actions: Another Level of Obstruction

Political actors with Trumpist values have done their best to impose their antidemocratic themes wherever possible, including all facets of American government from local city councils to national campaigns. Among the deniers' targets, the states have been ripe targets for exploitation. Below we consider gerrymandering and state voting laws as examples of Trumpist efforts to overturn American democracy.

Gerrymandering

If you're looking for an example of abstract political art, gerrymandering is a good place to start. The concept was named for Massachusetts Governor Elbridge Gerry, who didn't invent the idea as much as he perfected it. In the early 1800s, Gerry signed legislation allowing the leaders of his political party to design legislative district boundaries that would dilute the clout of opponents by splitting their numbers into several neighboring districts. As a result, the majority party would receive an overall artificial boost in some legislative districts, with more election winners than their proportion of the state's population would have expected to yield. Wisconsin is an example. Trump won the 2024 presidential election by less than a single percentage point, but six of the state's eight congressional districts had Republicans. Gerrymandering became a staple of those in power and has continued ever since.

Voting rights activists have long viewed gerrymandering as a political barrier to fair elections. Beginning in 1962, the US Supreme Court addressed the issue, at first, in terms of unevenly populated districts and decided that people in larger populated districts lacked the same representation as people in less populated districts. As the decade went on, subsequent cases focused on gerrymandering as a form of racial discrimination by minimizing the power of racial minorities.[54] Much of gerrymandered racial discrimination was found with southern states, along with less impactful instances elsewhere scattered throughout the nation.

In 1965, the US Congress passed the Voting Rights Act of 1965, a seminal piece of legislation with several provisions dedicated to eradicating racial discrimination in all aspects of voter participation. A key section required seven southern states and parts of five other states to preclear their apportionment maps following each decennial US census with the US attorney general prior to their implementation. The Voting Rights Act was strengthened and readopted by Congress in 1970, 1975, and 1982. As a result, states were much less likely to discriminate in the formation of their legislative districts.

The efforts to prevent racial discrimination via gerrymandering came to a screeching halt with the Supreme Court's *Shelby v. Holder* decision in 2013. In that case, the court's increasingly conservative majority held that the portion of the 1965 Voting Rights Act requiring preclearance was no longer needed because minority voter participation had approached White percentages. Subsequent cases decided by the court made it even more difficult for the federal government to review and stop gerrymandered discrimination.

The 2020 census was a turning point for gerrymandering proponents. No longer constrained by the 1965 Voting Rights Act, several states went about redistricting in ways that skewed their districts in favor of Whites and against non-Whites, which were reservoirs for Republican support. Their legislative efforts produced stunning results. Just over half of all the seats on the House of Representatives were carved out through gerrymandering: 177 seats in 19 states in legislatures controlled by Republicans and 49 seats in 7 states in legislatures controlled by Democrats. Most of the rest were designed either by independent commissions or state courts.[55]

These numbers give Republicans a 128-seat advantage in generating the boundaries of congressional districts, a net gain that would seem to favor the party to building a majority in the 435-member House of Representatives of 218. That's because gerrymandering usually produces "safe" districts sufficiently one sided in political party voter registration that the political candidate of the party in power has a tremendous advantage if he or she seeks election or reelection. This shield has other advantages as well. It should not be surprising that of the 139 House Republicans who voted against confirming Joe Biden on January 6, 2021, eighty-five came from states where Republicans had full control over the redistricting process. In other words, because of gerrymandering, they had little concern about a backlash in their districts.[56]

There have been occasional victories for reformers, such as when the Supreme Court gave a modest victory to redistricting activists in an Alabama case.[57] Nevertheless, as of 2024, cases brought by African Americans, Latinos, Native Americans, and multiracial groups about unconstitutional gerrymandering in nine states remained without resolution.[58] For the most part, the recent rulings on gerrymandering by the US Supreme Court have blended well with Trumpist goals of voter suppression.

State Voting Laws

It didn't take long for some states to take advantage of the *Shelby v. Holder* decision. Data compiled by the Brennan Center for Justice show that in the ten years following the landmark decision, legislatures in twenty-nine states enacted ninety-four laws in several critical areas of voting rights including increased voter registration requirements, reduced voting opportunities, smaller numbers of available voting places, limited voter assistance, and curbs on mail voting. A disproportionate majority of the most repressive laws came in states that produced large Republican majorities for Donald Trump.[59]

Many of the new state laws came in response to the surge of voters who participated in the 2020 presidential election. The large number of mail votes arriving late in the election cycle convinced the Trump campaign to allege without any evidence that Biden-friendly forces had managed to add millions of last-minute ballots.[60] In fact, the large numbers stemmed from a dramatic increase in voter turnout, 66.8 percent compared with 59.2 percent in 2016, leading to an additional 23 million voters. Then again, the Trump campaign was more concerned with unfounded accusations than facts.

A few of the restrictions have been struck down by the courts as excessive, and some states have actually increased voting opportunities. For example, after the 2020 election, eight states actually passed legislation making it easier to vote. Still, the overwhelming cumulative effect from the *Shelby* decision is that communities of color have suffered disproportionately.[61] Simply put, these groups have found it harder to vote.

Independent research on voter turnout since *Shelby* has found a growing gap in turnout between Blacks and Whites in precisely the same counties released from federal control. According to the study, by 2022, the turnout gap between Whites and non-Whites in areas shielded by *Shelby* was 9 percent, compared to 5 percent in similar demographic voting areas not protected by the case. At first glance, those percentages might seem insignificant in determining the outcome of a national election, yet they add up to a turnout gap of as many as 9 million votes.[62] And in a close election, that can easily mean the difference between victory and defeat. That number is all the more important, given that in the 2020 presidential election, 87 percent of the Black vote went to Democrat Joe Biden! The potential impact of those lost votes in 2024 could well be a turning point in the election. Clearly, state voting laws in the post-*Shelby* era have imposed a deleterious impact on Black participation, leaving a chink in the nation's democracy armor and giving an electoral advantage to Republicans.

Overcoming Trumpism

It would be an overstatement to characterize all of the many state efforts to restrain voter participation as examples of Trumpism. It would be just as wrong to suggest that all repressive voting laws and gerrymandered districts were at the hands of Republicans. Nevertheless, at a minimum, there is a synergy of Trumpism values with the aforementioned efforts to control elections and their outcomes.

Separating Fact from Fiction

This is a moment when we need to separate Trumpist bogus claims from reality. "The greatest rigged election in history," as Trump called it, allegedly contained missing ballots, stuffed ballot ballots, stolen ballots, and illegally mailed ballots. None of those claims carried a kernel of truth. Yet, we have clear evidence of Trump and his minions attempting to falsify the votes, organizing phony electors in seven states to overturn the outcomes, and staging a violent insurrection against the Capitol as a last ditch effort to overturn the election.

We also see Trumpist efforts to rig the system occur in states with Republican-controlled legislatures much more than Democratic-controlled states. Additionally, more than ever, in the post-*Shelby* era, largely Republican-controlled states have passed laws that discourage turnout by groups that would vote disproportionately Democratic. Who's been trying to rig elections? The answer is clear.

The point is, there are many access points to undermining an election. Taking advantage of them can have the effect of destabilizing democracy. For his part in the deceitful drama, Trump caught every break imaginable in avoiding trial. Indeed, Harry Houdini, the unparalleled escape artist, would have been impressed by Trump's success.

NOTES

1. "Delay, Delay, Delay: Trump's Legal Strategy Proves Effective as Election Nears," *The Guardian*, October 2, 2024, https://www.theguardian.com/us-news/2024/oct/02/trump-legal-strategy-election.
2. "Trump's Use of Campaign Funds to Pay Legal Bills," The Brennan Center for Justice, May 10, 2024, https://www.brennancenter.org/our-work/research-reports/trumps-use-campaign-funds-pay-legal-bills.
3. "Trump Delivers Fiery Post-Indictment Speech: 'They're Coming After You,'" NBC News, June 10, 2023, https://www.nbcnews.com/politics/donald-trump/trump-deliver-fiery-post-indictment-speech-georgia-rcna88561.

Disrespect, Destruction, Disenfranchisement

4   See Jason Stanley, *How Fascism Works: The Politics of Us and Them* (New York: Random House, 2020), pp. 26–27.
5   See "Fact Check: 2020 Presidential Election Results Are Still Valid, Biden Is Legitimate Winner," *USA Today*, https://www.usatoday.com/story/news/factcheck/2022/11/04/fact-check-2020-presidential-election-results-still-legitimate-trump-biden/10649174002/, "Fact-Checking the Breadth of Trump's Election Lies," *The New York Times*, August 17, 2023, https://www.nytimes.com/2023/08/17/us/politics/trump-election-lies-fact-check.html, and "10 Trump Election Lies His Own Officials Called False," CNN, June 16, 2022, https://www.cnn.com/2022/06/16/politics/fact-check-trump-officials-testimony-debunking-election-lies/index.html.
6   "New Details Shed Light on Ways Mark Meadows Pushed Federal Agencies to Pursue Dubious Election Claims," CNN, December 2, 2021, https://www.cnn.com/2021/12/02/politics/mark-meadows-election-fraud-liaison/index.html.
7   "Officials Fight Donald Trump's Claims of a Rigged Vote," *The New York Times*, October 16, 2016, https://www.nytimes.com/2016/10/17/us/politics/donald-trump-election-rigging.html.
8   "Trump Tells Wisconsin: Victory Was a Surprise," Politico, December 13, 2016, https://www.politico.com/story/2016/12/donald-trump-wisconsin-232605.
9   Quoted in "Trump Sees a 'Rigged Election' Ahead. Democrats See a Constitutional Crisis in the Making," Politico, May 25, 2020, https://www.politico.com/news/2020/05/25/donald-trump-rigged-election-talk-fears-274477.
10 "Fact-Checking the Breadth of Trump's Election Lies," *The New York Times*, August 17, 2023, https://www.nytimes.com/2023/08/17/us/politics/trump-election-lies-fact-check.html.
11 "Democrat Candidates Get 10,000 Missing Voted After 'Human Error,'" *Newsweek*, March 28, 2024,
12 "USPS Processed 150,000 Ballots after Election Day, Jeopardizing Thousands of Votes," *The Washington Post*, November 6, 2020, https://www.washingtonpost.com/business/2020/11/05/usps-late-ballots-election/.
13 "Biden's Statement on Trump's 2020 Mail Voting Is Half True," Politifact, January 13, 2022, https://www.cnn.com/2021/12/02/politics/mark-meadows-election-fraud-liaison/index.html.
14 "Fact-Check: Trump's Bogus Claim on Fox News That Ballots in 2020 Were 'Fake,'" Politico, June 22, 2023, https://www.newsweek.com/democrat-candidates-get-10000-missing-votes-after-human-error-1884430. https://www.politifact.com/factchecks/2023/jun/22/donald-trump/fact-check-trumps-bogus-claim-on-fox-news-that-bal/.
15 "FACT FOCUS: Gaping Holes in the Claim of 2K Ballot 'Mules,'" AP, May 3, 2022, https://apnews.com/article/2022-midterm-elections-covid-technology-health-arizona-e1b49d2311bf900f44fa5c6dac406762.
16 "Creator of '2000 Mules' Apologizes to Man Falsely Accused of Ballot Fraud in the Film," NPR, December 2, 2024, https://www.npr.org/2024/12/02/g-s1-36527/dinesh-dsouza-2000-mules-apology.

17. "Why Does It Take So Long to Count Mail Ballots in Key States? Blame Legislatures," The Brennan Center for Justice," November 7, 2022, https://www.brennancenter.org/our-work/analysis-opinion/why-does-it-take-so-long-count-mail-ballots-key-states-blame-legislatures.
18. "Flashback: The Call That Got Trump in Trouble in Georgia," Axios, April 14, 2023, https://www.axios.com/2023/08/15/trump-georgia-election-interference-call.
19. Liz Cheney, *Oath and Honor* (New York: Little, Brown, 2023), p. 1.
20. "'He Knows He Lost:' Cassidy Hutchinson Testified That Trump Acknowledged He Lost the 2020 Election," CNN, December 22, 2022, https://www.cnn.com/2022/12/22/politics/cassidy-hutchinson-trump-fighting-secret-service/index.html.
21. Indictment, *United States v. Donald J. Trump*, August 1, 2023, https://www.justice.gov/storage/US_v_Trump_23_cr_257.pdf.
22. "How Trump's 2020 Election Lies Have Gripped State Legislatures," *The New York Times*, May 22, 2022, https://www.nytimes.com/interactive/2022/05/22/us/politics/state-legislators-election-denial.html.
23. "Poll: 70 Percent of Republicans Don't Think the Election Was Free and Fair," Politico, November 9, 2022, https://www.politico.com/news/2020/11/09/republicans-free-fair-elections-435488.
24. "CNN Poll: Percentage of Republicans Who Think Biden's 2020 Win Was Illegitimate Ticks Back up to Near 70%," CNN, August 3, 2023, https://www.cnn.com/2023/08/03/politics/cnn-poll-republicans-think-2020-election-illegitimate/index.html.
25. "Widespread Election Fraud Claims by Republicans Don't Match the Evidence," The Brookings Institution, November 22, 2023, https://www.brookings.edu/articles/widespread-election-fraud-claims-by-republicans-dont-match-the-evidence/.
26. Ken Block, *Disproven* (Nashville, TN: Forefront Books, 2024), p. 114.
27. "Joint Statement from the Elections Infrastructure Government Coordinating Council and the Election Infrastructure Sector Coordinating Executive Committees," Cyberstructure and Infrastructure Security Agency, November 12, 2020, Washington, DC, https://www.cisa.gov/news-events/news/joint-statement-elections-infrastructure-government-coordinating-council-election.
28. "Trump's Bogus 'Simple Private Action' Defense of the Stormy Daniels Payment," *The Washington Post*, December 10, 2018, https://www.washingtonpost.com/politics/2018/12/10/trump-gops-dishonest-minimizing-stormy-daniels-payment/.
29. "District Attorney Bragg Announces 34-Count Felony Indictment of Former President Donald J. Trump," Press Release, April 4, 2023, https://manhattanda.org/district-attorney-bragg-announces-34-count-felony-indictment-of-former-president-donald-j-trump/.
30. "Trump Guilty Verdict Makes Minimal Impact on Public Opinion," Ipsos, June 2, 2024, https://www.ipsos.com/en-us/trump-guilty-verdict-makes-minimal-impact-public-opinion.

Disrespect, Destruction, Disenfranchisement

31 "Trials Have Little Impact on 2024 Race," Monmouth University, June 13, 2024, https://www.monmouth.edu/polling-institute/reports/monmouthpoll_us_061324/.

32 "Trump Avoids Punishment for Hush-Money Conviction and Calls Case 'Terrible Experience,'" *The Guardian*, January 10, 2025, https://www.theguardian.com/us-news/2025/jan/10/trump-hush-money-sentencing-new-york.

33 "Here's the Full Transcript and Audio of the Call between Trump and Raffensperger," *The Washington Post*, January 5, 2021, https://www.washingtonpost.com/politics/trump-raffensperger-call-transcript-georgia-vote/2021/01/03/2768e0cc-4ddd-11eb-83e3-322644d82356_story.html.

34 "Read: Full Transcript of Donald Trump's Call to Brad Raffensperger," Atlanta News First, February 15, 2023, https://www.atlantanewsfirst.com/2023/02/15/read-full-transcript-donald-trumps-call-brad-raffensperger/

35 For a complete text of the charges and individuals involved, see https://d3i6fh83elv35t.cloudfront.net/static/2023/08/CRIMINAL-INDICTMENT-Trump-Fulton-County-GA.pdf.

36 "Georgia Appeals Court Disqualifies Fani Willis from 2020 Election Subversion Case," Democracy Docket, December 19, 2024, https://www.democracydocket.com/news-alerts/georgia-appeals-court-disqualifies-fani-willis-from-2020-election-subversion-case/.

37 See "Trump Had a Direct Role in Plan to Install Fake Electors. Key Takeaways from the Fourth Jan. 6 Hearing," CNBC, June 22, 2022, https://www.cnbc.com/2022/06/22/jan-6-probe-takeaways-trump-had-a-direct-role-in-plan-to-install-fake-electors.html, and "An Intriguing New Detail on Trump's 'Fake' Electors," *The Washington Post*, July 26, 2022, https://www.washingtonpost.com/politics/2022/07/26/trump-fake-electors-arizona/.

38 The seven states and their electoral votes were Arizona (11), Georgia (11), Michigan (16), Nevada (6), New Mexico (5), Pennsylvania (20), and Wisconsin (10).

39 "Timeline: How Two Extremist Groups Planned for Jan. 6," *The Washington Post*, https://www.washingtonpost.com/politics/2022/03/15/timeline-how-two-extremist-groups-planned-jan-6/.

40 Christian Fuchs, "How Did Donald Trump Incite a Coup Attempt," *Journal for a Global Sustainable Information Society*, 19, no. 1 (2021), file:///Users/gerstondocs/Downloads/1239-Article%20Text-5291-2-10-20210125.pdf.

41 "The High-Water Mark of the Jan. 6 Prosecutions," Lawfare, January 6, 2025, https://www.lawfaremedia.org/article/the-high-water-mark-of-the-jan.-6-prosecutions.

42 "Republican Lawmakers Claim January 6 Rioters Were Just Friendly Guys and Gals Taking a Tourist Trip through the Capitol," *Vanity Fair*, May 12, 2021, https://www.vanityfair.com/news/2021/05/capitol-attack-tourist-visit.

43 "A GOP Congressman Compared Capitol Rioters to Tourists. Photos Show Him Barricading a Door," *The Washington Post*, May 18, 2021, https://www.washingtonpost.com/politics/2021/05/18/clyde-tourist-capitol-riot-photos/.

44 "'January 6 Never Ended': Alarm at Trump Pardon Pledge for Capitol Insurrections," *The Guardian*, January 6, 2024, https://www.theguardian.com/us-news/2024/jan/06/trump-pardon-january-6-rioters-if-elected-president/

45 "U.S. to Pay Nearly $5 Million to Family of Jan. 6 Rioter Ashli Babbitt," *The Washington Post*, May 19, 2025, https://www.washingtonpost.com/national-security/2025/05/19/ashli-babbitt-lawsuit-settlement/.

46 "Proud Boys Convicted in Jan. 6 Attack Sue Government on Claims of 'Political Persecution,'" *The New York Times*, June 6, 2025, https://www.nytimes.com/2025/06/06/us/politics/proud-boys-jan-6-lawsuit.html.

47 "Fact Sheet: President Donald J. Trump Strenthens America's Law Enforcement to Pursue Criminals and Protect Innocent Citizens," The White House, April 28, 2025, https://www.whitehouse.gov/fact-sheets/2025/04/fact-sheet-president-donald-j-trump-strengthens-americas-law-enforcement-to-pursue-criminals-and-protect-innocent-citizens/.

48 For complete details of the investigation, see The January 6 Select Committee, *The January 6th Report* (New York: Random House, 2023).

49 "Trump's Presidential Immunity Argument, Explained," Democracy Docket, April 17, 2024, https://www.democracydocket.com/analysis/trumps-presidential-immunity-argument-explained/.

50 Quoted in "Delay, Delay, Delay," *The Guardian*, October 2, 2024.

51 For example, see Andrew Weissmann, "Three Flaws in the Supreme Court's Decision on Presidential Criminal Immunity," Just Security, July 17, 2024, https://www.justsecurity.org/97781/three-flaws-supreme-court-immunity/.

52 "Judge Cannon Should Be Removed from Trump Case, Watchdog Group Argues in New Legal Filing," ProPublica, September 3, 2024, https://www.propublica.org/article/judge-aileen-cannon-trump-documents-case-ethics-complaint-crew-jack-smith.

53 Quoted in "Trump Would Have Been Convicted over 2020 Election, Says Special Counsel," *The Guardian*, January 25, 2025, https://www.theguardian.com/us-news/2025/jan/14/donald-trump-2020-election-conviction-special-counsel-report-jack-smith. For the entire report, see "Final Report of the Special Counsel Under 28 C.F.R. 600.8," U.S. Department of Justice, January 7, 2025, http://justice.gov/storage/Report-of-Special-Counsel-Smith-Volume-1-January-2025.pdf.

54 For a history of gerrymandering in the United States, see "Gerrymandering Explained," The Brennan Center for Justice, June 9, 2023, https://www.brennancenter.org/our-work/research-reports/gerrymandering-explained.

55 "Who Controlled Redistricting in Every State," The Brennan Center for Justice, October 5, 2022, https://www.brennancenter.org/our-work/research-reports/who-controlled-redistricting-every-state?amp=.

56 "How Gerrymandering Will Protect Republicans Who Challenged the Election," *The New York Times*, November 17, 2021, https://www.nytimes.com/2021/01/19/us/politics/republicans-gerrymander-trump-election.html.

57 The case was *Allen v. Milligan*, 599 U. S. 1 (2023).

58 See "Redistricting Fights in These States Could Determine Which Party Controls U.S. House, CNN, January 24, 2024, https://www.cnn.com/politics/redistricting-states-congressional-maps-house/index.html.

59 "States Have Added Nearly 100 Restrictive Laws since SCOTUS Gutted the Voting Rights Act 10 Years Ago," The Brennan Center for Justice, June

23, 2023, https://www.brennancenter.org/our-work/analysis-opinion/states-have-added-nearly-100-restrictive-laws-scotus-gutted-voting-rights.
60 "President Trump's False Claims of Vote Fraud: A Chronology," *The Washington Post*, November 5, 2020, https://www.washingtonpost.com/politics/2020/11/05/president-trumps-false-claims-vote-fraud-chronology/.
61 "States Have Added Nearly 100 Restrictive Laws," The Brennan Center for Justice, June 23, 2023.
62 "Growing Racial Disparities in Voter Turnout, 2008–2022," The Brennan Center for Justice, March 2, 2024, https://www.brennancenter.org/our-work/research-reports/growing-racial-disparities-voter-turnout-2008-2022.

CHAPTER 5
UNDERMINED INSTITUTIONS

"Total control" is a key concept for Trumpists, who are determined to rule American society with their goals, on their terms, and without interference or obstruction. To achieve their objective, they must have total control, which is nothing less than a synonym for Trumpism. But the question remains, how to achieve it?

Whatever the challenges, winning elections is the most economical way for Trumpists to gain total control of the levers of government and American society.[1] Whatever their costs, election victories are easier and faster to achieve than civil wars, which can drain a nation of valuable resources and potentially lead outside powers to join the conflict.

Many modern dictatorships often begin through legitimate election victories. It works like this: An autocrat running as a would-be reformer wins high office at the polls, and then over time uses the power of the office to slowly manipulate institutions in such a way that they fall under his management.[2] Subsequent elections become much easier for authoritarians because by that time, they control most, if not all, of the levers of power. And with that, bit by bit democracy becomes history. Judging from Trump's attempts to use various government agencies to stay in power after his election defeat in 2020, he fits the would-be authoritarian mold. Trump failed only because he had not yet achieved total control during his first presidency.

In a democracy, guardrails exist to discourage, and hopefully prevent, authoritarian ascendance and rule. Every democracy has its own unique combination of political mechanisms for resisting deterioration. Yet, there is a commonality among democracies in that the legitimacy of their leaders depends upon the system of governance accepted by the people, and that the people routinely have the right to decide who leads them through the franchise. But the people alone are not enough to assure success.

A key attribute of American democracy is the commitment to separate representative institutions and the willingness of their leaders to maintain them. Members of Congress are elected directly by the people. The president is elected indirectly through the votes accumulated in the Electoral College. Judges and justices are not elected directly or even indirectly; they are appointed. However, given that they are nominated by the president and subject to confirmation by the US Senate, members of the judiciary are connected, albeit indirectly, to the public through those who have been elected to the executive and legislative branches. In theory, there exists a dedicated, ongoing relationship between the governed and the governors, along with checks and balances guardrails.

Along with formal, constitutionally organized institutions, American democracy is supported by a series of informal institutions. They're called "informal" because these entities contribute to the well-being of the democratic environment, even though they are not mentioned in the Constitution or are officially part of the governing structure. Unlike formal institutions, their members are neither elected nor hold official positions of power, yet they can be influential in promoting democracy. Here we speak of the press and political parties.

In a democracy, a free press has the ability to hold officials accountable through its independent investigations, discussion of issues of importance to the public, and oversight of government officials as well as those seeking to influence government. If the press is muzzled or intimidated, then it loses its independence and no longer functions as a check on those in power or who seek it.

Political parties also loom large for the connective role they play between the people and the leaders voted into office. That's because candidates gain the nomination of their respective parties through earning the support of the voters. Upon election, candidates-turned-office holders represent their state or congressional district. However, with each election they must achieve voter approval to remain in office.

Historically, Americans have largely accepted and abided by our eclectic network of formal and informal structures of governance. Despite what may seem to some as awkward relationships, they have operated to keep government on the straight and narrow either through formal checks and balances among government institutions, informal pressure exerted by the press, political party leaders, or a combination of these. For the most part, this somewhat inelegant arrangement has preserved American democracy. Until now.

This chapter explores the extent to which Donald Trump and his allies have attempted to control virtually every lever of power found in America's formal and informal political institutions. As the remaining portions show, Trump has little regard for our institutions and norms, other than that they are the wellsprings of control and potential domination. In some instances, he and his allies have attempted to manipulate them, in others ignore them, and in others still run over them. Never before have our building blocks of democracy suffered the possibility of their undoing as they do today.

Puncturing Formal Institutions

Visit any civics class in just about every K–12 grade and you'll learn about the executive, legislative, and judicial branches of American government as the sources of political power and authority. In real life, that simple description breaks down quickly, with power operating through blurred arrangements. When those arrangements are abused however, democracy suffers. That has occurred with Donald Trump's assault on these key institutions.

Abusing the Presidency

Over time, the American presidency has become the most powerful office in the country, if not the world. Still, following the checks and balances doctrine embedded in the US Constitution, the presidency is not omnipotent nor was it designed to be so. Yet, Donald Trump has thought otherwise. At one point in the midst of his presidency, Trump declared during a speech, "I have an Article II [of the U.S. Constitution] where I have the right to do whatever I want as president."[3] The Constitution awards no such blanket authority to anyone. Nevertheless, repeatedly Trump attempted to pierce the boundaries of his office both domestically and internationally.

Early on in his first presidency, Trump met with the FBI Director James Comey who made Trump aware of his agency's investigation of possible interaction between Trump campaign officials and Russian agents. Uncomfortable with Comey's probe, Trump demanded the director's total loyalty, including FBI tasks that Trump opposed. Comey countered that his allegiance was to the Constitution. After four uncomfortable months of putting up with Comey's independence, Trump fired the FBI director. That was only the first of many instances in which Trump placed personal fidelity above any other quality. It was also an early sign of Trump repeatedly abusing the powers of his office. Consider a few of the most obvious instances of malevolent behavior and abuse of power by Trump during his first term:

- According to John Kelly, a former chief of staff, Trump wanted Kelly to pressure the IRS to probe the tax returns of two FBI agents who had investigated the possible connections between Russian go-betweens and the Trump 2016 campaign. Despite Trump's contempt for the two, there was no indication of illegal work by the agents.[4]
- Under the direction of Trump, Attorney General Jeff Sessions fired FBI Deputy Director Andrew McCabe for initially authorizing the investigation of the interaction between the Russian representatives and the Trump campaign team in 2016.
- In 2018, Trump demanded that Sessions reopen a closed investigation on 2016 Democratic presidential opponent Hillary Clinton for allegedly illegally keeping thousands of government emails on her private computer. Sessions refused to reopen the investigation, calling it unnecessary, and Trump fired him.
- In 2019, Trump forced Deputy Attorney General Rod Rosenstein to resign for Rosenstein's appointment of former FBI Director Robert Mueller as special counsel to head the investigation of possible ties between Trump's presidential campaign and Russian agents.
- In 2020, Trump fired New York–based federal prosecutor Geoffrey Berman for investigating Trump's personal attorney Rudy Giuliani, who was later charged for conspiring to overturn the 2020 presidential election.
- In 2020, Trump fired Lt. Colonel Alexander Vindman, his Ukraine expert on the National Security Council. Vindman had testified in Trump's first impeachment hearing that Trump had vowed to withhold military aid from Ukraine president Volodymyr Zelenskyy unless Zelenskyy manufactured false information against Hunter Biden, the son of then-Democratic presidential opponent Joe Biden.
- In 2020, Trump fired Michael Atkinson, the independent inspector general for the Intelligence Community because Atkinson passed on a whistleblower's complaint that contributed to the first of two charges against Trump in the 2019 impeachment trial.
- After the 2020 presidential election, Trump fired Christopher Krebs, the US Cybersecurity and Infrastructure Security Agency, after Krebs declared the election (and Trump's defeat) "the most secure in American history."

Note that in every case, the dismissals of Trump appointees were not for incompetence or abuse of their responsibilities; rather, these officials were terminated for activities that left Trump threatened, angry, or both.

Against Trump's abuse of authority, there were a few occasions where government guardrails miraculously held against Trump's intention to protect himself against legitimate investigations. For example, after Trump fired FBI Director Comey, pressure grew in Congress for an investigation about the possibility of a cover-up connected with Trump's 2016 presidential campaign. As noted, then-Attorney General Jeff Sessions recused himself from choosing a special counsel because of his participation in the Trump campaign. Trump was furious. Then, Deputy Attorney General Rod Rosenstein appointed Robert Mueller, a former FBI director with impeccably impartial credentials, to lead an investigation of the entire affair. As the enquiry progressed, Trump became so concerned about possible damning information that he set about to fire the special counsel. Upon learning of the plan, then-White House Counsel Donald McGahn threatened to resign in fear that Mueller's termination would appear as an obstruction of justice. Faced with repercussions from a McGahn resignation, Trump relented.[5]

In another instance, six weeks after Trump lost the 2020 presidential election, he asked then-Attorney General Bill Barr whether the Justice Department could seize voting machines from states where Trump suspected foul play leading to more votes for opponent Joe Biden. Barr responded that there was "no basis for the allegations."[6] Next, Trump wanted the Department of Homeland Security to confiscate voting machines on the basis of foreign interference with the election apparatus. In a heated discussion, Department of Homeland Security officials repeatedly told Trump that the government had no authority to do so. Trump backed off.[7]

Lastly, shortly before the January 6, 2021, insurrection, Trump met with Acting Defense Secretary Chad Miller about a rally scheduled for earlier in the day before the crowd marched to the Capitol, where some of the attendees would arrive with weapons. In the meeting, Trump wanted Miller to provide National Guard troops to protect the insurrectionists from harm by Capitol police, even though he was aware that many of the protesters were prepared for violence![8] According to Miller, Trump's words were, "Do whatever is necessary to protect demonstrators that were executing their constitutionally protected rights." Miller never carried out the order.[9] Ironically, when members of Congress, including House Republican Minority Leader and Trump ally Kevin McCarthy pleaded with Trump for National Guard personnel to repel the bloody attack and restore order, Trump didn't respond with any assistance for more than three hours.

The information presented above clearly reveals the extent to which Donald Trump labored to extend the reach of his presidency beyond constitutionally established boundaries. It also shows instances where Trump-appointed personnel resisted what they perceived as illegal demands from Trump. It all augurs the question, what if Trump had more cooperative appointees who would carry out his orders without any resistance? Signs of an answer to this question emerged in 2024 well before the election. In the words of former National Security Adviser John Bolton, rather than focus on expertise in key positions, "the chief requirements for duty will be how quickly you say 'yes, sir.'"[10]

As he campaigned for a second term, Trump pointedly outlined his postelection plans that made his first term look like child's play. The focus of his intentions centered on a governing concept known as the "unitary executive theory," which posits that the Constitution gives the president complete control of all levers in the executive branch.[11] Further, with sweeping powers, the theory holds, the president can minimize, if not ignore, the power of Congress.[12]

We don't know the extent to which Trump accepts unitary executive theory as a policymaking framework, but his expressed intentions for a second term of office strongly suggested agreement at least for his purposes. In his "interpretation" of the Constitution's Article II about the executive branch when he was in office, Trump said: "I have the right to do whatever I want as president."[13] That approach to governance coincided with some of Trump's publicly stated objectives for 2025 and beyond. If elected, Trump promised to

- appoint a special prosecutor to target Joe Biden and his family as well as other Trump enemies for what Trump referred to without any evidence as corruption;[14]
- invoke the Insurrection Act of 1807 to use the military for quelling violence in what Trump referred to as "crime-infested" cities, although the act is intended for cases of rebellion or extreme disorder;[15]
- conduct the largest deportation of noncitizens in American history, including as many as 11 million people without legal status;[16]
- defund the FBI to keep it from conducting "witch hunts" and "corrupt" investigations against people like Trump;[17]

- abolish the US Department of Education, a Cabinet department created by the US Congress;[18]
- place independent agencies such as the Federal Communications Commission, Federal Trade Commission, Federal Reserve, and National Labor Relations Board under direct presidential control, thereby limiting their effectiveness;[19]
- make every executive branch federal employee subject to the hiring and dismissal by the president without any explanation, thereby gutting at least fifty thousand civil service positions.[20]

Trump's promises for a second term paralleled many of his unfulfilled intentions in his first term. If nothing else, his governing goals were incredibly transparent. The only difference is that with four years of governing under his belt, he developed a deeper understanding of how to achieve his goals. Whether Trump's true aspirations were fully appreciated by the voters in what loomed to be an extremely close election was less apparent.

Taking on Congress

The American presidency may be the nation's most powerful office, but as we know, power in American government is distributed constitutionally among several institutions. President Donald Trump learned that governance lesson the hard way as early as 2017. One of his first policy objectives was to dismantle the Affordable Care Act, a signature piece of national healthcare legislation passed under the Obama administration. To do so required approval from Congress, which passed the law in 2011. With Republicans controlling the presidency as well as both chambers of the legislative branch, Trump felt confident that he would succeed. The House of Representatives voted for repeal of the act, leaving the Republican-led Senate to complete the process. But that didn't happen. Three Senate Republicans joined forty-eight Democrats to deny Trump's proposal, and he was livid. That outcome was enormously instructive for Trump who learned that holding the nation's highest office didn't necessarily mean his goals would be automatically realized. So, how does a president get what he wants?

More than a half century ago, Richard Neustadt, a well-respected presidential historian, wrote that a president's greatest effectiveness in governance comes with his "power to persuade." That power, Neustadt contended, stems from the president's unique "vantage points in government, together with his reputation in the Washington community and his prestige outside."[21] But as president, Trump relied on a different set of tools for his successes.

For Trump, presidential effectiveness stemmed from his ability to threaten and bully those who oppose him. Nowhere was that more evident than Trump's response to the ten House Republicans who voted to impeach him for inciting the January 6, 2021, insurrection against the Capitol. He vowed to "primary" them for their 2022 reelection campaigns, that is, support another Trump-devoted Republican in the same district for the nomination. With that threat hanging over their heads, four of the ten announced they would retire. Of the remaining six, four were primaried and only two were reelected. For many of the remaining Republican national office holders and future colleagues, that real-life event made an indelible impression. Result: many became Trump converts in the name of self-survival.

During the 2024 presidential campaign, congressional Republicans remained mindful of Trump's capabilities. Increasingly, Republicans conformed their politics along Trumpist lines, often reversing former public positions on important issues. Clearly, Trump's style of "persuasion" has paid off—at least with a large number of congressional Republicans. These days, particularly in the House of Representatives, a sizable segment of the Republican congressional delegation has a distinct Trumpian tone and willingly takes their cues from him.

Recent examples of Republican co-optation make this point incredibly clear on congressional activity. In December 2023, the House Ways and Means Committee, the unit responsible for tax policy, drafted a bill to extend tax credits for businesses and extend the child tax credit and walked Trump through various portions of the bill in advance of the vote. Committee Chair Jason Smith viewed Trump's approval as key to getting Republican buy-in because, he said, "President Trump is the leader of the Republican Party. People may not want to admit that. But he has been for a long time."[22] And so, Smith paid homage to Trump, who gave his approval. In January 2024, the bill sailed through the House.

Other cases have revealed the Trump imprimatur more as a barrier to lawmaking than as a passageway to success. In 2024, after years of bitter stalemate, arch-conservative US Senator James Lankford from Oklahoma worked with colleagues to produce a bill on border security. The bill was part of a package that included military aid for Ukraine, Israel, and Taiwan, along with money for humanitarian assistance in several global hotspots. Ukraine, particularly, was in dire need of the military assistance. Dubbed the most conservative border legislation in memory, Lankford and Senate

Republicans convinced Senate Democrats to pass the legislation. The bill had the support of the National Border Patrol Council, the agency responsible for keeping the southern border safe from undocumenteds and which had endorsed Donald Trump for president.[23] Finally, after decades of bitter disagreement on a troubling policy issue, the stars seemed to be aligned. It looked to be a rare moment of bipartisan harmony on substantive legislation.

As the Senate prepared to officially approve the package, Trump announced his opposition to the border bill: "As the leader of our party, there is zero chance that I will support this horrible open borders betrayal of America," he told a rally in Las Vegas.[24] Shortly thereafter, Republican House Speaker Mike Johnson (LA), a Trump ally, declared the bill "dead on arrival" in his chamber.[25] A week later, Trump directed his opposition squarely at Lankford, declaring with a not-so-subtle hint of payback, saying that Lankford's compromise was "a very bad bill for his career, especially in Oklahoma."[26] The Oklahoma Republican Party quickly chimed in by censuring Lankford and demanded that the Senator "cease and desist jeopardizing the security and liberty" of the United States.[27] Lankford was stunned, given his deeply conservative reputation. In the end, all but three Senate Republicans opposed the bill that most had endorsed before Trump's opposition.

It's worth taking a moment to ponder why Trump would undermine the most conservative immigration legislation in decades, given his strident views on the topic. Near-border and *Arizona Republic* political columnist E. J. Montini reasoned that Trump torpedoed the Lankford bill so that he could go to the border during the presidential campaign "to complain about a crisis that he personally wanted to exist."[28] There may be value to that assessment, except that it may not go far enough. Given Trump's lack of interest in legislation on the immigration in 2025, it's possible that he didn't want any so that he could keep the immigration issue prominently on the public agenda. After all, Trump is a master at creating chaos and benefitting from it.

Regarding the Ukraine issue, a brief glance at the changing assessment of longtime Ukraine supporter US Senator Lindsey Graham (SC) represents another example of Trump's influence on Congress. Initially, Graham was a vocal sponsor of the proposed military package, particularly as it applied to Ukraine, which Graham viewed as the bulwark against Russian aggression into Europe. At an October 1, 2023, interview on *Face the Nation*, Graham was asked about his commitment to Ukraine. He replied, "Do you think

I would leave Ukraine? I don't believe that one bit.... [Congress] will produce in the United States Senate $60 or $70 billion [in additional foreign aid for Ukraine]."[29] Yet, in early 2024, with Trump firmly opposed to the package, Graham did an about face. When asked why he flipflopped on the proposed bill, Graham candidly responded, "I talked to President Trump today and he's dead set against this [military aid for Ukraine] package."[30] Overnight, Graham the foreign policy internationalist became an isolationist.

The rejection of foreign aid to Ukraine by Trump was particularly significant for historical reasons. The first Article of Impeachment against Trump in December 2019 cited him for availing US foreign aid to Ukraine President Volodymyr Zelenskyy on the condition that the Ukrainian government produce a series of false charges against Hunter Biden, which Zelenskyy refused to do.[31] Bearing in mind those dark days, denying help for Zelenskyy may have been retribution for Trump as much as anything else.[32]

But on the Ukraine foreign aid package, Republican House Speaker Mike Johnson (LA) in a rare dissent broke with Trump. As Speaker, Johnson was privy to sensitive national security information not available to most colleagues. After receiving critical intelligence material from various government agencies and Republican Senators on key committees, Johnson agreed that the aid was necessary and allowed a vote, which passed with overwhelming approval from members of both political parties. Senate Republican Minority Leader Mitch McConnell, a longtime Trump opponent, also managed to convince enough Republicans to join the Democrats. On this infrequent occasion, Trump lost.

Let's remember that in the early months of 2024, Trump was neither president nor a member of Congress. In fact, he wasn't even the Republican Party nominee for president. Nevertheless, on most critical policy issues, he often seemed to set the conditions for congressional Republicans, who were only too happy to fall into line. Without Trump's buy-in, a large portion of his party's members in Congress was hesitant to move, lest they suffer his wrath downstream. So much for checks and balances.

Challenging the Courts

Some combinations in politics just don't gel well. A perfect example would be Donald Trump and the courts: they are about as well suited for each other as oil and water. It's not for any lack of experience. One examination of Trump's numerous lawsuit history found that from his earliest days in business through 2019, Trump had been a party in at least 3,500 legal

Undermined Institutions

disputes.[33] Add all the many civil and criminal lawsuits from 2019 through the present day and the number may well have approached four thousand. Or more. Over four decades, most of Trump's involvement stemmed from countersuits against those who sued him. Also, most have been civil suits—disputes relating to contractor arrangements and related real estate issues. Clearly, there is a litigious strain in Donald Trump.

During his first term as president, Trump sought to select judges who would support his ideas. He nominated 226 federal judges and 3 US Supreme Court justices. His overall opportunities to "stack" the federal courts weren't particularly unusual. Among recent presidents who served four years, his judicial nomination numbers were between George H. W. Bush (187) and Jimmy Carter (261). Where Trump scored was with Supreme Court appointments, the most of any one-term president since Warren Harding (1921–3). The vast majority of Trump's judicial nominees were preapproved by the conservative Federalist Society, which served as an unofficial vetting agent for Trump.

Compared with the previous two presidential administrations, Trump's judicial appointments were disproportionately White and averaged five years younger than the Obama appointees. But just because Trump appointments fulfilled his conservative goals doesn't mean that he has always been particularly happy about the American judicial system. That's because the federal judiciary, like Congress, is designed to be independent from the presidency, which means out of Trump's control—even if he appointed them! That's been a sore wound for Trump, who doesn't like what he can't control.

While president, Trump was never hesitant to attack judges or affiliated personnel. The list below includes just a few examples:

- Shortly after assuming the presidency in February 2017, Trump questioned the right of federal judges to stem his executive order preventing immigrants from seven Muslim nations.
- In 2018, after a US Court of Appeals ordered the Trump administration to accept migrant asylum claims, Trump said that an Obama-appointed judge on that court couldn't be fair.
- Also, in 2018, when a district court judge blocked the Trump administration's effort to end the Deferred Action for Childhood Arrivals (DACA) program, Trump lambasted the judge of being out of touch.
- In 2020, he attacked a federal district court judge who presided over a case where Trump ally Roger Stone was convicted of lying to Congress, witness tampering, and obstructing a House of Representatives investigation.[34] Trump later pardoned Stone.

Trump's 2024 vice presidential nominee, US Senator JD Vance, shared Trump's contempt for the judicial system to the point of dismissing its value as a key federal institution. In expressing his support of Trump's plan to fire thousands of civil servants and replace them with "our people," Vance added, "Then when the courts stop you, stand before the country like [President] Andrew Jackson did and say 'The chief justice has made his ruling. Now let him enforce it.'"[35] Neither Trump nor Vance had any room for the courts unless the courts ruled for what they wanted.

It's fair to say that few people know the wrinkles of the judicial system better than Trump. It's also fair to say that Trump abused the judicial process more than others. He has a rich history of attacking appendages of the judicial network beyond judges and prosecutors. For example, in 2018, during the time a jury considered the sixteen-count tax-and-fraud trial of former Trump campaign Chair Paul Manafort, then-president Trump told reporters "I think the whole Manafort trial is very sad . . . [Manafort] happens to be a very good person."[36] It's hard to see those words as anything other than jury tampering. At the end of its deliberations, the jury convicted Manafort, and the judge imposed a forty-seven-month sentence. Manafort didn't complete his sentence, however; he was among the many convicted Trump cronies who Trump pardoned in December 2020.

At a minimum, Trump violated the spirit of the "Separation of Powers" concept defined in the US Constitution. In almost every case he was involved in, Trump went after the assigned trial judge, the prosecuting attorney, or both. With the Washington, DC, case alleging that Trump caused the January 6, 2021, insurrection against Congress, he condemned federal district judge Tanya Chutkan as "highly partisan" and "unfair." In the Georgia case alleging that Trump directed a conspiracy to overturn the presidential election, Trump slammed Black Fulton County District Attorney Fani Willis for being a racist. In most cases, Trump attacked his judicial enemies, either through Truth Social, his new social media site, or rallies.

Regardless of the venue or type of case, the only time a judge has been "fair" has occurred with a Trump victory in court. But when Trump has been on the losing end of a case, the cause of the defeat always included the claim of an unfair judge. That's been a constant up to the present day, including two defeats in sexual abuse and defamation cases with E. Jean Carroll. In 2023, Trump was found guilty in a civil suit for sexual abuse of Carroll and fined $5 million. In 2024, Trump was assessed another $83 million in damages payable to Carroll for continued defamation. Again, Trump accused the judge of being unfair.

Undermined Institutions

Despite several losses in the courts, Trump did have a couple of significant victories. On July 1, 2024, by a 6-to-3 vote, the US Supreme Court declared that Trump may have had immunity in some of the circumstances connected with insurrection charges in the Washington, DC, case. The justices directed the district court judge initially overseeing the charges to determine the activities where the then-President Trump may have acted in his "official" capacity, raising the distinct possibility that some of the charges would be dropped.[37] The decision guaranteed that the trial would be delayed until well after the 2024 presidential election. But between Trump's 2024 election victory and the immunity decision, Special Counsel Jack Smith saw no reason to pursue the case and asked for dismissal.

Two weeks after the immunity decision, Trump caught another break with the National Archives case, when Trump-appointed District Court Judge Aileen Cannon dropped a bombshell by dismissing the entire case. Cannon ruled that Special Council Jack Smith had been appointed to his position improperly because his appointment was not based on the provisions in any federal law.[38] Cannon's decision sent shock waves throughout the constitutional law community where one after another, experts declared that the judge violated long-standing legal rulings.[39] Smith lost an appeal before the 11th Circuit Court of Appeals, after which he dropped the charges against Trump.[40]

Trump's attacks on judges, prosecutors, and others involved with judicial administration have become a template for Trumpists to do much the same. According to the US Marshalls Service, the federal organization charged with protecting federal judges, judicial personnel, and court buildings, the annual average number of threats against these elements of the judicial network more than tripled from 1,180 in 2015, the year when Trump declared his presidential candidacy, to 3,810 in 2022.[41] Never before had they grown at such an astounding rate. Similar threats against federal prosecutors more than doubled from 68 to 155 during the same period.[42] Some cases were stunning. For example, after US District Court Judge James Robart ruled against the Trump administration's initial travel ban executive order in February 2017, Trump referred to Robart as a "so-called judge" and tweeted "if something happens, blame him [the judge] and the court system." Following that, Robart received more than one hundred death threats.[43]

Beyond the federal judicial system, attacks on election personnel have become commonplace during American elections. Inspired by Trump's claims stemming from his 2020 presidential defeat that the presidential election was "rigged" and fraudulent, doubters of the election's system integrity have turned against election personnel. Again, the data and outcomes of these attacks are disconcerting, to say the least. Interviews of more than ten thousand state and local election personnel by the Brennan Center found that 30 percent "were personally abused, harassed, or threatened in 2020; 51 percent expressed concern that they would suffer" similar abuses in future elections; and one-third responded that they were worried about "facing pressure to certify election results in favor of a specific candidate." The result: 21 percent of local election officials who served in the 2020 election were unlikely to return in 2024.[44] Another survey of election personnel in eleven Western states learned of an average turnover rate from 2020 to 2024 of 40 percent, with Arizona having the highest projected drop-off rate as high as 80 percent![45] Common sense suggests that with reduced expertise of the officials observing and counting ballots, the possibilities for errors increase—this because of the fright instilled in election officials by election deniers.

Lest there be any doubt between the cause and effect of Trump's assaults on the judiciary, consider the words of retired Ohio Supreme Court Chief Justice Maureen O'Connor, a Republican, who said "Donald Trump set the stage. [He] gave permission by his actions and words for others to come forward and talk about judges in terms not just criticizing their decisions, but disparaging them and the entire judiciary."[46] O'Connor was not alone in her concern for the welfare of judges. In a rare rebuke of Trump by a sitting federal judge, Republican-appointed US District Court Judge Reggie Walton criticized Trump's social media attacks on judges as precursors to violence and tyranny, and attacks on the rule of law.[47]

Trump's persistent interference with the judiciary has illustrated again and again his belief in two sets of rules: one set for the public, and a separate set for him. As far as Trump is concerned, no aspect of government should be beyond his grasp. That's because he sees himself as *the* government.

Taking over Informal Political Institutions

As discussed above, Donald Trump's post-2020 election antics threatened the future of key American political institutions, especially the presidency and Congress. What's less known has been his ability to reach and impact portions of the political process outside of government. Here we refer to the national Republican Party and the media.

Undermined Institutions

The Republican Party

We begin with the Republican Party National Committee (RNC), which has become a virtual wing of the Trump political machine. To be clear, it's not unusual for a temporary amalgamation of sorts between a presidential nominee's campaign and the national machinery of his political party. That's because after the party nominee is determined at its national convention, the nominee gains immediate loyalty and assistance from the national committee staff and other parts of the political party machinery.[48] Polling, research, fundraising, outreach, and coordination with state political party organizations all become temporary "property" of the candidate from the moment of becoming the official party nominee through the presidential election.

Should the nominee prevail with a November victory, the official party organization remains close at hand throughout the presidential term, particularly if the incumbent is eligible to run for a second term of office. So close was the Republican relationship with then-incumbent Donald Trump in 2020, that at its national nominating convention, the delegates refused to pass a party platform, a traditionally lengthy document outlining the hopes and expectations of the party over the next four years. Instead, the delegates voted unanimously to "enthusiastically support the President's [Trump] full agenda." That's it! The "announcement" went on to explain that between their satisfaction with Trump and the medical concerns associated with COVID-19, no party platform was necessary.[49]

Meanwhile, the Democrats, meeting under similar circumstances to select Joe Biden as their presidential nominee, passed a ninety-one-page party platform. Clearly, the Republican National Convention was little more than a Trump political instrument. That was the state of the 2020 Republican National Convention.

Fast forward to conditions after the Trump defeat to Democrat Joe Biden in 2020. Historically, should the party nominee lose the national election, the party national committee traditionally resumes neutrality until the next party nominee four years later, when the temporary loyalty would be repeated. Further, if an incumbent left office for whatever reason, the party organization would assume neutrality during the next prenomination period and through the party primaries, lest the organization be accused of playing favorites. That's the way matters had proceeded in the past. However, for Republicans, the relationship between the defeated candidate, Trump, and the organization continued unofficially after his departure from the presidency on January 20, 2021. From the earliest moments of his candidacy announcement for the 2024 election on June 16, 2022, the RNC gave Trump an unmistakable advantage over other Republicans seeking the party nomination.

How did he do it? In the month following November 3, 2020, election day, Trump raised a whopping $207 million through his Save America, a political action committee that divided proceeds, with 75 percent for Trump's political activities and 25 percent for the RNC that was in dire financial need.[50] Thus, the financial linkage between the former candidate and the party continued. In the days following his 2020 loss, Trump also prevailed upon the RNC to retain Chair Ronna McDaniel, who was first chosen by Trump to lead the party after his 2016 nomination. McDaniel had earned her keep by supporting Trump during the postelection insurrection through providing support for Republican state attorney generals who had opposed Biden victories in their states.[51] The combination of Trump funneling money into the Republican Party and the continuation of McDaniel as Chair placed the former president in an ideal place to influence party activities and rules.

At the RNC midterm meeting in 2022, the body censured Liz Cheney and Adam Kitzinger, Republican members of Congress who had joined the Democratic-run House of Representatives Select Committee probing the causes of the January 6, 2021, insurrection. The Republican Party resolution condemned the two for their "persecution of ordinary citizens engaged in legitimate political discourse" at the insurrection on January 6,[52] more than nine hundred of whom had been found guilty of various federal crimes. Trump had not been shy about attacking the two House Republicans for their harsh criticism of his behavior on the day of the infamous attack. Thus, throughout the period after his presidency, the Republican leadership stayed with Trump, despite the fact that many Republicans slammed the rebellion at the time of its occurrence.

Toward the end of 2023, RNC Chair McDaniel had outlived her usefulness to Trump. A series of Republican election losses in 2022 and 2023 led Trump to demand her resignation, arguing that some Republican leaders had been "rigging the system for their own self-gain."[53] In fact, many of those Republicans had pointed fingers at Trump for election losses because of his obsession with his 2020 defeat when campaigning for Republican candidates. Nevertheless, he successfully turned the tables on them. With that, McDaniel resigned.

Meanwhile, Trump's control continued without missing a beat. He insisted that his longtime political strategist Michael Whatley be installed as

RNC Chair, and that Lara Trump, his daughter-in-law, be installed as RNC co-Chair despite the fact that she had no political experience in campaign management. Now in charge, Whatley fully remarried and energized the RNC with the Trump campaign. Said longtime Trump ally Chris LaCivita shortly after the leadership shake-up, "The RNC is as much a part of the Trump campaign as the Trump campaign is part of the RNC."[54] To no one's surprise, the 2024 Republican Party platform read like "an homage to Trump, repeatedly name checking him and mirroring his unmistakable writing style."[55] Whether in or out of an official position of power, Trump now was the Republican Party.

As part of the melding between Trump forces and the RNC, in 2024, Jake Hoffman, a fake Arizona 2020 elector and state senator indicted for his participation in the scheme, was elected to the RNC as a national committeeman for that state. In an even more audacious move, the RNC named Arizona attorney Christina Bobb, also indicted for attempting to overturn the 2020 presidential election, to oversee the RNC's new Election Integrity Team. The unit was designed to prevent election fraud, a rich irony in itself given the only massive illegal efforts to overturn the 2020 election were conducted by Republicans!

These events underscore the extent to which virtually no daylight existed between the Trump machine and the Republican Party from the time of his nomination in 2016 through the 2024 presidential election. In effect, both entities share responsibility for the havoc they imposed on the nation in the months and years to come.

The Media

Independent media are critical to the well-being of democracies. Media inform the public of issues, events, and problems that they might not know about otherwise.[56] We're reminded that the First Amendment of the Constitution prohibits interference with a free press. Without an unencumbered press, people would not have access to critical issues of the day. To this end, it's imperative that the fourth estate remain just that, free of interference or manipulation by those who would use the press to their advantage. The press is also accountable for the accuracy of their content. On that note, if reporters or their employers abuse the conveyance of their information, they will lose their credibility as reliable sources.

There is a potential ugly side to the press as suppliers of information, mainly the extent to which it can be manipulated by a communicator to influence those on the receiving end with tainted "news." On this issue, journalists guard against passing on inaccuracies and, for that matter, report them as such. This is key to the reputations of reporters and their news outlets. If reporters fail to distinguish false claims from the truth, the media loses its neutrality and can become a valuable instrument for would-be authoritarians to control their audience.

With more than a decade as the host of *The Apprentice* television show as a backdrop, presidential candidate Trump viewed the press as a conduit for shaping and carrying out his messages. He was different, more like an entertainer than a traditional politician. The press was simultaneously tantalized and dismayed by this unusual candidate who focused on grievances and outrage as the foundations of his campaign, and it paid off. The more Trump insulted and belittled his targets, the more the press focused on him. During the twelve-month period between September 2015 and September 2016, Trump received $4.6 billion worth of earned media (news reports), compared with Democratic presidential nominee Hillary Clinton who earned $2.5 billion. Unwittingly, journalists became megaphones for Trump's anger and unsubstantiated allegations.

With the media as his communications instrument, Trump has acclimatized large numbers of Americans, particularly Republicans, to view his false claims as news. Yes, journalists often correct his inaccurate assertions, but they never seem to equal his unbelievable pomposity. Any challenges to Trump's statements automatically fall into the category of "fake news," with the Trump admonition that disputes should be dismissed. By employing this formula of "information" dissemination over and over again, Trump prepares his audience to reject criticisms of his statements because the press doesn't want the people to know the "truth." He does so purposely and with the intention of weakening public acceptance of truthful information about him. Ruth Ben-Ghiat describes this approach as "a kind of insurance policy," which insulates the person making inaccurate statements.[57] When journalists question misleading or illegal behavior, the public is less likely to accept because of the persistent bombardment they have received prior to the press report. Thus, the information is rejected as "fake news."

Trump has often endorsed violence as a means of keeping reporters in line. On numerous occasions at his rallies, Trump has pointed to the back of the room and spoken of the press as "the enemy of the people."[58] He's actually called out reporters by name, belittling them in the process as purveyors of hate. At a September 2020 rally in Minnesota, Trump commented (incorrectly) on a situation where MSNBC anchor Ali Velshi was hit by a tear gas cannister while covering a protest. Trump called the violence "the most beautiful thing . . . It's called law and order." The audience roared with approval.[59] During another rally, Trump referred to a situation where a Republican member of Congress body-slammed a reporter after being asked about a piece of legislation. Trump praised the congressman as a "fighter and a winner."[60]

An account of Trump's deceptive statements by *The Washington Post* shows that increasingly larger portions of American society have come to believe him over time. Some examples from the investigation included issuing falsehoods such as citing an inflation rate of 50 percent, alleging 1 million jobs once held by native-born Americans lost to immigrants, and claiming that millions of fraudulent votes caused his 2020 presidential election loss to Joe Biden. All of these statements were totally without any foundation, yet large percentages of Americans have come to accept them as accurate.[61] The same pattern was adopted for the 2024 election. In a single speech at a July rally, Trump made ten false claims including that his administration had the lowest illegal immigration in history; states allow abortions "in the ninth month, and even after birth," and that countries send prisoners and mental health patients to the United States.[62] And that's just from one speech.

Many of Trump's followers accept his claims as validation of their own inaccurate perceptions. For example, when Trump lies about the evils of immigrants, most supporters agree because they feel that way to begin with.[63] Nevertheless, Trump's reinforcement of their beliefs further bind his supporters with their leader. Simply put, they are validated. Particularly among Republicans, the mainstream media is beneath contempt. Given the opportunity to believe Trump or the press, sizable numbers routinely accept whatever Trump says. According to a 2019 analysis, 85 percent of Republicans who strongly support Trump agreed that reporters have "very low" or "low" ethical standards.[64]

In his 2024 "hush-money" trial, Trump used his six-week case to campaign for the presidency nonstop. Three or four times a day before he went into court and after he left court, Trump would complain about a sham trial, a corrupt judge, a hateful prosecutor, and how Joe Biden and the Democrats had conspired to tie him down into court to prevent Trump from campaigning for the presidency. But, in fact, Trump was campaigning in front of reporters, a seemingly captive audience, with cameras putting him on air live. Then, at the end of every encounter with the reporters, television analysts would regurgitate, interpret, and in many cases rebut Trump's wild assertions. It really didn't matter to Trump, for reporters were his best messengers. To this day, the mainstream press that he publicly disdains is Trump's best weapon. No one plays the press more effectively than Trump.

Trump's behavior has been even more irresponsible in social media. Social media should not be taken lightly. One recent analysis finds that 14 percent of adults—one out of seven—consider social media as their "most important" source of election news; viewed through a wider lens, 62 percent of US adults get some news via social media.[65]

Unlike mainstream media, social media operate in a kind of "no man's land" with little government oversight. Mainstream media broadcasting companies can be punished by the Federal Communications Commission for indecency, hoaxes, news, vilification, and a variety of other violations. The legal system also provides a way for someone who feels victimized by the mainstream press to take action mainly through the courts. That's what happened when Dominion Voting Systems sued Fox Corporation for $1.6 billion in damages after Fox news anchors alleged that the media company intentionally altered its 2020 presidential election vote tabulations. In 2023, Fox settled out of court with Dominion for $787 million, one of the largest settlements of its kind in history. Newspapers and print media can also be sued by individuals for defamation and other wrongdoings if they knowingly make false statements. That precedent was established long ago in the famous 1964 US Supreme Court case, *New York Times v. Sullivan*.

With social media, however, there are fewer restraints from government and individuals. That's because these companies by law are exempt from most civil lawsuits,[66] courtesy of the language in Section 230 in the Communications Decency Act of 1996. Focusing on the "freedom of speech" clause in the First Amendment of the Constitution, social media websites have no responsibility or liability for what's published on their platforms. In everyday terms, the language in Section 230 allows almost anyone to write or say anything on social media. As if to provide a virtual guarantee for his own behavior, on May 28, 2020, then-president Donald Trump issued an "Executive Order on Preventing Censorship,"[67] which provided immunity for social media companies carrying controversial material. Upon assuming office in January 2021, President Joe Biden revoked Trump's order,[68] but the concept of federal immunity for social media remains in place.

For the most part, Donald Trump has taken to social media with reckless abandon. Until his own Truth Social platform began in 2022, he turned to Twitter as a megaphone for his grievances. There Trump has raged about his political enemies, unmanaged immigration, birtherism, climate change claims, the state of the economy, and numerous other objections. In a video to the rioters released on Twitter toward the end of the January 6, 2021, Capitol insurrection, Trump released a short video where he repeated his lie that "the election was stolen from us." Shortly thereafter, Twitter and the other major social media platforms banned Trump from publishing on their sites because of the violence connected with his messages. In effect, his mic was cut off. Yet, even that punishment was relatively temporary. Under the leadership of new owner Elon Musk, Trump was invited to return to Twitter (rebranded as X) in August 2023. Facebook and YouTube had allowed Trump to return earlier in the year, once again giving Trump free rein to espouse endless falsehoods without any accountability.

Trump's outrageous comments on social media have become even more extreme with his messages on Truth Social, his social media website created in 2022, where he has 7.8 million followers. Between November 2022 and March 2024, he averaged 29 posts per day, higher than the 18 per day average he posted on Twitter, where he had 91.2 million followers as of 2024.[69] Among his topics have been descriptions of Special Counsel Jack Smith as "deranged" and "sick," persistent denial of the 2020 presidential election outcome, damnation of the FBI and Department of Justice for framing him with federal charges, the "perfect" phone call in Atlanta where he asked for votes, the corrupt Manhattan district attorney, the New York state attorney general scam, and the out-of-control immigration invasion.

Trump, the Master Puppeteer of American Political Organizations

Whether through reorganization of formal institutions or informal means of personal interaction, Donald Trump and his allies have succeeded in altering American politics and democracy in potentially harmful ways. This represents a sea change from Trump's first administration when the road to total control of the government was often blocked, thanks to a few heroic Trump appointees who insisted on honoring the rule of the law and respected political traditions over autocratic domination. Nevertheless, as a "student" of power, Trump has taken a different approach to governance in his second term.

Rather than appoint people with solid credentials, he has resorted to loyalists who in many cases have little or no expertise in their appointed positions.[70] Then again, for Trump, personal allegiance is far more important than capability. As a result, the country faces a period where key officials are likely to decide major policy issues more by their unquestioned commitment to Trump than devotion to the Constitution and the interests of the nation.

NOTES

1. Steven Levitsky and Daniel Ziblatt, *How Democracies Die* (New York: Penguin Random House, 2019), p. 3.
2. Ruth Ben-Ghiat explains this process as the modern *modus operandi* for authoritarian emergence in her *Strongman: Mussolini to the Present* (New York: W.W. Norton, 2021).
3. "While Bemoaning Mueller Probe, Trump Falsely Says the Constitution Gives Him 'the Right to Do Whatever I Want,'" *The Washington Post*, July 23, 2019, https://www.washingtonpost.com/politics/2019/07/23/trump-falsely-tells-auditorium-full-teens-constitution-gives-him-right-do-whatever-i-want/.
4. "All the Ways Trump, Not His Foes, Sought to 'Weaponize' the Government," *The Washington Post*, July 10, 2023, https://www.washingtonpost.com/politics/2023/07/10/all-ways-trump-not-his-foes-sought-weaponize-government/.
5. "Trump Ordered Mueller Fired, but Backed off When White House Counsel Threatened to Quit," *The New York Times*, July 25, 2018, https://www.nytimes.com/2018/01/25/us/politics/trump-mueller-special-counsel-russia.html.
6. "Former Attorney General Says Trump Asked to Seize Voting Machines," CNN, July 12, 2022, https://www.cnn.com/politics/live-news/january-6-hearings-july-12/h_7a924eaf7abda74b87d99f9bee0d34fc.
7. "Exclusive: National Security Officials Tell Special Counsel Trump Was Repeatedly Warned He Did Not Have the Authority to Seize Voting Machines," CNN, April 6, 2023, https://www.cnn.com/2023/04/05/politics/election-voting-machines-trump-national-security/index.html.
8. "Trump Was Informed of Prohibited Items in Jan. 6 Crowd, His Driver Testified," Politico, March 12, 2024, https://www.politico.com/news/2024/03/12/trump-jan-6-rally-driver-testified-00146630.
9. "Trump Wanted Troops to Protect His Supporters at Jan. 6 Rally," Reuters, May 12, 2021, https://www.reuters.com/world/us/congresswoman-says-trump-administration-botched-capitol-riot-preparations-2021-05-12/.
10. Quoted in "The Prospect of a Second Trump Presidency Has the Intelligence Community on Edge," Politico, February 26, 2024, https://www.politico.com/news/2024/02/26/trump-intelligence-agency-national-security-00142968.
11. See Russ Vought, "Executive Office of the President of the United States," *Mandate for Leadership: Project 2025*, The Heritage Foundation, Washington, DC, 2023, p. 43, https://static.project2025.org/2025_MandateForLeadership_CHAPTER-02.pdf.
12. Peter M. Shane, "Legislative Delegation, the Unitary Executive, and the Legitimacy of the Administrative State," *Harvard Journal of Law and Public Policy*, 33, no. 1 (September 2010), https://journals.law.harvard.edu/jlpp/wp-content/uploads/sites/90/2010/01/shane.pdf.
13. "While Bemoaning Mueller Probe," *The Washington Post*, July 23, 2019.
14. "Trump Vows to Appoint Special Prosecutor to 'Go after' Biden if Former President Wins in 2024," The Hill, June 12, 2023, https://thehill.com/homenews/campaign/4045934-trump-vows-to-appoint-special-prosecutor-to-go-after-biden-if-former-president-wins-in-2024/.

Undermined Institutions

15 "Trump Hints at Expanded Role for the Military within the US. A Legacy Law Gives Him Few Guardrails," AP, November 26, 2023, https://apnews.com/article/trump-military-insurrection-act-2024-election-03858b6291e4721991b5a18c2dfb3c36.

16 "Trump and Allies Planning Militarized Mass Deportations, Detention Camps," *The Washington Post*, February 21, 2024, https://www.washingtonpost.com/politics/2024/02/20/trump-mass-deportations-immigration/.

17 "Trump Says Republicans in Congress Should 'Defund' Justice Department, FBI," *The Washington Post*, https://www.washingtonpost.com/politics/2023/04/05/trump-defund-fbi-justice-department/.

18 "Ending the U.S. Department of Education: What It Would Mean and Why Trump and Project 2025 Want It," Chalkbeat, August 23, 2024, https://www.chalkbeat.org/2024/08/24/if-trump-abolished-the-department-of-education-what-would-happen/.

19 "Trump Targets Independent Agencies in Potential Second Term," Yahoo News, January 17, 2024, https://news.yahoo.com/trump-targets-independent-agencies-potential-123843426.html.

20 "Trump Plan to Gut Civil Service Triggers Pushback," Reuters, December 22, 2023, https://www.reuters.com/world/us/trump-plan-gut-civil-service-triggers-pushback-by-unions-democrats-2023-12-22/.

21 Richard E. Neustadt, *Presidential Power: The Politics of Leadership* (New York: Signet Books, 1964), p. 150.

22 "Republicans in Congress Are Bending to Trump's Demands. Some Are Frustrated," Politico, February 2, 2024, https://www.politico.com/news/2024/02/02/trump-congressional-republicans-influence-00139061.

23 "Border Patrol Union Backs Senate Immigration Bill Despite House GOP Opposition," ABC News, February 6, 2024, https://abcnews.go.com/Politics/border-patrol-union-backs-senate-immigration-bill-despite/story?id=106969976.

24 "Trump Brags about Efforts to Stymie Border Talks: 'Please Blame It on Me,'" *The Washington Post*, January 28, 2024, https://www.washingtonpost.com/politics/2024/01/27/trump-border-biden/.

25 "Speaker Johnson: Senate Border Deal 'Dead on Arrival' in House," The Hill, January 26, 2024, https://thehill.com/homenews/house/4431375-speaker-johnson-senate-border-deal-dead-on-arrival-in-house/.

26 "Trump Says Border Bill 'Very Bad' for Lankford's Career," The Hill, February 5, 2024, https://thehill.com/homenews/senate/4449600-trump-border-bill-very-bad-lankfords-career/.

27 "US Sen. James Lankford Censured by Oklahoma Republican Party over Bipartisan Work," The Oklahoman, January 30, 2024, https://www.oklahoman.com/story/news/politics/2024/01/30/oklahoma-sen-james-lankford-censured-border-immigration-negotiations/72405419007/.

28 "Donald Trump Killed the Bipartisan Border Bill to Save His Campaign," AZCentral, August 22, 2024, https://www.azcentral.com/story/opinion/op-ed/ej-montini/2024/08/22/trump-border-bill-arizona-visit/74898253007/.

29 "Transcript: Sen. Lindsey Graham on 'Face the Nation,' October 1, 2023," CBS News, October 1, 2023, https://www.cbsnews.com/news/lindsey-graham-face-the-nation-transcript-10-01-2023/.
30 "Lindsey Graham, Longtime Foreign Policy Hawk, Bows to Trump on Ukraine," *The Washington Post*, February 14, 2024, https://www.washingtonpost.com/politics/2024/02/14/lindsey-graham-ukraine-trump/.
31 See Articles of Impeachment against Donald John Trump, December 18, 2018, https://www.congress.gov/116/bills/hres755/BILLS-116hres755enr.pdf.
32 "Why Donald Trump 'Hates Ukraine,'" Politico, April 18, 2024, https://www.politico.eu/article/why-donald-trump-hates-ukraine-us-congress-kyiv-war/.
33 See "Trump and His 3,500 Suits: Prosecutor and Author Reveals in Interview His Portrait as 'Plaintiff in Chief,'" *ABA Journal*, April 20, 2020, https://www.abajournal.com/web/article/attorney-and-author-on-his-portrait-of-donald-trump-through-more-than-3500-lawsuits.
34 The preceding events are part of the collection found in "In His Own Words: The President's Attacks on the Courts," The Brennan Center for Justice, February 14, 2020, https://www.brennancenter.org/our-work/research-reports/his-own-words-presidents-attacks-courts.
35 "How JD Vance Thinks about Power," *The New York Times*, August 8, 2024, https://www.nytimes.com/2024/08/03/us/politics/jd-vance-donald-trump-2024-campaign.html. It seems that Vance was referring to an 1832 US Supreme Court case, *Worcester v. Georgia*, where after the US Supreme Court declared a treaty between the state of Georgia and the Cherokee Nation unconstitutional, then-US president Andrew Jackson is alleged to have said, [US Chief Justice] John Marshall has made his decision; now let him enforce it." See "The Indian Removal Act and the Trail of Tears," *National Geographic*, https://education.nationalgeographic.org/resource/indian-removal-act-and-trail-tears/. The idea was that the courts had no power over the executive branch.
36 "Manafort Jury Ends Second Day of Deliberations after Trump Defends His Ex-Campaign Chair," *The Washington Post*, August 17, 2018, https://www.washingtonpost.com/local/jury-begins-deliberations-in-paul-manaforts-tax-and-bank-fraud-trial/2018/08/16/d2b0f486-a170-11e8-8e87-c869fe70a721_story.html.
37 "Justices Give Presidents Immunity for Official Acts, Further Delaying Trump's Trial," *The Washington Post*, July 1, 2024, https://www.washingtonpost.com/politics/2024/07/01/trump-immunity-supreme-court-ruling/.
38 "Judge Dismisses Classified Documents Case against Trump," *The New York Times*, July 17, 2024, https://www.nytimes.com/live/2024/07/15/us/trump-documents-case-dismissed.
39 See "Dismissal Brings New Scrutiny to Judge with a History of Unorthodox Decisions," *The New York Times*, https://www.nytimes.com/2024/07/15/us/politics/judge-aileen-cannon-trump-documents-case.html, and "Judge Cannon Shredded by Expert for Constant 'Bonkers' Favors to Trump," *The New Republic*, June 25, 2024, https://newrepublic.com/post/183058/judge-cannon-torched-inept-trump-case.

40 "Court Drops Remaining Classified Documents against Trump's Aides," NPR, February 11, 2025, https://www.npr.org/2025/02/11/nx-s1-5293113/trump-document-case-nauta-de-oliveira.
41 "Judges in Trump-Related Cases Face Unprecedented Wave of Threats," Reuters, February 24, 2029, https://www.reuters.com/investigates/special-report/usa-election-judges-threats/.
42 "Exclusive: Threats to US Federal Judges Double since 2021, Driven by Politics," Reuters, February 13, 2024, https://www.reuters.com/world/us/threats-us-federal-judges-double-since-2021-driven-by-politics-2024-02-13/.
43 "As Threats Intensify, Judges Urge Colleagues to Speak Out," The American Bar Association, August 2019, https://www.americanbar.org/news/abanews/aba-news-archives/2019/08/as-threats-intensify-judges-urge/.
44 "Local Election Officials Survey," The Brennan Center for Justice, New York, April 2023, file:///Users/gerstondocs/Downloads/April2023_LocalElectionOfficialSurvey%20(3).pdf.
45 "A Movement to Help Embattled and Stressed Election Workers," Governing, October 3, 2023, https://www.governing.com/work/a-movement-to-help-embattled-and-stressed-election-workers.
46 Ibid.
47 "Republican-Appointed Judges Raise Alarm over Trump Attacks on Law," The Washington Post, March 31, 2024, https://www.washingtonpost.com/dc-md-va/2024/03/29/trump-judge-attacks-violence/.
48 Mark D. Brewer and L. Sandy Maisel, *Parties and Elections in America* (Lanham, MD: Rowman & Littlefield, 2019), p. 293.
49 "Resolution Regarding the Republican Party Platform," The American Presidency Project, presidency.ucsb.edu/documents/resolution-regarding-the-republican-party-platform, August 24, 2020.
50 "Trump Campaign Press Release—Trump, RNC Announce Massive $207.5 Million Raised since Election Day," The American Presidency Project, December 3, 2020, https://www.presidency.ucsb.edu/documents/trump-campaign-press-release-trump-rnc-announce-massive-2075-million-raised-since-election.
51 "How Ronna McDaniel Backed Trump's Early Bid to Hold Power," *The New York Times*, March 27, 2024, https://www.nytimes.com/2024/03/26/us/politics/ronna-mcdaniel-trump-nbc.html.
52 "G.O.P. Declares Jan. 6 Attack 'Legitimate Political Discourse,'" *The New York Times*, February 4, 2022, https://www.nytimes.com/2022/02/04/us/politics/republicans-jan-6-cheney-censure.html.
53 "Trump Fully Devours the Republican Establishment," *The New York Times*, February 16, 2024, https://www.nytimes.com/2024/02/16/us/politics/trump-republican-party-establishment.html.
54 "Trump Takes Control of the RNC with Mass Layoffs, Restructuring," *The Washington Post*, March 12, 2024, https://www.washingtonpost.com/politics/2024/03/12/rnc-trump-firings-takeover/.
55 "Trump Remade the GOP in His Image—and Its Platform in His Words, *The Washington Post*, July 15, 2024, https://www.washingtonpost.com/elections/interactive/2024/republican-platform-changes-trump/.

56 Doris Graber explores these vital themes in her *Mass Media and American Politics*, 10th edition (Washington, DC: CQ Press, 2010).
57 Ruth Ben-Ghiat, *Strongmen* (New York: W.W. Norton, 2021), p. 95.
58 "Trump Ramps up Rhetoric on Media, Calls Press 'the Enemy of the People,'" The Hill, April 5, 2019, https://thehill.com/homenews/administration/437610-trump-calls-press-the-enemy-of-the-people/.
59 "Trump Turns Attack on MSNBC Journalist into Rally Fodder," *The New York Times*, September 23, 2020, https://www.nytimes.com/2020/09/23/business/media/trump-ali-velshi.html.
60 "Trump Crosses a New Threshold for Anti-Media Rhetoric, Jokingly Praising a Congressman for Assaulting a Reporter," *The Washington Post*, September 7, 2018, https://www.washingtonpost.com/politics/2018/09/07/trump-jokingly-praises-congressman-assaulting-reporter/.
61 See "Which Trump Lies Stick? Republicans Believe Some Falsehoods More Than They Did Six Years Ago, Our Poll Finds," *The Washington Post*, April 9, 2024, https://www.washingtonpost.com/politics/2024/04/09/some-trump-falsehoods-stick-more-than-others-fact-checker-poll-finds/.
62 "Here's a Look at Some of the False Claims Made during the Biden and Trump's First Debate," Associated Press, June 28, 2024, https://apnews.com/article/fact-check-misinformation-election-debate-trump-biden-577507522762aa10f6ee5be3a0ced2bb#.
63 "What Trump Supporters Believe and Expect," Pew Research Center, November 13, 2024, https://www.pewresearch.org/short-reads/2024/11/13/what-trump-supporters-believe-and-expect/.
64 "Study Shows Hostility toward Journalists by Trump Fans," PBS News Hour, December 12, 2019, https://www.pbs.org/newshour/nation/study-shows-hostility-toward-journalists-by-trump-fans.
65 Hunt Allcott and Matthew Gentzkow, "Social Media and Fake News in the 2016 Election," *Journal of Economic Perspectives*, 31, no. 2 (Spring 2017), p. 211, https://pubs.aeaweb.org/doi/pdfplus/10.1257/jep.31.2.211.
66 "Five Common Social Media Activities That Are Illegal," Non.Stop.Justice, June 23, 2023, https://www.nonstopjustice.com/blog/five-common-social-media-activities-that-are-actually-illegal/.
67 See "Executive Order on Preventing Online Censorship," May 28, 2020, Executive Order 13925, https://trumpwhitehouse.archives.gov/presidential-actions/executive-order-preventing-online-censorship/.
68 See "Revocation of Certain Presidential Actions and Technical Amendment," May 14, 2021, Executive Order 14029.
69 "Trump Averages More Than 24 Truth Social Posts a Day and He Was Even Busier during the V P Debate," Roll Call, October 2, 2024, https://rollcall.com/2024/10/02/trump-averages-more-than-24-truth-social-posts-a-day-and-he-was-even-busier-during-the-vp-debate/.
70 "Trump Taps Loyalists with Few Qualifications for Top Jobs," Reuters, November 14, 2024, https://www.reuters.com/world/us/trump-taps-loyalists-with-few-qualifications-top-jobs-2024-11-13/.

CHAPTER 6
WEAKENED SOCIOPOLITICAL FABRIC

Happiness is a social condition that occurs on many levels of life. At one end of the emotional spectrum, we can feel joy from an experience with a good book, a challenging hike, or a delicious meal. Those are momentary sources of happiness that give us satisfaction. At another part of the spectrum, we may find fulfillment from a vocational career, a long-term social relationship, or perhaps the policies from those in political power. The relationship between happiness and politics is the starting point of this chapter. Why? Research shows that happy people are more active, connected, engaged, and likely to participate in democratic processes.[1]

At the opposite end of the social spectrum, sadness can occur in situations stemming from disappointment from something like a movie, a broken personal relationship, or even a political system that has gone amuck. Particularly in the latter case, we may feel alone, removed from those around us in a world in which events leave us with too much negativity to cope and feel joy. Of course, few among us are always happy or always sad. But to the extent that people feel sad and lonely as a general emotional condition, they are vulnerable to manipulation for the purposes of others. Along those lines, research reveals that lonely individuals are significantly associated with xenophobia, a lower tolerance for distress, and right-wing authoritarianism.[2] Unfortunately, that condition is very much the case today for tens of millions of Americans.

Authoritarian anti-democratic zealots thrive on peoples' alienation and disinterest, qualities often related to loneliness. The isolation of people from politics and government gives anti-democrats the opportunity to win over lonely, estranged souls with ammunition for replacing democracy with authoritarianism. Seizing on the public's disquiet, autocratic adherents don't promote authoritarianism per se, but instead couch their guarantees for happiness with promises such as "security," "calm," and "stability" in an unsteady political environment.

It would be inaccurate to portray all lonely people as vulnerable to aberrant behavior. However, for many individuals with that condition, there is the predisposition for susceptibility to a withdrawn existence. As Jonathan Gruber writes, "loneliness not only stokes negative emotions, but it also stifles the prosocial behaviors that people hone through connection."[3]

The extent to which loneliness has increased in American society has presented Trumpists with a huge target for influence as well as a source of negative political energy. That transformation occurs through Trumpism providing an emotional security blanket for the disenchanted and lonely who feel left out in the cold. In a unique way, Trumpism can serve as an artificial solvent of comfort and consolation for unsatisfied, dejected sectors of the polity. Yet, Trumpism doesn't cure their sociopolitical ailments; rather, it actually heightens their pain through focusing on society's disappointments.

Loneliness isn't the only factor that has left some people less engaged in American society. Increasingly, a sizable segment of American society is less educated and politically uninformed. In recent years, the public as a whole has grown weary of the way democracy works in the United States, but the deepest decline of satisfaction by far has come from those with a high school education or less, according to a 2024 Gallup Poll.[4] Their lack of information leaves them more distrustful of American institutions. Along with loneliness and social isolation, this combination of circumstances leaves large numbers vulnerable to "leaders" with simple answers to our complicated political condition. Not surprisingly, it's an invitation to authoritarianism. That's where Trumpism steps in as the remedy.

Another concern of our sociopolitical framework lies with news dissemination. The twenty-first century has witnessed the rearrangement of how many of us learn news. Traditional sources such as newspapers have decreased in numbers, content, and the quality of coverage. Digital media, their "replacement" in name only, often disseminate unvetted, and hence potentially unreliable information, often leaving their readers confused, angry, and distrustful of the mainstream news outlets.[5] Along those lines, a 2023 Gallup Poll found only 32 percent of Americans trust the mass media, coinciding with the low established in 2016,[6] the year when Trump was elected to the presidency. In the absence of reliable media foundations, many Americans turn to less dependable sources that often produce untruthful or misleading information packaged as "news." With that, often the loudest and most inaccurate voice prevails, creating a poisoned information environment. Here, too, are opportunities for authoritarian-generated material posing as news to influence users.

The threat of authoritarianism in the United States is more real than we might think. The combination of a polarized American society, alienation and loneliness, a general lack of efficacy, growing ignorance, and disappointment with policymakers leaves people vulnerable to authoritarians who are ready to "save" us from collective dismay.[7] Our challenge here is to understand the causes of our political malaise as well as the sinister political forces that discourage us from dedicating ourselves into the democratic process.

All of which brings us back to the subject at hand. Some observers view the political malaise in the United States as the result of Trumpism; to the contrary, the origins of widespread political discontent go back long before Trumpism. But the means of dissemination today are more varied and less controlled in the age of social media.

That's where Trumpists come in. With statements such as "Only I can fix it" and "I am your retribution," Donald Trump and his minions have presented themselves as the remedy to the untreated assortment of social problems and economic conditions endured by the politically dispossessed. In other words, Trumpists offer the simple "cure" for the "disease" with other more complex prescriptions for our political problems often drowned out. That cure could kill our democracy.

This chapter focuses on the weakened sociopolitical fabric of American society and the extent to which a sizable swath of Americans has become exposed to and embraced antidemocratic values and behavior as the best way to manage problems. We begin with a discussion of sociopolitical change in America and its implications for our politics and society. That analysis is followed by attention to the problems of an increasingly uninformed society and its attendant openness to extremism. We conclude with an examination of how Trumpist authoritarians have attempted to convert disconnected Americans to believers in totalitarian government, where their feelings of isolation and loneliness would be acknowledged and allegedly attended.

Social Change in America

The ancient Greek philosopher Heraclitus once said that "The only constant in life is change." His words from nearly three thousand years ago are as profound today as they were then about the conditions in much of the world, including the United States. We are evolving, and not necessarily for the better. Countless terms are dedicated to explaining the dramatic changes in this country over its relatively brief history. Some historic examples include the transitions from agrarianism to industrialism to postindustrialism, from family-centric social units to individual choice, and more recently, from individualistic to collective behavior.

But what about American politics and democracy? Accounting for the transformation of American politics over time has its own unique explanations. Lawrence Quill discusses the advent of television as a fundamental indicator of our change. Its development and widespread use exemplified movement of Americans from "mass democracy," where the population relied on relatively few sources of information transfer, to what Quill describes as "segmented democracy," where different shows catered to "different markets based on class religion, race, and age."[8] No doubt, the introduction of social media has segmented markets and political audiences even further. The point is that just like economic, social, and psychological changes, American politics have changed as well, leaving some parts of the population segmented and politically distant from others. Such isolation is not good for democracy.

Fewer Group Attachments

The sense of people finding comfort in association with others like them has long been a staple of American society. Think of scouting, religious institutions, and antique car clubs as some examples of belonging. In these situations, and others, people with like-minded interests bond periodically over participation in activities relevant to their organization. From social involvement, members gain satisfaction and security.

And so it is with politics. People with like-minded political and economic concerns sometimes organize into collectives with the intent to gain benefits for their members. Groups like the Pharmaceutical Research and Manufacturers of America (PhRMa), state chapters of the Sierra Club, or a local taxpayers association are among the thousands of examples that often interact with governments at all levels. Although not officially parts of government, sometimes they are viewed as de facto elements of policymaking centers. Some of these economic organizations are stronger today than ever, often garnering criticism in some quarters for their excessive influence on the governmental process.[9]

Our concern here, however, turns to small groups in local communities, who provide havens—almost sanctuaries—for connecting people with common concerns, interests, and values. In these organizations, sometimes the level of intimacy is such that if you're absent, the others know. If you're not there, you're missed! Rather than seek something from government, these grassroots clusters exist mainly as social islands for people who share specific interests. For example, if you belong to a model airplane club, such elements as religious attachment, political party affiliation, and vocation have no effect on your status—only your commitment to the model airplane experience matters. These social sanctuaries help to perpetuate political stability by promoting cohesion over conflict.

If all this sounds a bit like exploring another time in history, it's because for many people it is. These days, for many of us, social groups are so time-intensive that we don't see much of a return for investment. Instead, we remain couched in our separate worlds. Something like online card games for "members" substitute for face-to-face group contacts, or that's the intent anyway. On the surface, that seems like efficiency. But recent research has uncovered an unanticipated consequence from diminished numbers of local communities of people with like-minded interests.

Robert Putnam's well-received work, *Bowling Alone*, chronicles the decline of group participation as a source for "civic malaise" and individual isolation.[10] The numbers of grassroots groups in America have decreased dramatically, and many of those remaining have become single-purpose units designed to promote narrow self-interests. As a result, there is diminished interest in the common good. This is unfortunate, Putnam writes, because in addition to bringing people together in a communal context, "informal groups of civic engagement instill in their members habits of cooperation and public-spiritedness, as well as the practical skills necessary to partake in public life."[11]

Putnam's identification of "public spiritedness" brings us to the connection between groups and political participation. With less group-inspired civic engagement, there is less public spiritedness, or concern with the welfare of others in society, or what we might call the "collective good." It then follows that with less public spiritedness, interest in politics wanes. So, why is that necessarily a problem? In a democracy, the lack of interest in politics and institutions can have negative consequences for the polity. As one study points out, participation "shapes the quality of democratic discourse."[12] The more civic participation, the more likely that democracy thrives. Conversely, less participation leaves a society susceptible to undemocratic alternatives.

Working at Home

Remote work, another invention in modern society, has become a contributor to the loss of community. Much of the recent employment environment emerged as a necessary byproduct of the COVID-19 pandemic, when the need to isolate from others was paramount to avoid contracting the virus. Prior to the pandemic, only 5 percent of the employed worked at home or at locations other than their place of business. During the pandemic, as many as 50 percent of the employed worked at their residence.[13]

While the pandemic eventually receded, remote working remained and became a popular alternative to being at a site with others. As of 2023, nearly 30 percent of full-time employees still worked from home, with as many or more employees working a hybrid schedule where the work week was split between the workplace and home.[14] While these new settings may be desirable for their personal convenience, they leave workers removed from others, and that circumstance leaves them less connected and isolated.

Proponents of remote work cite countless benefits from the arrangement, among them more productivity, lower company costs, less employee turnover, a wider talent pool, and fewer absences from the job. At first glance, these benefits would seem advantageous for both the employer and the employed. But there may be an unanticipated consequence. With the remote workforce located away from the workplace, there are fewer social interactions with others as well as less attachment to the employer. With that physical and psychological distance, the employed individual who works remotely is likely to experience increased loneliness.[15] Thus, the benefits of increased productivity may be offset by the sense of social isolation from fellow workers who, collectively, would otherwise operate as a community.

Loneliness

While loneliness is connected with remote work, its pervasiveness extends well beyond the place of employment. A national poll by Yahoo/YouGov in 2024 found that nearly one-fifth of American adults experienced loneliness "always" or frequently. Among young adults between ages eighteen and twenty-nine, 29 percent felt lonely. As to the factor most responsible for their loneliness, 12 percent cited the lack of a romantic relationship, 11 percent mentioned difficulty in making friends, and 11 percent noted "spending too much time online" as the three most common reasons.[16]

Drilling down to young people, a Harvard study found that in some ways they are the most at-risk members of American society. According to the report's researchers, young people "tend to be especially dependent both on social media and peer norms and peer approval, making them particularly vulnerable to social media's harms, including the production of false selves, the deluge of people enjoying others' company, and ostracism and bullying."[17] Simply put, loneliness can be harmful to individuals and, in the larger context, society.

Isolated people often struggle for social direction. If they feel targeted or marginalized by others, their separation can lead them to pursue political extremist groups. In the process of searching for a sense of belonging, they may hope to gain acceptance and fulfilment. Being part of a radical group may give an otherwise lonely person a community of sorts. Jesselyn Cook found these links with individuals who migrated to the QAnon movement, perhaps the most radical of the conspiracy groups loyal to Donald Trump.[18]

Loneliness is also connected with levels of education. Specifically, the less education for an individual, the more likely he or she is prone to experience loneliness and isolation.[19] Conversely, Sidney Verba and his colleagues have found that education channels opportunities beyond the obvious characteristics such as occupation and income; it also "places individuals in institutional settings where they can be recruited to political activity; and it fosters psychological and cognitive engagement with politics."[20] Without education, people are less inclined to become involved and influential in the political process. Less educated people are also not as likely to have had experience working with others in groups where different ideas are sorted out.[21]

It's clear that loneliness is problematic for American society, and not just in a psychological or even political sense. A lengthy investigation by the federal Department of Health and Human Services found that loneliness can account for increases in heart disease, stroke, and even premature death. So extensive is loneliness that the US surgeon general in 2023 listed loneliness and isolation as an American epidemic.[22]

The bottomline is that Americans are more fragmented than ever. Sizable numbers of us spend little time with each other, feel pretty crummy about our lives, and know little about the world around us. For these people, democracy is an abstract concept with little application to their lives. Is everyone like this all the time? No, but increasing numbers of Americans seem to fall into isolated social silos that leave them access to little political knowledge. The data show that being less engaged comes at a price: the possibility of alienation and vulnerability to simple explanations for life's problems. As a consequence, this condition has a profound negative effect on the politics of its victims. It leaves people susceptible to authoritarian values that purport to bring purpose to their lives.

Overcoming Trumpism

Abandoning News

Democracies are known for the relatively mutual commitments between citizens and their governments. In a sense, each of these elements depends upon the other for its legitimacy and value in the democratic environment. Elections, of course, are the essential glue between citizens and those they choose to serve in positions of governance. But how do citizens determine who they want to govern? In part, they make their assessments of leader preferences by what they learn about how officeholders as well as candidates for office might respond to their concerns as well as political conditions of the day.

Of course, there's no way for even the most diligent citizens to know all the activities of government, especially one as complicated as ours. That's where responsible media come in. These critical linkage institutions gather and provide information to citizens and government leaders alike. They are essential to helping people become aware of issues, developments, crises, and just about anything that would help us understand what is happening all around us.[23] Just as important, the press helps keep government accountable through the information they share with the public. It follows that most of us have counted on news media to facilitate digestion of the myriad circumstances that frame our political world. We rely upon these sources to help us learn about those things we can't see or experience personally.

Research shows that the average adult in the United States spends nearly half of his or her available free time connecting with television, radio, newspapers, magazines, or the Internet. Some of that time is dedicated to gathering, understanding, and reacting to news,[24] although interest in news has plummeted over the past fifteen years. According to Gallup, those with "very close" interest in political news have dropped from 43 percent in 2008 to 32 percent in 2023.[25] Given that news often becomes important to the ways we act politically, its availability and credibility are key to how we evaluate the actions of our leaders. Yet, if people have little interest in the world around them, they wind up operating with a "knowledge void" leaving them to get their news from less than credible sources.

Bye, Bye Traditional Media

Newspapers, radio, television, and magazines are often described as "traditional media" news foundations. Radio and television remain abundant through the United States as "go to" sources. That's not been the case with magazines and newspapers. Magazines have experienced a dramatic decline, with the number of US magazine companies declining by 31 percent between 2012 and 2022.[26] Some magazines have stemmed the tide by printing both paper and digital issues. Still, between 2017 and 2022 alone, total audiences for magazine companies dropped by a staggering 38 percent.[27]

By far, the most significant decline in the mass media space has occurred with newspapers. An examination by the Pew Research Center found that the circulation of daily newspapers in the United States was just under 63 million in 1985, the high point for the industry. By 2021, weekday newspaper circulation had fallen to 22.7 million, down by nearly two-thirds from the 1985 zenith.[28] Some publishers have attempted to overcome their circulation downfall by shifting to a combination of print and digital formats in the Internet age. That has generated something of an upward movement in growth. Circulation estimates in 2022 for the dual delivery format stood at just under 43 million—higher than the most recent print circulation figures, but still almost one-third less than the 1985 peak. But once we include the population growth between 1985 and 2022 (237 million versus 333 million), the increase of news readership is meaningless.

We dwell on these data because of the distinction between newspapers and other forms of information transmission. Print brings a certain level of confidence for the reader not found in other news delivery formats. Specifically, reporters and publishers are accountable by virtue of their names and titles next to their stories. Newspapers also provide the luxury of detail and sources that are often not found in television or radio formats. Consider that the typical television report lasts between 1 and 2 minutes, or approximately 60 to 120 words. Now consider that the average story in *The New York Times* exceeds six hundred words; in *The Washington Post*, the typical story is just over five hundred words. Other newspapers may offer less coverage averages, but the point is this: newspapers are likely to be more comprehensive and detailed than television, including more source materials and color, or descriptions of the circumstances in the story.

There's another unfortunate point regarding newspapers: declining availability. Yes, you can pick up a national newspaper like *The New York Times* or *USA Today* almost anywhere, with information on the latest big events and controversies. But as the late US House of Representatives Speaker Tip O'Neill once pointed out, "all politics is local," because local news carries a special, almost intimate currency for its readers. For that assessment we turn to the circulation of local and regional newspapers, where availability to readers has suffered greatly. Between 2005 and 2023, the number of newspapers in the United States declined from 8,900 to about 6,000,[29] or almost one-third. Most were weeklies, but they were the only news available to local communities or counties. During that same period, 70 percent of the nation's newspaper journalists lost their jobs.[30] Today, there are now about 200 of the nation's 3,143 counties without any news outlet, and 1,562 counties with only one—typically a weekly. The bottomline is that independent news sources are vanishing in the United States, leaving people less connected with the larger political, social, and economic environments.

Hello, Social Media

Against the decline of traditional news outlets we find the extraordinary rise of social media. The information sources that are available through the Internet run the gamut politically, but few offer distribution of real news. Some platforms such as Facebook, Instagram, TikTok, X, and YouTube, have wide audiences. Other "alternative" platforms like Parler, Rumble, and Truth Social, a Donald Trump–based site, appeal to niche audiences.

Some social media sources are largely benign to the extent of not taking a particular bent on political issues of the day. With these social networks, people share information in various formats online. Long-lost friends are found, and new online friendships are created. In a throwback to the past, online user groups have sprouted on social media sites, covering just about every subject imaginable. Facebook alone accounts for more than 70 million of what are described as "virtual communities," groups of people who share a particular interest. Businesses also utilize these free social media sites as vehicles for connecting with potential customers. And for good reason. Many social media platforms provide huge potential customer bases. With more than 2 billion monthly "visitors" (users) on social media, companies have the ability to reach huge audiences.

To a great degree, social media has replaced traditional media as information conduits. According to a Reuters investigation, reliance by Americans on social media sites as their prime sources of news swelled from 27 percent in 2013 to 48 percent in 2024. Meanwhile, the dependence on print as the prime source of news declined from 47 to 16 percent during the same period.[31] Clearly, social media has assumed prominence as a primary agent of information dissemination. However, a problem lies with the accuracy of the material that appears on these sites and the willingness of so many viewers to perceive what they read as "news" when it's often anything but.

Dealing with the intersection of social media material, news, and viewers has been vexing for those concerned with the presentation of real facts. Social media platforms can be important sources of information, but information should not be confused with news. Often, news, opinions on the issues of the day, and social chatter become so intermingled that social media users have difficulty distinguishing truth from misinformation. Part of the reason is that anyone on social media can become an instant "news" source by virtue of posting their "content," which can be devoid of truth. Worse, the more outrageous the claims on social media, the more the alleged news is shared between users with little regard for its veracity.[32]

Although many social media platforms have been largely politically neutral, some major sites have been criticized for allowing information of questionable taste, or in other cases, untruthful political ads. Instagram has been condemned for directing teens to provocative social videos,[33] while Meta (formerly known as Facebook) has been chastised for allowing altered footage of President Joe Biden along with other inaccurate information by a group loyal to his political opponent.[34] In the past, the social networking website actually conducted research on nearly seven hundred thousand users to see if its posts could manipulate emotions of those who read them without the consent of the users.[35] Considerable criticism followed.[36]

Sometimes social networking sites simply produce false information as news; a study of TikTok videos in 2022 found that 20 percent of its videos contained inaccurate material about drugs.[37] So erratic are social media outlets in their content that US surgeon general Vivek Murthy has asked Congress to pass legislation forcing social media platforms to contain a warning by the surgeon general to "regularly remind parents and adolescents that social media has not proved safe."[38]

Beyond the basic personal exchange component, some social media sites are largely political by design, and often with right-wing perspectives. Most of these have relatively small audiences, while their messages are beyond provocative. By far, the most incendiary material has appeared on numerous right-wing social platforms that have been banned or censored by traditional social media sites for their content. *Gab*, for example, has been a hotbed for antisemitic and racist discussions. *Parler* has been a hub for support of the January 6, 2021, insurrectionist effort. *Rumble* has been an alternative site for political conspiracy theorists. Research on X found that since its purchase by Elon Musk in 2022, the site has been transformed from a more neutral stance to embracing "a culture of rapid production of unlinked or ambiguously sourced content" encouraged by the new owner.[39]

Musk's endorsement of Donald Trump for his 2024 presidential run on his site eliminated any thought of his platform's neutrality. Worse, Musk violated an X policy instituted in 2023 that prohibited placement of synthetic, manipulated, or out-of-context media on his site. During the 2024 presidential campaign, he shared a political ad with an artificial voice mimicking Democratic nominee Kamala Harris saying that she became her party's nominee because of President Joe Biden's senility and that she didn't "know the first thing about running the country." Musk called the ad a parody, but the post, viewed 98 million times, surely had the potential of misleading or at least confusing X users.[40] Musk has also used his platform to embrace conspiracies that Jews promote "hatred against whites"[41] and that Black students have lower IQs than Whites.[42] It shouldn't be surprising that within days of Musk assuming control over X, hatred posts on the site soared.[43] Meanwhile, as Musk buddied up to Republican presidential candidate Trump both politically and financially with a staggering $277 million in campaign contributions,[44] X labeled accounts supporting Democratic candidate Kamala Harris as spam.[45]

The fact is that many social media sites are anything but benign distributors of information. Clearly, social media has become the wild west of interpersonal communications. Sadly, there is no sheriff (think government) in town to separate fact from fiction.

All this might provide a level of amusement, considering the outrageous material delivered as "news" that often originates in social media, except for the fact that about one in five Americans get their political news primarily through these pathways. Disproportionately, they tend to be younger, White, less educated, and less engaged than the rest of society and, as such, open to conspiracy theories and other false claims about American politics.[46] As such, this population subset is ripe for manipulation, which is a key phase for population control by authoritarians.

Some of the problems on social media originate abroad. In the past decade or so, foreign interests have become adept at using social media to weigh in on elections, often with misleading information. Beginning in 2016, Russian trolls with false identities bought online ads intended to influence targeted election groups.[47] The *Mueller Report* on Russian interference in the 2016 presidential election campaign cited thousands of social media ads purchased by Russian-controlled companies designed to support Donald Trump and oppose Hillary Clinton. These ads reached more than 126 million people who had no idea of their origins.[48] Similar social media activity by Russian actors occurred during the 2020 presidential campaign,

Weakened Sociopolitical Fabric

again on behalf of Trump and in opposition of Democratic nominee Joe Biden.[49] A half dozen other nations attempted to influence election politics, but their activities were not anywhere close to the involvement of Russian elements.

In 2024, US intelligence officials again warned that Russia would again attempt to influence the outcome of the election.[50] There is no proof that Trump had any direct connection with these Russian-based activities, but we do know about the extent to which Trump admires Russian president Vladimir Putin. Enough said. Beyond Russia, Justice Department officials also learned that TikTok had collected massive amounts of personal data on sensitive topics including gun control, abortion, and religion for ByteDance, its Chinese-owned parent company—this, despite a US law banning the practice.[51]

Clearly, the value of social media has two sides. It can make available all kinds of material to users who wouldn't have it otherwise. At the same time, social media exposes users to a variety of potential problems ranging from personal manipulation to national security concerns.

Enter Authoritarians and Trumpism

Earlier in this chapter, we pointed out that nearly one out of every five Americans experiences loneliness on a regular basis, which in numerical terms could include as many as 65 million residents. Lonely people don't connect with others; that's why they're lonely. Because lonely people are isolated, generally less educated, and tend to be at risk, they are particularly vulnerable to someone or something that promises to ease their pain or anger. At first glance, it would seem that social media could be an antidote to loneliness because of the relative ease in making connections via the Internet. But it's not that simple.

It turns out that interaction with social media only makes lonely people feel worse than they would otherwise. Studies reveal that when lonely people turn to social media, they often feel isolated.[52] It shouldn't be a surprise, moreover, that research also points out that lonely people are frequently vulnerable to gravitating to extreme groups.[53] Combined, loneliness, extremism, and the Internet take us to the world of Trumpism, where authoritarian sources and like-minded proponents impact the alienated and dispossessed with their messages. This leads to instability and uncertainty among millions of people in the body politic.

Overcoming Trumpism

Casting Doubt about Government

For years, Donald Trump has used social media to express his grievances about government agencies and those who run them. Many of his claims have been outright lies, which nonetheless flow into society's news pockets along with traditional media. Whether on Twitter or Truth Social, his own social media platform since 2022, Trump has issued endless tirades against government agencies, including voting officials for "rigging" his election loss in 2020, the FBI, the entire United States intelligence community, the courts, his attorney general, the US Department of Justice, the US military, and the press. Many of these attacks occurred during his first presidency, while others came before and after. Adding a touch of conspiracy to his list, Trump characterizes many of these institutions and their custodians as elements of the "deep state," a secret corrupt network of government officials dedicated to acting in their own self-interest. How much of this is provable? None. But for the angry, less educated, and socially isolated individual, these claims are just what the doctor ordered.

Trumpists have become adept at using social media both to build support for antidemocratic groups and to impact the public at large with messages designed to cast doubt on elected officials of American government institutions. These efforts come right out of the authoritarian playbook, which works to persuade citizens of a government that is inattentive, corrupt, and harmful to the public good.[54] With social media, Trumpists have staying power because of federal legislation and court decisions that allow most antidemocratic material to be distributed without any ability by the government to stop what's said, no matter how demonstrably false.

Trump's attacks on American institutions have spawned a new political industry among far-right leaders and organizations. Without any evidence, in 2021 then-Fox television host Tucker Carlson accused the National Security Agency of spying on Fox. Other outrageous incidents include the following:

- US House of Representatives member Marjorie Taylor Greene claiming that there was no evidence of a hijacked plane crashing into the Pentagon on 9/11.[55]
- Elon Musk permitting pro-Nazi content on his *X* social media platform.[56]
- Florida governor Ron DeSantis repeatedly attacking Dr. Anthony Fauci, head of the National Institute of Allergy and Infectious Diseases, for proposing mask mandates to combat COVID-19.[57]

- Kari Lake, a former television journalist and Republican nominee for a US Senate seat in Arizona, declaring that all the news is "full propaganda."[58]

And how's this for size? After the bullet of an attempted assassination grazed Donald Trump's ear at an open-air Pennsylvania rally on July 6, 2024, then-US senator and soon to be Trump's vice presidential nominee JD Vance implied on X that President Biden was responsible for the attack![59] Add the 147 Republican members of Congress who voted against certifying the 2020 presidential election and you have some of the best-known Republican leaders in the United States speaking out against some of the nation's most important institutions.

There's more. At the 2024 Republican national convention to accept the presidential nomination, Trump began his acceptance speech by disavowing the heated rhetoric of the campaign (most of which had been brought about by Trump and his sycophants) and called for unity. He wanted, Trump said, to be president of all Americans and not just the half that elected him. Then, in practically the next breath, Trump blew up his conciliatory words with a barrage of jabs against the Department of Justice, demanding that Democrats stop weaponizing the justice system and that partisan witch hunts against him must stop. At three points during his ninety-minute speech, Trump blamed the Democrats for using COVID-inspired election chicanery in the form of mail-in ballots to prevent his 2020 election victory.[60] Never mind that Trump had benefitted from recent Supreme Court decisions regarding presidential power, the questionable dismissal of the documents case by a Trump-appointed district court judge, and that no evidence had ever presented even a whiff of illegality in the 2020 presidential election. The old Trump was alive and accusative after all.

Republican political leaders weren't the only ones to succumb to Trumpism. Right-wing White supremacy groups have been all too eager to connect with Trump because of his racist statements. Ever since Trump announced for the presidency in 2015, violent right-wing groups have been active in supporting his campaign and bringing harm to those who opposed it. They have been particularly violent at Trump outdoor rallies, often attacking peaceful Trump opponents. For his part, Trump hasn't been shy about raising the profile of racist groups and welcoming them as supporters for his presidential campaigns. One glaring example occurred during a 2020 presidential debate with then-Democratic candidate Joe Biden. In an exchange with moderator Chris Wallace about far-right extremist organizations, Trump was asked to condemn the Proud Boys, a notorious neofascist right-wing group. After denying any support for the group, Trump said "Proud boys, stand back and stand by." Stand by! The Proud Boys and other similar violent right-wing groups considered that comment as an acknowledgment of their value to Trump and an invitation to continue their violent tactics.[61] In effect, they were legitimized—at least in their minds. And their violent, disruptive activities increased. Of note is that more than sixty Proud Boys participated in various aspects of the January 6 insurrectionist Congress and the federal government.[62]

Of course, the Trump rants would be meaningless without boogeymen assigned blame for America's ailments. Bad guys are an essential part of the authoritarian playbook because someone has to be responsible for the nation's failures. To that end, Trump's attacks on government and the media have been accompanied by his insistence that elected leaders have allowed millions of non-White immigrants in the United States with the intent of "poisoning the blood" of America, changing American culture, taking American jobs, and voting illegally.[63] This one-two combination—immigrants and the failed governance—was foundational to Trump's rise to power.

That so many key leaders in and out of government have made outrageous comments about American government and politics has not gone without notice. In 2018, the nineteen-year-old White man who killed seventeen high school students in Parkland, Florida, was a Trump admirer;[64] the 21-year old White man who killed 22 people at an El Paso Walmart in 2019 had written a manifesto with language similar to that used by Donald Trump;[65] in 2020, a White man punched a Latino gas station attendant in the head and ended his attack saying, "This is for Trump."[66] These are instances where assassins mentioned Trump specifically. Dozens of other attacks have been conducted by Whites loyal to racist values and organizations that gained prominence during the Trump presidency.[67] Clearly, Trumpists have created a disgruntled citizen army of sorts ranging from right-wing extremists to demented individuals ready to advance the goals of authoritarian provocateurs.

The Vulnerable Society

We began this chapter with a discussion of loneliness in American society. Those who are lonely, alienated, and uneducated are vulnerable to someone or something all too ready to heal their despair. Change has left them behind and adrift, struggling as lonely, powerless, helpless, and angry individuals.

Such people "seek certitude of what is known rather than the certainty of the unknown."[68] That newfound faith comes from a source that basically offers to rescue the dispossessed with an array of "solutions" responsive to their pain. It may matter little that these promises often have authoritarian tinges and are fraudulent, based on dividing the aggrieved from those leaders who have been labeled as their enemies. What matters is that authoritarians offer hope.

With little knowledge and awareness of the conditions around them, lonely people rely on their rescuers for salvation. They tend to pay little attention to real news. Instead, they gather most of their information from social media, which fills them with conspiracies that they are all too ready to accept as their reality. In some ways, the lonely and alienated are the most vulnerable members of society.

That's where Trumpists come in. Authoritarian in nature, Trumpists fill the void in the lives of the weak and angry members of society who are looking to get even for their plight. Trumpists identify the troublemakers as immigrants and non-Christians as ready to steal the jobs of lonely, alienated Whites and undermine what they define as "our culture." Trumpists disparage the mainstream media for not telling the truth about America's condition. And finally, Trumpists blame the government for conspiring to keep the dispossessed in a permanent depression and devoid of any real happiness. Or these people bring hope.

Unwittingly, the downtrodden become the foot soldiers for Trumpists. Some are right-wing extremists who have been searching for an ideology that fits their values and are willing to fight for it. More likely, many of the others are willing to make their case at the voting booth. Authoritarianism and loneliness go well together.

Let's remember that not all alienated people are Trumpists, nor are all Trumpists lonely people. Some Trumpists identify as such because they see benefits from ruling the rest of society; other Trumpists appreciate the fiscal advantages that accrue from generous tax relief policies; other Trumpists still accept the approach for its obsession with immigrants, dedication to antiabortion dogma, or other specific policies.

But the case has been made here that a sizable swath of American society is desperate enough to see Trumpism as the cure for their troubled emotional, financial, and political conditions. They accept extremist violence as a necessity to protect what's left of their beaten down lives and welcome authoritarian rule as assurance that they will be saved from those seeking to take their place in society. In a tight election, this group of alienated

Americans can make the difference in the outcome of that important political event.

NOTES

1. Chris Barker and Brian Martin, "Participation: The Happiness Connection," *Journal of Public Deliberation*, 7, no. 1 (October 19, 2011), https://delibdemjournal.org/article/392/galley/4683/view/.
2. Kory Floyd, "Loneliness Corresponds with Political Conservative Thought," *Research in Psychology and Behavioral Sciences*, 5, no. 1 (2017), pp. 13–21, http://pubs.sciepub.com/rpbs/5/1/3.
3. "All the Lonely People: Why Americans' Isolation Is a Threat to Our Democracy," *USA Today*, September 16, 2022, https://www.usatoday.com/story/opinion/2022/09/16/how-loneliness-breeds-resentment-threatens-american-democracy/8004713001/.
4. "Record Low in U.S. Satisfied with Way Democracy Is Working," Gallup Poll, January 5, 2024, https://news.gallup.com/poll/548120/record-low-satisfied-democracy-working.aspx.
5. Martha Minow, *Saving the News* (New York: Oxford University Press, 2021), pp. 25–35.
6. "Media Confidence in U.S. Matches 2016 Record Low," Gallup Poll, October 19, 2023, https://news.gallup.com/poll/512861/media-confidence-matches-2016-record-low.aspx.
7. Marc J. Hetherington and Jonathan D. Weiler make this point in their *Authoritarianism and Polarization in American Politics* (New York: Cambridge University Press, 2009), p. 9.
8. Lawrence Quill, *Nostalgia and Political Theory* (New York: Routledge, 2024), p. 134.
9. For an intriguing analysis of interest groups in American politics, see Theodore J. Lowi, *The End of Liberalism*, 2nd edition (New York: W.W. Norton, 1979).
10. Robert H. Putnam, *Bowling Alone: The Collapse and Revival of American Community* (New York: Simon & Schuster, 2000).
11. Ibid., p. 338.
12. Sidney Verba, Kay Lehman Schlozman, and Henry Brady, *Voice and Equality* (Cambridge, MA: Harvard University Press, 1995), pp. 506–7.
13. "Monthly Labor Review," U.S. Bureau of Labor Statistics, March 2022, https://www.bls.gov/opub/mlr/2022/article/telework-during-the-covid-19-pandemic.htm.
14. Jose Maria Barrero, Nicholas Bloom, Shelby Buckman, and Steven J. Davis, "How Much Work from Home Is There in the United States," ITAM, Hoover Institution and Stanford University, January 27, 2024, https://wfhresearch.com/wp-content/uploads/2024/02/How-Much-WFH-in-the-US.pdf.

15 Liad Bareket-Bojmel, Lily Chernyak-Hai, and Malika Margalit, "Out of Sight but not Out of Mind: The Role of Loneliness and Hope in Remote Work and in Job Engagement," *Personality and Individual Differences*, 202 (February 2023), https://wfhresearch.com/wp-content/uploads/2024/02/How-Much-WFH-in-the-US.pdf.
16 "19% of U.S. Adults Report Frequently or Always Feeling Lonely, New Yahoo/YouGov Poll Finds. Here's Why—and Which Age Group Is Affected Most," yahoo!life, May 20, 2024, https://www.yahoo.com/lifestyle/19-of-us-adults-report-frequently-or-always-feeling-lonely-new-yahooyougov-poll-finds-heres-why--and-which-age-group-is-affected-most-090036452.html.
17 Richard Weissbourd, Milena Batanova, Virginia Lovison, and Eric Torres, "Loneliness in America," Making Common Care Project, Harvard Graduate School of Education, Cambridge, MA, February 8, 2021, https://static1.squarespace.com/static/5b7c56e255b02c683659fe43/t/6021776bdd04957c4557c212/1612805995893/Loneliness+in+America+2021_02_08_FINAL.pdf.
18 See Jesselyn Cook, *The Quiet Damage* (New York: Brown Books, 2024).
19 "Loneliness Damages not Just Children's Mental Health, but Their Grades as Well," *Forbes*, February 9, 2022, https://www.forbes.com/sites/nickmorrison/2022/02/03/loneliness-damages-not-just-childrens-mental-health-but-their-grades-as-well/.
20 Verba et al., *Voice and Equality*, p. 433.
21 Russell Brooker and Todd Schaefer, *Public Opinion in the 21st Century* (New York: Houghton Mifflin, 2006), pp. 264–6.
22 Vivek Murthy, "Our Epidemic of Loneliness and Isolation," Department of Health and Human Services, Washington, DC, 2023, https://www.hhs.gov/sites/default/files/surgeon-general-social-connection-advisory.pdf.
23 Jan E. Leighley, *Mass Media and Politics* (Boston, MA: Houghton Mifflin, 2004), p. 6.
24 Doris A. Graber, *Mass Media and American Politics*, 8th edition (Washington, DC: CQ Press, 2010), p. 3.
25 "U.S. Attention to Political News Slips Back to Typical Levels," Gallup Poll, October 25, 2023, https://news.gallup.com/poll/513128/attention-political-news-slips-back-typical-levels.aspx.
26 Dean Talbot, "Magazine Publishing Statistics," *Wordsrated*, April 4, 2023, https://wordsrated.com/magazine-publishing-statistics/.
27 Ibid.
28 "Newspapers Fact Sheet," Pew Research Center, US PIRG, November 10, 2023, https://www.pewresearch.org/journalism/fact-sheet/newspapers/.
29 The data in the paragraph come from "The State of Local News, 2023 Report," Northwestern University, November 26, 2023, https://localnewsinitiative.northwestern.edu/projects/state-of-local-news/2023/report/.
30 "The State of Local News, 2022," Local News Initiative, Northwestern University, October 4, 2022, https://localnewsinitiative.northwestern.edu/assets/the_state_of_local_news_2022.pdf.

31 "Reuters Institute Digital News Report 2024," June 23, 2024, https://reutersinstitute.politics.ox.ac.uk/sites/default/files/2024-06/RISJ_DNR_2024_Digital_v10%20lr.pdf.
32 "How Misinformation on Social Media Has Changed News," US PIRG Education Fund, November 22, 2023, https://pirg.org/edfund/articles/misinformation-on-social-media/.
33 "Instagram Recommends Sexual Videos to Accounts for 13-Year-Olds, Tests Show," *The Wall Street Journal*, June 21, 2024, https://www.wsj.com/tech/instagram-recommends-sexual-videos-to-accounts-for-13-year-olds-tests-show-b6123c65.
34 "Oversight Board Rebukes Meta's Policies after Altered Biden Video Spreads," *The Washington Post*, February 5, 2024, https://www.washingtonpost.com/technology/2024/02/05/meta-oversight-board-deepfake-president-biden/. In April 2024, Meta did impose new rules on political advertising, including recommendations on political content. See "As Meta Flees Politics, Campaigns Rely on New Tricks to Reach Voters," *The Washington Post*, April 21, 2024, https://www.washingtonpost.com/technology/2024/04/21/social-media-trump-biden-politics-instagram-facebook/.
35 Adam D. Kramer, Jamie E. Guillory, and Jeffrey T. Hancock, "Experimental Evidence of Massive-Scale Emotional Contagion through Social Networks," *Proceedings of the National Academy of Sciences of the United States of America*, June 2, 2014, https://www.pnas.org/doi/full/10.1073/pnas.1320040111.
36 "Facebook Emotion Study Breached Ethical Guidelines, Researchers Say," *The Guardian*, June 30, 2014, https://www.theguardian.com/technology/2014/jun/30/facebook-emotion-study-breached-ethical-guidelines-researchers-say.
37 Jack Brewster, Lorenzo Arvanitis, Valeria Pavilonis, and Macrina Wang, "Beware of the 'New Google:' TikTok's Search Engine Pumps Toxic Misinformation to Its Young Users," *NewsGuard*, September 14, 2022, https://www.newsguardtech.com/misinformation-monitor/september-2022/.
38 See "Surgeon General Calls for Social Media Warning Signs," *The Washington Post*, June 17, 2024, https://www.washingtonpost.com/technology/2024/06/17/surgeon-general-social-media-warning-labels/.
39 Mike Caulfield, Mert Can Bayar, and Ashlyn B. Aske, "The 'New Elites' of X: Identifying the Most Influential Accounts Engaged in Hamas/Israel Discourse," Center for Informed Public, The University of Washington, October 20, 2023, https://www.cip.uw.edu/2023/10/20/new-elites-twitter-x-most-influential-accounts-hamas-israel/.
40 "Elon Musk Shares Manipulated Harris Video, in Seeming Violation of X's Policies," *The New York Times*, July 27, 2024, https://www.nytimes.com/2024/07/27/us/politics/elon-musk-kamala-harris-deepfake.html.
41 "Elon Musk Endorses Antisemitic Conspiracy Theory that Jews 'Push Hatred' on White People," Spectrum News 1, November 23, 3034, https://ny1.com/nyc/all-boroughs/politics/2023/11/16/elon-musk-endorses-antisemitic-conspiracy-theory-about-jews-welcoming-in--hordes-of-minorities-.
42 "Elon Musk Cosigns Racist Claim That Black Students Have Low IQs," Yahoo! News, January 11, 2024, https://www.yahoo.com/news/elon-musk-cosigns-racist-claim-153400769.html.

43 "X Content Moderation Failure," The Center for Countering Digital Hate, September 2023, https://counterhate.com/wp-content/uploads/2023/09/230907-X-Content-Moderation-Report_final_CCDH.pdf.

44 "Elon Musk Spent At Least $277 Million Backing Trump and the GOP: Here's Where All That Money Went," Business Insider, December 6, 2024, https://www.businessinsider.com/elon-musk-260-million-spending-trump-republican-party-2024-12.

45 "Elon Musk's X Accused of Bias after Pro-Harris Accounts Labeled as 'Spam,'" The Washington Post, August 7, 2024, https://www.washingtonpost.com/technology/2024/08/07/musk-x-harris-bias/.

46 "Americans Who Mainly Get Their News on Social Media Are Less Engaged, Less Knowledgeable," Pew Research Center, July 30, 2020, https://www.pewresearch.org/journalism/2020/07/30/americans-who-mainly-get-their-news-on-social-media-are-less-engaged-less-knowledgeable/.

47 See Jelena Vicic, "How Foreign Governments Sway Voters with Online Manipulation," Scientific American, April 29, 2024, https://www.scientificamerican.com/article/how-foreign-governments-sway-voters-with-online-manipulation/.

48 "Report on the Investigation into Russian Interference in the 2016 Presidential Election," The Washington Post, 2019, p. 88, https://www.washingtonpost.com/graphics/2019/politics/read-the-mueller-report/.

49 "Foreign Threats to the 2020 U.S. Federal Elections," National Intelligence Council, Washington, DC, March 15, 2021, https://www.dni.gov/files/ODNI/documents/assessments/ICA-declass-16MAR21.pdf.

50 "U.S. Intel Officials Warn Russia Plans to Target Swing States in 2024 Elections with Influence Operations," CNN, July 11, 2024, https://www.cnn.com/2024/07/09/politics/russia-2024-election-influence-operations-intellignce/index.html.

51 "TikTok Collected U.S. Users' Views on Gun Control, Abortion and Religion, U.S. Says," The Wall Street Journal, https://www.wsj.com/tech/tiktok-collected-u-s-users-views-on-gun-control-abortion-and-religion-u-s-says-4fcf19f6.

52 'Does Social Media Make You Feel Lonely? Here's Why and How to Avoid It," Kaiser Permanente, January 12, 2023, https://healthy.kaiserpermanente.org/health-wellness/healtharticle.have-healthier-relationship-with-social-media.

53 See Emma J. Renstrom, Hanna Black, and Molly M. Knapton, "Exploring a Pathway to Social Radicalization: The Effects of Social Exclusion and Racial Sensitivity," Group Processes and Intergroup Relations, 23, no. 8 (December 2020), pp. 1204–29, https://doi.org/10.1177/1368430220917215, and Masa Markovic, Aleksandra Nicovic, and Marko Zivanovic, "Contextual and Psychological Predictors of Militant Extremist Mindset in Youth," Frontiers in Psychology, February 10, 2021, https://www.ncbi.nlm.nih.gov/pmc/articles/PMC7902909/.

54 Karen Stenner, The Authoritarian Dynamic (New York: Cambridge University Press, 2005), p. 326.

55 "QAnon Candidate Marjorie Taylor Greene Is a 9/11 Conspiracy Theorist Who Claimed That There's No Evidence a Plane Crashed into the Pentagon," MediaMatters, August 8, 2020, https://www.mediamatters.org/congress/qanon-candidate-marjorie-taylor-greene-911-conspiracy-theorist-who-claimed-theres-no.

56 "Elon Musk Will Reinstate Neo-Nazi on Twitter," *Los Angeles Magazine*, May 2, 2024, https://lamag.com/internet/elon-musk-will-reinstate-neo-nazi-on-twitter.
57 "DeSantis and Other GOP 2024 Prospects Target Public Health Officials with Political Attacks," CNN, July 31, 2021, https://www.cnn.com/2021/07/31/politics/desantis-fauci-coronavirus-republican-2024-race/index.html.
58 "Kari Lake: Interviewing the Election Denier Who Ran for Arizona Governor," BBC, November 14, 2022, https://www.bbc.com/news/world-us-canada-63593153.
59 "Ohio Sen. JD Vance, a Top VP Contender, Blames Trump Shooting on Biden 'Rhetoric,'" *Cincinnati Enquirer*, July 15, 2024, https://www.cincinnati.com/story/news/politics/2024/07/13/trump-rally-shooting-jd-vance-blames-biden-campaign-rhetoric/74397100007/.
60 "Read the Transcript of Donald J. Trump's Convention Speech," *The New York Times*, July 19, 2024, https://www.nytimes.com/2024/07/19/us/politics/trump-rnc-speech-transcript.html.
61 "Trump to Far-Right Extremists: 'Stand Back and Stand by,'" Associated Press, September 30, 2020, https://apnews.com/article/election-2020-joe-biden-race-and-ethnicity-donald-trump-chris-wallace-0b32339da25fbc9e8b7c7c7066a1db0f.
62 "Capitol Attack: More Than 60 Proud Boys Used Encrypted Channel to Plan, Indictment Says," *The Guardian*, March 20, 2021, https://www.theguardian.com/us-news/2021/mar/20/four-proud-boys-leaders-indicted-capitol-riot-donald-trump.
63 "Trump's Return to Anti-Immigration Message Takes Hold among Republicans," *The Washington Post*, January 9, 2024, https://rollcall.com/2024/01/09/why-trumps-return-to-anti-immigration-message-could-be-bad-news-for-biden/.
64 "Nikolas Cruz, Suspected Parkland Shooter, Espoused Racism in Chats; Bragged of Writing Trump: Report," Associated Press, February 17, 2018, https://apnews.com/article/shootings-race-and-ethnicity-racial-injustice-nikolas-cruz-5574fe53ea088e1ed1fc6a48804b4bc8#.
65 "El Paso Shooting Suspect's Manifesto Echoes Trump's Language," *The New York Times*, August 4, 2019, https://www.nytimes.com/2019/08/04/us/politics/trump-mass-shootings.html.
66 "'No Blame?' ABC News Finds 54 Cases Invoking 'Trump' in Connection with Violence, Threats, Alleged Assaults," ABC News, May 30, 2020, https://abcnews.go.com/Politics/blame-abc-news-finds-17-cases-invoking-trump/story?id=58912889.
67 See "The GOP Had an Uneasy Relationship with the Far Right. Until Trump," *The Washington Post*, September 16, 2020, https://www.washingtonpost.com/outlook/2020/09/16/gop-far-right-trump/, and "The Rise of Far-Right Extremism in the United States," Center for Strategic and International Studies, Washington, DC, November 7, 2018, https://www.csis.org/analysis/rise-far-right-extremism-united-states. à
68 Michael J. Diamond, *Ruptures in the American Psyche* (Bicester, Oxfordshire, England: Phoenix, 2022), p. 38.

CHAPTER 7
DESTABILIZING PUBLIC EDUCATION

It's no secret that democracies have the potential to be the least stable forms of government. To begin with, in democracies, citizens agree on elections as the method of choosing leaders, including the peaceful acceptance of outcomes. Along with general agreement on the rules, democracies depend upon widespread consensus among the citizens about inclusiveness and equal status for the members of society, or what William Hudson describes as a shared sense of community.[1] Most societies fall short of meeting these fundamental requirements because of deep social, religious, racial, or economic fissures; as such, to various degrees they exhibit characteristics of undemocratic governments.[2]

Other than the Civil War, the United States has managed to avoid democratic collapse, although moments such as the January 6, 2021, insurrection against Congress certainly threatened our political stability. So then, how is such a consensus built that enables democracy?

No doubt, several factors come into play, including tradition, culture, relative homogeneity of the population, and institutional stability for starters. Along with these elements, however, an educated population has long been viewed as a major source of basic community maintenance.

Education has a critical role in a democracy. Beyond analytical thinking and writing skills, education nurtures a democratic environment and serves as a guardian of sorts from society succumbing to authoritarianism.[3] At least in theory. John Dewey, an early twentieth-century philosopher and public education expert, noted that democratic societies "must have a type of education which gives individuals a personal interest in social relationships and control, and the habits of mind which secure social changes without introducing disorder."[4] Dewey wasn't alone. His observations are in line with those of Alexis de Toqueville, an early foreign observer of the United States, who wrote that "in the United States the education of the people powerfully contributes to the maintenance of a democratic republic."[5]

The outline of American federalism consigned education activity largely to the states. No doubt, in part, that placement occurred because although the US Constitution provides numerous guarantees to Americans, it does not contain any right to a public education. That omission places the United States apart from more than 120 countries that provide such a right in their constitutions. Thus, from the earliest times of the Republic, this policy issue has resided largely outside of the federal government's domain.

Nevertheless, these days, the federal government contributes about 10 percent of the overall cost of public education in the states, but federally dictated policies for education in the states are relatively rare. In recent years, in fact, the somewhat small federal education policy footprint has diminished because of US Supreme Court decisions all but wiping out the 1954 *Brown v. Board Education* decision that ordered desegregation of the public schools,[6] as well as a recent US Supreme Court decision seriously lessening authority of bureaucracies such as the federal Department of Education.[7] As a result, although states have some common objectives for schools, their requirements on various programs and issues can differ substantially.

Which takes us to contemporary state education policies in the Trump era. In the current learning environment, key aspects of public education that were once rather largely uncontroversial have become incredibly politicized, and often with a radically conservative bent. In some states, policymakers have introduced themes and concepts totally out of step with long-standing pluralistic democratic values.

For example, the separation of church and state has long been accepted as a given in public education, as declared in a 1980 US Supreme Court case.[8] Yet, in 2024, Oklahoma, Texas, and Louisiana adopted policies to include the Ten Commandments and various themes in the classroom. In 2025, a federal appeals court overturned Louisiana's adoption,[9] with observers expecting a ruling by the US Supreme Court in the near future. Until final resolution, K–12 public education students in some states are receiving religious instruction in an environment where such information was excluded. In other cases, students are kept from exposure to some themes increasingly commonplace in modern society. The lack of discussion about climate change in many states is a case in point.[10] Either way, public education policies and components have become incredibly controversial in some parts of the United States.

This chapter centers on serious policy threats by Trumpists and antidemocratic allies to the public education enterprise, particularly in light of reduced federal financial involvement. We focus on how some state governments have severely weakened a once relatively open public education environment with instructional curricula that limit a well-rounded

Destabilizing Public Education

education by denying history in some cases and rewriting the present in others. So, what does that have to do with democracy?

In numerous states and political settings, the treasured concept of public education as a guarantor for democracy through an informed and enlightened citizenry is no more. Instead, the open quest for truth has been replaced by a Trumpism-inspired rigid system that emphasizes strict dogma over open inquiry. Discussions about provocative ideas and values have been omitted from curricula, leaving students in the dark and teachers apprehensive about a distorted educational environment. The result is an existential danger to American society that could threaten the future of our democracy for generations to come. It's a danger that once again illustrates the long-term efforts of Trumpism, in this instance through injecting the "us" versus "them" division into the public education framework, with the "thems" consisting of non-Whites, non-Christians, and non-heterosexual individuals.

Trump's Approach to Public Education

In his run up to the presidency during the 2016 campaign, Trump sought to take the federal government out of the public education business completely. Upon assuming the presidency, he pursued initial steps to fulfill that objective. His first budget plan proposed to reduce, if not end, a variety of federal education initiatives to help those most in need, including after-school programs, childcare for low-income parents, teacher training, and class sizes. He also dissed *Common Core*, a comprehensive standards-setting program that set minimum learning objectives in English Language, History, Science, and Technical Subjects. That voluntary plan was created under the auspices of the National Governors Association and was agreed to in all or in part (eight states) by all fifty states. Ironically, even a states-generated plan for public education wasn't good enough for Trump. Overall, he called for a 13.6 percent decrease in federal education spending.[11]

Trump argued that education policies should be established and governed at the local level, ideally in private hands, which would pave the way for tremendous disparities in instruction, large class sizes, inconsistent standards, and little security for teachers. He also sought to increase federal spending only for charter schools along with vouchers for private and religious schools. Fortunately, Congress had little interest in most of Trump's education initiatives, leaving the status quo largely in place.

Overcoming Trumpism

Little changed for Trump between 2016 and 2020 other than refinement of his plan to obliterate federal involvement in public education. During his 2024 presidential campaign, he offered a more targeted approach to education reform. This time, Trump promised that if elected president, he would eliminate federal funding "for any school or program pushing Critical Race Theory [more on that later], gender, ideology, or other inappropriate racial, sexual, or political content on our children." Trump also pledged to "veto the sinister effort to weaponize civics education" and work for "the direct election of school principals by the parents,"[12] which effectively would remove public education policies from the hands of professionals.

Toward the end of the 2024 presidential campaign, Trump doubled down on his disdain for public education. Claiming that public schools "have been taken over [by] the radical Left maniacs," Trump repeated his original pledge of his first administration to abolish the federal Department of Education altogether.[13] At the root of his concern was federal funding for public schools that recognize gender identity, teach critical race theory (CRT), and require COVID vaccines.[14]

In many cases, Trump's words left considerable room for interpretation, such as "inappropriate racial, sexual, or political content" and "weaponized civic education." Reading between the lines for the true intent became something of an art. For example, "inappropriate racial, sexual, or political content" has been interpreted in conservative circles as classroom discussion of racism (because there isn't any according to Trumpists!); education about sexuality, gender differences, puberty, and transgender issues are unnecessary (those topics would be for parents only); and dialogue on political differences and approaches to controversial issues don't belong in classrooms (no reason to confuse kids with radical gibberish). And that's what has happened in many states with conservative state governments.

Trump has had help with his effort to place education squarely in the hands of the states and local communities. For some time, conservative political organizations and evangelical religious bodies have pushed for state control of education for complementary reasons. For political conservatives, state control offers the possibility of retooling the education system with state-sponsored private schools, charter schools, and voucher systems. Allowing states maximum leverage in education opens the way for local control can be one-sided and narrow in the approach to various subjects. The possible use of federal money to achieve these goals would be frosting on the cake. In its *Project 2025: Mandate for Leadership*, the Heritage Foundation, long viewed as the intellectual framework for a second Trump administration, actually proposed these themes,[15] and Trump was only too happy to include them as part of his executive branch reorganization.

For evangelicals, local control of public education offers the opportunity to include a Christian framework. They claim that with faith-based education initiatives, student knowledge comes from the Bible, the Ten Commandments, and other religious themes that build character, patriotism, and good citizenship. Evangelicals also believe that faith-based education allows students to "learn the arts and sciences through a spiritual lens and build who they are in Christ."[16] With such a learning framework, there is no room for nor interest in non-Christian views as well as the views of those with no religious beliefs.

Combined, conservative groups and evangelicals have provided much of the support and energy for retooling approaches to state education policies. Several states have restructured curricula to the point of denying widely accepted scientific facts and rewriting portions of American history.

Restricted Curriculum

Trump's commitment to minimize, if not end, federal participation in public education programs has made it easy for states to fill the void and pursue their own, often narrow approaches to the discipline. In the past, state efforts to ignore discrimination against LGBTQ students, racial prejudice, students with non-Christian beliefs, and laws limiting introduction of religion into the classroom were thwarted by federal rules. But between Trump's disinterest in federal guarantees and increasing conservative successes in the federal courts, states now have firm control of these sensitive topics. Of course, not all states have reconstructed education policies on religious-based themes, but the introduction of revisionist curricula in more than two dozen states has trashed the notion of any "common core." That agreed upon approach to basic subject areas we should remember was created originally by the states, not the federal government. Below we examine the major difficulties produced by different state laws on race, gender, and religion.

Race

Since 2020, fifteen states have enacted legislation restricting instruction relating to race and racism.[17] Some new rules are quite specific. However, many of these laws are vaguely worded, creating interpretation problems for teachers and administrators alike. Either way, the intent in these states legislating on racism has been to avoid the issue as an academic subject, thereby denying existence of historical and present-day inequities. In addition, these laws have often included severe penalties for teachers who ignore them. With such threats, teachers have refrained from instruction on controversial issues. As a result, racial minorities and their histories have been minimized, if not delegitimized, altogether not only in the classroom, but by extension in society.

Examples abound. In 2024, the Alabama legislature enacted legislation restricting classroom curricula on racial diversity, equity, and inclusion. During the same year, Louisiana legislators gave parents the right to see that their child's school did not make their child feel racially oppressed by curricula dealing with race. Also, Utah legislators forbade schools from holding mandatory instruction or training for students that relate to moral character and race. And Florida forbade K–12 schools from "distorting" historical events relating to systemic racism, oppression, and privilege. In that state, Governor Ron DeSantis, perhaps the most radical of the race revisionists, went so far as to eliminate Advanced Placement courses in African American studies offered by the College Board.[18]

DeSantis set the tone for revision of racism education in America. In discussing the history of slavery, he defended enslavement as actually useful for African Americans, claiming that "slaves developed skills which, in some instances, could be applied for personal benefit after their freedom."[19] In other words, there was no reason in Florida to teach about slavery because it was actually Florida's version of a job training program!

Most educators find themselves at odds with state laws that restrict or forbid teaching about issues related to race. In a national poll of teachers about discussing race in the classroom, nearly two-thirds of the respondents believed it was important for students to learn about the legacy of slavery and its impact on today's students.[20] Nevertheless, the intentional ambiguity of race-centered legislation in many states and the potential punitive response by school administrators have made it almost impossible for teachers to do their jobs on the subject of racism.[21] Meanwhile, racial minorities often find themselves as outcasts in an educational setting that seems to have little room for them or their historical experiences. Such an approach makes a mockery of equality, not to mention the truth.

One major area of criticism for Trumpists has been their obsession with a once-arcane academic concept known as "Critical Race Theory." Conceived nearly a half century ago by philosophical and legal scholars, CRT focuses on the role of racism as foundational in virtually all social, political, and economic aspects of American society. As such, CRT finds that conditions such as slavery, segregation, and present-day systemic discrimination of African Americans are not products of historical racism, but the precursors of virtually all aspect of modern life.

Without evidence, Trump and his allies have argued that CRT is routinely taught in K–12 classes in such a manner as to foster blame on today's White children for historical tragedies associated with racism. From there, many state-elected officials have gone berserk. As of 2024, eighteen states banned the teaching of CRT in K–12 schools, with nine more considering legislation. The irony is that despite the hysteria created by Trumpists, there is little proof that CRT is taught anywhere in K–12 education, if for no other reason because the theory is much too sophisticated for young students to grasp.[22] Instead, in the words of one assessment, CRT has become "a new bogey man for people unwilling to acknowledge our country's racist history and how it impacts the present"[23]—a bogeyman that allows states to restructure our national past.

In 2020, then-president Trump took the false narrative of CRT to another level. He labeled CRT as "unAmerican propaganda" and instructed federal agencies to stop teaching it to employees as part of their racial sensitivity training programs.[24] Trump continued that promise with his 2024 education platform. He was a critic of treatments such as the award-winning *The 1619 Project*,[25] which discussed the origins and consequences of slavery as a key element of the American narrative, which he viewed as anti-American. Thus, Trump wrote in his "Agenda 47: President Trump's Ten Principles for Great Schools Leading to Great Jobs" that he would eliminate "decades of poor scholarship [that] have vilified our Founders and principles they championed." Instead he would "ensure our children know the truth about the American Founding…" and "come to appreciate the United States as the freest, most prosperous, most virtuous nation in the history of the world."[26] For Trump, there was no room for any education pointing to historical blemishes in America's history.

Avoiding discussion of race only encourages racism because of unnecessary knowledge gaps. Studies show that conversations about different racial appearances have the effect of fostering positive views of other races and decreasing the possibility of racial bias. Conversely, classroom environments without such discussions allow negative feelings by various groups against the others.[27] So, why don't Trumpists embrace dialogue between the races instead of excluding any discussion in the classroom environment? Perhaps because dialogue would counter their not-so-subtle promotion of White superiority in the "us" versus "them" paradigm. Accordingly, the absence of a racial enemy might make it easier for the population to focus on the real issues affecting American government, including irresponsible leaders.

Gender

For decades, public schools and universities have been ground zero for debates on gender equality. During much of that period, discussion focused on whether girls were receiving the same education opportunities as boys. Over time, that issue was largely resolved through various state and federal initiatives such as affirmative action, especially Title IX of the Education Amendments signed into law by Republican President Richard Nixon in 1972 and executive orders signed by Presidents John F. Kennedy and Lyndon Johnson.[28] Out of this compilation came guarantees that females would be given opportunities similar to those given to males. That delicate balance ended in 2023 when the US Supreme Court overturned affirmative action, vastly diminishing federal clout on gender issues at the university level.[29] Yet, change emerged out of the forty-five-year affirmative action period. These days, larger percentages of girls than boys attend college and graduate into professional jobs.

During Trump's first presidential administration, the federal Department of Education refused to consider teenage transgender student complaints of discrimination for disallowing their use of bathrooms that comported with their gender identity. That policy decision reversed protections that had been provided by the Obama administration.[30]

Recently, a different kind of gender scrutiny has focused on the K–12 education environment. At issue is the management of LGBTQ issues in the twenty-first-century public school classroom. Similar to the controversy over race-related topics in the classroom, public sentiment on gay and transgender matters has now become a focal point in public education, with great divisions of opinion.

Meanwhile, large numbers of evangelicals are clear on LGBTQ issues, and they have successfully demanded that states adopt legislation on a variety of gender policies and the role of schools in informing parents in situations regarding a child's anti-heterosexual orientation. Between 2023 and 2024 alone, seventeen states passed more than thirty LGBTQ-related laws on topics such as bathroom assignments, sports participation, restrictions on the use of pronouns, curricula, and instruction on LGBTQ issues, with punishments and potential dismissals for teachers and administrators who violated these laws.[31]

Most of the new anti-transgender laws include requirements for teachers and administrators to inform parents about their transgender children, "outing" them in the process. As a result, affected children with gender issues feel abandoned and vulnerable to abuse by their fellow classmates.[32] There is reason for their concern. An FBI study of anti-LGBTQ hate crimes in the public schools between 2015 and 2022 revealed a dramatic increase of more than 350 percent in states with restrictive laws on gender conversations, compared to an increase of 104 percent in states without restrictive legislation.[33] Clearly, denying any discussion of LGBTQ-related issues actually allows for more hostility than in states permitting discussion of the topics.

More than ever, anti-transgender forces have found a friend in Donald Trump, who has a long record of disparaging transgender students.[34] As with racial minorities, Trump and his allies have identified members of the transgender community and their supporters as part of the undesirable "them." During his 2024 presidential campaign, Trump said at one point, "On day one [of his second presidential term], I will sign an executive order instructing every federal agency to cease the promotion of sex or gender transition at any age."[35] Late in the campaign, Trump's team and pro-Trump groups spent $37 million on anti-transgender ads, accusing opponent Kamala Harris of being soft on the issue—this, even though less than 1 percent of the nation identifies as transgender.[36] For those concerned with the uncomfortable possibility of transgender dialogue and accommodation in the public schools, Trump's promise was manna from heaven.

Trump wasted little time in dealing with the transgender issue upon his reelection. Within ten days of taking office, Trump issued an executive order that ended federal support for gender transition for anyone under the age of nineteen.[37] He also announced in another executive order that henceforth, the federal government would recognize two genders, male and female. Shortly thereafter in February 2025, Trump issued an executive order denying federal education funds to those states that allowed transgender females to participate in competitive sports.[38] Some pro-transgender schools sued the Trump administration,[39] but the issue, like so many civil rights–related questions, would be settled only by the US Supreme Court at a future point in time.

Despite Trump's rhetoric and the hysteria of others, trepidation about gender issues in the schools seems to be more of a problem for politicians than the public or teachers. More than three-quarters of adults feel that politicians use debates on transgender issues to distract attention from more pressing priorities, according to a 2024 national poll.[40] It turns out that more than two-thirds of K–12 teachers say that themes such as sexual orientation and identity rarely or never occur in their classrooms.[41] Add to these findings the fact that 70 percent of parents want sex education to be part of the school curriculum, and we see a political dispute over what is essentially a nonissue for everyone except a small minority of extremists.[42] Yet, Trump and his evangelical allies have made the issue seem like the number one concern on the nation's educational agenda. It isn't. Simply put, concerns about gender issues in the schools come from a small minority.

Nevertheless, Trump's pronouncements on gender-related issues coincide well with the values of the evangelical community, where most of the members have supported him with predictable endorsements at the ballot box. Estimates for the 2020 Trump vote from White evangelicals ranged between 76 and 81 percent, making them one of the most, if not the most loyal voters in Trump's orbit.[43] An almost identical evangelical vote for Trump emerged in the 2024 presidential election.[44] Given that evangelicals were 23 percent of all voters, there was little reason for Trump to accept the claims of transgender population as equals in American society. He knows where his bread is buttered.

Religion

Early on in the effort to establish education opportunities, the first American schools often attached the study of Christian religion and values as part of the curriculum; they typically began each school day with a prayer. As compulsory public education evolved, many public schools removed religion in favor of more secular instruction. But questions remained about the appropriate relationship between religion and the classroom. In 1962, the US Supreme Court in *Engle v. Vitale* struck down school prayer as a violation of the First Amendment guarantees of freedom of and from religion. That decision seemed to set a precedent. Nearly twenty years later, in referencing the Kentucky case discussed above, the US Supreme Court rendered its decision denying the posting of the Ten Commandments in classrooms because of its plainly religious connotations, giving further support for separating religious items from governmental buildings.

Since then, the new generation of justices on the Supreme Court have reconsidered the topic, permitting religion in the schools on relatively narrow terms such as silent prayer on school grounds, clergy-led prayers at graduation ceremonies, and prayers after football games. No court decisions have welcomed widespread religious activity in educational or public arenas, however—at least to this point.

These days, the movement for Christian prayer in the public school setting is making a comeback. As discussed above, evangelicals argue that religion in state-supported public schools facilitates "truly experience spiritual freedom" and character development. They further claim that without religious education, students are not fulfilled.[45] Evangelicals have had some success in addressing the issue at the state level. In 2023, the Montana state legislature made it legal to begin the school day with a prayer in the classroom. As of 2024, Florida, Louisiana, and Texas allowed schools to bring in religious chaplains for student counseling. While many of these questions have been declared unconstitutional by the US Supreme Court in the past, they are likely to be reconsidered by the current collection of US Supreme Court justices.

Donald Trump is fully on board with the evangelical movement's objective of connecting public education and Christianity. During his presidency, he advocated for school prayer. When he campaigned for a second term in 2024, he wrote on his Truth Social site in caps, "I LOVE THE TEN COMMANDMENTS IN PUBLIC SCHOOLS, PRIVATE SCHOOLS, AND MANY OTHER PLACES, FOR THAT MATTER." In his "Agenda 47: President Trump's Ten Principles for Great Schools Leading to Great Jobs," Trump promised to "fiercely protect the First Amendment right to pray in public schools—and . . . ensure that every American's fundamental to the Free Exercise of Religion does NOT end when you walk into a classroom."[46]

But there's another side to the question. As discussed above, critics of religion in the schools contend that minority faiths are given little attention, if any, rendering them second-class status. They also argue that any teaching of religion should include critical thinking skills that allow students to thoroughly examine theological claims.[47] Without a healthy dialogue on religious propositions, opponents continue, religious instruction imposes a rigor that actually denies students creativity and freedom of thought. Another concern comes from skeptics who rely on science for explanations of human events and conditions. Spirituality and other religious explanations of life, they say, interfere with fact finding.

Clearly, this brief discussion is not about to answer heady questions about the value of religion in our lives. One thing is certain, however: evangelicals who seek to make Christian teachings a cornerstone of the public education experience bring with them the Ten Commandments and teachings along with a series of other tenets that include assessments on marriage and divorce, sexuality, abortion, the role of government, and even an ordering of society by who is religiously observant and who is not. Such instructions and evaluations take us back to the "us" versus "them" belief system, with the "thems" being a religious version of second-class citizens. Given that, religion in the classroom has the potential for creating the framework of society that embraces some members and excludes others. No wonder evangelicals see benefits from religion in the schools.

The Restructured Classroom

Under a second Trump administration, the classroom would most likely undergo radical change as an impartial depository of knowledge and discussion, thanks in part to the lessening of federal oversight. In fact, the transformation has already begun. Along with a flurry of recent legislation on race, gender, and religion, many states have delegated control of the education environment to parents and private organizations, reducing—if not eliminating—the roles of educational experts. For the most part, these "reformers" have little understanding of what goes into a well-rounded secular learning environment and seek to restructure education in line with their own narrow values. Below, we examine book bans, the transfer of pedagogy control, and the crisis of teachers, many of whom have moved on to other careers because of the arduous constraints placed on roles in the public school classroom.

School Book Bans

Book bans in the United States precede the Declaration of Independence. In 1637, the Puritans of Massachusetts colony banned a book challenging old world customs as heretical. Ever since, there have been moments in US history when authors and their books have been banished by some states, usually at political tipping points. During the Civil War era and decades after, several southern states banned books dealing with slavery-related issues. At times, the federal government has been involved with book bans as well. In 1873, Congress passed the Comstock Act, which made it illegal for anyone to possess or mail obscene or immoral books and articles. The reading matter portion of the law was overturned by the US Supreme Court in 1957, although the portion that outlawed the mailing of contraceptives and related material remains on the books to this day.

For the rest of the twentieth century and early years of the twenty-first century, book bans occurred at public libraries at rates between five hundred and eight hundred per year. At various junctures, state officials and local leaders objected to material dealing with sexuality, race, communism, anarchy, satanic rituals, and assorted themes that were considered socially inappropriate. In most cases, controversies came and went with the times.

Book bans at schools and their libraries were also fairly rare until recently, when they emerged as major topics of political discussions and action. The surge has been led largely by evangelicals and conservative antigovernment groups aligned with Trumpism. BookLooks.org, Moms for Liberty, and Citizens Defending Freedom are among the organizational leaders of the contemporary book ban movement. To the casual observer, words like "liberty" and "freedom" may sound innocent enough, but actually they mean "liberty" from controversial themes such as gender, race, and religious beliefs their members see as harmful to a White Christian society. Likewise, evangelicals and conservative antigovernment groups view "freedom" as the right to impose narrow values and doctrines compatible with their beliefs.

Their purging efforts have had some success over time. During the 2021–2 school year, 1,145 book titles were pulled from library shelves. The number of banned books from schools increased to 1,586 during 2022–3, and soared to an astounding 4,240 during the 2023–4 academic year.[48] Although book bans occurred in forty-two states between 2021 and December 31, 2023, a few states stood out as leaders of the movement, namely Florida (3,135), Wisconsin (481), Iowa (142), Texas (141), and Kentucky (100+). The largest areas of dispute focused on sexuality and LGBTQ+ issues, race, and religion.

Part of the confusion associated with the book banning movement is that it has been demanded by a relatively few protesters. As a case in point, a *Washington Post* examination in 2023 found that of one thousand book challenges, eleven people filed most of the complaints.[49] The small number of activists have given the impression that the undertaking has had much more citizen involvement than has actually taken place. Still, according to PEN America, more than ten thousand books were banned throughout the United States in classrooms and school libraries between 2021 and 2024.[50] But there's a collective institutional defensive response to the book banning issue as well. Anticipating public anger, as many as 41 percent of the book removals in libraries and public schools have resulted from directives originally brought by elected officials or school administrators—a preemption of sorts designed to avoid contentious public debates and government investigations.

State and local policies for school book bans have been anything but consistent, in part because of vaguely worded state laws that cause discomfort for teachers and principals trying to follow them. Generally speaking, someone challenging a book is supposed to read it and write the exact issue of concern either to the school principal or the board of education. If there is a challenge as to a book's worthiness at a school, state or district officials must then determine whether to remove certain passages, make it available to appropriate grade levels only, or keep the book off the shelf altogether.

Beyond these general rules, the outcomes of these confrontations vary greatly.[51] Some public school district officials pull books after a challenge regardless of its merits, often against the wishes of teachers. Other administrators remove books without reading them just to avoid any potential conflict with accusers. In fact, the only common theme with book challenges is that the districts want to dispense with the problem as soon as possible lest they face the wrath of local boards of education or members of the community. So contagious is the book ban frenzy that in many states, advocates don't even have to live in the school district or have any students in schools to make their claims!

Book ban opponents in schools argue that the prohibition efforts are little more than draconian attempts to keep children from controversies that are reflected in American society today. Studies show that rejected young children's books often include character combinations of diverse races; rejected young adult books frequently have LGBTQ elements. Researchers have also found that the majority of rejected books were written by people of color or women, often offering points of view that differ from those of White males.[52]

Many of the books banned from public schools have won national and international awards. A few examples and their "objectionable" content: Alice Walker's *The Color Purple* (explicit sexuality and drug use); George Orwell's *Animal Farm* (political theories); Harper Lee's *To Kill a Mockingbird* (race); John Steinbeck's *The Grapes of Wrath* (profanity and sexuality); William Faulkner's *The Sound and the Fury* (obscenity); and William Golding's *Lord of the Flies* (racism, misogyny, and sexuality). Clearly, book bans focus disproportionately on themes dealing with the "thems" in American society—the same "thems" that the Trumpists need to motivate the "us" groups as part of their effort to restructure the composition of American society.

The Costs of Censorship

Widespread censorship and other revisionist changes in public education policy have taken a toll on America's K–12 teachers.[53] These efforts to control the educational narrative have also denied students a full understanding of reality in a multifaceted society. A Pew Research Center national survey of teachers in 2024 found that most were dissatisfied with their profession; in fact, many have reached career tipping points. Some of the results: 77 percent described their job as frequently stressful, 68 percent said the pressure was overwhelming, 70 percent commented that their school was understaffed, and 52 percent stated bluntly that they would not advise a young person starting out to become a teacher.

In today's banned book environment, many teachers now labor figuratively with one hand tied behind their backs. More than ever, they don't know what or how to teach key subjects that they were otherwise trained in. In a major survey by Rand Research of teachers in seventeen states impacted by restrictive policies on race, gender, and "divisive" subjects, more than a quarter have become bewildered on how to (or not to) teach those issues. More than one-third felt limited by either the state, school district, or both with respect to the material they could choose for instruction. Teachers of color were even more confused; 41 percent felt uncertain of what to teach and how.[54] In the words of one educator, "We were told not to teach critical race theory—no one was. The past two years have made me nervous about teaching Frederick Douglass (a famous leader of the abolitionist movement) because I don't think people in my community know the difference between teaching [Black] history and teaching critical race theory."[55] He wasn't alone. In the Rand Research survey, about one out of five teachers "reported that they avoided or were now more hesitant and less willing to engage in controversial topics with students."[56]

Because of endless pressures from elected officials, low teacher morale has become pervasive in public education. In a 2023 survey of 1,500 educators, 71 percent viewed book banning as undermining their expertise and saddled with community distrust.[57] These were not happy campers.

In addition to the impacts of book banning on educators, there is also the impact on students. In a national survey, 41 percent of educators see censorship and other pressures having a deleterious effect not only on students, but also on what they learn.[58] Responding to the book ban crusade in Florida, one school librarian noted, "If the broad aim of education is to prepare students to become citizens in a pluralistic, often contentious society, trying to maintain this difficult balance can be stultifying."[59]

The public has weighed in on the book ban issue as well. A national poll by NPR/Ipsos in 2023 found 65 percent of Americans opposed to school book bans by school boards, compared with 21 percent who supported them. On the question of whether state lawmakers should ban books, 69 percent of the respondents were in opposition, compared with 17 percent who offered support.[60] Simply put, there is little public support for the issue, yet like so many issues in these times, a small minority has intimidated a sizable majority.

Then there's the impact on what students experience in their own lives. With so many social and cultural topics off the educational table, students—particularly those at risk—are denied the ability to express themselves on particularly sensitive issues as well as understand the issues of others. As sociologist Alyssa Lyons notes, "Banned books can inform students' beliefs on how gender and sexuality work (or doesn't); whether (and how) White supremacy and how anti-Black racism impacts people's lives, identities and material realities; or even help students establish baseline knowledge about lives different from their own."[61] Whether their own circumstances or the experiences of others, students shielded from reality are prevented from fully understanding their own concerns as well as the world around them. Moreover, ignorance of the harm from systemic discrimination allows students to maintain their own prejudices, thereby perpetuating the "us" versus "thems" hierarchy in American society.

But there's more, for research shows that ignorance breeds hate. In 2024, *The Washington Post* released the results of student hate crimes between 2015 and 2022. While hate crimes went up everywhere, there emerged a stark difference between states that prevented discussion of controversial social issues and those that did not. In twenty-eight states with laws curbing transgender student rights and restricting teachers from discussing gender issues, hate crimes increased at twice the rate over those states without restrictions.[62] The US Department of Justice discovered similar data about hate crimes on school campuses. According to its findings, hate crimes more than doubled in K–12 schools between 2018 (392 incidents) to 2022 (890 incidents). In order from most to least, hate crime offenses occurred against Blacks, Jews, and lesbian/gay/bisexual/transgender categories.[63] Meanwhile, during the same period nationwide, hate crimes went up 56 percent. Schools are a hotbed for hate crimes, compared to the nation. To the extent that teachers are prevented from discussing these issues, public schools are breeding grounds for these offences.[64]

Teachers on the Run

In the United States, the public education profession is troubled by teacher shortages. The numbers of teachers across the nation dwindled from 3.8 million in 2020 to 3.2 million in 2024 as the population of K–12 students grew. Much of the problem centers on the decreasing attractiveness of the vocation. A study produced in November 2022 found that interest in the teaching profession by high school and college freshmen fell by 38 percent from the level of interest in 2010; not surprisingly, the number of students entering the profession dropped by a third over the same period.[65]

It would be an oversimplification to attribute this decline to any one source; in fact, there are many factors for the growing disinterest, including working conditions, heavy workloads, burnout, financial compensation, and even the dislocations from the COVID-19 pandemic to name a few. However, it would be disingenuous to not include a relatively new cause of teacher disinterest, namely restrictions against teaching about topics such as race and gender issues and the fears of punishment or reprisals. A *Washington Post* analysis in 2022 found that 160 teachers lost their jobs as a result of what has become known as "the culture war."[66] But that statistic is only the tip of the culture war iceberg. A 2023 study by Rand Research discovered that 5 percent of the school districts throughout the nation disciplined teachers for "violating" policies that restrict dialogue about race, gender, or sexuality issues in the classroom since the 2020–1 academic year.[67] More to the point, the message has reached its targets. In the same Rand national study, one-third of the teachers reported that state restrictions against instruction of race- or gender-related topics influenced their selection of curricula and instruction.[68]

Teachers in Florida represent a massive example of a public education system turned upside down. In what has become the epicenter of the school culture war, Governor Ron DeSantis and the state legislature passed a series of laws and regulations that criminalized classroom discussions on race, gender identity, and historical events that allegedly make White students feel guilty or suffer from any other psychological angst. One new law, HB 1467, requires every Florida school to publicly publish every book in the school's library and allows *anyone* living in the county to file an objection.[69]

Given an unbearable working environment, Florida teachers took flight *en masse*. In 2019, when DeSantis assumed the state's highest elected office, K–12 public schools had 2,217 teacher vacancies. By 2023, Florida had almost seven thousand unfilled teaching positions.[70]

Overcoming Trumpism

Curriculum restrictions coupled with the threat of discipline or termination have changed the K–12 education landscape in Florida as well as sizable portions of the nation. Those are difficult conditions for anyone to bear. In the end, of course, it's the students who suffer from narrow-minded policies.

Redefining "Public" in Public Education: A Trumpist Weapon for the Future

Education is fuel for knowledge, and knowledge gives us the ability to think and make decisions about life. If our education regarding controversial social issues is incomplete, denied, or filled with inaccuracies and misinformation, our life experiences may well be molded accordingly by untruths and misperceptions. Such a chain of events must be stopped before it gains too much strength.

That's what we face in the United States today: an education system where large portions of American youth are intentionally prevented from learning the truth about history, society, and in some situations, themselves, as well as vital information about today's issues, problems, and circumstances. This approach to gaining knowledge and the ability to think is closer to political indoctrination than public education. It's merely the fictitious reflection of what the privileged "us" segment wants the "thems" to believe as reality. Under these conditions, public education is anything but an access point for the marketplace of ideas and guarantor of democracy.

The value of the preceding discussion extends well beyond Donald Trump and his minions. It points to the potential of long-term implications for American society where the truth for many will be dictated by the fears, denials, and prejudices of the few. If today's students are programmed thoroughly with Trumpist values, they may well become adults all too willing to accept the bigoted conditions designed by Trumpist leaders. That compliance is an essential element in an authoritarian society. It's particularly important for Trumpists who look to White Christian males to protect and pursue their version of American "democracy," which is likely to be anything but. It's equally tragic for various racial, religious, ethnic, gender minorities who don't fit in with the American stereotype defined by the majority.

The extent to which Trumpist values dominate the public education enterprise reveals the hypocrisy of how Trumpists really feel about government. It's worthwhile remembering that Trumpists eschew the idea of the federal government interfering with public education, particularly with respect to guarantees and protections for minorities. Yet, they are all too willing to use the federal government for their own purposes to keep states from what they see as harmful policies. Trumpists are also willing to accept the role of state governments restructuring the educational environment along narrow parochial lines as long as their policies comport with insular Trumpist values. And that's the point. Trumpism is not necessarily a movement to reduce the size and power of the federal government. Rather, it's a movement to impose narrow values on national and state populations.

The restructuring of public education in a manner consonant with profoundly authoritarian hues is harmful to basic liberal education values as well as several populations of American society. It is a draconian threat to the general welfare of our democracy and must be stopped.

NOTES

1 William E. Hudson, *American Democracy in Peril*, 9th edition (Thousand Oaks, CA: Sage, 2021), p. 315.
2 Suzanne Mettler and Robert C. Lieberman, *Four Threats: The Recurring Crises of American Democracy* (New York: St. Martin's Press, 2020), p. 19.
3 Richard D. Brown, *The Strength of a People: The Idea of an Informed Citizenry in America, 1650–1870* (Chapel Hill, NC: University of North Carolina Press, 1986), p. 113.
4 John Dewey, *Democracy and Education* (Middlesex England: Echo Library, [1916] 2007), p. 74.
5 Alexis de Toqueville, *Democracy in America*, translation by Gerald E. Bevan (London, England: Penguin Books, [1840] 2003), p. 74.
6 See Erwin Chemerinsky, "The Segregation and Resegregation of American Public Education: The Courts' Role," *North Carolina Law Review*, 81 (2003), pp. 1597–622, https://scholarship.law.duke.edu/faculty_scholarship/805.
7 The decision was *Loper Bright Enterprises v. Raimondo* (2024).
8 The case was *Stone v. Graham* (1980).
9 "Appeals Court Blocks Louisiana Law Requiring Public Schools to Display Ten Commandments," CBS News, June 20, 2025, https://www.cbsnews.com/news/louisiana-law-schools-ten-commandments-court/.
10 "Why Isn't My Kid Learning about Climate Change in Their High School Classroom?" Ask MIT Climate, July 6, 2022, https://climate.mit.edu/ask-mit/why-isnt-my-kid-learning-about-climate-change-their-high-school-classroom.
11 "Trump's First Full Education Budget: Deep Cuts to Public School Programs in Pursuit of School Choice," *The Washington Post*, May 17, 2017, https://www.washingtonpost.com/local/education/trumps-first-full-educat

ion-budget-deep-cuts-to-public-school-programs-in-pursuit-of-school-cho ice/2017/05/17/2a25a2cc-3a41-11e7-8854-21f359183e8c_story.html.

12 "President Trump's Plan to Save American Education and Give Power Back to Parents," Donald J. Trump for President, July 24, 2024, https://www.donaldjtr ump.com/news/da7f3c42-76b5-42c0-9beb-475d649030ae.

13 Quoted in "Here's Where Trump and Harris Stand on 6 Education Issues," NPR, September 8, 2024, https://www.npr.org/2024/09/08/nx-s1-5103698/trump-harris-election-platforms-education-views.

14 "Trump Drives the Education Debate with Big, Contradictory Ideas," *The Washington Post*, October 10, 2024, https://www.washingtonpost.com/educat ion/2024/10/10/trump-harris-education-platforms/.

15 *Project 2025: Mandate for Leadership* (Washington, DC: The Heritage Foundation, 2023), p. 319, https://static.project2025.org/2025_Mandat eForLeadership_FULL.pdf?fbclid=IwY2xjawEqWWBleHRuA2FlbQIxM AABHWQh7jBYxHZvK29QmmF2sHg3O2CSDiBbM7-sBKAZcrQLHcB-kZKabZmiQg_aem_mCnntRyZGgc3iYEyk_RDsg.

16 "4 Benefits to Religious Educational Programs (Gradeschool to College)," The Corelink Solution, https://thecorelinksolution.com/4-benefits-to-religious-educational-programs/.

17 The examples in this paragraph come from "Which States Are Restricting, or Requiring, Lessons on Race, Sex and Gender," *The Washington Post*, June 13, 2024, https://www.washingtonpost.com/education/2024/education-laws-sta tes-teaching-race-gender-sex/.

18 "DeSantis Takes on Florida's Education Establishment, and Builds His Brand," *The New York Times*, February 1, 2023, https://www.nytimes.com/2023/01/31/ us/governor-desantis-higher-education-chris-rufo.html.

19 "DeSantis Doubles Down on Claim That Some Blacks Benefited from Slavery," *The Washington Post*, July 22, 2023, https://www.washingtonpost.com/polit ics/2023/07/22/desantis-slavery-curriculum/.

20 "Most Teachers Think Students Should Learn That the Legacy of Slavery Still Affects Black Americans Today," Pew Research Center, February 12, 2024, https://www.pewresearch.org/social-trends/2024/02/22/race-and-lgbtq-iss ues-in-k-12-schools/st_24-02-22_lgbtq-race-in-schools_00_06-png/.

21 "Teachers Wary of New Laws Limiting Instruction on Race," AP, June 12, 2021, https://apnews.com/article/tn-state-wire-laws-racial-injustice-race-and-ethnic ity-5da643d3fd15e425adbde2b4e0340ad4.

22 See "Anti-'Critical Race Theory' Laws Are Working. Teachers Are Thinking Twice about How They Talk about Race," *Time*, June 30, 2022, https://www. brookings.edu/articles/why-are-states-banning-critical-race-theory/.

23 "Why Are States Banning Critical Race Theory?" Brookings, November 2021, https://www.brookings.edu/articles/why-are-states-banning-critical-race-theory/.

24 "Trump Tells Agencies to End Trainings on 'White Privilege' and 'Critical Race Theory,'" NPR, September 5, 2020, https://www.npr.org/2020/09/05/910053 496/trump-tells-agencies-to-end-trainings-on-white-privilege-and-criti cal-race-theor.

25 See Nikole Hannah-Jones, Caitlin Roper, Ilena Silverman, and Jake Silverstein, eds, *The 1619 Project: A New Origin Story* (New York: Random House, 2024).
26 "Agenda 47: President Trump's Ten Principles for Great Schools Leading to Great Jobs," September 13, 2023, https://www.donaldjtrump.com/agenda47/agenda47-president-trumps-ten-principles-for-great-schools-leading-to-great-jobs.
27 "In Schools, Honest Talk about Racism Can Reduce Discrimination," *Scientific American*, August 19, 2022, https://www.scientificamerican.com/article/in-schools-honest-talk-about-racism-can-reduce-discrimination/.
28 See Executive Order 10925, March 6, 1961, and Executive Order 11246, September 24, 1965.
29 The cases were *Students for Fair Admissions Inc. v. University of North Carolina* and *Students for Fair Admissions Inc. v. President & Fellows of Harvard College*, June 29, 2023.
30 "Trump Admin to Transgender Kids: We Won't Deal with Your Civil Rights Complaints," The Hill, January 6, 2018, https://www.huffpost.com/entry/transgender-office-for-civil-rights_n_5a5688ade4b08a1f624b2144?ncid=engmodushpmg00000004.
31 "Over 30 New LGBTQ Education Laws Are in Effect as Students Go Back to School," NBC News, August 2023, https://www.nbcnews.com/nbc-out/out-politics-and-policy/30-new-lgbtq-education-laws-are-effect-students-go-back-school-rcna101897.
32 "Trans Students Should Be Treated with Dignity, not Outed by Their Schools," ACLU, January 26, 2023, https://www.aclu.org/news/lgbtq-rights/trans-students-should-be-treated-with-dignity-not-outed-by-their-schools.
33 "In States with Laws Targeting LGBTQ Issues, School Hate Crimes Quadrupled," *The Washington Post*, March 13, 2024, https://www.washingtonpost.com/education/2024/03/12/school-lgbtq-hate-crimes-incidents/.
34 See "Fact Sheet: Donald Trump on LGBTQ Issues: Transgender Americans," GLAAD, August 20, 2024, https://glaad.org/fact-sheet-trump-transgender/.
35 Quoted in "American Autocracy: Tracking Trump's Threats to Gender-Affirming Care and the LGBTQ+ Community," *MS Magazine*, May 20, 2024, https://msmagazine.com/2024/05/10/trump-trans-gay-sports-gender-care-usa-democracy/.
36 "Why Anti-Transgender Ads Are Dominating the Airwaves This Election," PBS, November 2, 2024, https://www.pbs.org/newshour/show/why-anti-transgender-political-ads-are-dominating-the-airwaves-this-election.
37 "Protecting Children from Chemical and Surgical Mutilation," Executive Order, January 28, 2025, https://www.whitehouse.gov/presidential-actions/2025/01/protecting-children-from-chemical-and-surgical-mutilation/.
38 "Keeping Men Out of Women's Sports," The White House, February 5, 2025, https://www.whitehouse.gov/presidential-actions/2025/02/keeping-men-out-of-womens-sports/.
39 "Minnesota Sues Trump Administration over Limits on Transgender Athletes," *The New York Times*, April 22, 2025, https://www.nytimes.com/2025/04/22/us/minnesota-trump-transgender-athletes.html.

40 "Increasing Understanding of LGBTQ+ Health Equity Issues," NORC/L.A. Times Poll, January 18–26, 2024, https://www.norc.org/content/dam/norc-org/pdf2024/norc-lgbtq+-health-equity-topline-final.pdf.
41 "Race and LGBTQ Issues in K–12 Schools," Pew Research Center, February 22, 2024, https://www.pewresearch.org/social-trends/2024/02/22/race-and-lgbtq-issues-in-k-12-schools.
42 "70% of Parents Want Better Sex Education for Their Kids," Parents, July 19, 2023, https://www.parents.com/the-state-of-sex-education-today-7497738.
43 "Religious Group Voting and the 2020 Election," Gallup, November 13, 2020, https://news.gallup.com/opinion/polling-matters/324410/religious-group-voting-2020-election.aspx.
44 "Exit Polls from the 2024 Presidential Election," *The Washington Post*, December 2, 2024, https://www.washingtonpost.com/elections/interactive/2024/exit-polls-2024-election/.
45 See Richard A. Baer and James C. Carper, "Spirituality and the Public Schools: An Evangelical Perspective," ascd, 56, no. 4 (December 1988), https://ascd.org/el/articles/spirituality-and-the-public-schools-an-evangelical-perspective.
46 "Agenda 47," September 13, 2023.
47 Annie Laurie Gaylor, "The Dangers of Religious Instruction in Public Schools," *Religion and Politics*, January 7, 2014, https://religionandpolitics.org/2014/01/07/the-dangers-of-religious-instruction-in-public-schools/.
48 See "Today's Book Bans Might Be More Dangerous Than Those from the Past," *The Washington Post*, September 12, 2022, https://www.washingtonpost.com/made-by-history/2022/09/12/todays-book-bans-might-be-more-dangerous-than-those-past/, "The Freedom to Write, PEN America" https://pen.org/report/narrating-the-crisis/, and "Banned and Challenged Books," American Library Association, https://www.ala.org/bbooks/book-ban-data.
49 "Objection to Sexual, LGBTQ Content Propels Spike in Book Challenges," *The Washington Post*, June 9, 2023, https://www.washingtonpost.com/education/2023/05/23/lgbtq-book-ban-challengers/.
50 "New Report Finds Unprecedented Surge in School Books Bans," PEN America, April 16, 2024, https://pen.org/press-release/new-report-find-unprecedented-surge-in-school-books-bans/.
51 "Banned in the USA: Rising School Book Bans Threaten Free Expression and Students' First Amendment Rights," PEN.org, April 2022, https://pen.org/banned-in-the-usa/#what.
52 Marcelo S. O. Goncalves, Isabelle Langrock, Jack LaViolette, and Katie Spoon, "Book Bans in Political Context: Evidence from U.S. Schools," PNAS Nexus, 3, no. 6 (June 2024), https://academic.oup.com/pnasnexus/article/3/6/pgae197/7689238.
53 The data in this paragraph are from "What's It's Like to Be a Teacher in America Today," Pew Research Center, April 4, 2024, https://www.pewresearch.org/social-trends/2024/04/04/whats-it-like-to-be-a-teacher-in-america-today/#:~:text=77%25%20say%20their%20job%20is,today%20to%20become%20a%20teacher.

54 These data come from "Walking on Eggshells—Teachers' Responses to Classroom Limitations on Race- or Gender-Related Topics," Rand Research Report, January 25, 2023, https://www.rand.org/pubs/research_reports/RRA 134-16.html.
55 Ibid.
56 Ibid.
57 "New First Book Study Tackles National Issue of Banned Books," First Book, October 3, 2023, https://firstbook.org/blog/2023/10/03/new-first-book-study-tackles-national-issue-of-banned-books/.
58 "Race and LGBTQ Issues in K–12 Schools," Pew Research Center, February 12, 2024, https://www.pewresearch.org/social-trends/2024/02/22/race-and-lgbtq-issues-in-k-12-schools/.
59 "Teacher Voice: How the Sad Shadow of Book Banning Shuts Down Conversations and Lacerates Librarians," *The Hechinger Report*, September 12, 2022, https://hechingerreport.org/teacher-voice-how-the-sad-shadow-of-book-banning-shuts-down-conversations-and-lacerates-librarians/.
60 "Poll: Americans Say Teachers Are Underpaid, about Half of Republicans Oppose Book Bans," NPR, June 2, 2023, https://www.npr.org/2023/06/02/1177566467/poll-teachers-underpaid-republicans-book-bans.
61 "Book Bans Impact Students' Worldviews," Contexts: Sociology for the Public, April 26, 2023, https://contexts.org/blog/book-bans/.
62 "In States with Laws Targeting LGBTQ Issues, School Hate Crimes Quadrupled," *The Washington Post*, March 13, 2024, https://www.washingtonpost.com/education/2024/03/12/school-lgbtq-hate-crimes-incidents/.
63 "Reported Hate Crime at Schools: 2018–2022," US Department of Justice, January 2024, https://www.justice.gov/hatecrimes/reported-hate-crimes-schools/dl?inline=.
64 See "2018 Hate Crime Statistics Released," US Department of Justice, November 2019, https://www.fbi.gov/news/stories/2018-hate-crime-statistics-released-111219, and "2022 FBI Hate Crime Statistics," US Department of Justice, October 2023, https://www.justice.gov/crs/highlights/2022-hate-crime-statistics.
65 Matthew A. Kraft and Melissa Arnold Lyon, "The Rise and Fall of the Teaching Profession: Prestige, Interest, Preparation, and Satisfaction over the Last Half Century," EdWorkingPaper No. 22-679, Annenberg Institute, Brown University, November 2022, https://edworkingpapers.com/sites/default/files/Kraft%20Lyon%202022%20State%20of%20the%20Teaching%20Profession_0.pdf.
66 "Caught in the Culture Wars, Teachers Are Being Forced from Their Jobs," *The Washington Post*, June 16, 2022, https://www.washingtonpost.com/education/2022/06/16/teacher-resignations-firings-culture-wars/.
67 "Staffing, Budget, Politics and Academic Recovery in Districts," Rand Research, March 14, 2024, https://www.rand.org/pubs/research_reports/RRA 956-19.html.
68 "The Diverging State of Teaching and Learning Two Years into Classroom Limitations on Race and Gender," Rand Research, March 12, 2024, https://www.rand.org/pubs/research_reports/RRA134-22.html.

69 See "House Bill 1467, K–12 Education, School District Responsibilities," Florida Department of Education, June 3, 2022, https://info.fldoe.org/docushare/dsweb/Get/Document-9557/dps-2022-83.pdf.
70 "Florida Educators Face Off with State Officials over a Teacher Shortage," *The Week*, September 7, 2023, https://theweek.com/education/1026335/teacher-shortage-florida.

CHAPTER 8
2024: DONALD TRUMP RETURNS TO THE PRESIDENCY

Donald Trump has had a bizarre political life. He is the only US president ever to be impeached by the House of Representatives twice, although never convicted by the US Senate. After losing a 2020 reelection bid by more than 7 million popular votes, he was indicted by a federal grand jury for attempting to remain in office through inspiring a violent insurrection against the US Capitol by thousands of followers. That rebellion threatened to overturn the legitimate victory of the 2020 presidential election by Joe Biden and caused the nation's most serious constitutional crisis since the Civil War.[1] But there's more, so much more. He was also indicted by a second federal grand jury for intentionally withholding important government documents from the National Archives, held liable by a New York jury for sexual abuse, indicted by a Georgia grand jury for conspiring to overturn the presidential election in Georgia, and convicted by another New York jury on thirty-four felony counts of falsifying business records to keep an affair with a porn star from becoming public.[2]

Despite all of that, shortly after the 2022 midterm elections, Donald Trump announced his candidacy for a second term as president of the United States. Trump didn't just run for another term; he ran to reclaim his status as the paramount political heavy weight of America. After publicly aggrieving nonstop for four years about alleged electoral thievery in the 2020 presidential balloting, he viewed the 2024 presidential rematch as his chance for redemption, to show that his 2020 loss only occurred because it was "rigged." His 2024 victory would verify his claim and his rightful place in history, he emphatically claimed. What's more, he won what many pundits describe as the greatest election comeback in American political history.

Had you had been reading this summary of events in the fiction section at the local library, you would have probably found it beyond unbelievable. How could anyone with such a past win the presidency? Twice? Yet it was all so true, every bit of it.

Overcoming Trumpism

Despite condemnation by his detractors for his role in the January insurrection debacle and the litany of other nauseating activities, Trump began his journey on the road to political redemption with a head of steam. His coalition from 2016 and 2020 was largely intact, and this time his campaign would be run by experienced professionals, not the disorganized rag-tag collection of earlier years. He also had a clear enemy in the name of incumbent Joe Biden, who Trump believed was responsible, at least in part, for rigging the outcome of the 2020 presidential election as well as the series of successive federal and state indictments. Over time, Trump added to his enemies the members of the Select House Committee charged with investigating the insurrection against the Capitol on January 6, 2021.

With that, Trump went about attacking his foes and making his case for another presidential term. Beyond his enemies, he focused on what he described as uncontrolled immigration that brought rising crime to cities increasingly beleaguered by thousands—sometimes tens of thousands—of undocumented immigrants who sucked up precious government resources. To that ugly picture Trump added his condemnation of an economy ravaged by inflation that had eaten away at 20 percent of the nation's purchasing power in a mere four years. Repeatedly, Trump claimed that none of these problems occurred during his presidency and that only he could restore the nation's health, the likes of which transpired during his four years in office. Somehow the chaos that dominated Trump's first term drifted to the back waters of history and was no longer in public memory.

Still, Trump was fighting the trappings of Biden's incumbency, which normally give a compelling advantage to the person in office. Before Trump's loss to Biden in 2020, not since 1992 had a presidential incumbent failed to land a second term, when George H. W. Bush lost to Bill Clinton. But not this time.

Just because four years transpired between Donald Trump's terms of office doesn't mean that Trump changed, or that the country stepped away from Trumpism. Were it not for COVID-19 and Trump's callous mismanagement of it, some experts believe that he would have won the 2020 presidential election.[3] Regardless, his grievances about an allegedly rigged 2020 election were blended into Trump's predictions of the same manipulated outcome in 2024. As with the 2016 and 2020 campaigns, the only way Trump would agree about the election's fairness would be if he won. Meanwhile, Trump allies remained in place and stood fully prepared to fight for their leader in 2024.

2024: Donald Trump Returns to the Presidency

Preparing for Battle

Two months *before* the 2024 presidential election, Trump's legal team had already filed more than ninety lawsuits challenging voting rules and operations in swing states and crucial counties throughout the country. Their vigilance produced more than three times the number Trump lawyers initiated before the 2020 presidential election. The targeted areas of suspicious activities included allegations of corrupt voting machines, illegally registered voters, mailed ballot containers, inflated voter rolls, and poorly protected mail voting procedures.[4]

Many of the lawyers leading the lawsuit barrage were veterans from the 2020 presidential election legal fights where virtually all claims were rejected by state and federal courts. This time, however, they were much better organized and sponsored by well-funded conservative organizations including the Election Integrity Network, America First Legal, the American First Policy Institute, and the Heritage Foundation. They were committed to assuring a Trump victory.

Aside from legal efforts, Trumpists prepared to do battle for a 2024 election victory with his ground game. In voting locations throughout the nation, they planned protests against what they perceived as Democratic election shenanigans. In several instances, alt-right Trump loyalists threatened election workers who might not provide the "right" result on election day.[5] Local chapters of the Proud Boys mobilized throughout the nation in preparation for violence. Many of these same members that had recently been in prison for their participation in the January 6 insurrection were ready to return to battle.[6] Not much of a civics lesson learned there. Other far-right hate groups posted images of armed men ready to fight for a Trump election victory.[7] FBI agents and local police arrested election denialists who promised officials reprisals varying from home hoax calls to assassinations. Some polling sites provided drones, barriers, and even snipers to protect against domestic extremists.[8]

Meanwhile, Democrats had their own problems. On April 25, 2023, eighty-year-old Joe Biden declared what by then everyone expected, but what a small, but growing number of detractors feared: he would seek a second presidential term.[9] Still, Biden's announcement was not without a certain gravitas, given his remarkable record with Congress, especially during the first half of his term. With the legislative branch narrowly controlled by fellow Democrats, Biden had scored major victories on COVID-19 financial assistance, infrastructure repair and expansion, climate change, and domestic microchip manufacturing. National unemployment had dropped to a post–Second World War all-time low, the economy was humming, and the nation enthusiastically endorsed his leadership of a Western military alliance committed to saving Ukraine from brutal Russian aggression. Now in 2024, Biden claimed, it was time to "finish the job,"[10] an intention that seemed to contradict Biden's description of himself in 2020 as a "transition" candidate between generations. Predictably, the party *literati* lined up behind him, although in several national polls most Democratic voters opposed a second term by large margins even before Biden announced his intention.[11]

The rest, as they say, is history, but not the history one might have expected. Biden's campaign focused on the imperatives of preserving democracy from what they described as Trump's authoritarian views. However, over time, Biden himself had problems dealing with an economy that had become shaky particularly because of increasing inflation. He repeatedly talked about record number of jobs, but what good were jobs if salaries couldn't overcome dramatically increased costs of goods and services? Then there was the lingering question of Biden's stamina. Even though only three years separated the two candidates, by 2024, the voters saw vast differences. In a February 2024 national poll, only 23 percent agreed that Biden had the necessary mental and physical stamina to be president, down from 41 percent in October 2020. In the same poll, 46 percent agreed that Trump had the necessary mental and physical acuity for the job, up from 41 percent in October 2020.[12] By comparison, 77-year-old Donald Trump was the youngster in the race!

The question of Biden's well-being was answered in Atlanta on June 27, 2024, during a presidential debate between Biden and Trump. Trump dominated the event with direct attacks on the incumbent's record and, indirectly, his stamina. For his part, Biden appeared flummoxed much of the time with a vacuous stare, often unable to provide coherent statements. In the words of one post-debate analysis "If the debate was the president's [Biden's] best chance to turn around a tight race with Trump, which has him in deep peril of losing reelection, it was a failure."[13] According to a post-debate poll, two-thirds of the 51 million registered voters watching the debate reached the same conclusion.[14]

Suddenly, the Democratic Party was in a severe downward spiral. Within days, once-cautious, often whispered concerns about Biden swelled into public demands from growing numbers of Democratic leaders for Biden to step down—an unprecedented move to say the least. But then again, no one could recall a time in modern history when such a meltdown of a presidential candidate occurred so quickly. Within three weeks the drama regarding Biden's health was over. On July 21, 2024, incumbent Joe Biden announced that he was stepping aside as the Democratic nominee for president.

From that point on, movement in Democratic ranks was swift and determined. Vice President Kamala Harris had been a loyal Biden defender throughout the entire collapse. Immediately, after Biden's announcement, Harris took to the phone, making more than a hundred calls the rest of the day to key Democratic members of Congress, governors, and major campaign contributors, as well as labor and civil rights principals.[15] Harris's masterful attention to the precarious political conditions and concerns among Democratic leaders assured that she would not have major opposition in securing the presidential nomination. Running a successful national presidential campaign in 107 days rather than the usual average of 18 months, however, would be another story.

Beating Back the Ghost of COVID-19

As the 2024 presidential campaign shifted into high gear, most Americans were unhappy with their condition; they wanted change and wanted it badly. A *YouGov* national poll taken during the first days of the year found 63.3 percent of the respondents saying that the United States was headed in the wrong direction. Their mood was prescient of what was to come. Nearly a year later and just days before the November 2024 presidential election, 64.6 percent of the respondents felt the same way.[16] The question was, which vision for repairing their woes would the voters prefer, the one from Trump or Harris? Voting for the status quo never works for a population mired in misery, and for that reason, if no other, Harris would have her hands full.

Enter, or to be more accurate, re-enter Donald Trump, who was once described by a biographer as "too much of a showman to be embarrassed by a single disastrous performance,"[17] in this case, his presidency. He did so by revising historical events almost as quickly as they occurred. In fact, few people rewrite history faster and more convincingly than Trump. Whether it's his repeated false claims of a 2020 presidential election victory or reconstructing the history of his business "successes" in a career that brought bankruptcy to his company at least six times, Trump has made a career of reshaping facts and events to his liking and benefit.

Thus, it was with Trump's presidency once he assumed office after his 2016 election victory, where he stunned favored Democratic opponent

Hillary Clinton. Among Trump's false recreations of the facts during his first term: he rescued the Affordable Care Act (Obamacare) from Congressional termination, prevented thousands of undocumented immigrants in caravans from entering the United States, and forced Mexico to cover all building costs of the wall at the southern border. But these falsehoods were just the tip of the Trump fabrication iceberg.

Research by *The Washington Post* found that during his first presidential administration alone, Donald Trump made more than thirty thousand (that's not a typo) false or misleading statements. But perhaps the most damaging transgression by Trump came with countless statements over his stewardship of COVID-19, where he lied about a series of related topics ranging from the numbers of infected Americans to his prediction of imminent and magical disappearance of the pandemic.[18] Trump rejected criticisms of his management of the medical catastrophe, instead faulting the Centers for Disease Control and Prevention (CDC) for developing defective vaccines that slowed the nation's ability to deal with the pandemic.[19] He further castigated a long list of miscreants, including state governors who were inept or unwilling to deal with the virus; the media for overreacting in their coverage of the pandemic; the Obama administration for poor advance preparation for responding to a pandemic; and, of course, China for not controlling the spread of COVID-19.[20] In Trump's eyes, just about everyone but Trump was at fault for the COVID-19 tragedy.

Undaunted by the national disaster, Trump had campaigned for reelection in 2020 with a nostalgic description focused on the good old days of his presidency when the economy was healthy, inflation was low, immigration was under control, and the nation was without involvement in any serious global conflict. In fairness, those elements were a sizable part of Trump's first presidency. However, their value meant little in the face of the runaway onslaught by the pandemic that would ultimately infect 104 million Americans, while claiming more than 1.1 million American lives. Who knows how many lives would have been saved if Trump had acknowledged reality sooner?

To longtime Trump aid Kellyanne Conway, Trump's interpretation of disastrous events such as the administration's botched handling of COVID-19 weren't lies, but simply his reliance upon "alternative facts;"[21] in other words, convenient distortions of the truth. Former Trump White House Press Secretary Stephanie Grisham put the matter differently when she explained Trump's marching orders to lie in her meetings with reporters about COVID-19 as well as any other matters: "It doesn't matter, Stephanie. Just say it over and over again, [and] people will believe it."[22] Such repositioning of history is often a political weapon of sorts used by fascists who are also anxious to replace unpleasant historical facts with revised accounts that are easier for the public to swallow and more expedient for their own needs.[23] More times than not, the approach worked for Trump in discussion about COVID and other controversies.

Traditionally, the president assumes responsibility for managing national disasters. That's what then-President Harry S Truman meant when he famously said about the office, "The buck stops here." But not President Donald Trump, which is why independent observers viewed his portrayal of the "facts" surrounding the pandemic with alarm. In their biography of the Trump presidency during 2017–21, respected journalists Peter Baker and Susan B. Glasser described Trump's lies about the deadly COVID-19 episode as among the most egregious of his presidency.[24] Apparently, so did the voters, at least at the time. Days before the 2020 presidential election, polls showed that nearly 60 percent of the voters, including 58 percent of independents, disapproved of Trump's management of COVID-19.[25] In the end, Trump may have been the pandemic's most significant political victim in the form of his 2020 reelection defeat.[26] Yet, any lessons from Trump's lies and mismanagement would not be memorable to most voters a mere four years later. But we're getting ahead of the story.

Trump Campaign: Returning to a Winning Formula

By 2024, Trump's persistent lies and revisionist history seemed to work on a public all too anxious to overlook, if not forget, COVID-19. He positioned himself as the "outsider" with no responsibility for his administration's problems that fully matured during the Biden/Harris administration. Self-cleansed of any past misjudgments, Trump went to war initially with Biden, and then Harris after July 21, 2024. Of the many factors that led to Trump's victory, three stand out: his focus on an economy ravaged by inflation, endless complaints against "deep state" bureaucrats and a radical press, and relentless attention to unrestrained immigration that brought out-of-control crime.

The Economy

During the 2024 campaign, Trump boasted of the "good old days" provided by his previous administration, when unemployment was low, inflation remained under control, good manufacturing jobs returned, and illegal immigration was contained. Compared to Biden's record, Trump's claims on jobs and manufacturing were good but hardly standouts; he did have a point on inflation, however, although even that required an asterisk. Given the wild gyrations associated with the COVID-19 pandemic in 2020 and 2021, we'll compare the Trump administration between 2017 and 2019 with Biden's from 2022 through 2024.

With respect to jobs during the first Trump presidency, the nation's unemployment fell from 4.7 to 3.5 percent just before the pandemic. As for Biden, unemployment hovered between 3.5 and 4.2 percent. The point is that, on this issue, both administrations fared well, with Biden having an edge.[27] But what about those manufacturing jobs, which have had a history of leaving the United States over the past several decades due to globalization? During the Trump administration between 2017 and 2019, the American economy added 438,000 manufacturing jobs. During the Biden administration between 2022 and November 2024 (the last official Bureau of Labor Statistics data), the American economy added 349,000 manufacturing jobs.[28] On this comparison, Trump gets the edge.

Last, we examine inflation, a problematic statistic. During the Trump years between 2017 and 2019, inflation rates were 2.1 percent (2017), 1.9 percent (2018), and 2.3 percent (2019). During the Biden years of 2022 through 2024, inflation rates were 6.5 percent (2022), 3.4 percent (2023), and 2.9 percent (2024). Looking at this significant data point, there is a substantial difference between the two administrations, and perhaps a reason why so many voters chose Trump—at least that's what they answered in the exit polls. But there is one major consideration: In the last year of Trump's administration, Congress passed the Coronavirus Aid, Relief, and Economic Security Act (CARES), amounting to $4.8 trillion. During the first year of Biden's administration, Congress also passed the American Rescue Plan, which totaled $2.1 trillion. Combined, these two massive COVID-19 assistance bills amounted to almost 7 trillion dollars.

With much of the economy shut down because of COVID-19, the huge infusion of capital kept Americans afloat for eighteen months until the pandemic abated. Yet, there was an unanticipated consequence as the country began its return to normal. High demand for goods and limited supplies produced a sharp tick upward in inflation—a situation that was neither the fault of Biden nor Trump, for that matter,[29] but one that Trump and the public successfully blamed on Biden's poor management of the economy.

Why Harris and the Democrats didn't explain the relationship between the massive COVID-19 financial infusions and the unfortunate inflation byproduct remains a mystery. In the absence of any Democratic statement, Trump's assessment prevailed. Since Vice President Harris was now running for president in Biden's place, she suffered the consequences.

Neutralizing the "Deep State" Bureaucrats and the Radical Press

Blaming America's problems on the stewards of government and mainstream media has long been part of Trump's condemnation arsenal. This approach to politics is right out of a would-be dictator's handbook. In his *How Fascism Works,* Jason Stanley notes that "Fascist politics seeks to undermine the credibility of institutions that harbor independent voices of dissent,"[30] thereby leaving the public demanding change. And so it has been with Trump, who has spent most of his political life disparaging national institutions as enemies of the people. The idea is to persuade the public that the very foundations of our political system are corrupt and that someone must rescue us from this downward spiral. Only he, Trump would say, is positioned to save us from the evils brought forth by the corrupt bureaucracy and dangerous media. These are notorious elements of what Trump and his allies refer to as the "deep state." Of course, rigged elections are also part of the conspiracy against Trump, for they were managed by enemies within the deep state. How else could he lose an election?

Trump was unyielding in putting major institutions on the defensive. Leaders of the "deep state" must be controlled, if not eliminated, he insisted. Throughout his first term, he attacked judges, generals, the FBI, the CIA, the IRS, the Federal Reserve Board, and the FDA as either incompetent or in cahoots with corrupt "deep state" opponents seeking to prevent him from doing his job. Often, Trump's attacks focused on the very people he hired. Upon their departures from their respective appointments, Trump's harsh public recriminations would usually replace effusive praise he offered at their times of appointment; personnel initially deemed brilliant by Trump were reclassified as dumb, lazy, incompetent, or all of the above, and more.

Trump also liked bringing on temporary department heads instead of permanent appointees so that he could avoid senatorial confirmation. Denied the ability to question nominees as part of the confirmation process, the Senate, part of a coequal branch of government, was hindered in its ability to fully assess and weigh in on Trump's approaches to various policies. Such a tactic allowed Trump to "safely advance his deregulatory goals, weakening government oversight" with diminished congressional oversight, enhancing his own power in the process.[31] Keeping other institutions in disarray gave Trump maximum control of many levers of government, especially in the executive branch.

Then there was the mainstream media. Whether outside of or inside government, Trump often considered the press his biggest problem, chiefly because he could not control the Fourth Estate in the same way he could dominate the executive branch. En route to, during, and after his first term as president, Trump labeled the mainstream press "enemy of the people" who consistently spewed "fake news," which generally translated to information he didn't like. Collectively, Trump complained, reporters and their companies (except Fox) were complicit with, if not fully integrated members of, the "deep state."

At his rallies, Trump routinely badgered reporters covering the political events. He would single out reporters in the crowd, leaving them vulnerable to verbal assaults. Sometimes members of the press were physically attacked by attendees. Trump often refused to take questions at scheduled press conferences from reporters he despised; on other occasions, he wouldn't meet with the press altogether. Here again, Trump's goal was to neutralize what he viewed as a challenge to his authority. Beyond his own damnations, Trump created a political environment generally hostile to the press. In the words of the chief executive of PEN America, a nonprofit organization promoting free expression, "By denigrating journalists so often, [Trump] has degraded respect for what journalists do and the crucial role they play in a democracy."[32]

Trump's hostility toward the press continued throughout the 2024 presidential campaign. The more that reporters described occurrences or situations in ways that Trump deemed potentially harmful to his campaign, the more that Trump attacked his adversaries. Toward the end of the campaign, Trump warned that he would urge the Federal Communications Commission (FCC) to strip away the licenses of television networks that, in his words, defamed him.[33] Given that Trump would be appointing a new chair of the FCC, the warning was not taken lightly. Trump also threatened upon his election to jail reporters who refused to reveal confidential sources to their stories. Soon after he won his second term in 2024, he instructed Senate Republicans to block the proposed PRESS act, a bill designed to protect reporters from divulging confidential sources, even though the bill had passed unanimously in the Republican-led House of Representatives.[34] Senate Republicans jettisoned the proposed legislation.

In his effort to dominate those around him, Trump has diminished the ability of others to question his rule; he routinely singles out and attempts to ostracize anyone who takes him on, whether inside or outside of government. Such behavior, Ruth Ben-Ghiat writes, is the work of a strongman, for whom "politics is always personal."[35] For Trump, the presidency was *his* presidency. It followed, therefore, that the president's appointees would be required to be loyal to him first, and the nation's needs second in that order. The public saw virtue in Trump's strongman concept. In a U.S. News and World Report worldwide survey of public opinion weeks before the 2024 presidential election on whether "My country's leader should have total, unchecked authority," an astounding 57.4 percent of Americans agreed with the statement.[36] Clearly, Trump was on to something. No doubt, some of the public's frustration was due to declining support for the public institutions so often denigrated by Trump.[37]

Immigration

Trump has long made immigration a cornerstone of his "us" versus "them" distinction. The "us" group consists largely of White Christians, the alleged stewards of "our culture" by Trump's account. The "thems" are largely non-White, non-Christians, those who seek to replace "our culture" with theirs, according to Trump. This is an important distinction because Trump really wasn't opposed to immigration as much as he was opposed to immigration by non-Whites and non-Christians. In fact, at his rallies, Trump said he would be content with immigrants from "nice" countries such as Denmark, Norway, or Switzerland, all overwhelmingly White and Protestant.[38] By Trump's own statements, race was the determining factor between desirable and undesirable immigrants.

It's unclear whether Trump's racist bent stirred Americans or was in sync with Americans already moving in that direction. Either way, the synergy was powerful. Data compiled between 2012 and 2016, the year of Trump's first presidential election, showed that White Americans hardened their attitudes toward immigrants and Muslims, perfect scapegoats for Trump's "us" versus "them" dichotomy.[39] There was nothing new about this approach to politics and campaigns. Historically, it's been a focal point of Trump's public persona, served as a foundation of his successful 2016 presidential campaign, and became a staple of his presidency.[40] Trump thought, if menacing talk of the problems caused by immigration worked to garner votes for him in 2016, why not revive the pitch in 2024?

Overcoming Trumpism

Trump blamed Biden, and later Harris, for being soft on illegal immigration. While the number of undocumented people hovered around 11 million for more than a decade, Trump and JD Vance, his Vice Presidential nominee, frequently claimed without proof numbers as high as between 20 million and 25 million. In fact, the number of undocumented migrants grew by about 2.3 million under the Biden administration, largely because of a new humanitarian policy that allowed mostly families to remain in the United States while their claims for asylum were processed.[41] With COVID-19 immigrant restriction rules no longer in place, however, migrant numbers grew largely due to inadequate border staffing. That was the rub. From the earliest days of his administration, Biden repeatedly asked help from Congress to provide more border assistance, chiefly more personnel and judges. None was forthcoming, thanks to a decades-long disagreement between congressional Republicans and Democrats over the appropriate solution.

Still, by 2024, both Republicans and Democrats began to seriously search for a comprehensive agreement on a policy that might curb illegal immigration. After extensive negotiations, a conservative package of immigration bills addressing those questions was about to move through Congress and on to Biden's desk with the leaders of both political parties onboard. Shortly before an important vote on the bill, Trump demanded that conservative Republicans back off a bill that they largely drafted.[42] They did, largely so that Trump could keep illegal immigration front and center on the presidential campaign stage.[43]

With the southern border remaining a controversial topic in 2024, Trump repeatedly condemned immigrants as scum responsible for crime, exhausted government coffers, and unseemly, if not illegal behavior offensive to the United States. It didn't matter that crime rates for undocumented immigrants were lower than for US-born citizens.[44] What mattered were the rare cases of attacks by undocumenteds on US citizens, which played into Trump's claims of danger to "us" imposed by the "thems."

Then, there were the denunciations of race-related cultural cruelties. Who can forget when, Trump Vice Presidential nominee JD Vance, followed by Trump, falsely accused legal Haitian immigrants in Springfield, Ohio, of stealing and eating pets owned by Springfield residents?[45] That bogus claim along with countless similar spurious assertions appeared during the campaign, only to be quickly disproven every time. In fact, Vance later admitted that he "created" (his word) the entire Springfield story just to make the public aware of a problem that didn't exist.[46] Created? Vance's little narrative was simply a self-admitted lie. But just like so many other

Trump-produced racial slurs, there were ugly consequences. Suddenly in Springfield, there was a widespread presence of guns, bomb threats, and racial slurs. Hate groups suddenly appeared seemingly from nowhere. Republican governor Mike DeWine lamented about a changed community: "It's not about Trump talking about pets anymore. Now you have white supremacists declaring a war."[47] Meanwhile, ignoring the facts, Trump pledged to deport the Haitians upon winning reelection even though the vast majority were in the United States legally.[48] Similar unfortunate repercussions took place in other cities, resulting from unfounded claims.

Unlike previous immigration spurts over the nation's history, most of the immigrants to the United States over the past half century have been non-Whites. This did not bode well with the changing mindset of many Americans. A 2024 Gallup poll data found that 56 percent (88 percent Republicans, 28 percent Democrats) agreed that immigration should be decreased; by contrast, 34 percent of the public felt that way in June 2015 approximately when Trump began his first campaign for the presidency.[49] Trump's nonstop haranguing of immigrants paid off.

Given that most of the migrants attempting residence in the United States were non-White, Trump conveniently warned his audiences that Kamala Harris, a woman of color, was one of "them." This time, rather than focus on then-Democratic presidential candidate Barack Obama's birthplace as he did years earlier, Trump's 2024 version centered on how Harris allegedly "turned Black" to get a job.[50] His racial denigration of Harris was just a twist of the same strategy he had used in the past. Repeatedly during the campaign, he mispronounced Harris's name, ridiculed her Jamaican/Indian heritage as non-American, and described her as mentally impaired, to the delight of most rally attendees.[51] Implied was that immigrants are shifty, they'll do anything to get ahead, and you just can't trust them. Trump knew exactly what he was doing. By the campaign's end, immigration, race, and Harris were presented as part of the same problem—a threat to the American way of life.

With Trump leading the charge, the most important issue in the 2024 presidential campaign really wasn't so much about the economy and inflation, but the combination of race and gender. Just two weeks before the 2024 presidential election, You/Gov asked, "Is America Ready to Elect a Black Woman President?" To that, 74 percent answered "yes," while 26 percent replied "no."[52] That meant that one-fourth of the electorate rejected Harris even before voters considered proposed policies, experience, and anything else about Harris related to the campaign. Put it all together, and there was no way Harris could win.

Overcoming Trumpism

The Harris Campaign: From Boom to Bust

With a whirlwind start out of the gate, Kamala Harris began the seemingly impossible. She had 107 days to do what most winning presidential candidates manage over 18 months, or longer: introduce herself to the public, go on an extensive listening tour, test various campaign messages, offer cures of the country's ills, and persuade Americans that she was worthy of their votes. Yes, Harris had effectively sealed the nomination within twenty-four hours of her announcement, thereby sparing the Democrats of an ugly fight most likely at the party's nominating convention in August. But the absence of traditional political vetting through candidate debates and party primaries deprived the voters of learning about her in depth and brought pause for some.

Still, early indications signaled that Harris had a chance to succeed. The first polls seemed to acknowledge that something palpable had occurred. Just before Biden stepped away from the nomination, he was trailing Trump by anywhere between two and five points. But Harris's presence changed the lay of the land. Not only did she start out running even with Trump, but she also had much higher favorability than the controversial former president. At times, Harris actually led Trump in some national polls. More to the point, a sizable swath of the voters who had been committed to Trump now expressed a willingness to consider the merits of a Harris campaign.[53] What seemed impossible at the start of it all began to look doable. But as we all know, looks can be deceiving, and eventually that proved to be the case with the Harris campaign.

Being vice president brings benefits and challenges. The good news is that the vice president has a certain cache that differs from other officeholders and political leaders. She is, as they say, a heartbeat away from the presidency; present at countless meetings and events; and has prominence in those dramatic moments in the US Senate where her vote breaks a tie in generally the weightiest proposed legislation. But there's also a substantial challenge for a sitting vice president to campaign for and win the nation's highest elected office. Since Vice President Martin Van Buren's presidential victory in 1836, only once has that transition been accomplished, when George H. W. Bush won the nation's highest office in 1988. That statistic alone reveals volumes about the challenge for an incumbent vice president.

In touting her experience on the campaign trail, Harris frequently told her audiences how she was "the last person in the room" in moments when Biden was confronted by a tough decision on a crisis. That implied

2024: Donald Trump Returns to the Presidency

Harris was not only a participant in critical discussions, but also that she was particularly valued for her input. Implied was that Harris was part of the decision-making process. Such status may have a positive impact if the president is popular, but Biden was not. In fact, for most of Biden's presidency, he was underwater in terms of public approval. According to data compiled by fivethirtyeight.com, Biden's unpopularity exceeded his popularity from September 2021 through the end of his presidency. On July 21, 2024, when he announced he would not seek a second term, 56 percent of the nation disapproved of Biden's presidential performance, compared with 39 percent who approved.[54] By virtue of her role in Biden's administration, Harris now carried some of that baggage. The question was, how much?

Harris found herself seemingly stuck between a rock and a hard place. On one hand, she defended the Biden/Harris administration for shepherding legislative responses to COVID-19, a threatened environment, renewed innovation, and infrastructure repair, along with the administration's ability to rally European support for defending Ukraine against Russian invasion. On the other hand, Harris frequently positioned herself as a change agent. Repeatedly, at her rallies and in interviews with the press, Harris positioned her candidacy as a timely opportunity to "turn a page" from the past, whereas Trump was portrayed as little more than a repeat of a failed presidency. So, who was she? Biden 2.0 or a change agent? She couldn't be both.

In October 2024, Harris herself seemed to answer the question, at least from the Trump campaign's point of view. When asked in an interview whether she would do anything differently than Biden during his stay in office, she replied, "There's not a thing that comes to mind . . . and I've been part of the decisions that have had the most impact."[55] Whoops! Harris's description of her place in the Biden administration only accentuated the attack that had been coming from the Trump campaign almost since the very day she sealed the Democratic nomination: that Harris and Biden were two peas in the same presidential pod, and that Harris was as responsible as Biden for our border woes, runaway inflation, and a messy foreign war where the United States was pouring billions of dollars into Ukraine with no end in sight.

Harris could never extricate herself from that conundrum. The Trump campaign basically used her own words against the vice president, basically saying that the Harris promise to "turn a page" meant a continuation of failed Biden policies and that Americans deserved better. At a time when the voters cried for change, they perceived Trump as the candidate most likely to provide it. Ironically, Trump's definition of change meant returning to a political version of *status quo ante bellum*—in this case, a return to the policies of the first Trump administration. So, why would the voters take a giant step backward? Perhaps her campaign focused on the wrong themes. Three elements that failed to work out for Harris included the inability to successfully separate her campaign from President Joe Biden, a campaign that relied on democracy and freedom as key themes; the inability to capitalize on the reproductive freedom constituency; and the triple whammy challenge of racism, misogyny, and abortion.

The Democracy and Freedom Theme Goes Flat

Throughout his presidency, Democrats repeatedly accused Donald Trump of a high-handed, bitter, and often inept governing style that trampled democratic norms. Such behavior, they warned, would be even more undemocratic if Trump was elected to a second term. The Harris team had good reason for reaching that conclusion. Hundreds of examples of questionable behavior ranged from Trump accepting Russian dictator Vladmir Putin's denial of interference in the 2016 presidential over the CIA's blunt assessment to offering unproven and dangerous medical remedies for ending the COVID-19 pandemic.[56]

But no Trump-orchestrated commotion was more criticized than Trump's reaction to the 2020 presidential election when he not only claimed it was rigged, but also called for his supporters to convene January 6, 2021, for a march to the Capitol. While Trump did not join them, he exhorted his supporters to "take back our country" from corrupt election officials who stole the election from the American people. Said Trump to his incensed audience toward the end of his hour-long speech, "We fight. We fight like hell. And if you don't fight like hell, you're not going to have a country anymore." And with that urging, thousands of Trump supporters invaded the Capitol to stop Congress from carrying out its Constitutional mandate to confirm the 2020 presidential election result. Out of control, the mob searched out members of Congress with the intent to harm them. Many chanted "Hang [Vice President] Mike Pence" for his unwillingness to stop the confirmation process. More than 140 police were hurt during the unprecedented rampage that lasted more than two hours.

Behind it all was Donald Trump. In a YouGov national poll taken later that day after the failed insurrection, 55 percent of the respondents assigned a "great deal of blame" to Trump for the rebellion, compared with 22 percent who maintained that Trump was "not at all to blame."[57] Subsequently, the

2024: Donald Trump Returns to the Presidency

rash of federal and state indictments against Trump and hundreds of others only added to the one-sided sentiment. That tragedy was the birthplace for the Harris campaign's promise to prevent 2024 opponent Trump from undermining democracy.

As discussed earlier, democracy is much, much more than the outcome of an election campaign. It's a national commitment to a positive relationship between leaders and those whom they govern from offices that they temporarily hold. In a democracy, citizens and their leaders pledge to obey time-honored rules and norms that were present well before any election and remain long after. It's the collective pledge to solve differences peacefully, while living in a framework of toleration and inclusivity. That commitment includes the loser of an election stepping aside to allow a peaceful transition.

In a democracy, the system is designed with checks and balances from other parts of government to keep anyone from acting illegally or unconstitutionally. Most of all, freedom is a cornerstone of democracy. Given the January 6 assault on democracy and the horrific events that followed, the Harris team viewed the call to preserve fundamental freedoms as an election campaign theme that couldn't miss. They were wrong.

It turns out that these days precious few Americans really understand the meaning of democracy. How could they, given the assault emerging from election denial? It follows, if you don't really understand democracy, why would you be concerned with freedom? Even voting, the activity that so many people view as a core element of democracy, doesn't meet with unanimity as a democratic value. Recent data gathered by Pew Research found that 57 percent of American adults regard voting as "a fundamental right," while 42 percent classify the activity as a "privilege that can be limited."[58] That's hardly a mandate.

There's more. Remarkably, a sizable percentage of Americans would just as soon do away with the checks and balances element of democracy as keep it. While nearly nine out of ten Americans say they believe in democracy, more than 40 percent in a recent study prefer a "strong leader who doesn't have to bother with Congress and election," while nearly another fifth would prefer "army rule."[59] If you support freedom and democracy, you don't support a dictator unless you don't really understand the concept.

Perhaps the most dispiriting aspect of the disconnect between so many Americans and democracy is found with the lack of understanding and commitment found in young American adults. In a 2023 national survey of more than four thousand adults between the ages of eighteen and twenty-four, only 4 percent showed high civic knowledge levels on topics such as the intent and design of the US Constitution, the Bill of Rights, and current events. The study found that higher levels of civic knowledge correlated with a greater desire to participate and a deeper understanding of democracy.[60] Likewise, individuals with little civic knowledge had less commitment to democratic norms and values.

With the approach of the 2024 presidential election, the preservation of the democracy theme simply didn't score with the voters. A Gallup poll taken just days before the November 5th election found that the economy drew most concern from voters, 21 percent, followed by immigration (13 percent), and abortion (9 percent).[61] Only a paltry 8 percent of the electorate made preservation of democracy as their most important issue. Democracy was the second most important issue for Democrats at 14 percent, but not nearly enough to overcome concerns about the economy. A related problem for the Democrats came in the form of low enthusiasm. Whereas Trump received 2.5 million more votes in 2024 than in 2020, Harris received 6.8 million fewer votes in 2024 than Biden received in 2020. With little knowledge about democracy and a strong belief by many of a strongman to solve their problems, the election took its course. The voters spoke.

Missed Assessment of the Abortion Constituency

For much of her time as Vice President, Kamala Harris toiled in the backwaters of the Biden administration. Yes, as a woman of color, her selection by Biden as his running mate seemed to inoculate two major components of the Democratic coalition, women and people of color, from temptation to Donald Trump and the Republicans. But did it, and what was she about, anyway?

Harris's tenure as Biden's vice president began with neither a bang nor a whimper, to build on a line from T. S. Eliot, but more like a "whatever." Dutifully, in her role as vice president, over the first two years, she broke a tie twenty-nine times in the Senate where Democrats and Republicans were evenly split. In terms of major responsibilities, Biden appointed Harris to look into and report on the Central America chaos, which had led tens of thousands of frightened people to migrate north to the United States, but the assignment was far from the "border czar" label that Republicans inaccurately tied to Harris through her presidential candidacy.[62] Other than that project and breaking Senate ties, Harris functioned largely as cheerleader for Biden's policies which, though potent, failed to generate public support. A year into his presidency, Biden's popularity was at a dismal 38 percent;

Harris's popularity was even lower at a record 28 percent.[63] Between the never-ending border issue, reported tiffs with her staff, and gaffes in key interviews with the press, Harris just wasn't clicking.

Then came *Dobbs v. Jackson Women's Health*, the 2022 US Supreme Court decision, where a majority of justices overturned *Roe v. Wade*, a nearly fifty-year-old precedent that had established the constitutional right of women to have abortions. Reaction to the *Dobbs* case was swift and loud. Within days, the Pew Research Center released a poll showing disapproval of the Supreme Court decision, 57 to 41 percent; among women, disapproval outdistanced approval 62 to 36 percent.[64] A year later, survey data showed even more opposition to the *Dobbs* decision.[65] Clearly, the question of a woman's control of her body was an issue that was not about to go away. More significantly, studies revealed that during the 2022 midterm congressional elections, large numbers of voters favoring abortion rights shifted from Republican candidates to Democratic candidates, turning preelection projections of a massive red wave to a red trickle. With the huge negative reaction to the Dobbs decision, the Democrats were in business. So was Harris.

Political fallout from the *Dobbs* case gave Kamala Harris a voice far more explosive and determined than before the decision. Always an advocate for a woman's right to choose, the Vice President could now speak on the abortion issue with clarity, commitment, and a bit of outrage. Explained then-Emily's List President (and later, briefly US Senator) Laphonza Butler, Harris "helped the country to have a national conversation and come to a clear consensus on where we stand as a nation [and] on who should be making these decisions."[66] From that point on, Harris became the Biden/Harris administration spokesperson on a woman's right to choose and related issues. Her newfound voice was a relief to Biden, who as a devout Catholic, was all too happy to stay in the background on the issue.

Fast forward to July 21, 2024, when Harris quickly all but secured the Democratic Party presidential nomination after Biden stepped aside. Throughout the campaign, Harris spoke forcefully on the abortion issue to receptive crowds. Yes, she campaigned on a litany of other issues, including the economy, inflation, healthcare, public education, climate change, taxes, Israel/Gaza, and Ukraine. But nothing excited her rally audiences with greater passion and enthusiasm than Harris on abortion. She frequently promised to take on the issue immediately upon assuming the presidency—a promise she would never be able to keep.

Democrats viewed the abortion issue as their potential political slingshot to a 2024 presidential victory. They were cautiously optimistic and had reason to be so. After all, they thought, the post-*Dobbs* 2022 congressional election results served as a powerful undercard of the main event that would take place in the form of the 2024 presidential election. The Democrats were further encouraged after the *Dobbs* decision in 2022 and 2023, when seven states including conservative voters in Kansas and Ohio passed voter-initiated pro-abortion laws. In addition, ten more states would have the abortion issue on the ballot in 2024, which was all the more reason for Democrats to expect a massive turnout benefitting Harris whose candidacy would be on the same ticket. Meanwhile, Trump presented a stark contrast, given that a few months earlier he—as a resident—voted for a new Florida law that limited a woman's abortion to the first six weeks of pregnancy.

Preelection polls showed huge gender gaps of as much as 25 percent, with a sizable percentage of men voting for Trump, offset by an even larger percentage of women voting for Harris. This offered more hope for the Haris campaign. Because there were more female voters than male voters, and because females were more likely to vote than males, Democratic leaders believed that the abortion issue could be *the* factor that made the difference between winning and losing the election.

But it wasn't to be so. As the election approached, a swath of otherwise torn prochoice Republicans opted to solve the conflict by voting for Trump. For example, seven of the ten states where the abortion carried on the ballot—including the swing states of Arizona and Nevada—voted for Trump. The point was underscored by a study of voters in Arizona, Missouri, and Nevada, which found that about three in ten prochoice voters supported Trump.[67] Even though Harris was the issue's champion and Trump voted for a six-week abortion ban in Florida earlier in the year, sizable numbers of abortion rights voters went with Trump. Simply put, the abortion controversy didn't carry the same sway in 2024 as it did in 2022 or even 2023. The issue that Democratic strategists expected to carry their nominee over the top fell flat, and the huge gender gap found in polls throughout the fall fell back to a ten-point difference that had existed for the past several presidential elections.

Racism, Misogyny, and Abortion: The Missing Pieces?

Long before the 2024 presidential election, the issues of racism and misogyny were staples in American culture. Yet, when voters were asked about the

2024: Donald Trump Returns to the Presidency

most important issues, those concerns were never on the list. How could they be, given their controversy and the reluctance of people to discuss them as part of the nation's political backdrop? Yet the question lingered: could it be that some voter reasons for choosing Trump over Harris were not so much about the economy or inflation as the Trump voters often said, and more about racism and misogyny?

It may well have been the case for some, but not others. Voters chose African American Barack Obama for the presidency in 2008 and 2012. Hillary Clinton won the popular election against Trump in 2016, by 2.5 million votes, although she failed to garner enough electoral votes to win. But a female and person of color was a first. Could that combination be enough to put the kibosh on the Harris candidacy?

The results of the YouGov poll discussed earlier bring the issue into focus. Recall that one-fourth of the respondents in a national poll said that America wasn't ready to elect a Black woman president. Still, we have never seen voter data based on those public opinion results. And why would we, given that people often are not willing to share what some would see as prejudices? The abortion issue, however, may give us a clue.

Could it be that race and gender were sufficiently worrisome for Whites to cast their votes for Trump? We can't say for sure, but it does appear that voter defections of White pro-abortion voters cost Democrats dearly in the 2024 presidential election. When we compare the abortion issue with the Harris vote by race, 60 percent of Whites were prochoice, but only 43 percent of Whites voted for Harris. That's a significant drop off. Meanwhile, 59 percent of Latinos were prochoice, with 53 percent of Latinos voting for Harris, showing little change. Among African Americans, 73 percent of African Americans were prochoice, with 86 percent of African Americans voting for Harris.[68] Combine race, the issue of choice, and the vote, and it appears that prochoice Whites were the biggest drop off from Harris.

This is not to say that the defection of prochoice Whites alone cost Harris the election. In terms of the total vote, 4.2 million fewer people participated in 2024. But the drop off was far from evenly distributed with Trump increasing his vote by 2.5 million over 2020 and Harris losing 6.8 million from Biden's vote that year. In addition, no doubt some voters were more concerned with questions like inflation or taxes more than anything else irrespective of the abortion question. Nevertheless, given what we know, in a close election, the race/gender/abortion connection may well have made the difference.

Overcoming Trumpism

To the Victor Goes the Nation

Rarely does any one event or fact decide the outcome of an election, especially a presidential election that is filled with too many variables to count. But we do know this: judging from the vote tabulations, Trump didn't win the 2024 presidential election as much as Harris lost it. Coupled with a narrow three-seat victory in the House of Representatives and a comfortable 53-to-47 margin in the US Senate, Republican Donald Trump emerged from the election with a president's dream—his political party's control of both chambers of the Congress. Trump immediately claimed that the voters had given him a huge mandate, even though the numbers indicated otherwise.[69] Nevertheless, he would now be the beneficiary of a political trifecta—Republican control of the presidency, House of Representatives, and the US Senate. Incredibly, after overcoming one daunting obstacle after another, Donald Trump stared at a political obstacle course with no obstacles in sight. And he was more than ready to seize the moment.

NOTES

1   The January 6 Select Committee, *The January 6th Report: Findings from the Select Committee to Investigate the January 6th Attack on the United States Capitol* (New York: Random House, 2023).
2   "How Donald Trump Got Convicted at His Hush Money Trial," Reuters, May 30, 2024, https://www.reuters.com/legal/how-donald-trump-got-convicted-his-hush-money-trial-2024-05-30/.
3   See Marcus Noland and Eva Yiwen Zhang, "COVID-19 and the 2020 US Presidential Election," Working Paper, Peterson Institute for International Economics, March 2021, https://www.piie.com/sites/default/files/documents/wp21-3.pdf.
4   "Trump Allies Bombard the Courts, Setting State for Post-Election Fight," *The New York Times*, September 29, 2024, https://www.nytimes.com/2024/09/29/us/politics/trump-2024-presidential-campaign-election-lawsuits.html.
5   "With Armed Guards, Drones, Poll Workers Brace for Deniers," *The Wall Street Journal*, October 22, 2024, https://www.wsj.com/public/resources/documents/dHjlwwb9QHyQiq8KqYcK-WSJNewsPaper-10-22-2024.pdf.
6   "The Proud Boys Have Regrouped and Are Signaling Election Plans," *The Wall Street Journal*, November 4, 2024, https://www.wsj.com/politics/national-security/the-proud-boys-have-regrouped-and-are-signaling-election-plans-de7a1f45.
7   "On Telegram, a Violent Preview of What May Unfold on Election Day and After," *The New York Times*, November 6, 2024, https://www.nytimes.com/2024/11/04/technology/telegram-right-wing-groups-election.html.

8. "Election Officials Face Torrent of Threats as Nov. 5 Looms," *The New York Times*, https://www.nytimes.com/2024/10/25/us/politics/election-officials-workers-threats.html.
9. "Biden Campaign Works to Ease Democratic Anxiety over Reelection Chances," *The Washington Post*, November 19, 2023, https://www.washingtonpost.com/politics/2023/11/19/biden-campaign-democrats-anxiety-trump/.
10. See "Biden Dives Back in, Announces Reelection Bid," Politico, April 25, 2023, https://www.politico.com/news/2023/04/25/biden-reelection-00093662.
11. For example, see "Most People Think Biden Should Not Run for Office," AP-NORC Poll, January 26–30, 2023, https://apnorc.org/projects/most-people-think-biden-should-not-run-for-reelection-in-2024/.
12. "Biden's Age and Fitness Top the List of Voters' Concern, Poll Finds," NBC News, February 6, 2024, https://www.nbcnews.com/politics/2024-election/bidens-age-fitness-top-list-voters-concerns-poll-finds-rcna137212.
13. "Biden's Disastrous Debate Pitches His Reelection Bid into Crisis," CNN, June 28, 2024, https://www.cnn.com/2024/06/28/politics/biden-trump-presidential-debate-analysis/index.html.
14. "CNN Flash Poll: Majority of Debate Watchers Say Trump Outperformed Biden," CNN, June 28, 2024, https://www.cnn.com/2024/06/28/politics/debate-poll-cnn-trump-biden/index.html.
15. "Kamala Harris on Phone with Biden, 100 Other Democrats as She Makes Her Case to Be Nominee," *Los Angeles Times*, July 22, 2022, https://www.cnn.com/2024/06/28/politics/biden-trump-presidential-debate-analysis/index.html.
16. "Direction of the United States," You/Gov, October 27, 2024, https://today.yougov.com/topics/politics/trackers/direction-of-the-united-states.
17. Wayne Barrett, *Trump: The Deals and the Downfall*, 2nd edition (New York: Regan Arts, 2020), p. 28.
18. "Trump Made 30,573 False or Misleading Claims as President. Nearly Half Came in His Final Year," *The Washington Post*, January 23, 2021, https://www.washingtonpost.com/politics/how-fact-checker-tracked-trump-claims/2021/01/23/ad04b69a-5c1d-11eb-a976-bad6431e03e2_story.html.
19. "Despite Covid 'Amnesia,' the Pandemic Simmers beneath the 2024 Race," *The New York Times*, October 30, 2024, https://www.nytimes.com/2024/10/29/us/politics/trump-harris-covid-rfk-vaccines.html.
20. "Everyone and Everything Trump Has Blamed for His Coronavirus Response," *The Washington Post*, March 31, 2020, https://www.washingtonpost.com/politics/2020/03/31/everyone-everything-trump-has-blamed-his-coronavirus-response/.
21. "Kellyanne Conway's Legacy: 'The Alternative Facts'-ification of the GOP," *The Washington Post*, August 24, 2020, https://www.washingtonpost.com/politics/2020/08/24/kellyanne-conways-legacy-alternative-facts-ification-gop/.
22. Quoted in "Grisham: Trump 'Knows He Can Basically Say Anything and His Base Will Believe,'" The Hill, January 7, 2004, https://thehill.com/homenews/campaign/4394676-grisham-trump-knows-he-can-basically-say-anything-and-his-base-will-believe/.

23 Jason Stanley, *How Fascism Works: The Politics of Us and Them* (New York: Random House, 2020), p. 21.
24 Peter Baker and Susan B. Glasser, *The Divider: Trump in the White House 2017–2021* (New York: Doubleday, 2022), p. 644.
25 See "Democrats Are Increasingly 'Very Worried' about COVID-19," YouGov, October 29, 2020, https://today.yougov.com/politics/articles/32771-democrats-increasingly-very-worried-poll.
26 See John Sides, Chris Tausanovitch, and Lynn Vavreck, *The Bitter End: The 2020 Presidential Campaign and the Challenge to American Democracy* (Princeton, NJ: Princeton University Press, 2022), p. 161.
27 "The Economy under Trump vs. Biden," *The Wall Street Journal*, October 12, 2024, https://www.wsj.com/economy/joe-biden-donald-trump-economy-compared-90d2d0b6.
28 "Databases, Tables, and Calculators by Subject," US Bureau of Labor Statistics, November 23, 2024, https://data.bls.gov/timeseries/CES3000000001, and "U.S. Job Growth Surged in November, Adding 227,000 Jobs," CNN, December 6, 2024, https://www.cnn.com/2024/12/06/economy/us-jobs-report-november-final/index.html.
29 See "Unpacking the Causes of Pandemic-Era Inflation in the US," National Bureau of Economic Research, September 1, 2023, https://www.nber.org/digest/20239/unpacking-causes-pandemic-era-inflation-us.
30 Stanley, *How Fascism Works*, p. 38.
31 "The Clock Is Ticking on President Trump's Temporary Appointments," *The Washington Post*, January 17, 2019, https://www.washingtonpost.com/outlook/2019/01/17/clock-is-ticking-president-trumps-temporary-appointments/.
32 "Trump Has Sown Hatred of the Press for Years. Now Journalists Are under Assault from Police and Protesters Alike," *The Washington Post*, May 30, 2020, https://www.washingtonpost.com/lifestyle/media/trump-has-sown-hatred-of-the-press-for-years-now-journalists-are-under-assault-from-police-and-protesters-alike/2020/05/30/1e6b81ae-a2a3-11ea-81bb-c2f70f01034b_story.html.
33 "Trump Ratchets Up Threats on the Media," *The New York Times*, October 21, 2024, https://www.nytimes.com/2024/10/21/business/media/trump-media-broadcast-licenses.html.
34 "Trump Tells Republicans to 'Kill' Reporter Shield Bill Passed Unanimously by the House," *The New York Times*, November 20, 2024, https://www.nytimes.com/2024/11/20/us/politics/trump-press-act-freedom-reporters.html.
35 Ruth Ben-Ghiat, *Strongmen: Mussolini to the Present* (New York: W.W. Norton, 2021), p. 51.
36 "A Leader with 'Unchecked Authority? Americans Might not Mind," US News and World Report, September 11, 2024, https://www.usnews.com/news/u-s-news-decision-points/articles/2024-09-11/survey-high-american-support-for-authoritarianism-as-trump-harris-clash.
37 See "Americans' Deepening Mistrust of Institutions," Pew, *Trend Magazine*, October 17, 2024, https://www.pewtrusts.org/en/trend/archive/fall-2024/americans-deepening-mistrust-of-institutions.

2024: Donald Trump Returns to the Presidency

38 "Trump Bemoans Lack of Immigrants from Majority-White Countries to the US," *The Guardian*, April 8, 2024, https://www.theguardian.com/us-news/2024/apr/08/trump-immigration-north-europe.

39 John Sides, "Race, Religion, and Immigration in 2016," Democracy Fund Voter Study Group, June 2017, https://www.voterstudygroup.org/publication/race-religion-immigration-2016.

40 See Larry N. Gerston, *Trumpism, Bigotry, and the Threat to American Democracy* (Lanham, MD: Lexington Press), pp. 111–37.

41 "Biden at the Three-Year Mark: The Most Active Immigration Presidency yet Is Mired in Birder Crisis Narrative," Migration Policy Institute, January 12, 2024, https://www.migrationpolicy.org/article/biden-three-immigration-record.

42 "GOP Senators Seethe as Trump Blows up Delicate Immigration Compromise," CNN, January 25, 2024, https://www.cnn.com/2024/01/25/politics/gop-senators-angry-trump-immigration-deal/index.html.

43 "Donald Trump Killed a Bipartisan Border Security Deal to Help His Political Campaign," National Security Action, March 2024, https://nationalsecurityaction.org/messaging-guidance-trump-killed-a-bipartisan-border-security-deal.

44 See "Debunking the Myth of Immigrants and Crime," American Immigration Council, October 17, 2024, https://www.americanimmigrationcouncil.org/research/debunking-myth-immigrants-and-crime.

45 "Trump Repeats Baseless Claim about Haitian Immigrants Eating Pets," BBC, September 15, 2024, https://www.bbc.com/news/articles/c77l28myezko.

46 "JD Vance Admits He Is Willing to 'Create Stories' to Get Media Attention," *The Guardian*, September 15, 2024, https://www.theguardian.com/us-news/2024/sep/15/jd-vance-lies-haitian-immigrants.

47 "'Used as a Pawn:' How the US Election Has Poisoned Springfield, Ohio," *The Guardian*, September 30, 2024, https://www.theguardian.com/us-news/2024/sep/30/springfield-ohio-republicans-haitian-immigrants-lies.

48 "Trump Pledges to Deport Haitians in Ohio City, but Most Are in US Legally," *USA Today*, September 24, 2024, https://www.usatoday.com/story/news/politics/elections/2024/09/14/trump-pledges-to-deport-haitians-in-springfield-ohio/75224212007/.

49 "Sharply More Americans Want to Curb Immigration to U.S.," Gallup Poll, July 12, 2024, https://news.gallup.com/poll/647123/sharply-americans-curb-immigration.aspx.

50 "Donald Trump Falsely Suggests Kamala Harris 'Happened to Turn Black,'" CNN, July 31, 2024, https://www.cnn.com/2024/07/31/politics/donald-trump-kamala-harris-black-nabj/index.html.

51 "Not One of Us: Trump Uses Old Tactic to Sow Suspicion about Harris," *The New York Times*, October 2, 2004.

52 "CBS News Harris–Trump Poll Has Closer Look Inside Gender Gap as Candidates Draw Even," October 28, 2024, CBS News, https://news.gallup.com/poll/647123/sharply-americans-curb-immigration.aspx.

53 "Poll: Presidential Race Hits a Reset with Harris vs. Trump," NPR, July 23, 2024, https://www.npr.org/2024/07/23/nx-s1-5048890/elections-poll-biden-harris-trump.

54 "How Popular/Unpopular Is Joe Biden?" fivethirtyeight.com, November 27, 2024, https://projects.fivethirtyeight.com/biden-approval-rating/.
55 Quoted in "On Differences with Biden, Harris Says, 'Not a Thing That Comes to Mind,'" *The Washington Post*, October 8, 2024, https://www.washingtonpost.com/politics/2024/10/08/harris-biden-differences-view-howard-stern/.
56 For a long list of Trump's violations of norms, see Amy Siskind, "This Is Not Normal," *The Washington Post*, October 16, 2020, https://www.washingtonpost.com/graphics/2020/outlook/siskind-list-trump-norms/.
57 "Most Voters Say the Events at the US Capitol Are a Threat to Democracy," YouGov, January 6, 2021, https://today.yougov.com/politics/articles/33604-US-capitol-trump-poll.
58 "Wide Partisan Divide on Whether Voting Is a Fundamental Right or a Privilege with Responsibilities," Pew Research Center, July 20, 2021, https://www.pewresearch.org/short-reads/2021/07/22/wide-partisan-divide-on-whether-voting-is-a-fundamental-right-or-a-privilege-with-responsibilities/.
59 Lee Drutman, Joe Goldman, and Larry Diamond, "Democracy Maybe: Attitude on Authoritarianism in America," Democracy Fund, June 20, 2020, https://today.yougov.com/politics/articles/33604-US-capitol-trump-poll.
60 "The Civic Outlook of Young Adults in America," Institute for Citizens and Scholars, September 2023, https://citizensandscholars.org/wp-content/uploads/2023/09/Citizens-Scholars-Civic-Outlook-of-Young-Adults-in-America-Executive-Summary.pdf.
61 "Economy, Immigration, Abortion Democracy Driving Voters," Gallup Poll, November 1, 2024, https://news.gallup.com/poll/652970/economy-immigration-abortion-democracy-driving-voters.aspx.
62 "Kamala Harris Dives into Migration Diplomacy as GOP Aims to Make Her the Face of the Border Crisis," *Time*, April 1, 2021, https://www.cnn.com/2021/04/01/politics/kamala-harris-migration-border/index.html.
63 "Gloomy Landscape for Democrats in Midterms as Biden's Approval Drops to 38% in *USA Today*/Suffolk Poll," *USA Today*, November 7, 2024, https://www.usatoday.com/story/news/politics/2021/11/07/biden-approval-falls-38-midterms-loom-usa-today-suffolk-poll/6320098001/.
64 "Majority of Public Disapproves of Supreme Court's Decision to Overturn *Roe v. Wade*," Pew Research Center, July 6, 2022, https://www.pewresearch.org/politics/2022/07/06/majority-of-public-disapproves-of-supreme-courts-decision-to-overturn-roe-v-wade/.
65 See "The Supreme Court Dramatically Changed Public Opinion on Abortion," Politico, June 24, 2023, https://www.politico.com/news/2023/06/24/supreme-court-public-opinion-abortion-00103493.
66 "The Dobbs Decision Made Kamala Harris a Powerful Voice on Abortion. Has It Made a Difference?" *San Francisco Chronicle*, June 30, 2023, https://www.sfchronicle.com/politics/article/kamala-harris-abortion-rights-18167987.php.
67 "They Split the Ticket. Meet the Abortion Rights Voters Who Also Went for Trump," NPR, November 9, 2024, https://www.npr.org/sections/shots-health-news/2024/11/08/nx-s1-5184539/trump-election-abortion-votes-harris.

68 These data come from "Public Opinion on Abortion," Pew Research Center, May 13, 2024, https://www.pewresearch.org/religion/fact-sheet/public-opinion-on-abortion/, and "How Voting Demographics Changed between 2020–2024 Presidential Election," NBC4 Washington, November 6, 2024, https://www.nbcwashington.com/decision-2024/2024-voter-turnout-election-demographics-trump-harris/3762138/.

69 "Trump Claims a 'Massive' Mandate, but Presidents Often Overread Their Victories," NPR, December 16, 2025, https://www.npr.org/2024/12/16/g-s1-38003/trump-mandate-presidents.

CHAPTER 9
TRUMPISM 2.0

For Donald Trump, the 2024 presidential election had its own distinct characterization, compared to his first two efforts. Trump's first victory in 2016 came almost as a complete shock to him. Public bravado notwithstanding, he didn't even have a prepared acceptance speech for his apparent victory on election night but scrambled with aides to put one together the next day when the outcome was clear.

Trump's election defeat in 2020 was devastating to him personally; it pierced his public shield of invincibility. But more to the point, Trump was the victim of his persona on *The Apprentice*, where he would belt out to a hopeful contestant, "you're fired." Trump was tortured by the 2020 presidential election result to the point that he repeatedly denied his loss for the next four years and continues objection to this very day.

The 2024 presidential contest, however, brought Trump neither surprise nor anguish. This time, the amateurism connected with his 2016 campaign staff was gone, as were the public's memories from the debacle coming with Trump's mismanagement of the 2020 COVID-19 pandemic. This time Trump won, exuberant with confidence. He was in charge, and everyone knew it. On January 20, 2025, otherwise known as Inauguration Day, Trump was ready to roll full throttle.

Well before the November 5th presidential election, the Trump team was busy at work, boldly organizing his second term in the nation's highest office. He and his team promised a political revolution of sorts by vastly reducing the federal bureaucracy footprint, purging the nation infested by unwanted immigrants, and organizing the employees of the executive branch in such a way so as to owe their jobs to the president and no one else. Most of all, a second presidential term would enable Trump to finally get even with every single person and office that had made his life miserable from the assortment of indictments, trials, and embarrassing publicity. He would have his retribution.

Trump's team would embrace his revival with relish and determination. As he worked his will, both friends and foes wondered whether America would ever be the same at his term's end. It seemed to nearly everyone connected with the 2024 presidential election that the very future direction of the United States was on the line. The unanswered question was, to what extent would Trump succeed with his bold outline, and relatedly, could he be stopped?

This chapter delves into the many drastic changes planned, and in many cases, executed by Trump and his acolytes. We begin with the controversy surrounding Trump's expanded view of the executive branch. Following that, we turn to the interaction occurring between the Trump presidency and the two other branches of the federal government. Another issue centered on the recurrent tensions between the federal and state governments over key public policies, a sensitive political relationship otherwise known as federalism. Finally, we discuss the frightening question of whether his rule would clearly identify Trump as a living synonym for dictator.

Whatever the initial perceptions, any conclusions about Trump's reign must be tentative, given that his term will not end until January 20, 2029. Issues before the federal courts particularly seem to have lives of their own, confounding administrative deadlines with seemingly endless turning points. Still, within a year or two, we're likely to have a pretty good idea of the country's direction under Trump and its impact upon American democracy.

Wasting No Time Reformulating the Executive Branch

Donald Trump and his loyalists had a governing plan well before settling into the presidency on January 20, 2024. Trump had long insisted that he would overhaul major components of the executive branch, among them the Department of Justice, Department of Homeland Security, the Department of State, the Department of Education, the Department of Veteran Affairs, the Department of Health and Human Services, the IRS, FBI, CIA, and CDC. He also promised to replace merit-based civil service positions with "at will" appointees who could be easily fired if they failed to carry out Trump's objectives.[1] The clear intent was to streamline the executive branch with personnel who were 100 percent loyal to their leader.[2] There would be no room for deviation from the plan.

Most of the changes to the executive branch, Trump claimed, would be in the name of ending the outrageous "weaponization" of government agencies and departments. Various governmental units, he declared falsely, had been dedicated to charging Trump with election interference, orchestrating the insurrection, and related illegalities. Trump's revenge would come from punishing those individuals responsible for these injustices as well as the reorganization of their agencies or departments so that this malicious behavior could never occur again. Not on his watch, anyway. Just as the alleged conspiracy against him had been massive in scope, he promised, so would be the retribution. By the time he began his second term, Trump added fraud and waste among the concerns generating his massive overhaul of the executive branch. Change wasn't so much in the wind as it was in the form of an unprecedented political tornado.

Ironically, given the legitimacy of the various 2020 election-related charges by federal and state agencies against him, it was Trump who weaponized government agencies, not the other way around. That shouldn't have been surprising, given that dictators often charge their enemies with doing what they, the dictators, do. Richard Stanley summarizes such behavior as simply fascist. He writes that "Fascist politicians characteristically decry corruption in the state they seek to take over, which is bizarre, given that fascists themselves are invariably vastly more corrupt than those they seek to supplant or defeat."[3] In other words, the idea is to accuse those whom you criticize of the misdeeds you carry out. That has been Trump's *modus operandi* again and again.

The Impact of Project 2025

Trump's plans and more were meticulously laid out by the candidate's key supporters during the 2024 presidential campaign. Most of the major proposals originated via *Project 2025*, a massive book of nine hundred-plus pages written under the auspices of the Heritage Foundation, a well-funded conservative think tank.[4] The book smacked of Trump's values from cover to cover. More than 140 individuals who had worked in the previous Trump administration authored major portions of the pro-MAGA volume.[5] By one account, twenty-five of the thirty chapters in the book had been written by former Trump officials.[6] Further, many of Trump's top appointed administrative officials during the second term came from *Project 2025* ranks.[7] The connection was unmistakable.

During the 2024 presidential campaign when some of *Project 2025*'s proposals surfaced, Trump maintained he had never heard of the volume. Said Trump in July: "I know nothing about *Project 2025*. I have not seen it,

Overcoming Trumpism

I have no idea who is in charge of it and . . . [I] had nothing to do with it."[8] Nevertheless, the MAGA imprint was unmistakable through the swarm of administrative appointments and executive orders issued by Trump from the first day of his second term and beyond.

Among the first cache of Trump appointments was Russell Vought, the leading architect of *Project 2025*, who Trump appointed to lead the Office of Management and Budget (OMB). This office was key for overseeing all executive branch departments and occupied by Vought during the first Trump presidency. In Vought's view, government employees working in the executive branch should be loyal to the president and nobody else: "Civil servants should be oriented to accomplishing the agenda of the president, not the office of the president, not their institutions, Office of Management [and] Budget, or the EPA or Department of Justice. They should be working for the agenda of a president that gets elected by the voters."[9] Beyond political loyalties, Vought had little use for federal employees, saying at one point, "We want the [federal] bureaucrats to be traumatically affected ... . When they wake up in the morning, we want them to not want to go to work, because they are increasingly viewed as villains. We want their funding to be shut down."[10] Pure and simple, this was the philosophical essence of *Project 2025*. Moreover, it became the basis of the massive political dismissals in executive branch departments once Trump assumed office in January 2025. Civil servants were of little value and easily expendable.

The Expanded Power of the Trump Presidency

Not content to wait for legislation from majorities in both the US Senate and House of Representatives, Trump went to work shrinking the federal government's footprint and purging those employees deemed to be enemies of his administration. During the first month alone, he signed seventy-four executive orders at a rate exceeded only by former president Franklin D. Roosevelt who presided over the Great Depression as well as America's involvement during the Second World War. Of the many disruptive Trump administration commands, elimination of programs focusing on undocumented immigrants; diversity, inclusion, and equity (DEI); ending US Agency for International Development (USAID) programs; and the hollowing out of the federal civil service are four examples worth examining.

Deporting Undocumented Immigrants

For Donald Trump's voters, immigration had become increasingly important. In a national poll of Trump voters taken just before the 2020 presidential election, 61 percent labeled immigration a "very important" issue; in 2024, 82 percent of Trump voters cited immigration as a "very important issue," a sizable jump.[11] Their concern dovetailed well with Trump's anti-immigrant history as a major plank of his campaign platform. Now with a second opportunity to take on this highly toxic topic, Trump went to work, pulling numerous levers of the national government to accomplish his intended result of removing immigrants from the United States.

Trump tackled the immigration issue on two levels: first, preventing entry into the United States, and second, removing undocumenteds living in the United States. The first task would be accomplished by shutting down the border with Mexico and quickly removing those who still managed entry. Almost immediately after taking office in January 2025, Trump issued a presidential proclamation that described illegal immigration as an "invasion" that would require an expanded US military role at the US border. By March 2025, the Trump administration announced that border encounters with would-be unauthorized immigrants dropped by an astounding 95 percent from March 2024 to 7,181 apprehensions.[12]

Deporting undocumented immigrants would be a much thornier problem for Trump. With his second term, he committed to deporting at least 1,000,000 per year, more than triple the 267,000 removals in 2019.[13] Doing so would be extremely difficult for a variety of reasons ranging from greatly increased personnel costs to the lack of cooperation from sanctuary states and cities. Nevertheless, Trump and his team went to work.

Trump found a huge potential group of more than five hundred thousand immigrants from Venezuela, Cuba, Haiti, and Nicaragua, who previously had been accorded Temporary Protected Status (TPS) by the Biden administration. Traditionally, TPS is granted when migrant petitioners submit evidence of suffering from armed conflicts, natural disasters, or extraordinary situations that make it temporarily unsafe for petitioners to return to their country. With approval from the US Supreme Court, the administration began the process of finding and deporting these individuals.[14] But that would take time.

But Trump needed more tools and opportunities to meet his objective. By invoking the Alien Enemies Act of 1798, a rarely used law that allows the president to deport foreigners in wartime, the Immigration and Customs

Enforcement (ICE) agency of the Department of Homeland Security was able to seize and remove suspected immigrant criminals without allowing them "due process" in the courts. The revered Fifth Amendment Constitutional guarantee requires the government to explain why people are in custody and allows the accused to argue their case. Use of the Alien Enemies Act—again with approval from the US Supreme Court—allowed ICE to swiftly remove thousands of "suspected" undocumented criminals. However, even these numbers of deportations would be relatively small.

The key to deportation of massive numbers of undocumenteds emerged with ICE raids throughout the nation usually in communities likely to have immigrant populations. In spring 2025, ICE began "Operation At Large," a sweeping national crackdown of the undocumented population with the goal of detaining and eventually deporting three thousand unauthorized immigrants per day.[15] From factories to immigration court hallways to public schools, ICE agents seized anyone believed to be an undocumented immigrant, regardless of whether they had criminal records. In the words of ICE director Tom Homan, "If you're in the country illegally, you're not off the table."[16] And so began a nationwide sweep of unprecedented proportions. And what about these allegedly vicious foreigners so frequently condemned for their brutality by Trump and his acolytes? A study of more than two hundred thousand undocumented immigrants arrested for deportation found that 93 percent had not been convicted of any violent crimes.[17] So much for the rapists, murderers, and gangsters overriding our country. In fact, they were an insignificant portion of the deportees.

Negative reactions to the increased aggressive stance by ICE slowly percolated. By early June, anti-ICE anger began to boil over. On June 6, a relatively small crowd gathered at the Los Angeles office of ICE to protest the agency's raids in several parts of the city. Some violence and arrests occurred. By the next day, the crowd size increased substantially with more arrests and violence. Even though LA police chief Jim McDonnell described most of the protestors as nonviolent,[18] President Trump ordered two thousand National Guard (later four thousand) members, and along with seven hundred marines, to quell the disturbance. In fact, the federalized troops did nothing other than guard federal buildings; LA police dealt with crowd management. California governor Gavin Newsom accused Trump of intentionally inflaming a manageable situation and called the president an authoritarian, saying "Authoritarian regimes begin by targeting people who are least able to defend themselves. But they did not stop there. Trump and his loyalists thrive on division because it allows them to take more power and exert even more control."[19] Over the next few days, protests occurred throughout the nation. Still unknown was whether the behavior of ICE would lead to more tension in the months to come.

In all, 561 protestors were arrested in Los Angeles with the largest categories of criminality being failure to disperse and curfew violation categories.[20] No one was killed in what President Trump described as a violent riot populated by "animals" and a "foreign enemy."[21]

Public opinion has taken a turn on the Trump administration's treatment of undocumented immigration. Prior to the 2024 election, 54 percent of the voters favored mass deportation of undocumented immigrants.[22] Six months into the second Trump administration and massive ICE raids, only 38 percent supported deporting all illegal immigrants living in the United States to their home country.[23] Clearly, the approach to deportation taken by the Trump administration is now viewed as a major negative, particularly since immigration was Trump's biggest campaign theme. There have been too many examples of innocent people detained, the denial of constitutional rights to those arrested, families broken up, and law-abiding undocumented people seized and deported only for being found at the wrong place at the wrong time. Trump has overplayed his hand.

Doing Away with DEI

Among Trump's earliest targets were all federal curricula dealing with DEI and their employees. Originating in the 1960s, this array of programs focused on sensitivity training and practices relating to promoting racial, cultural, and gender equality as well as the issues of other identity groups. The idea was to extend equal employment and promotion opportunities to those who had been historically underrepresented or victims of discrimination and who may have been unaware of opportunities known to others. Over time, DEI training programs were created to help employees understand different cultures as well as how to discover when diverse identity groups were discriminated against. Moreover, the idea spread. Whereas DEI programs were originally applied to the public sector, many companies in the private sector adopted the approach for their own employees.

National tumult over race and gender has always been a way of diverting attention from other problems, and Donald Trump throughout his career had often weighed in against women and people of color and in favor of White males.[24] For Trump and his allies, DEI was the latest iteration of punishing Whites. They viewed DEI programs as intentionally dividing

American society, contending without evidence that such programs unfairly favored women and racial minorities over others. Trump's translation: White males looking for employment or advancement were disadvantaged, often by those less qualified than they were.

Abolishing DEI programs promised a huge political benefit for Trump. White males had become a core segment of the Trump voter universe,[25] and Trump's focus on the issue during the 2024 campaign was well received by them. Thus, in his executive order, Trump described DEI programs as "illegal" and full of "immense public waste and shameful discrimination" against those who didn't fit into any DEI categories, in other words, White males. He ordered that all DEI instruction and implementation in federal programs cease immediately.[26]

Beyond the federal government, the Trump administration informed government contractors that they would need to certify that they didn't utilize DEI programs, which had been described as "illegal." Failure of the contractors to abide by Trump's executive order would result in a cessation of government work.[27] Most major companies succumbed to Trump's anti-DEI demands. A few, however, did not. Apple, Costco, Coca-Cola, Disney, J.P. Morgan, Marriott, and Proctor and Gamble, emerged among the heroes of the anti-DEI resistance.[28]

But Trump didn't stop there. In April 2025, he ordered the US Department of Education to cease all federal grants to any universities or K–12 schools that employed DEI programs, used DEI as part of the method of hiring their employees, or taught about the concept.[29] Education groups sued on the grounds that the move was unconstitutionally vague and violated First Amendment rights. In three separate cases, they quickly obtained an order requiring the Trump administration to pause any action against the education institution. The Trump administration appealed, with the outcome to be determined.[30]

Nonprofits also suffered from the Trump backlash to DEI. To begin with, nonprofits over the past several years have received between one-quarter and one-third of their funds from the federal government.[31] For most, DEI policies had been part of their DNA, with approximately two-thirds of these entities employing DEI values and standards.[32] Forced with abandoning this core quality as the price for continued support, several sued the Trump administration for violating their free speech. Like so many other disruptive changes brought about by the Trump administration, clear resolution of the issue has awaited final judicial action. Meanwhile, several frightened corporations toed the new Trump line not only internally but also with respect to eliminating or reducing their sponsorships of nonprofits that remained committed to DEI.[33]

It doesn't take a rocket scientist to recognize that Trump's focus on DEI was the latest iteration of his talent for seizing and benefitting from differences in American society. Now, instead of outright bigotry or complaints about losing "our culture," Trump made DEI the nation's bogeyman. His goal, as always, has been to pit elements of society against one another, while personally benefitting from the chaos and animus. DEI personnel affected by Trump's order sued the administration and, as with other controversial Trump executive orders, prepared for a lengthy court battle. In the meantime, both sides of the DEI debate stewed as confusion reigned throughout the nation's education community, the levels of government, businesses, and the nonprofit sector.

Minimizing Foreign Aid

Another Trump executive order struck down a key component of the nation's foreign aid program, long viewed by Trumpists as the source of wasteful government spending. Upon taking office, Trump placed a ninety-day pause on almost all foreign aid, with exceptions for Israel and Egypt.

Among foreign aid programs, the Trump administration all but obliterated the USAID, whose initiatives were popular abroad for often helping the poorest of nations. The agency ran food distribution programs; anti-malaria programs; reproductive health programs; airport exit screenings to guard against virus outbreaks reaching the United States; several medical programs ranging from pregnancy to HIV management; and infrastructure projects in more than 170 countries throughout the world, with particular emphasis in Africa. Recent projects in developing countries included women's health, clean water, landmine clearances in war zones, anti-corruption, and energy security. Those kinds of projects spewed the stench of Marxism, according to Trump ally Elon Musk who wrote on X, "USAID is a criminal organization… . Time for it to die."[34]

To the contrary, USAID had a worldwide reputation for promoting democracy while saving lives. It was the classic example of what Joseph Nye, Jr., defined as "soft power," where the United States used economic, social, and medical assistance for desperate populations to win friendship and loyalties.[35] According to a congressional report prepared during the first Trump administration, USAID supported democracy programs on electoral participation, judicial reform, law enforcement reform, municipal governance, human rights, and the rule of law.[36] Somehow, Trump and his

Republican congressional friends forgot about these attributes between the end of his first administration and the beginning of the second.

Terminating so many USAID projects without any systematic order or review was marked with poor judgment and waste. When the USAID inspector general informed the Trump administration that $500 million in food awaiting distribution could be lost if not immediately delivered, he was fired, along with almost all the agency's ten thousand employees.[37] As with so many other thoughtless program dissolutions, the Trump administration's effort was also placed on hold while lawsuits wended their way through the judicial system. But the damage was done. With US influence throughout Africa largely gone, even if temporarily, it was expected that China would increase its presence in developing countries,[38] thereby undoing years of cultivation of potential allies by the United States. If there was ever an example of the phrase "penny wise and pound foolish," the huge long-term loss of American political clout as a result of ending USAID was it.[39]

Lost in the virtual termination of foreign aid was its relative financial insignificance in terms of its portion of the federal budget. In the most recent fiscal years leading up to Trump's reelection, all US foreign aid totaled $72 billion, approximately 1 percent of the nation's entire federal budget.[40] Budget cutters weren't about to save much there, but then again ending foreign aid had the symbolic effect of telling the world that the United States would no longer be in the business of helping anyone but itself. Given the inward approach of Trump's "America First" agenda, that was just fine.

Opponents of the foreign aid shutdown sued, objecting that the stoppage was unconstitutional. The case went up the three-tier federal judicial adder in a matter of weeks, with the US Supreme Court deciding by a 5-to-4 vote that the issue should be contested in US district court. Challengers to the USAID shutdown were exuberant over their victory, but their joy was short-lived. Trump circumvented closure of the agency by merging it with the State Department, where more than 90 percent of its programs and employees disappeared.[41] Only Congress could stop the change, but there was little appetite for such from the Republican majority. For all intents and purposes, USAID suffered an ignominious death. Worst of all, innocent former international recipients paid the price.

Dismembering Federal Employment

Claiming without any evidence that the federal civil service was bloated, on January 29, 2025, Trump's Office of Personnel Management emailed a memorandum offering buyouts to almost all federal employees, with a February 6, 2025, deadline (later extended to February 12), to accept or reject the offer. Fearing dismissal if they refused, about 75,000 of the 2.4 million federal employees accepted the offer, uncertain whether they would be paid or could ever come back. Some employees sought relief through the federal courts. Like so many other contested Trump executive orders, the constitutional outcome of their complaints may not be known for months at least, and probably years.

Shortly after the buyout period, the Trump administration swept through every agency and department with termination notices effective immediately. During February 2025, nearly all of the 220,000 probationary federal employees on the job for less than a year were particularly vulnerable, given that little explanation was necessary for their dismissal. Many were terminated. Within the first three months alone of Trump's new term, about 120,000 federal employees were let go,[42] in addition to the 75,000 "voluntary" departures, and at least that many more expected to be on the chopping block within the coming months. As of June 2025, additional expected departments and agencies included Veterans Affairs (30,000), Department of Defense (5,400), Department of Agriculture (6,000), Forest Service (3,400), Department of Health and Human Services (10,000), Department of the Treasury (6,000), Department of Housing and Urban Development (4,000), Department of Education (1,300) Internal Revenue Service (11,000), and the Social Security Administration (7,000). By the end of the purge, the numbers of dismissed and retired employees were expected to approach three hundred thousand, equaling about 12.5 percent of the federal workforce.

Some areas critical to the welfare of the United States paid dearly with their employee terminations. For example, inside the cuts in the Department of Health and Human Services, 6 percent (1,165) of the employes at the National Institutes of Health; 19 percent (3,000) of the employees at the Centers for Disease Control and Prevention; and 26 percent (5,200) at the Food and Drug Agency 5 percent (1,000) were let go. Given the nation's recent assault by COVID-19, it's hard to comprehend the extent to which the nation has become vulnerable. As Democratic Congresswoman Rosa De Lauro, a key member of the House of Labor, Health, Human Services, and Education Committee put it, "This [the cuts] does not lower costs for families as Trump promised he would. Instead, it tells them they are on their own."[43]

Other terminations were equally difficult to digest. Some examples: At the Department of Energy, hundreds of employees charged with protecting the nation's nuclear stockpile were let go, only for the terminators rushing to retain them after the "efficiency experts" were made aware of their potentially disastrous move. The US Cybersecurity and Infrastructure Agency dealing with sensitive intelligence issues lost 130 employees; the Department of Homeland Security (DHS) lost 400 employees, including 200 from the overwhelmed Federal Emergency Management Agency (FEMA) responding to recent hurricanes and West Coast wildfires; and several hundred employees from the Federal Aviation Administration (FAA) just weeks after a fatal collision between a passenger jet and military helicopter at Washington's Reagan National Airport.[44] So many of these changes just didn't make sense, given the pressing needs for their expertise.

Beyond employment reductions, Trump, via an executive order, instructed the Office of Personnel Management to redesignate more than fifty thousand senior executives across the federal bureaucracy from career civil service status to political appointees.[45] Under their new descriptions, these high-level appointees now serve at the pleasure of the president, which allows the president to fire them whenever he wishes.[46] In typical Trump fashion of reversing cause and effect, the administration wrote that the change would respond to "unaccountable, policy-determining federal employees who put their own interests ahead of the American people's."[47] In fact, the change simply made it easier for Trump to dismiss political bureaucrats who failed to stay in line with the administration's priorities, thereby severely weakening roles of independent civil servants dedicated to program management over political directives.

But there was more carnage to come. On February 8, 2025, Office of Management and Budget director Russell Vought ordered the Consumer Financial Protection Bureau (CFPB) to shut down immediately. How effective was that agency? Operating with a budget of $721 million in 2023, it brought in $2.5 billion in civil fines from banks with illegal practices. In 2024, the agency brought in another $2.2 billion in civil fines.[48] In other words, the agency paid for itself three times over.

In a very few cases, workers let go were rehired when management personnel realized they were essential to the mission of the agency or department. Case in point: Within days of their termination, the Trump administration rehired 180 workers at the National Nuclear Security Administration, the agency that manages the US nuclear weapons arsenal and radioactive materials. Specialists in sensitive areas such as pandemic management and airport management were not among the rehired, however, nor were key forest management personnel. And there's the Department of

Homeland Security which let four hundred employees go only to receive authorization in the 2026 federal budget to hire twenty thousand.

Fallout from the Cuts

While Trumpists raved over cutting government programs, in most cases, time would tell whether the costs were truly cost effective. In some cases, problems occurred almost in sync with the employee terminations. In the Department of Veterans Affairs where the largest cuts took place, the agency was attracting record numbers into the system as help declined—not a good combination. The announced cuts of seventy thousand employees came at a time when the VA already had sixty-six thousand vacancies. Between 2023 and 2024, the VA admitted four hundred thousand veterans into the system, a staggering increase of 30 percent compared to the previous year.[49] Internal VA memos warned of veterans who would be turned away for treatment along with "the inability to track oncology treatment and recurrences."[50]

At the FAA, the Department of Transportation released four hundred employees who worked in maintenance, safety, and nautical information. These personnel were critical to assisting the overtaxed controllers. A former FAA technician familiar with the agency noted that the loss of personnel would have "long-term safety implications—just work that simply can't be done."[51] Whether a crash between a commercial airliner and a military helicopter at Reagan International and the forced reduction of flights at Newark due to staff shortage and antiquated equipment resulted from layoffs was unknown, but the optics looked awful.

Similar problems occurred in the Social Security Administration serving 74 million Americans. In the post-workforce reduction environment, the agency struggled with website crashes, overloaded servicers, and long lines at field offices. Because of a vastly undermanned phone call network, recipients were forced to rely more on an online portal that was challenging to customers who were used to communicating through phone calls. Meanwhile, the average time from scheduling an appointment to a field office meeting has increased from 32 days to 34 days.[52]

In the aftermath of the mass firings, the Trump administration realized that they had gone too far. Bit by bit, the administration sought to rehire former employees from many agencies, including the Food and Drug Administration, the Department of Agriculture, the IRS, the State Department, the National Weather Service, and the Department of Housing and Urban Development. Some former employees returned; others wanted nothing to do with returning because of the chaos associated with their dismissal.[53] For the moment, huge expertise gaps in the federal bureaucracy remained.[54]

Special Trump Retribution for the FBI

We can't end this section without turning to Trump's animus toward the FBI. Between the agency's involvement in the investigation of Trump's possible association with Russian agents in 2016 and subsequent federal indictments over his outrageous behavior in 2020, Trump repeatedly lambasted FBI agents as "fascists" who "weaponized" their agency against him. The agency was corrupt through and through, Trump would say, even though he had handpicked its director, Christopher Wray to replace James Comey, who Trump fired in 2017. During the 2024 campaign, Trump stated his intent to fire Wray, bringing about yet another leadership disruption to the agency.[55]

Immediately upon commencing his second term, Trump's aides in the Department of Justice went to work. Emil Bove, Trump's acting deputy attorney general, fired eight FBI senior executives, including those involved in the January 6, 2021, insurrection of the Capitol. But that wasn't enough. On January 31, Bove demanded a list of the agents and staff members having anything to do with the insurrection investigation, or face termination. Facing a deadline of February 4, the Department of Justice received information on more than five thousand of the agency's thirty-eight thousand personnel. While the DOJ leadership said it had no immediate plans to make the names public, at least two lawsuits were filed by agents to protect their anonymity. Nevertheless, the message to agents was loud and clear. In the words of one agent, "This is a massacre meant to chill our efforts to fight crime without fear or favor. Even for those not fired, it sends a message that the bureau is no longer independent."[56] Given Trump's proclivities, it's likely that the message was meant for just about everyone in the federal bureaucracy.

All of this begs the question: Who was weaponizing the federal government, the FBI that investigated serious crimes such as the January 6 insurrection or the person who desperately sought to rewrite history by destroying those seeking to uphold the law? The answer was clear.

The Musk Factor

Much of the shrinkage of the federal workforce was orchestrated by Elon Musk and a small taskforce of cost cutters brought aboard by the billionaire. Musk's work began one week after Trump's election and well before his inauguration, when Trump set about to restructure the executive branch. During the 2024 presidential campaign, Musk had boasted that he could cut $2 trillion in "waste" from the $6.8 trillion annual budget.[57] Trump appointed him and fellow billionaire Vivek Ramaswamy to head the Department of Government Efficiency (DOGE), with the responsibility of uncovering wasteful expenditures and unduly burdensome regulations in departments throughout the federal government.[58] In early January 2025, Ramaswamy left to prepare a campaign for the Ohio governorship in 2026. That left Musk, the richest man in the world and a $277 million donor to the Trump campaign, to run the "department" that had no official standing in government other than the benefit of an executive order by Trump upon his inauguration. Musk and his group systematically went through numerous federal departments and agencies in search of waste and corruption.

Between full permission from Trump and his "break it first, and fix it later" mentality, Musk had little tolerance for anyone getting in his way in his effort to restructure (some said, "destructure") the federal government. Any judge who put a pause or dared to stop Musk's efforts was automatically condemned for interfering with the DOGE machine: "A corrupt judge protecting corruption.... He needs to be impeached NOW,"[59] Musk wrote on X after one judicial rebuke.

Musk never provided a methodology for his recommendations. But if his techniques in the corporate world are any guide, a company's stockholders would be in for a world of hurt. That's because there was no methodology other than stripping the government down to its bare bones without any thought of the consequences. As one reviewer commented at the time, Musk "has been unabashed about slashing costs to the point that corporate processes—and sometimes even product safety—break down, philosophizing that he can just fix things later."[60] But can that process work when it comes to minimizing medical research or cutting back costs for air traffic controllers or terminating valuable members of the CIA? What happens when a new pandemic erupts, or an air traffic disaster occurs, or an intelligence agent is compromised in the wake of these cuts?

In one particular instance, Musk and the DOGE crew dismembered the financial regulator one week after CFPB discussed a new payment system about to be brought online by X for people purchasing goods on the site. The agency worried about protecting consumers because, unlike banks, the X program was not insured to shield consumers against losses.[61] But any possibility of CFPB investigating X disappeared with DOGE's shutdown of the federal agency. Talk about the fox guarding the henhouse . . .

Overcoming Trumpism

At the start of the second Trump administration, Elon Musk and his DOGE team had a tremendous impact on the dismantlement of the American government. But it must not be forgotten that DOGE was acting at the behest of President Donald Trump whose orders mimicked major portions of the recommendations written in *Project 2025*.[62] To be clear, anyone blaming Musk for the massive, erratic downsizing of the federal government must remember that his "authority" came directly from Donald Trump, and Trump's orders were intimately connected with Project 2025.

While the federal job cuts created financial upheavals for more than two hundred thousand government workers and their families, their losses of income represented a small percentage of the $2 trillion in savings sought by Musk. Research by the Congressional Budget Office on federal salaries for 2022 found that the salary totals for all civilian employees amounted to $271 billion.[63] Even adding government contributions to employee Social Security accounts didn't get close to the desired savings. The real "savings" would come not from firing federal employees but from the programs they worked on.

But what about all the alleged "waste," the basis of Musk's promise to cut $2 trillion from the budget? In just six short weeks after tunneling through two dozen federal departments and agencies, Musk claimed that DOGE had found $65 billion in savings largely by elimination of contracts, leases, and unnecessary government employees. According to an examination by *The New York Times*, the DOGE report was riddled with misstatements. Some examples: a claimed "savings" of $8 billion was actually $8 million; an alleged contract savings of $655 million was counted three times; and a contract cancellation of $1.9 billion was actually done during the Biden administration. All told, the true savings were no more than $10 billion, and quite possibly less.[64] The point is, DOGE produced great headlines, but little credibility and even less success.[65]

Then there was the question of Musk's potential conflict of interests with many of the government agencies DOGE was investigating. According to one report, at least eleven federal government agencies were involved in thirty-two investigations of five Musk companies. The National Labor Relations Commission alone was engaged in twenty-four inquiries into Musk companies. Other examples included FAA fines against Space X for safety violations; the Security and Exchange Commission (SEC) demanding as much as $150 million for violation of federal securities laws by X; and the (now defunct) CFPB fielding hundreds of complaints against Tesla about automobile loan issues.[66] When asked about the possibility of any conflicts

Trumpism 2.0

of interest in investigating agencies impacting his companies, Musk dodged the question by answering, "I'm not the one filing the contract [with the government] ... . It's the people at Space X" and other Musk companies directly interacting with the government.[67] Such logic failed any sense of credulity. Clearly, Musk was investigating agencies that were investigating his companies—clear conflicts of interest!

Not everything done by Musk has escaped scrutiny. A brief mutiny of sorts erupted in March 2025 when, at a cabinet meeting, Musk and Secretary of State Marco Rubio clashed over who was in charge of revamping the State Department. It turned out that similar concerns had been expressed by Treasury Secretary Scott Bessent, Defense Secretary Pete Hegseth, and FBI director Kash Patel. After a while, Trump intervened, complimented the offended cabinet members, and went on to say that he would coordinate with Musk biweekly to assure more tailored reductions.[68] Whether the strain was indicative of a serious break or just a temporary tiff remained to be seen. For the moment, it appeared the latter was the case.

A Trumpist Twist to Isolationism

In its purest form, isolationism occurs when a country turns away from involvement with other nations and foreign relationships. Soon after his assumption of office in January 2017, President Donald Trump promised just that with his "America First" policy that included everything from turning away from international commitments to protecting the American border from the entry of illegal migrants.

Trump's inward lurch wasn't novel. Various versions of "America First" have occurred throughout this nation's history.[69] But after the Second World War, national security requirements and the overriding desire to contain American enemies abroad led the United States in a different direction. Shortly after the end of the Second World War and for the next three-quarters of a century, the United States created and/or joined numerous treaties with nations around the world to pursue mutual interests.

With his "America First" policy, Donald Trump saw little need for the United States to be part of any regional or international organizations. Thus, during his first term, Trump withdrew from the Paris Climate Agreement, which worked on climate change; the Trans-Pacific Partnership, which created the largest trading bloc in the world designed to increase the tariff-free flow of goods among members; the United Nations Educational, Scientific, and Cultural Organization, which was designed to deal with poverty, promote sustainable development, and facilitate cultural dialogue; and the World Health Organization, which shared information on communicable diseases and emerging epidemics. Other than the Trans-Pacific Partnership, almost every country belonged to these organizations. In each case, Trump withdrew because of opposition to cost or policy. Ignored were the benefits from communication, mutual interests, and global considerations.

When Joe Biden became president in 2021, he resumed American membership in all of these organizations except the Trans-Pacific Partnership, which was then formed during the Trump administration without the United States. Biden explained the benefits of collaboration in a 2023 speech at the United Nations: "The United States seeks a more secure, more prosperous, more equitable world for all people because we know our future is bound to yours."[70] Such were the goals of a foreign policy based on internationalism, a cooperative spirit among nations for the common good. That policy had been the international objective of the United States since the Second World War, other than Trump's first four-year term.

With his election to a second term in 2024, Trump returned the nation to his approach of "America First" and isolationism. He quickly removed the United States from the organizations he had shunned in 2017. Beyond the organizational departures, Trump's first major move was to distance the United States from helping Ukraine stave off Russia, which had ruthlessly invaded the nation in 2022. Although Russia's invasion of the Ukrainian democracy was universally recognized, Trump flipped the war's causality by falsely claiming that Ukraine started the war.[71] He also falsely claimed that the United States had spent nearly three times the amount of money as Europe in defending Ukraine. In fact, European countries had spent more than the United States.[72]

Worst of all, by negotiating with Russia's Putin to end the war in Ukraine, Trump basically ignored Russia's violation of the Budapest Memorandum, a four-nation agreement including Russia, Great Britain, and the United States, which was signed in 1994. The essence of that agreement provided that in exchange for Ukraine turning over about two thousand nuclear weapons to Russia, the three countries agree to protect Ukraine from any aggression.[73] Russia violated that agreement, first by attacking and seizing Ukraine's Crimea peninsula in 2014 and second by invading the rest of Ukraine in 2022. As if to add insult to injury, on February 23, 2025, at Trump's direction, the US delegation at the United Nations voted against a resolution that condemned Russia for invading Ukraine.[74] Some of the other "no" votes included Russia, Sudan, and North Korea, not exactly democratic countries. It's hard to imagine a more twisted arrangement than the United States refusing to condemn an authoritarian nation for invading a democracy that received so much American military and financial support until Trump's return to the presidency.

In June 2025, after a half-hearted attempt to secure an agreement between Ukraine and Russia to end invasion, Trump said that the United States would no longer be involved in ending the conflict. With the decision to stop defending Ukraine, the United States also became a party to violating the memorandum, making this country just as unreliable as Russia as a treaty guarantor. However, in July, Trump announced that the United States would resume arms shipments to Ukraine due to Russia's unwillingness to negotiate an end to the war.[75] Even then, the "resumption" was in the form of selling weapons to NATO countries, which then would ship them to Ukraine. In other words, there would be no cost to the United States. How long Trump's new tepid commitment toward helping Ukraine would last was anyone's guess, given his erratic behavior and unwillingness to take on Putin.

Trump's isolationism had an unusual twist. While he zigzagged on Ukraine, and to a significant extent, Western Europe, he attempted to exercise America's muscle elsewhere. Within days of resuming the presidency, Trump proposed that Denmark sell Greenland, its autonomous territory, to the United States;[76] invited Canada to become the fifty-first state;[77] and warned Panama[78] that the United States might invade the country if Panama didn't adjust its shipping charges to US ships traversing the canal. He also initiated a trade war by implementing substantial tariffs on Canada and Mexico, two of America's largest trading partners, as well as almost all of the other nations doing business with the United States. In other words, Trump wanted no part of helping other nations, even allies, but he was not above pushing around other nations for his needs. Such an approach has done nothing to maintain long-term friendships or trust, but there's little reason to believe that Trump had any interest in either objective.

A classic example of Trump's America First policy came in spring 2025, with the troubled Red Sea shipping route. Historically, the United States has led multination efforts to protect ships traveling busy international sea lanes when pirates, rebels, or other hostile groups have attempted to interfere with seagoing international commerce. Ever since the October 7, 2023, renewed hostilities between Israel and Hamas, Iran-backed Houthi rebels in Yemen attacked ships moving through the corridor. At first, the United States and other countries stepped in with military presence to repel the Houthis, but after the Houthis and the United States agreed to a ceasefire between the two countries, the US Navy pulled out. Other countries using the Red Sea corridor would be on their own, clearly showing the extent that the United States had walked away from its international presence.[79]

There is another exception to Trump's isolationist foreign policy approach that bears mention. On June 21, 2025, Trump ordered a massive bombing of Iran's nuclear facilities. The strikes came as a result of years of uranium enrichment by Iran, leading many critics to believe that the country was on the verge of developing a nuclear weapon. After failed international efforts to persuade Iran to stand down, Trump ordered the attack. At first, such activity appeared out of character for Trump, the isolationist. However, a closer look points to the close relationship between Trump and evangelicals, Trump's most important constituency, who have long viewed Iran as a threat to Israel, home to the most sacred Christian values.[80]

Lastly, we turn to Trump's use of tariffs as a foreign policy tool. Claiming with no basis that for decades the United States had been "looted, pillaged and raped" by trading partners, on April 2, 2025, Trump announced that the United States would impose minimum 10 percent tariffs on every nation.[81] The tariffs would bring in hundreds of billions of dollars to the US Treasury, Trump predicted, at no cost to Americans. He further announced that unless trading partners agreed to new terms with the United States within ninety days, much harsher tariffs would be applied. That deadline came and went, with only two countries in toe, and Trump issuing varying rates to countries. By August, Trump had "negotiated" tariffs with other nations that went as high as 50 percent in some cases. The average US tariff rate soared to 17.7 percent, the highest since 1934.[82] In 2024, the rate had been 2.5 percent. Most economists viewed the new approach harmful to the American consumer who would actually be picking up the tabs through passed on costs.[83]

Put it all together and we see a series of incredible outcomes from Trump's international realignment of American foreign policy. Between Trump's wishy-washy attitude toward Ukraine, disregard for traditional allies, his embrace of Russia's Putin, and his foreign interests elsewhere, the world was becoming a less secure place.

From Draining the Swamp to Living in It

When he ran for president in 2016, Donald Trump described himself as a reformer who would "drain the swamp" of corruption, excessive lobbying, and influence peddling.[84] He also promised to bring ethics reform to Washington. During his first term, Trump broke a historic norm by refusing to release his tax returns, failing to separate from his businesses, holding Republican party events at the White house, and using the power of the presidency for monetary gain through the International Trump Hotel at the DC Old Post Office. Miraculously, all these peccadillos seemed forgotten by enough of the voters by the time Trump secured a second term in 2024. Quickly we saw Trump's lack of ethics embodied in the very swamp that he sought to drain. It's hard to imagine, but the collection of ethical miscues during the first term paled to Trump's behavior the second time around.

The growing list of unethical behavior is incredible. Unlike 2017 when Trump went through the charade of allegedly keeping his businesses at arm's length, this time he didn't even bother to go through the exercise. The family business remained well within arm's length. But this time there is so much more without any pretense of suggesting that Trump has separated from his business practices.

Shortly after his election in December 2024, Trump joined a crypto venture firm as the "chief crypto advocate," entitling him to a cut of all revenues.[85] Three days before taking office in 2025, Trump partnered in another new venture, $Trump, a meme coin company where 1 billion coins were made available for sale, with Trump getting a portion of every transaction. On this investment, President Trump held a special dinner at his Virginia golf course with the 220 largest purchasers. Another potential conflict of interest occurred with Trump's acceptance of a $400 million Boeing 747-8 jumbo jet from the Qatari royal family for his use until new presidential planes under construction were ready, with the plane donated to Trump's presidential library after his presidency. Then there was the $28 million paid to First Lady Melania Trump by Amazon for the purpose of producing two documentaries about her. And how about the multibillion dollar deals in the Middle East put together by Trump's sons, Donald Trump, Jr., and Eric Trump? It's not that the relatives of previous presidents haven't benefitted from leveraging their names. But in these cases, White House records show that President Trump benefits directly from most of the deals.[86] That's the difference.

It would take an unbelievable dose of naivete to believe that these arrangements were made out of the goodness of the donors' hearts. In the case of the Melania Trump deal, we must remember that Amazon does billions of dollars of business with the federal government.[87] With respect to Qatar, the royal government and Trump signed a $1.2 trillion trade deal during

Trump's visit;[88] the details have not been released. Almost simultaneously, the Trump family business announced new business deals in Qatar.[89] Would all of these deals have occurred had Trump not been elected to a second term? We'll never know. But an exhaustive examination of Trump's finances concluded, "Mr. Trump's wealth is now built on monetizing the family name in new ways and, intentionally or not, the office of the presidency."[90]

Much of the financial exchanges have occurred with nary a whisper of public resentment perhaps due to the furious pace of so many taking place simultaneously. But not everything has gone without public reaction. A Harvard CAPS Harris national poll taken in late May 2025 found that 62 percent of the respondents agreed that Trump's acceptance of the plane raised ethical concerns about corruption. Even 40 percent of Republicans voiced apprehension over the transaction.[91] Numerous Republican members of Congress complained that Trump's actions violated the Emoluments Clause of the Constitution in Article I, Section 9, which explicitly forbids anyone holding office from benefitting from foreign gifts, yet no formal efforts were taken against Trump perhaps because of the generous way that the Supreme Court has interpreted the president's actions.[92] Regardless, the Trump Corruption Express just kept moving seemingly at light speed. In the words of one government ethics expert, "There's nothing in the history of America that approaches the use of the presidency for massive personal gain. Nothing … . He's in the Hall of Fame of ripping off the presidency for personal gain."[93] However the legacy of the Trump presidencies may turn out, it's hard to believe that there won't be a chapter focusing on the long series of self-serving deals during his time in power.

The Other Two Branches

As Trump all but turned the executive branch into his personal fiefdom, political observers watched to see what action the Congress and federal courts might take to rein in his autocratic movements. There were good reasons for challenging Trump's actions. After all, from its earliest days, the governing process of the United States depended upon a system of checks and balances to prevent any one branch from dominating governance. This was a fundamental element of the "separation of powers" doctrine. Along those lines, the US Constitution declares, and the US Supreme Court has generally clarified, that "Congress has broad constitutional authority to establish and shape the federal bureaucracy."[94] Meanwhile, in the landmark case of *Marbury v. Madison (1803)*, the US Supreme Court early on interpreted its power to include a review of the legality of legislative and administrative acts. The bottom line is that the Constitution established both Congress and the federal courts as equal partners with the executive branch in the policymaking process.

Neither of these essential foundations of American governance seemed to matter to Donald Trump and his allies. In fact, these constitutional provisions interfered with the Trumpists' primary goal to amass as much power as possible in the hands of the president, thereby making it easy to transform the nation on their terms.

Congress

In the first few months of Trump's second presidency, his power over Republicans in Congress all but neutered the GOP members. In rapid succession upon taking office, Trump fired independent inspectors general overseeing key departments and agencies, terminated congressionally created agencies, and approved drastic cuts of congressionally authorized funds for various departments and agencies.

Rather than protest the loss of their power, Republicans in the once-equal branch of the national government showered Trump with approval for usurping their power. About all of this and more, Republican House of Representative Speaker Mike Johnson commented that Trump was "using his executive authority, I think, in an appropriate manner. He got a mandate from the American people."[95] But did "the mandate" of Trump's 1.5 percent popular vote victory over Kamala Harris include permission for him to single handedly restructure the organization of American government? No.

Then, there was the Republican problem of reducing $1.5 trillion from federal budget spending—largely in social and healthcare programs—to partially offset the continuation of a $4.5 trillion tax cut first passed in 2018, and extended in 2025, that would disproportionately help the wealthy. The $3 trillion gap between the "savings" and tax cut were added to the national debt, increasing it to $36 trillion—all to support financial benefits disproportionately for the wealthiest Americans while the poorest residents lost healthcare and food stamp benefits.[96] When asked whether Republicans would go along with Trump's demands irrespective of any financial harm to less fortunate elements of American society, Republican House Appropriations Committee Chair Tom Cole (OK) simply explained, "We're not going to shackle the president of the United States—can't do it."[97]

Of course they could. As the Constitution prescribes, it's Congress that does the appropriating, not the president.

Republican US Senator Lisa Murkowski (AK) offered a depressed assessment about deferring to Trump on matters before Congress. Said Murkowski, "We are all afraid .... I'm oftentimes very anxious myself about using my voice because [Trump's] retaliation is real. And that's not right."[98] Given Trump's well-demonstrated execution of political retribution when he doesn't get what he wants, Murkowski had reason to think twice about publicly opposing the president.

If anyone had any questions about Trump's firm control over Republicans in Congress, all they had to do was watch the way that Republicans twisted and turned to justify Trump's up-and-down orchestration of his tariffs plan in 2025. Between March and June 2025, Trump changed the way he would win acceptable trade agreements sometimes daily. Firm deadlines regarding agreements with other nations that he announced one day would disappear the next, leaving supporters and opponents alike gasping for certainty. Day after day, the US stock markets fluctuated sometimes by hundreds of points. During this period, consumer sentiment plummeted from 71.1 points in January 2025 to 50.8 points in May 2025.[99] Several congressional Republican economists winced, but they stood steadfast behind Trump.[100]

The fact is that Article I, Section 8 of the US Constitution clearly stipulates that Congress, not the president, has the power to regulate commerce with other nations and impose tariffs. A caveat exists, however, with the International Emergency Economic Powers Act (IEEPA). Under this law, the president can declare an emergency and establish tariffs.[101] Even then, the Congress can legislate to prevent the president from acting if they differ with the president's interpretation of the economic climate.

And what about the congressional Democrats? Yes, after the 2024 elections, they were underwater by three seats in the US Senate and three seats in the House of Representatives, and therefore out of power. Nevertheless, the opposition party is obligated to make itself heard with criticisms and arguments against those in power if for no other reason than for the voters to consider the merits of their choices in the next election. At least in the early going of Trump's second term, congressional Democrats focused more on drawbacks associated with Trumpism than a cogent set of propositions to make things better. Trump seemed all the more powerful given the Democrats' malaise.

Meanwhile, as Trump gambled with his tariff policy and Trump-ordered personnel carried out their objective of eviscerating the federal bureaucracy, public reaction showed signs of emerging opposition. During the spring and summer recesses in 2025, several Republican members of Congress found themselves confronted by angry crowds over the massive Trump-choreographed changes at town halls in their districts, with the discontent televised on local evening news programs.[102] Back in Washington, Republican leaders blamed the discontent on paid troublemakers, although they provided no evidence with the accusations. Nevertheless, in a closed-door meeting, Republican leaders urged their members to stop holding in-person meetings and instead do town halls where citizens could call in.[103] Whether that tactic would be enough to discourage public anguish remained to be seen.

The Federal Judiciary

In our constitutional system of checks and balances, the judiciary cannot be an independent coequal branch of the government if its decisions depend upon passing muster with another branch. Time after time, however, the Trump administration has sought to eliminate independent judicial responsibilities, lest any admonitions handed down by a federal court threaten Trump's efforts to tuck virtually all aspects of the federal bureaucracy under his direct control.

Donald Trump has a long history of disdain for the courts, both as a businessperson and as a politician. Typically, when Trump has lost a case or trial, he has blamed the judge for being unfair to him. He often attaches a racial or sexist element to his complaint. But at least on the federal level, Trump hasn't had much to complain about in recent years, particularly with respect to the Supreme Court's thoughts about his role as president between 2017 and 2021.

In a sense, the Supreme Court opened the door for Donald Trump's current incredible power grab of the executive branch. Just months before the 2024 presidential election, in *Trump v. United States*, the justices in a 6-to-3 decision held that the president was immune from prosecution for any official act. That sweeping decision led prosecutors to drop all the indictments in the four major cases awaiting trial, including the charge of Trump's involvement in the January 6, 2021, insurrection against Congress and withholding highly sensitive government documents from the government archives. It may also explain why Trump critics have been so reluctant to go after Trump for emolument violations. Think about it: Why prosecute the nation's chief executive who has been given a wide berth for his actions because of his role as president?

Officially, the Supreme Court's decision on immunity had nothing to do with Trump's bombardment of executive orders and actions immediately upon his second presidency at 1600 Pennsylvania Avenue. Still, without saying as much, the Court seemed to value the "unitary executive theory," which holds that the president has total authority over every aspect of the executive branch. This seemed to embolden Trump's sense of power. In fact, it looked as if Trump was determined to test the limits, if any, of the president's power. As Trump's former White House counsel Ty Cobb said, "Trump is determined to maximize the power of his presidency. He believes he's omnipotent and that anything he does is beyond reproach."[104] Why not? In Trump's mind, presidential power seemed to overlap with the Supreme Court's blessing to the extent that if the president is immune from prosecution for any official acts, it stands to reason that anything the president does is beyond challenge.

He had supporters. On X, Trump's Vice President JD Vance wrote, "Judges aren't allowed to control the executive's legislative power." In that single sentence, Vance viewed the president as the holder of legislative authority, wiping out the "separation of powers" concept in the US Constitution. Trump's deputy director of the FBI, Dan Bongino, argued that Trump should ignore court decisions that don't have his agreement. In fact, Bongino said, on issues important to Trump, a courtroom should be set up in the East Room of the White House, where Trump "can just start making judicial decisions."[105] Along those lines, several Republican members of the House of Representatives filed articles of impeachment against federal judges they viewed as unconstitutionally interfering with the efforts of Trump and Musk to overhaul the federal government.[106] The impeachment efforts never gained steam but many of the members did.

Within the first 90 days of the second Trump administration, opponents filed more than 150 lawsuits in various federal courts against DOGE, the Office of Personnel Management, the Office of Management and Budget, and, of course, President Donald Trump. Per constitutional organization, federal judges have been the backstop for challenges to the administration's executive branch restructuring efforts. At stake there have been the particularly massive amounts of energy designed to weaken, if not eliminate, various departments and agencies as well as their civil service employees. When a judge has ruled for the Trump team, the administration has cheered their wisdom; however, on occasions when a judge has ruled against the administration, members of the Trump team have been quick to criticize the outcomes and the "corrupt" judges who have interfered with their "reforms."

Examples of the Trump administration's disgust with federal judges abound. After a federal judge ruled against the DOGE team gaining access to some Treasury Department data, an angry Elon Musk wrote that the decision resulted from "a corrupt judge protecting corruption . . . He needs to be impeached NOW."[107] An equally angry Republican US Senator Mike Lee (UT) wrote in a media post, that "corrupt judges should be impeached and removed."[108] Such behavior, the American Bar Association wrote, is unacceptable for the simple reason that allows for judges to be removed "simply because we disagree with their ruling."[109] Trump himself was the loudest of all judicial critics, frequently describing them as "radical leftists."[110]

There can be considerable damage from this approach to policymaking evaluation. By alleging a connection between the judge's decision with a lack of integrity, Trumpists attempt to cast a pall not only on the judiciary, but also on a part of the foundation of our democracy. In fact, Trump has made "corrupt" government a theme of his entire political life, basically asking the voters to trust him instead. Portraying a corrupt judiciary as part of our "problem" leads to the next step, namely a turn to someone—Trump—who will clean up the mess. Truthful? No. But certainly effective.

Given the Supreme Court's recent decisions favoring the power of the executive branch, it's a mystery as to what extent the federal judiciary will stand up to Trump's massive overhaul of the federal government. It may well be that the court defers to Trump's reorganization of entities designed to be placed under executive purview such as the FAA or FBI, while denying Trumpists the ability to fiddle with congressionally authorized funds for such things as foreign aid. On more than one occasion, the Supreme Court has allowed the firing of independent agency-appointed officials, with the judges asserting that capability exists because of the president's oversight of activities in the executive branch.[111]

Of course, it's not that simple. For example, in March 2025, Trump announced that he was closing down the Department of Education, which was created by Congress in 1979. In response to a lawsuit protesting the elimination, in May 2025, a federal judge blocked Trump's effort. Like so many other lawsuits, this one would no doubt climb up the judicial ladder with a final decision by the US Supreme Court.

At first blush, it would seem that only Congress can change a department that it has created. But what if Trump reduces the number of employees in the Department of Education to a bare minimum, in effect rendering the department all but useless? Where does the Supreme Court draw the line? And to what extent will excessive deferral to the executive branch reduce the power of Congress to a point of impotence? These questions are not easy to answer, and in all likelihood may be resolved only after a long period of time. Until then, it's clear that Trump and his acolytes will be on the offense, testing the court's collective philosophical composition in case after case, while the future of American democracy hangs in the balance.

A particularly troublesome situation occurred in spring 2025 when the Trump administration announced that it had mistakenly deported Kilmar Abrego Garcia, an undocumented Salvadorian to El Salvador.[112] Garcia had fled to the United States in 2012 because of death threats from a gang in his home country, and records show that Garcia was not involved in any gangs during his stay in the United States. He was given protective status by a judge in 2021. On March 15, 2025, US Immigration and Customs Enforcement (ICE) deported Garcia to El Salvador along with several dozen Salvadoran gang members. Nevertheless, the Trump administration would not correct their error and bring Garcia back to the United States At first President Trump said he didn't have the ability to retrieve Garcia from another country. Shortly thereafter, Trump changed his response, now saying he could bring Garcia back, but that he wouldn't because he was a criminal—a claim with no substantiation.[113]

On April 10, 2025, the US Supreme Court ordered Trump to "facilitate and effectuate" the return of Garcia to the United States,[114] and ordered a federal district court judge to see the order through. Over the next two months, Trump administration attorneys offered several reasons to the district court judge managing the case as to why they were unable to comply, leaving the outcome of the case at a standstill. The judge countered that they were stalling.

Some constitutional experts cited the Garcia case as approaching a constitutional crisis. Inasmuch as the Supreme Court has final say over legal questions, the Trump administration was duty bound to honor the court's order. What would happen if Trump refused to comply? Would that basically negate the power of a coequal branch of government, paving the way for the president to be able to act unchallenged? The longer this unresolved issue continues, the more likely that the crisis will be a reality. Finally, on June 6, 2025, the standoff ended when US officials brought back Albrego Garcia, now with the intent to prosecute him for transporting undocumented migrants.[115] Uncertain was whether the charges against Garcia would secure his conviction.

Regardless of the inconsistent judicial applications in the second Trump administration, the examples above at least show that on more occasions than not, the justices have been willing to stamp approval of a more robust role for the chief executive. To the extent that allowance continues, Trump may well take even more liberties to exercise his perception of expanded power in the presidency.

What You See Is What You Get—and You Shouldn't Be Surprised

It's clear that Donald Trump seeks to stretch the powers of the presidency as far as possible. How much of what he does remains constitutional may not be known for some time because, if for no other reason, court battles tend to languish, sometimes for years, before there is any clarity.

Yet, there are some things we do know. For starters, at least in the first year of Trump's second term, Republican majorities in Congress were all too willing to accept, perhaps even welcome, his moves against traditional sources of potential countervailing power, including the legislative branch. This in itself is astonishing. Among its core responsibilities, Congress controls the federal purse. That power is the heart of Article II of the US Constitution. Under the terms of this financial clout, the executive branch can't refuse to spend funds authorized by Congress. That issue was settled in 1974, when Congress passed the Impoundment Control Act, which constrained the president's ability to withhold spending authorized by Congress. Through his actions, however, Trump seems to believe the act is unconstitutional. That issue is sure to come before the US Supreme Court sooner or later. Meanwhile, congressional Republicans have abandoned one of their most important roles, instead of offering their imprimatur to aid an authoritarian.

We also know that the fates of numerous federal agencies and departments as well as hundreds of thousands of federal employees remain in limbo until their cases are fully decided by the US Supreme Court one at a time. What we don't know is how much Donald Trump will be able to bend the other two branches into submission, effectively rendering checks and balances no longer a foundation of our democracy, where power is limited because of the three-part division of authority.

Left without any constraints by the other branches, President Donald Trump is poised to control the media and the public square; lessen federal regulations; minimize or even eliminate key components of the federal bureaucracy; dominate every aspect of the executive branch, including independent agencies; minimize US participation in global and regional

Overcoming Trumpism

initiatives; and reduce America's footprint abroad except where it fits his definition of America's interest (think control of the Panama Canal, the purchase of Greenland, and the addition of Canada as a US state). Most of all, during the second term, Donald Trump shows every indication of relying on three manipulative qualities that have become signature traits: hate, division, and intimidation. Increasingly, America's version of a strongman is showing his true colors, and they are very dark.

NOTES

1 "The President-Elect's Vision Will Lead to Sweeping Changes at Federal Agencies and the Employees Who Work in Them," Government Executive, November 6, 2024, https://www.govexec.com/management/2024/11/agency-agency-look-trumps-plan-overhaul-government/400885/.
2 "Want a Job in the Trump Administration? Be Prepared for the Loyalty Test," The New York Times, December 7, 2024, https://www.nytimes.com/2024/12/07/us/politics/trump-administration-loyalty-test.html.
3 Richard Stanley, How Fascism Works: The Politics of Us and Them (New York: Random House, 2018), p. 25.
4 "37 Ways Project 2025 Has Shown Up in Trump's Executive Orders," Politico, February 5, 2025, https://www.politico.com/interactives/2025/trump-executive-orders-project-2025/.
5 "All of the Trump Cabinet Picks That Have Ties to Project 2025," New York, November 29, 2024, https://nymag.com/intelligencer/article/trump-cabinet-picks-with-project-2025-ties.html.
6 "Former Trump Officials Wrote 25 of the 30 Chapters in the Project 2025 Playbook," The Revolving Door Project, July 16, 2024, https://therevolvingdoorproject.org/former-trump-officials-wrote-25-of-the-30-chapters-in-the-project-2025-playbook/.
7 See "Top Trump Picks Have Ties to Project 2025," Axios, November 26, 2024, https://www.axios.com/2024/11/26/trump-picks-project-2025-russ-vought, and "Trump Once Shunned Project 2025 as 'Ridiculous,' Now He's Staffing with Them," Politico, November 21, 2024, https://www.politico.com/news/2024/11/21/trump-taps-project-2025-authors-administration-00191047.
8 "Trump Calls Attempts to Link Him to Project 2025 'Pure Disinformation,'" The Hill, July 11, 2024, https://thehill.com/homenews/campaign/4765917-trump-denies-link-project-2025/.
9 Quoted in "If Trump Is Reelected, the Independence of Federal Agencies Could Be at Risk," NPR, August 16, 2023, https://www.npr.org/transcripts/1192432628.
10 "Russell Vought: Trump Appointee Who Wants Federal Workers to Be 'in Trauma,'" The Guardian, February 10, 2025, https://www.theguardian.com/us-news/2025/feb/10/who-is-russell-vought-trump-office-of-management-and-budget.

Trumpism 2.0

11 "What Trump Supporters Believe and Expect," Pew Research Center, November 13, 2024, https://www.pewresearch.org/short-reads/2024/11/13/what-trump-supporters-believe-and-expect/.

12 "CPB Releases March 2025 Monthly Update," US Customs and Border Protection, April 14, 2025, https://www.cbp.gov/newsroom/national-media-release/cbp-releases-march-2025-monthly-update.

13 "The First 100 Days of the Second Trump Administration: Key Immigration-Related Actions and Developments," National Immigration Forum, April 28, 2025, https://immigrationforum.org/article/the-first-100-days-of-the-second-trump-administration-key-immigration-related-actions-and-developments/.

14 "Supreme Court Allows White House to Revoke Temporary Protected Status of Many Migrants," *The Guardian*, May 30, 2025, https://www.theguardian.com/us-news/2025/may/30/supreme-court-trump-administration-revoke-temporary-protected-status.

15 "A Sweeping New ICE Operation Shows How Trump's Focus on Immigration Is Reshaping Federal Law Enforcement," NBC News, June 3, 2025, https://www.nbcnews.com/politics/justice-department/ice-operation-trump-focus-immigration-reshape-federal-law-enforcement-rcna193494.

16 Quoted in "Under Pressure from the White House, ICE Seeks New Ways to Ramp Up Arrests," *The New York Times*, June 11, 2025, https://www.nytimes.com/2025/06/11/us/politics/ice-la-protest-arrests.html.

17 "65% of People Taken by ICE Had No Convictions, 93% No Violent Convictions," CATO Institute, June 20, 2025, https://www.cato.org/news-releases/65-people-taken-ice-had-no-convictions-93-no-violent-convictions.

18 "What Started the LA Protests? Immigration Raids Sparked Outrage," *USA Today*, June 11, 2025, https://www.usatoday.com/story/news/nation/2025/06/10/los-angeles-immigration-ice-protests-trump-newsom/84129692007/.

19 Quoted in "Newsom Tells Nation That Trump Is Destroying American Democracy," *The New York Times*, June 11, 2025, https://www.nytimes.com/2025/06/10/us/newsom-speech-trump-la-protests.html.

20 "Los Angeles County DA Announces Additional Criminal Charges Filed in Connection with ICE Protests," CBS News, June 17, 2025, https://www.cbsnews.com/losangeles/news/los-angeles-county-da-additional-criminal-charges-ice-protests/.

21 "Trump Says He Will 'Liberate' Los Angeles in Speech to Mark the 250th Anniversary of the Army," AP, June 10, 2025, https://apnews.com/article/donald-trump-fort-bragg-6df36485dec1df2350d5b7be0882a703.

22 "Poll Tracker: Attitudes on Immigration in the 2024 U.S. Elections," AS/COA, October 25, 2024, https://www.as-coa.org/articles/poll-tracker-attitudes-immigration-2024-us-elections, and "Americans Have Mixed to Negative Views of Trump Administration Immigration Actions," Pew Research Center, June 17, 2025, https://www.pewresearch.org/politics/2025/06/17/americans-have-mixed-to-negative-views-of-trump-administration-immigration-actions/.

23. "Surge in U.S. Concern about Immigration Has Abated," Gallup Poll, July 11, 2025, https://news.gallup.com/poll/692522/surge-concern-immigration-abated.aspx.
24. See Larry N. Gerston, *Trumpism, Bigotry, and the Threat to American Democracy* (Lanham, MD: Rowman & Littlefield, 2024), pp. 91–108.
25. "As Trump Attacks Diversity, a Racist Undercurrent Surfaces," *The New York Times*, February 23, 2025, https://www.nytimes.com/2025/02/03/us/politics/trump-diversity-racism.html.
26. The order was Executive Order 14173.
27. "The Trump Administration's Diversity, Equity, and Inclusion (DEI) Executive Orders: A Brief Primer," SheppardMullin, April 4, 2025, https://www.governmentcontractslawblog.com/2025/04/articles/executive-orders/the-trump-administrations-diversity-equity-and-inclusion-dei-executive-orders-a-brief-primer/.
28. "These Companies Still Support DEI," The Advocate, May 21, 2025, https://www.advocate.com/news/companies-keeping-dei#rebelltitem2.
29. "Trump Admin. Tells Schools: No Federal Funds If You're Using DEI," EducationWeek, April 3, 2025, https://www.edweek.org/policy-politics/trump-admin-tells-schools-no-federal-funds-if-youre-using-dei/2025/04, and "Trump Signs Executive Orders Targeting Colleges, Plus Schools' Equity Efforts," AP, April 23, 2025, https://apnews.com/article/trump-executive-orders-education-9fb7e1f707f0df93e3b28d4eff984d04.
30. "Courts Block Trump from Withholding School Funds over D.E.I., for Now," *The New York Times*, April 24, 2025, https://www.nytimes.com/2025/04/24/us/trump-public-school-funds-dei.html.
31. "Nonprofit Trends and Impacts 2021–2023," Urban Institute, October 2024, https://www.urban.org/sites/default/files/2024-10/Nonprofit_Trends_and_Impacts_2021-2023_National_Findings_on_Government_Grants_and_Contracts.pdf.
32. "Despite Momentum, Many Nonprofits Still Struggle with Basic DEI Principles," The Chronicle of Philanthropy, December 15, 2023, https://www.philanthropy.com/article/despite-momentum-many-nonprofits-still-struggle-with-basic-dei-principles.
33. "The Corporate Retreat from DEI: A Symptom of Our National Fracture," *Westside Gazette*, May 8, 2025, https://thewestsidegazette.com/the-corporate-retreat-from-dei-a-symptom-of-our-national-fracture/.
34. Quoted in "Senior USAID Officials Put on Leave after Denying Access to Musk's Doge Team," *The Guardian*, February 3, 2025, https://www.theguardian.com/us-news/2025/feb/02/usaid-officials-put-on-leave-musk-doge.
35. For a discussion in depth of this topic, see Joseph S. Nye, Jr., *Soft Power: The Means to Success in World Politics* (Cambridge, MA: Perseus Books, 2004).
36. "Democracy Promotion: An Objective of U.S. Foreign Assistance," Congressional Research Service, January 4, 2019, https://crsreports.congress.gov/product/pdf/R/R44858.
37. "USAID Inspector Fired after Revealing Nearly $500m in Food Aid was about to Spoil amid Trump Funding Freeze," Yahoo News, February 12, 2025,

https://www.yahoo.com/news/usaid-inspector-fired-revealing-nearly-152421287.html.

38 "The Facts about the Pause on U.S. Foreign Aid," Better World Campaign, February 11, 2025, https://www.edweek.org/policy-politics/trump-admin-tells-schools-no-federal-funds-if-youre-using-dei/2025/04https://betterworldcampaign.org/funding/what-we-know-about-the-pause-on-u-s-foreign-aid.

39 Bintang Corvi Diphda, "The Closure of USAID: Is America Surrendering Its Foreign Soft Aid Power?" Modern Diplomacy, February 10, 2025, https://moderndiplomacy.eu/2025/02/10/the-closure-of-usaid-is-america-surrendering-its-foreign-aid-soft-power/.

40 "What the Data Says about U.S. Foreign Aid," Pew Research Center, February 6, 2025, https://www.pewresearch.org/short-reads/2025/02/06/what-the-data-says-about-us-foreign-aid/.

41 "Trump Administration Moves to Eliminate USAID, Firing Remaining Employees," The Hill, March 8, 2025, https://thehill.com/policy/national-security/5220447-trump-administration-to-end-usaid/.

42 "Analyzing the Scale of Trump's Federal Layoffs in His First 100 Days," CNN, April 29, 2025, https://www.cnn.com/2025/04/26/politics/federal-layoffs-trump-musk-dg.

43 Quoted in "BREAKING: Mass Layoffs Hit CDC, NIH, FDA," Healthcare Innovation, February 18, 2025, https://www.hcinnovationgroup.com/policy-value-based-care/article/55268713/breaking-mass-layoffs-hit-cdc-nih-fda. For other data sources, see "Experts: FDA Layoffs Will Slow Device Reviews, Impact Decision Making," Regulatory Focus, February 19, 2025, https://www.raps.org/news-and-articles/news-articles/2025/2/experts-fda-layoffs-will-slow-device-reviews,-impa, and "FDA Begins Layoffs as Trump Moves to Shrink Federal Workforce," Bloomberg Law, February 15, 2025, https://news.bloomberglaw.com/health-law-and-business/fda-begins-layoffs-as-trump-moves-to-shrink-federal-workforce.

44 See "How Many Federal Employees Have Been Fired and Laid Off: What We Know," NBC Washington, February 19, 2025, https://www.nbcwashington.com/news/local/how-many-federal-employees-have-been-fired-and-laid-off-what-we-know/3847944/, "Here Are All the Agencies Federal Workers Are Being Fired From," ABC News, February 19, 2025, https://abcnews.go.com/US/agencies-federal-workers-fired/story?id=118901289, and "Trump Begins Firings of FAA Staff just Weeks after Fatal DC Plane Crash," Federal News Network, February 17, 2025, https://federalnewsnetwork.com/workforce/2025/02/trump-begins-firings-of-faa-air-traffic-control-staff-just-weeks-after-fatal-dc-plane-crash/.

45 "Trump Administration Estimates 50,000 Federal Employees Will Lose Civil Service Protections," Federal News Network, April 18, 2025, https://federalnewsnetwork.com/workforce/2025/04/trump-administration-estimates-50000-federal-employees-will-lose-civil-service-protections/.

46 "Trump to Convert Some Top Career Roles to Political Appointments and Evaluate Execs on Adherence to President's Agenda," Government Executive, February 25, 2025, https://www.govexec.com/management/2025/02/

trump-convert-governments-top-career-roles-political-appointments-and-evaluate-execs-adherence-presidents-agenda/403277/.
47 Quoted in "Thousands of Federal Workers Would Be Easier to Fire under Trump Rule Change," NPR, April 18, 2025, https://www.npr.org/2025/04/18/nx-s1-5369550/trump-federal-workers-schedule-f.
48 "The Consumer Financial Bureau Budget: Background, Trends, and Policy Options," Congressional Research Service, December 9, 2024, https://crsreports.congress.gov/product/pdf/R/R48295/2.
49 "5 Reasons Federal Cuts Are Hitting Veterans Especially Hard," PBS News, March 16, 2025, https://www.pbs.org/newshour/politics/5-reasons-federal-cuts-are-hitting-veterans-especially-hard.
50 "Internal V.A. Emails Reveal How Trump Cuts Jeopardize Veterans' Care, Including to 'Life-Saving Cancer Trials,'" ProPublica, May 6, 2025, https://www.propublica.org/article/trump-veterans-affairs-budget-staff-cuts-jeopardize-cancer-research.
51 "Jobs Cut at the FAA Helped Support Air Safety, a Union Says," AP, February 19, 2025, https://www.yahoo.com/news/jobs-cut-faa-helped-support-184342970.html.
52 See "Customer Wait Times in the Social Security Administration's Field Offices and Card Centers," Office of the Inspector General, Social Security Administration, May 2024, https://oig.ssa.gov/assets/uploads/152307.pdf, and "Social Security Stops Reporting Call Wait Times and Other Metrics," The Washington Post, June 20, 2025, https://www.washingtonpost.com/politics/2025/06/20/social-security-wait-times-cuts/.
53 "Trump Administration Races to Fix a Big Mistake: DOGE Fired too Many People," The Washington Post, June 6, 2025, https://www.washingtonpost.com/business/2025/06/06/doge-staff-cuts-rehiring-federal-workers/?utm_campaign=wp_post_most&utm_medium=email&utm_source=newsletter&carta-url=https%3A%2F%2Fs2.washingtonpost.com%2Fcar-ln-tr%2F42eceeb%2F684313e9d2a65e782705f53d%2F596a5d109bbc0f0e09eaa923%2F11%2F65%2F684313e9d2a65e782705f53d.
54 "ATD Research: Government Agencies Face Current and Future Skills Gaps," Association for Talent Development, April 2, 2025, https://www.td.org/content/press-release/atd-research-government-agencies-face-current-and-future-skills-gaps.
55 Seeing Trump's intent, Wray resigned his position shortly after the November presidential election.
56 "Trump DOJ Demands List of Thousands of FBI Agents, Others Who Worked on Jan. 6 and Investigations for Possible Firing," CNN, January 31, 2025, https://www.cnn.com/2025/01/31/politics/fbi-agents-who-investigated-january-6-fired/.
57 "Musk Says He Can Cut $2 Trillion from Budget at Trump Rally," Fortune, October 28, 2024, https://fortune.com/2024/10/28/elon-musk-cut-2-trillion-federal-budget-trump-rally/.
58 "Trump Taps Musk to a 'Department of Government Efficiency' with Ramaswamy," NPR, November 12, 2024, https://www.npr.

org/2024/11/12/g-s1-33972/trump-elon-musk-vivek-ramaswamy-doge-gov ernment-efficiency-deep-state.

59 "Musk Calls for Annual Firing of Judges after Blocked DOGE Access at Treasury," The Hill, February 9, 2025, https://thehill.com/policy/technol ogy/5135170-musk-annual-firing-judges-doge/.

60 "Slash First, Fix Later: How Elon Musk Cuts Costs," *The New York Times*, November 24, 2024, https://www.nytimes.com/2024/11/16/technology/ elon-musk-cost-cuts.html.

61 "The CFPB Took Aim at Big Tech, Then Elon Musk Moved to Dismantle It," *The Washington Post*, February 11, 2025, https://www.washingtonpost.com/busin ess/2025/02/11/elon-musk-doge-cfpb-regulations/.

62 For example, see "How Directives by Trump Echo Project 2025," *The New York Times*, February 14, 2025, https://www.nytimes.com/interactive/2025/02/14/ us/politics/project-2025-trump-actions.html%C3%A7.

63 "Comparing the Compensation of Federal and Private-Sector Employees in 2022," Congressional Budget Office, April 2022, https://www.cbo.gov/publicat ion/60235.

64 For the list of DOGE errors, see "DOGE Claims Credit for Killing Contracts That Were Already Dead," *The New York Times*, March 2, 2025, https://www.nyti mes.com/2025/03/02/us/politics/doge-musk-contracts-errors.html.

65 For more examples of Musk's fraudulent claims, see "Fact Check: Eight Ways Elon Musk Has Misled Americans about Government Spending," CNN, February 23, 2025, https://www.cnn.com/2025/02/23/politics/government- spending-elon-musk-doge/index.html.

66 "Elon Musk's Business Empire Scores Benefits under Trump Shake-Up," *The New York Times*, February 11, 2025, https://www.nytimes.com/2025/02/11/us/ politics/elon-musk-companies-conflicts.html.

67 "At Oval Office, Musk Makes Broad Claims of Federal Fraud Without Proof," *The New York Times*, February 11, 2025, https://www.nytimes.com/2025/02/11/ us/politics/trump-musk-oval-office.html.

68 "Inside the Explosive Meeting Where Trump Officials Clashed with Elon Musk," *The New York Times*, March 9, 2025, https://www.nytimes.com/2025/03/07/us/ politics/trump-musk-doge-power.html.

69 For a thorough examination of this topic, see Charles A. Kupchan, *Isolationism: A History of America's Efforts to Shield Itself from the World* (New York: Oxford University Press, 2020).

70 "Remarks by President Biden before the 78th Session of the United Nations General Assembly," The White House, September 19, 2023, https://bidenwhi tehouse.archives.gov/briefing-room/speeches-remarks/2023/09/19/rema rks-by-president-biden-before-the-78th-session-of-the-united-nations-gene ral-assembly-new-york-ny/.

71 "Trump Falsely Says Ukraine Started the War with Russia. Here Is What to Know," *The New York Times*, February 19, 2025, https://www.nytimes. com/2025/02/19/world/europe/trump-zelensky-ukraine-comments.html.

72 "Ukraine Support Tracker," Kiel Institute for the World Economy, February 14, 2025, https://www.ifw-kiel.de/topics/war-against-ukraine/ukraine-support-tracker/.

73 "Ukraine, Russian Federation, United Kingdom of Great Britain and Northern Ireland and the United States of America," Memorandum on Security Assurances in Connection with Ukraine's Accession to the Treaty on the Non-Proliferation of Nuclear Weapons, Budapest, December 5, 1994, https://www.securitycouncilreport.org/atf/cf/%7B65BFCF9B-6D27-4E9C-8CD3-CF6E4FF96FF9%7D/s_1994_1399.pdf and "Treaty Series: Treaties and Agreements Registered or Filed and Recorded with the Secretariat of the United Nations," 3007 (2014), pp. 167–72, https://treaties.un.org/doc/Publication/UNTS/Volume%203007/v3007.pdf.

74 "U.S. Votes against U.N. Resolution Condemning Russia for Ukraine War," *The Washington Post*, February 24, 2025, https://www.washingtonpost.com/national-security/2025/02/24/united-nations-ukraine-russia-trump/.

75 "Trump Embarrasses the Pentagon with a U-Turn on Ukraine," *The Economist*, July 8, 2025, https://www.economist.com/united-states/2025/07/08/trump-embarrasses-the-pentagon-with-a-u-turn-on-ukraine.

76 "Why Does Trump Want to Buy Greenland? What to Know as Danish Prime Minister Says It's Not for Sale," *Forbes*, January 16, 2025, https://www.forbes.com/sites/saradorn/2025/01/16/why-does-trump-want-to-buy-greenland-what-to-know-as-danish-prime-minister-says-its-not-for-sale/.

77 "Trump Says He Seriously Wants Canada as 51st State," *Time Magazine*, February 9, 2025, https://time.com/7214321/trump-canada-51st-state-fox-super-bowl-interview/.

78 "Trump Threatens to Retake Control of Panama Canal," Reuters, December 23, 2024, https://www.reuters.com/world/americas/trump-says-he-might-demand-panama-hand-over-canal-2024-12-22/.

79 "Two Ships Desperately Tried to Fight Off Houthi Attacks. Help Never Arrived," *The Wall Street Journal*, July 11, 2025, https://www.wsj.com/world/middle-east/two-ships-desperately-tried-to-fight-off-houthi-attacks-help-never-arrived-c400a2a8?gaa_at=eafs&gaa_n=ASWzDAiU5e5Dshtjp_I7OI-FHjV3vWrE76aSb-jbZ4zOrLKPkyte8QNsWNLNGPU1aCo%3D&gaa_ts=68714685&gaa_sig=CpeAIg_4sMSMr4aMCZK6l1cg6-KKQAUnUHRJJjD6yAeatQAItQs5LUMgl1sFOCUMXUNaqrk2i8jmiB5QMGGRjg%3D%3D.

80 See "Trump Faith Leader to Former President: Time to Bomb Iran," *The Jerusalem Post*, January 30, 2024, https://www.jpost.com/international/article-784253, and "Texas Pastors Cite Bible in Support of Trump's Iran Strikes," Chron, June 23, 2025, https://www.chron.com/culture/religion/article/texas-pastors-trump-iran-20389536.php.

81 "Trump Announces Sweeping New Tariffs, Upending Decades of US Trade Policy," *The Guardian*, April 2, 2025, https://www.theguardian.com/us-news/2025/apr/02/trump-new-tariffs-liberation-day.

82 "State of U.S. Tariffs: August 7, 2025," The Budget Lab, Yale University, August 7, 2025, https://budgetlab.yale.edu/research/state-us-tariffs-august-7-2025.

83 "The Incoherent Case for Tariffs," *Foreign Affairs*, March 11, 2025, https://www.foreignaffairs.com/united-states/incoherent-case-tariffs-trump?check_logged_in=1.

Trumpism 2.0

84 "Trump Calls to 'Drain the Swamp' of Washington," *USA Today*, October 18, 2016, https://www.usatoday.com/story/news/politics/elections/2016/2016/10/18/donald-trump-rally-colorado-springs-ethics-lobbying-limitations/92377656/.

85 "Trump Crypto Venture Partners with Platform Linked to Middle East Militants," Reuters, December 12, 2024, https://www.reuters.com/technology/trump-crypto-venture-partners-with-platform-linked-middle-east-militants-2024-12-12/.

86 "Trump Sons' Deals on Three Continents Directly Benefit the President," *The New York Times*, May 5, 2025, https://www.nytimes.com/2025/05/05/us/politics/eric-donald-jr-trump-family-deals.html.

87 "Emails Shed Light on Amazon's Cozy Relationship with the U.S. Government," *New York Magazine*, December 2018, https://nymag.com/intelligencer/2018/12/emails-show-amazons-cozy-relationship-with-u-s-government.html.

88 "Fact Sheet: President Donald J. Trump Secures Historic $1.l2 Trillion Economic Commitment in Qatar," The White House, May 14, 2025, https://www.whitehouse.gov/fact-sheets/2025/05/fact-sheet-president-donald-j-trump-secures-historic-1-2-trillion-economic-commitment-in-qatar/.

89 "Luxury Skyscrapers, Golf Courses and Cryptocurrency: The Trump Family's Rapidly Expanding Middle East Businesses," CNN, May 13, 2025, https://www.cnn.com/2025/05/13/politics/trump-middle-east-business-invs.

90 "Trump's Finances Were Shaky. Then He Began to Capitalize on His Comeback," *The New York Times*, July 3, 2025, https://www.nytimes.com/2025/07/02/us/trump-finances-crypto.html.

91 "Most Voters Raise Concern of Trump's Acceptance of a $400 Million Plane," Harvard CAPS Harris Poll, May 2025, https://harvardharrispoll.com/search?s=qatari+plane&page=1&type=Key+Results&sort=last_12.

92 See Jack Landman and Bob Bauer, "Trump 2.0 and the Foreign Emoluments Clause," American Enterprise Institute, May 15, 2025, https://www.aei.org/op-eds/trump-2-0-and-the-foreign-emoluments-clause/.

93 Quoted in "As Trumps Monetize Presidency, Profits Outstrip Protests," *The New York Times*, May 26, 2025, https://www.nytimes.com/2025/05/25/us/politics/trump-money-plane-crypto.html.

94 "Congress's Authority to Influence and Control Executive Branch Authorities," Congressional Research Service, December 19, 2018, https://crsreports.congress.gov/product/pdf/R/R45442/2#:~:text=Congress%20may%20use%20its%20Article,offices%20are%20appointed%20and%20removed.

95 "Republicans Take a Back Seat as Trump Steamrolls Congress with Flurry of Unilateral Moves," NBC News, February 3, 2025, https://www.nbcnews.com/politics/congress/republicans-back-seat-trump-steamroll-congress-unilateral-moves-rcna190465.

96 "Here's Who Stands to Gain from the 'Big, Beautiful Bill.' And Who May Struggle," CNN, July 4, 2025, https://www.cnn.com/2025/07/03/business/trump-big-beautiful-bill-business-economy.

97 "Powers of Trump and Congress Collide as Government Shutdown Nears," *The Wall Street Journal*, March 1, 2025, https://www.wsj.com/politics/policy/trump-congress-budget-government-shutdown-threat-5781b817.

98 "'We Are All Afraid': Murkowski Says Fear of Retaliation from Trump Administration Is 'Real,'" Politico, April 17, 2025, https://www.politico.com/news/2025/04/17/lisa-murkowski-trump-retaliation-00295852.

99 "United States Michigan Consumer Sentiment," Trading Economics, May 2025, https://tradingeconomics.com/united-states/consumer-confidence

100 "Republicans in U.S. Congress Sweat Trump Tariffs' Hit to Retirees, a Critical Constituency," Reuters, April 9, 2025, https://tradingeconomics.com/united-states/consumer-confidence.

101 Scott Bomboy, "How Congress Delegates Tariff Powers to the President," The Constitution Center, April 2, 2055, https://constitutioncenter.org/blog/how-congress-delegates-its-tariff-powers-to-the-president/.

102 "Anger Erupts at Republican Lawmakers' Town Halls amid Tariff and DOGE Drama," USA Today, April 16, 2025, https://www.usatoday.com/story/news/politics/2025/04/16/anger-erupts-town-halls-lawmakers/83116024007/, and "A G.O.P. Congressman Faced Hometown Voters. It Wasn't Pretty," The New York Times, August 5, 2025, https://www.nytimes.com/2025/08/05/us/politics/mike-flood-town-hall.html.

103 "No More In-Person Town Halls, NRCC Chief Tells House Republicans," Politico, March 4, 2025, https://www.politico.com/live-updates/2025/03/04/congress/gop-town-halls-richard-hudson-00210024

104 "Trump's Blitz to Expand His Power Is Direct Threat to Democracy, Experts Say," The Guardian, February 7, 2025, https://www.theguardian.com/us-news/2025/feb/07/trump-executive-actions-democracy.

105 Quoted in "Dan Bongino Argues That Trump 'Should Ignore' Court Order Blocking Funding Freeze," Media Matters, February 11, 2025, https://www.mediamatters.org/dan-bongino/dan-bongino-argues-trump-should-ignore-court-order-blocking-federal-funding-freeze.

106 "Several Republicans Push Impeachment Bids against Judges Who've Stood in Trump's Way," MSNBC, February 25, 2025, https://www.msnbc.com/rachel-maddow-show/maddowblog/several-republicans-push-impeachment-bids-judges-ve-stood-trumps-way-rcna193678.

107 "Musk Calls for Annual Firing of Judges after Blocked DOGE Access at Treasury," The Hill, February 9, 2025, https://thehill.com/policy/technology/5135170-musk-annual-firing-judges-doge/.

108 Quoted in "Musk and Republican Lawmakers Pressure Judges with Impeachment Threats," The New York Times, March 2, 2025, https://www.nytimes.com/2025/03/01/us/politics/trump-musk-republicans-congress-judge-impeachment.html.

109 "The ABA Rejects Efforts to Undermine the Courts and the Legal Profession," American Bar Association, March 3, 2025, https://www.americanbar.org/news/abanews/aba-news-archives/2025/03/aba-rejects-efforts-to-undermine-courts-and-legal-profession/.

110 "Trump Asks the Supreme Court to Stop Judges from Blocking His Policies," MSNBC, March 21, 2025, https://www.msnbc.com/top-stories/latest/trump-supreme-court-injunctions-judges-rcna197457.

111 "Supreme Court Upholds for Now Trump's Firing of Two Independent Agency Officials," *Los Angeles Times*, May 22, 2025, https://www.latimes.com/politics/story/2025-05-22/supreme-court-upholds-trumps-firing-of-two-agency-officials.

112 For an overview of this case, see "What We Know about Kilmar Abrego Garcia, the Maryland Man Mistakenly Deported to El Salvador," NBC News, April 18, 2025, https://www.nbcnews.com/news/us-news/kilmar-abrego-garcia-deported-el-salvador-trump-immigration-what-know-rcna201708.

113 "Trump Says He 'Could' Return Abrego Garcia to US, but Won't," The Hill, April 30, 2025, https://thehill.com/homenews/administration/5274438-donald-trump-abc-news-interview-kilmar-abrego-garcia/.

114 The case was 24A949 *Noem v. Abrego Garcia* (April 10, 2025).

115 "Kilmar Abrego Garcia on Way Back to US to Face Criminal Charges: Sources," ABC News, June 6, 2025, https://abcnews.go.com/US/mistakenly-deported-kilmar-abrego-garcia-back-us-face/story?utm_source=facebook&utm_medium=social&utm_campaign=dhfacebook&utm_content=app.dashsocial.com/abcnews/library/media/539079708&id=121333122.

CHAPTER 10
RESTORING THE POWER OF THE VOTE IN A DEMOCRACY

We begin this section of *Overcoming Trumpism* with an important cautionary note: Don't expect an immediate solution to the plague of an authoritarian scourge decades in the making. Nor has it been the creation of a single narcissistic megalomaniac. The roots of our democratic decay are deep and wide. They will disappear only with the commitment to substantive long-term changes.

The essence of Trumpism began long before Donald Trump's emergence on the political stage. Along with attracting a fringe element of American society, it has been embraced by millions of Americans troubled by this country's direction as well as the circumstances of their own distressed lives. Trump is hardly a solitary figure in his effort to replace American democracy with his shade of despotism. Should he falter, there are all too many would-be autocrats with similar views who lie in wait for their opportunity to seize upon the democratic setting that defines the American political system.

So, painful as it may be, we need to temper any expectation of immediate relief as we pursue recommended remedies for the American polity to overcome the autocratic infestation that has penetrated many levels of governance. To disable the widespread stain of Trumpism, we require patience, persistence, and vigilance to alter our current course and firmly insulate American democracy from future assault. Most of all, we have to think outside of the box, and the American public must be willing to take bold action.

This is not to say that in a post-Trumpism world American democracy will be permanently secure. The fact is, democracy is always under threat by demagogues who would rule us if just presented with the opportunity. As noted in Chapter 2, because our political system depends upon the ongoing buy-in of the people, despots find it rather easy to uncover areas of societal weakness and penetrate the culture with meaningless promises of a better world. And given the polarized nature of American society today, we are particularly susceptible to tyrannical enemies. Yet, if recent events are an indication, rather sizable numbers of Americans are unaware of just how close we are to democratic implosion. On that observation, Barbara Walter writes that there is an irony about us in that Americans "are more prepared, as a country, to counter foreign enemies such as Al-Qaeda than we are to disarm the warriors in our midst, even though the latter are more virulent and dangerous."[1] It's when we—or at least a sizable number of us—collectively let our guard down at home that Trumpist-like political movements find their footing. Therefore, our vigilance against autocratic intrusion must be powerful and enduring. To that end, the material we present in this and in the remaining chapters may be our best opportunity to save our democracy for years to come.

This chapter spotlights institutional components of the American political system that are either out of date or have been abused in such a way as to no longer fulfill their originally intended purposes. In their totality, these government institutions now fail to promote democracy and help to facilitate authoritarian regimes such as Trumpism. They include the Electoral College, gerrymandered congressional districts, and the voting process. At first, these three elements may appear unrelated, but they all relate to the waning power of the individual in a democracy. At their root, they are connected with the part of the Fourteenth Amendment that confers to each citizen "equal protection of the laws." There can be no equal protection for each citizen unless each vote in an election carries the same clout as the vote of others. And lest we forget, equality is a lynchpin of democracy.

The discussion includes a series of recommendations to protect the voter from conditions that inhibit democracy and by extension facilitate Trumpism. Solving each concern will require leadership from Congress, which was designed by the framers as a coequal policymaking institution, and which faces its own problems from failing to control an unchecked and dangerous Trump presidency. We also need to seriously consider carefully tailored constitutional changes to make the document a bit more reflective of the changes that have occurred in our democracy. Beyond these recommendations, citizens need to think long and hard of the role we can play in electing government leaders willing to take bold action in troubled times.

Fixing these critical obstructions to democracy won't automatically prevent Donald Trump or another person with similar values from gaining the presidency. However, if put into place, these repairs, will go a long way toward making the American electoral system more democratic and less susceptible to electoral chicanery and incomplete representation.

Restoring the Power of the Vote in a Democracy

Eliminating the Electoral College

In terms of its function, the Electoral College is more of a temporary formal situation than an institution. It briefly becomes an integral part of the presidential election process after each state's presidential votes are tabulated and confirmed. Once that job is completed and validated, the Electoral College recedes from any official activity until the next presidential election. Still, for that brief period, the Electoral College is key to completing the presidential election.

There are no permanent members of the Electoral College, only individuals selected by the winning political party in each state to serve as temporary electors, people assigned to affirm the presidential vote result. Created as part of the Constitution in 1787, it was designed as a buffer between direct democracy and an elected president. As Anthony King put it, in the United States, "The electoral college institutionalizes a form of indirect democracy--of democracy, so to speak, at one remove."[2] Two hundred and forty years later, it's worth examining whether the "indirect democracy" element provided through the Electoral College is a good enough representation in a nation where democracy is on the line.

How It Works

The Constitution guarantees each state a minimum of one seat in the House of Representatives and two seats in the US Senate. By law, there are 538 electoral votes in recognition of the total number of US senators (100) and members of the House of Representatives (435) along with three electors for the residents of the District of Columbia per the Twenty-Third Amendment to the Constitution in recognition of its residents. The rest of the nation's congressional seats are assigned in response to the population of each state. Likewise, the number of a state's electoral votes is based on its number of elected members of Congress. Wyoming, the least populated state with its 576,000 residents, according to the 2020 national census, has the minimum 3 electors reflecting a single House member and 2 US senators. California, the state with the largest population with 39.5 million residents, has 54 electors—2 for its US senators and 52 for its congressional districts.

Every ten years after the results of a constitutionally assigned census of the US population, the electors for each state are reallocated on the same basis as reallocating the numbers of elected House members. After the 2020 census, Wyoming continued as the nation's least populated state and remained at three electors because of little change in its population. California, which had fifty-five electors after the 2010 census, gained population but less than several other states, and therefore lost a congressional seat, leaving the state with fifty-four electors. Texas, which gained more residents over the previous decade than any other state, grew enough in population to receive two additional congressional seats, which combined with its two Senate seats, expanded its total to forty electoral votes. And so it went for all the states with some gaining, some losing, and others remaining the same in their numbers of the House of Representatives, and as such, the numbers of presidential electors. The congressional and Electoral College assignments will remain in place until the 2030 census, when the reallocation process begins anew.

At the time of a presidential election voters in each state select their choice from a list of candidates on the ballot. Except for two states, the presidential candidate in a state that receives more votes than any other candidate wins all the state's electoral votes that are then presented at meetings of the Electoral College in each state on the first Tuesday in December after the second Wednesday.[3] Whichever candidate gathers at least 270 electoral votes, one more than half wins the presidential election. The results are then sent to Congress for a meeting on January 6 following the November election, where the vice president presides over a ceremony to accept the results.

For most presidential elections, the Electoral College has worked to the extent that it has accumulated a majority of state electors to produce a presidential victor. The only exception occurred in 1824 because of minor political party candidates who siphoned off enough votes to prevent an electoral vote majority. On that occasion, the election outcome was settled as per the prescription in the Twelfth Amendment where each state delegation in the House of Representatives had one vote. That cleared the way for John Quincy Adams to win.

More consequently, there have been four presidential elections where one candidate won the popular vote only to lose the electoral vote and outcome to another candidate. They occurred in 1876 (Rutherford B. Hayes defeated Samuel J. Tilden); 1888 (Benjamin Harrison defeated incumbent Grover Cleveland); 2000 (George W. Bush defeated Al Gore); and 2016 (Donald Trump defeated Hillary Clinton). Otherwise, the electoral and popular votes for the winners have been in alignment. But when the two vote outcomes differ, the dissonance between the popular vote winner and the electoral vote winner not only causes confusion but breeds distrust in the system.[4] In the current era, that's a serious problem.

The January 6, 2021, Debacle

The January 6, 2021, insurrection against the Capitol in part was also an insurrection against the Electoral College. During the very contentious 2020 presidential election campaign, designated Republican electors in seven states that produced a win for Democrat Joe Biden refused to accept the election certified results. Instead, they claimed without any evidence that the vote counts incorrectly awarded the results to Joe Biden. Independent audits in most of these states along with 60+ federal court decisions verified the Biden victories. Nevertheless, so incensed were the Republican electors about the results that they submitted "alternate" Republican Electoral College lists to Congress with the demand that their electoral votes be accepted as the official results. The number of alternate electoral votes was more than enough to shift the victory to Trump if the House accepted that scenario.

If Donald Trump's fingerprints weren't on the Republication fake elector lists, they were incredibly close. Trump campaign lawyers were heavily involved in the effort[5] and in several cases were indicted in their states. Ever since the November 3, 2020 presidential election, Trump had insisted without a shred of evidence that the election outcome had been "rigged" for Biden. As the January 6 ceremony neared, he became increasingly direct with his demand that Vice President Mike Pence accept the alternate list or at least send the election result to the House of Representatives where the number of Republican state delegations outnumbered the Democratic delegations, thereby guaranteeing a Trump victory.

At a nearby "Stop the Steal" rally just before the insurrection against the Capitol, Trump warned, "Mike Pence, I hope you're going to stand up for the Constitution and for the good of the country, and if you're not, I'm going to be very disappointed in you."[6] Shortly thereafter the historic riot ensued. Despite calls in the mob to hang him, Pence held firm, and despite the insurrection and some Republican opposition, counted the official electoral votes. With that, Joe Biden was officially elected as the nation's forty-sixth president.

Assessing the Electoral College in the 21st Century

Two of the past three presidential elections—2016 and 2020—have put the Electoral College to a stress test of sorts. In the first case, angst occurred because of the popular vote winner losing the electoral vote. In the second case, the loser attempted to tinker with the Electoral College process. Both situations were aggravated by social media posts, which added to the public's confusion. With these events as well as other historical Electoral College–related problems, we need to think about whether it should continue.

Arguments for the Electoral College

A Staple of Continuity

Defenders of the Electoral College cite several reasons for keeping it as part of the presidential election process.[7] To begin with, they argue that the Electoral College maintains horizontal federalism,[8] which focuses on the relationship between the states. Some states are largely rural, while others are urban; likewise, as we already know, some states are much more populated than others. Under the Electoral College arrangement, every state is represented in accumulating presidential electors. States with sizable populations can be offset by several small states with similar approaches to an election. Horizontal federalism recognizes the value of every state and its people.

Political Moderation

A second defense of federalism lies with the propensity for political moderation. Much of this benefit accrues from presidential candidates campaigning in so many different states. National issues consume a good deal of the candidates' time and energy, but they may be viewed very differently from state to state. Consider an issue like climate change. Some state populations may embrace alternate energy, while others may remain attached to fossil fuel. Recognizing the widely differing views on so many issues, candidates need to think of policy positions that cling closer to the middle than one extreme or another to avoid losing a large segment of the voter universe. Finding middle ground promotes moderation and stability.

Legitimacy of the Outcome

A third consideration focuses on the legitimacy of the election outcome provided by the Electoral College. With the winner-take-all aspect of elector accumulation in forty-eight of the fifty states, the electoral outcomes are often much more lopsided than the popular vote. The one-sided outcome provides a consensus of sorts as part of the election outcome, leading vote challenges in various states to appear unnecessary. In other words, there's a closure element that makes it easier for voters to accept the election outcome and go on to other issues.

Arguments against the Electoral College

Less Confusion about the Outcome

The two vote counts that are assembled at the end of a presidential election can be bewildering to the less informed and a source of voter stress. Most Americans focus on the popular vote as a guide to the outcome. The candidate tallies are massive, they come in from everywhere, and public opinion expects that the person with the most popular votes *should* win. Talk of the electoral vote seems so, well, confusing and unnecessary. It doesn't matter anyway since the winner accumulates more votes than the loser in the popular and electoral vote contests. But it's not always the case. Setting aside a few historical examples, for example, in 2000, when George W. Bush won the electoral vote over Al Gore 271-to-267, and yet Gore defeated Bush in the popular vote count by more than 500,000 votes. Differences in the two vote outcomes were even more extreme in the 2016 presidential when Donald Trump defeated Hillary Clinton by winning the electoral vote 306-to-232, while losing the popular vote by more than 2.8 million votes. Even though the electoral vote is the only vote that matters for determining the presidential winner, the popular vote gives people a clear indication of national sentiment. Furthermore, we live in an age where conspiracy theories about vote tampering appear in large numbers, and they seem to be more believable when the popular and electoral vote counts aren't the same. Of the two systems, it's clear that the popular vote is more understandable as well as a more accurate representation of public sentiment.

Increased Cultural Integration

At the time of the Constitution, the United States was much more of a political patchwork quilt than it is today. Slavery was paramount in the South while largely outlawed in the North. There were vast swaths of agriculture across the nation and large cities dotted in between. Two hundred and forty years later, the differences are not nearly as stark as they were at the time of the Constitution's birth. To begin with, Americans are mobile. About one out of eight Americans moves every year, and about one-fourth of those move more than five hundred miles.[9] In addition, the United States

Overcoming Trumpism

receives annual infusions of immigrants, further adding to our cultural diversity. Since the nation's earliest days, an estimated one hundred million immigrants came to the United States. As of 2024, 45.3 million lived here.[10] In recent years, Mexico, India, China, and the Philippines have contributed the largest numbers, but immigrants have come to the United States from dozens of other countries. The point is, Americans are no longer planted in the same places, removed from others who are not like them. Mobility has helped to reduce barriers. To be sure, there remain pockets where the same people's families had been ensconced for generations, but such examples become fewer with each generation. This development reduces the need for states to receive special protection because of their own idiosyncrasies.

An Impairment to Equal Representation

Finally, we focus directly on representation. For decades now, representation in the United States has been clarified by the "one person, one vote" decisions emerging from the Supreme Court's attention to the Fourteenth Amendment of the Constitution, which assures that every person's vote has the same value. But perhaps the most overlooked underrepresentation exists through the constitutionally prescribed organization of the Electoral College. By relying on the organization of Congress as its model, the Constitution assures that there will be huge representation issues in Congress and by extension the Electoral College. Let's go back to the Wyoming-California examples for a moment. Recall that with 576,000 residents, Wyoming has 3 electoral votes. With 39.5 million residents, California has 54 electoral votes. Here's where the math becomes interesting. While California has eighteen times the Electoral College membership of Wyoming, the Golden State has sixty-five times the population of the Cowboy State. Nothing is more undemocratic than those sets of numbers. If we really want equal representation for Americans, the Electoral College must be abolished. It's critical to assuring true democracy.

There will be those who scream about the sacred nature of the Constitution. To that, we offer two thoughts. First, by virtue of its many decisions over its existence, the Supreme Court has made *de facto* changes in the Constitution, beginning with its own self-defined power of judicial review. Second, much of the Constitution is as relevant today as it was at its beginning, but the population is different today on the representation issue in that we don't need to worry about various interests being artificially protected. We are one nation, where everyone deserves the same vote.

The public may have a consistent record of supporting the popular vote as the way to elect the nation's president. A 2024 poll found a nearly two-to-one majority for the idea, 63 to 35 percent.[11] Far from a one-time assessment, strong public support to use the popular vote for determining the outcome of a presidential election has been steady for some time.[12]

Unrepresentativeness of Gerrymandering

During his tenure as governor of Massachusetts (1812–14), Elbridge Gerry signed legislation creating oddly shaped state senatorial districts designed in such a way as to artificially keep his political party in power. So egregious was the shape of one district that the *Boston Globe* described its salamander-like appearance as a "Gerry-mander," reflecting upon the approval of its creation by the Massachusetts governor. Over time, the process of forming legislative districts intentionally designed to favor the political party in charge became known as "gerrymandering." The US Constitution mandates that a population census of all the states be taken every ten years. Based on the overall shifts of the national population, states frequently are assigned additional or fewer congressional districts. That's when states have the opportunity to apply gerrymandering.

Whether minimizing the clout of certain populations by spreading their numbers into several districts, or packing them disproportionately into a single district to diminish their influence elsewhere, gerrymandering puts "a thumb on the scale to manufacture election outcomes that are detached from the preferences of voters."[13] As a result, gerrymandered districts in a state often produce election results far different than the overall preferences of the voting population. Historically, this tactic has been used to limit the political power of people of color.[14] Because gerrymandering maximizes the power of some groups and minimizes the power of others, it is by definition undemocratic.

The gerrymandering problem was significantly weakened with the passage of the Voting Rights Act of 1965. This seminal legislation required seven southern states and parts of four others riddled with devious electoral manipulation to gain approval of the US Department of Justice before changing the voting rules. Informally, it also placed the rest of the states on notice that the federal government would be watching their election processes as they related to racial discrimination.

Federal oversight to prevent gerrymandering was upended when the Supreme Court handed down three redistricting-related decisions that essentially stripped the Department of Justice of its supervisorial powers on the questionable proposition that little racial discrimination of voters existed anymore. That's what the justices wrote, anyway.[15] These days, about half of the states place congressional redistricting in the hands of their state legislatures, where they still utilize the gerrymander. The remaining states rely upon independent commissions, the courts, or shared legislative responsibility for redistricting, all of which provide more representative formulas than gerrymandering.

Designation and reallocation of congressional districts after the 2020 census occurred in an environment largely free of federal involvement. The outcome was hardly surprising. An independent, nonpartisan examination found that gerrymandering was reintroduced in fifteen states, with one-sided overall benefits for Republicans. Research by the Brennan Center for Justice estimated that gerrymandered districts developed from the 2020 US Census gave Republicans sixteen more seats than they would have had from fair maps.[16] Legislative Democrats in four states gerrymandered a total of seven extra districts that elected Democratic candidates. Meanwhile, legislative Republicans in eleven states gerrymandered a total of twenty-three extra districts that elected Republican candidates.[17] Who knows how many of those fifteen states would have had different congressional compositions in gerrymandering-free political environments? Most significantly, racial underrepresentation continues despite court decisions that declared the end of racism in contemporary redistricting.[18]

Inasmuch as presidential elections have become incredibly close, the ability to artificially configure congressional districts has become an important topic of discussion. In the 2022 congressional elections, Republicans won control of the House with a four-seat advantage. Do the math on the gerrymandering and you'll see that the outcome could have resulted in the Democratic control of the House of Representatives if redistricting in all states had occurred by independent commission or another relatively neutral entity. Similar unrepresentative results also occurred in state legislative elections.

But there's more. Gerrymandering has the potential to elect an unrepresentative president. Here's why. We already know that in the event that Electoral College votes end in a 269-269 tie, the Constitution stipulates that the House of Representatives would break the tie. In such a situation, each state's delegation of representatives would have one vote. Thus, the political party in each state with a majority of seats controls that single vote. After the 2022 election, Republicans comprised a majority of House members in twenty-eight states and Democrats in seventeen; five had equal numbers. Had a similar outcome occurred in 2024, Republicans would have won the tiebreaker in the House, yielding a Republican presidential winner. Yet, if enough Democrats were elected in just a few of the gerrymandered states, the presidential votes of each state delegation might yield a different result. This dilemma underscores the unrepresentative nature of the Electoral College.

It would be tempting to view this discussion as hypothetical, and even more so, highly unlikely. Yet, given the closeness of recent elections, we could end up with a 269-269 tie in the Electoral College, paving the way for the state delegations to determine the outcome. Which takes us back to the gerrymandering discussion. If gerrymandering is outlawed, congressional districts in the states would in all likelihood be reasonably reflective of their population compositions. With that simple formula, at least the problem of unrepresentative state delegations would be eliminated.

The unfortunate fact is that the easiest way to end gerrymandering would be through the US Supreme Court overturning its own decisions that allowed this undemocratic practice to creep back into our electoral system. The current Supreme Court has demonstrated the ease with which majorities have overturned several precedents. Thus, there is no short-term cure. We can only hope that the gerrymandering issue becomes part of future presidential campaigns and that the voters will see the wisdom of electing a president who, if given the opportunity, appoints justices sympathetic to decisions more supportive of democratic concepts.

The Many Aspects of Voter Suppression

In addition to controlling the organization of legislative districts, states make the laws regarding election voter registration, election management, and voter intimidation. Sadly, examples abound of situations where states intentionally legislate to encourage turnout for some and discourage turnout for others. And to the extent that representation fades, so goes the well-being of democracy. In a 2021 analysis of more than four hundred recently enacted antivoter bills, the American Civil Liberties Union concluded "these measures disproportionately impact people of color, students, the elderly, and people with disabilities."[19] For all of these groups, the stakes are particularly large.

Voter Registration

People can't vote unless they are registered in advance of the event. Should state laws impose rigorous registration requirements beyond citizenship, they can shape the attributes of the qualified registrants, and as such, the collective composition of the overall vote. Although passage of the Fourteenth, Nineteenth, and Twenty-Sixth Amendments to the Constitution clarified the right for all citizens aged eighteen and older to vote, determining parochial requirements for registrants remained in the hands of the states and continues to the present day. Sleight-of-hand efforts to deny voter registration especially to people of color and young groups in some states have nevertheless continued.[20]

At one point, the Voting Rights Act of 1965 seemed to assure fair representation, thanks to a provision requiring states historically abusive of voting rights to gain approval of the attorney general in advance of legislative changes in election rules. However, recent Supreme Court decisions have reopened that once-closed door to voter discrimination by declaring major portions of the Voting Rights Act unconstitutional. Nowadays, states once again have near total control of election management.

In the wake of Trump's 2020 presidential defeat, new state laws discouraging registration have returned with a vengeance, particularly in states with Republican-controlled legislatures loyal to Donald Trump. In the post-2020 presidential election environment, the Brennan Center identified eleven states that passed legislation that interfered with the voting process.[21] Examples include demands for excessive voter documentation, barriers to same-day registration, the absence of automatic registration, legislation prohibiting registration support by independent voting assistance groups, and purging from the voter rolls those individuals who failed to vote in the previous election.

Recent Florida legislation serves as a case in point. Focusing on voter registration drives by independent groups, in 2021 the state legislature imposed a $1,000 fine on canvassers posing as election officials. A year later, state legislators raised the fine to $50,000. In 2024, the Florida legislature increased the fine to $250,000 along with new rules on how and where voting organizations could return the forms. Because of fears that they might inadvertently go awry with the costly law, most groups stopped their registration efforts. The outcome was predictable. Between 2018 and 2024, organized voter registration drives by independent groups went down by more than 90%, according to state data.[22] "As a consequence of all these threatening provisions, the League no longer collects paper voter registration applications," said the president of the League of Women Voters in Florida,[23] which is hardly considered a radical group.

Another example of potential state harm to would-be voters occurred in 2024 just days before the presidential election. On this occasion, the Supreme Court held that Virginia election officials had the right to purge 1,600 people from the voter rolls on the suspicion that some of them were noncitizens. Virginia Republican Governor Glenn Youngkin claimed that only noncitizens were removed, although the removal process classified the group as "possible noncitizens," giving the now-ineligible group just days to confirm their citizenship.[24]

Interference with voter registration comes at a cost to selected portions of the population, according to an elections expert. In her *One Person, No Vote*, Carol Anderson bluntly explains that "The goal of all the GOP voter ID laws is . . . to diminish the ability of blacks, Latinos, and Asians, as well as the poor and students to choose government representatives and the types of policies they support. Unfortunately," she adds, "it's working."[25] Registration differences by race and ethnicity support this claim.[26] The lack of opportunity for these groups to participate in exercising the franchise is nothing short of a red flag with respect to inequality at the ballot box as well as a stain on American democracy.

It's important to note that these laws came about because of alleged state concerns of widespread illegal registration and voting which, if true, could interfere with determining the final election results. But such claims simply aren't true. Returning to Florida for a moment, in 2022, Governor Ron DeSantis in a "major" news conference announced that in his state with 14.4 million voters, 20 people with prior felony records had illegally registered to vote.[27] Within days, at least eighteen of the twenty cases fell apart due to the fact that the accused had responded to voter registration cards mailed to them![28]

Another example: Upon reviewing six million votes in the 2020 presidential election, the Ohio Republican Secretary of State referred 641 voter fraud cases to authorities.[29] As of 2024, only twelve of the cases resulted in criminal charges.[30]

And here's a third instance: In fall 2024, just before the presidential election, Virginia Governor Youngkin announced that over his first two and one-half years in office, his office purged 6,303 noncitizens from the state's voting rolls. That sounds impressive enough, except that an examination of state court records and voting official interviews revealed that almost all of the cases involved innocent clerical errors. It turns out that between January 2022 and July 2024, three people had been prosecuted![31]

Finally, there was a case in Pennsylvania where, shortly before the 2024 presidential election, a Republican operative searching for voter fraud falsely accused fifty-three people registered at a monastery of not living there. The Benedictine Sisters of Erie who lived on the property begged to differ, leaving the Republican operative embarrassed, but not before fifty-eight thousand followers on X read the story.[32] Over and over again, state charges of voter fraud were themselves fraudulent.

Illegal voter registrations are indeed rare events, but suppressing voter registration is not. The facts are clear: sensationalized press conferences with outlandish claims of voter registration fraud never live up to their billing. Meanwhile, too many times the public buys into the exaggerated allegations of authorities without giving much thought as to their veracity. These kinds of unproven assertions are the breeding grounds for public distrust of "the system." Sadly, news of the facts fails to attract an audience equal to the number of those learning about the initial announcement.

Here's a prediction: As the 2026 election approaches, watch how many Republican governors, attorneys general, and secretaries of state scream about voter registration fraud. Then, check out their claims after the election. Expect history to repeat itself. The voter registration fraud issue will disappear.

Election Management

Oversight of the election process begins with the participation conditions before the vote and continues through casting the ballot, followed by the actual tabulations by election authorities. Here we consider such issues as restricting the voting process, toughening the requirements for voting, and limiting voting locations. As with the recent changes in voter registration laws, altered policies on election management have occurred in states where Trump lost the 2020 presidential election.

The Voting Process

Election research provided by the Brennan Center for Justice determined that eleven states dominated by Republicans enacted legislation restricting the voting process.[33] Although the lawmakers have justified the reformulated laws as assuring "election integrity" or "election efficiency," these laws have actually been designed to discourage "undesirable" portions of the voter universe from exercising the franchise. Some examples: In 2021, Alabama shortened the window for an absentee ballot request to seven days down from ten days.[34] Also in 2021, the Iowa state legislature passed a bill that reduced the time for early balloting by nine days, reduced the time for absentee ballot requests, and shortened hours for in person voting on election day.[35]

There's also the question of voting drop box venues, specified locations where absentee ballots and early voting ballots could be deposited in lieu of the voter appearing personally on election day. The idea behind drop boxes is to make voting more accessible, thus encouraging a higher turnout. Since 2020, seven states have prohibited the use of boxes, while two others have severely curbed their use. Almost all of these states were in the hands of conservative Republican legislatures.[36] As of the 2024 presidential election, eleven states banned drop boxes altogether, while five others placed limitations on their use. All told, as of 2024, 40 percent of the nation's voters live in states with these suppressive conditions.[37] This is not democracy.

Voting Requirements

As noted earlier, the Constitution originally had one simple requirement for voting in a federal election: an individual must be a US citizen. Subsequently, states passed the Nineteenth Constitutional Amendment allowing women to vote, followed by the Twenty-Sixth Amendment establishing eighteen years of age as the minimum age for voting. To protect the integrity of the vote, Congress passed the National Voter Registration Act of 1993, which requires citizens upon their voter registration to sign government forms that explain penalties for any falsifications. Beyond that, the Illegal Immigration Reform and Immigrant Act of 1996 unambiguously ban noncitizen voting in federal elections.

In recent years, some states and local governments have added a couple of opportunities for noncitizens with local races. San Francisco now allows noncitizens eighteen years or older to vote in school board elections, while Maryland and Vermont permit noncitizens to vote in municipal elections. Local governments have also tinkered with voting in terms of age. Beginning in 2024, sixteen- and seventeen-year olds in Newark, New Jersey as well as a few cities in California, Maryland, and Vermont are now allowed to vote in school board elections with the hope that voting at an early age will help create a lifelong habit.[38] In both of these experimental cases, the intent has been to inculcate the value of voter participation in democracy.

Overcoming Trumpism

Many states have tightened the registration and voting process allegedly to protect the integrity of the vote. With respect to stricter voting requirements for citizens, twenty-four states enacted such legislation between 2021 and 2024, according to data compiled by the Brennan Center. Described as reforms to protect the integrity of the vote, virtually all of the new laws actually have been intended to limit participation. Among them, in 2024, Idaho governor Brad Little signed into law a bill that prohibited ballot harvesting, a popular process in particularly remote areas where third-party volunteers collect ballots from voters for deposit in collection sites.[39] In 2023, the Indiana legislature tightened the conditions for mail-in ballots by requiring the ballot to contain two acceptable forms of identification.[40] No doubt, Texas looms as the most vote-suppressing state of all, courtesy of SB 1, passed by the legislature in 2021. That single law bans automatic vote-by-mail applications, prohibits twenty-four-hour voting, restricts assistance for people with disabilities and non-English speaking voters, and imposes criminal penalties for any violations.[41] Rather than protect the vote from electoral chicanery, the largest takeaway from these laws has come in the form of a growing gap in the turnout rate between Whites and people of color.[42] Voter discrimination continues to loom large in American society.

Voting Sites

Since 2013 when the *Shelby v. Holder* case overturned much of the Voting Rights Act of 1965, states have systematically reduced the number of voting sites. Fewer voting locations come at a cost that is disproportionately harmful for some groups more than others. Research by the Voting Rights Lab found that increased distance between polling places leads to significantly reduced turnout for Black and Latino voters when compared to Whites.[43] Moreover, those who vote have to wait longer because of fewer sites, which reduces turnout and leads to further disparities.[44]

A related issue concerns the decreased number of voting drop boxes, secure containers placed at locations to make it easier for people to drop off their ballots without visiting actual voting centers.[45] As with so many other conspiracies, anxieties about drop boxes exist without any proof of abuse. Particularly because of COVID-19 and the need to avoid crowds at voting centers, in the 2020 presidential election drop boxes were integral to managing the collection of ballots. In all, drop boxes throughout the nation collected 41 percent of the ballots for the 2020 election.[46] Some critics have described these containers as flimsy and subject to removal. Yet, Tammy

Patrick, the executive director of the National Association of Election Officials states that drop boxes are anything but physically fragile. In fact, drop boxes typically are "surveilled by camera, bolted to the ground, and constructed with fire-retardant chambers" so that even if a match were tossed in to a drop box, the ballots would not be destroyed.[47] Clearly, these vote collection receptacles facilitate conditions under which voters participate in elections while protecting the safety of the vote.

Of course, no voting system is perfect, and that includes drop boxes. In the closing days of the 2024 presidential election, vandals attacked three vote containers, two in Oregon and one in Washington, in what appeared to be related incidents. Most of the ballots were unharmed, thanks to retardants.[48] Nevertheless, the opposition to drop boxes is such that authorities must be vigilant in protecting the voter rights to exercise the franchise through this process.

On this matter, the Brennan Center found eleven states that have hampered access by reducing the number of ballot drop-off sites. In 2021, Georgia's SB 202 tightened its drop boxes program by establishing a policy providing one box per one hundred thousand voters. Worse yet, the new system made the boxes available only at indoor voting locations. That was a major departure from the 2020 presidential election, where numerous boxes were placed throughout counties at outdoor locations and available for use 24/7.[49] In 2023, the South Dakota state legislature passed a bill banning drop boxes altogether, instead requiring voters to return ballots by mail or in person to elections offices.[50] In these cases and others, increased difficulty for gaining access to voting locations in all likelihood changes the composition of the participating electorate.

Intimidation of Voters and Election Officials

Once was the time that voter intimidation was rare—at least after the civil rights and voting rights legislation during the 1960s. Then again, once was the time that American society was not nearly as politically polarized as it is today. Nowadays, intimidation is back. This bullying of those connected with voting includes behaviors such as registrars unreasonably questioning voters about their citizenship, officials denying otherwise qualified individuals the right to vote, and election personnel spreading false information about voter qualification. As discussed elsewhere in this book, election worker intimidation has also become all too present in the current political environment. Several national laws going back more than 150 years have made voter intimidation illegal,⁵¹ although that doesn't seem to have mattered in these contentious times when Trumpism thrives on bullying, violence and divisiveness.

One relatively recent form of intimidation has been found with the appearance of weapons at polling sites. At the time of the 2016 presidential election when Trump was first elected, eleven states allowed guns to be present in polling places.⁵² Trump's persistent (and unverified) claims of rigged voting led armed supporters to turn up at voting sites and tabulation centers to "protect" the sanctity of the vote.⁵³ By the time of the 2024 presidential election, the number of states allowing guns near voting venues had swelled to twenty-six.⁵⁴

The increased presence of firearms at voting sites comes at a huge psychological price for election participants. A 2022 poll by the Global Project against Hate and Extremism found that only 41 percent of Americans feel safe at polling places. Specifically, one-third of the respondents worried about people carrying weapons to the polling sites, with a similar number (32 percent) fearing a violent attack or shooting attack on election day. It's not surprising that the same poll found an astounding 63 percent of the sample (67 percent Democrats, 54 percent Republicans, and 54 percent Independents) support the prohibition of guns at voting sites.⁵⁵ Sadly, for many who engage in the process, voting has become a hazardous undertaking.

The last element of the voting experience centers on the tabulation of ballots. Every state relies upon special voting machines that tabulate the results with incredible speed and accuracy. Still, machines are only as fast as the times when they are put to work. And that's where doubts are sown for some critics. For years, Donald Trump has argued that only the votes from election day should be allowed and counted. Shortly after the November 3, 2020 presidential election, Trump declared that any votes received or counted by states after election day was illegal and was the basis for changing the outcome of the election.⁵⁶ Neither state election officials nor the courts agreed with him.

As of 2024, eleven states did not count absentee, mailed in, and provisional votes until all of the votes from election day were first counted.⁵⁷ That alone has often led to delays in announcing the final outcomes, sometimes for a few hours, other times for a few days. In addition, fourteen states allow votes as long as they are postmarked by election day and arrive by a specified time after the election.⁵⁸ This circumstance has been the source of discontent among those who want to know the results as soon as the polls close. Among Trumpists, the delayed counts are the basis of "rigged election" cries. More than one state has experienced the clamor of angry citizens outside the processing centers demanding that they be let to "watch" the tabulation process. Such situations are the potential precursors to anarchy.

Nevertheless, in today's voting environment, voters are confronted by intimidation in more states than not, and that's not helpful for attracting election turnouts. The inability of so many states to process the votes quickly only adds to the suspicion of those already concerned about the legitimacy of the voting experience, thanks to the persistent false claims by Donald Trump and his supporters, including Republican elected officials. Such situations are hardly encouraging for the well-being of democracy.

The Road to Repair

The right to equal political representation is a hallmark of democracy. Without the capacity for individuals to present their election voting choices in a safe, impartial setting and without intimidation, democracy is a tarnished enterprise, leaving its citizens unable to make their legitimate claims in an unfettered environment. So, what can be done to guarantee the integrity of the vote? We address this pressing question below.

Ending Gerrymandering

An answer to the gerrymandering problem exists as part of the proposed Freedom to Vote Act. Passed by the US House of Representatives first in 2019 and then again in 2021 largely along political party lines (House Democrats for, House Republicans against), the proposal contains several components to promote and allow voting access. One of the provisions would require all states to organize congressional districts by politically independent commissions consisting of five Democrats, five Republicans, and five Independents.[59] To ensure an impartial outcome, the concept also specifies a speedy process of judicial resolution in the event of a dispute so that challenges are addressed in a quick and orderly manner.

The thinking behind the anti-gerrymandering provision is that if the redistricting responsibility is removed from partisan state legislatures and placed into the hands of politically balanced state commissions, the process itself would at least be responsive to all ethnic, racial, and religious populations within the states. With such a change, every citizen would have the same influence in the voting process.

But what the House has been able to do twice the Senate has not been able to accomplish even once. In the case of this legislative effort, the failure of the House bill to move through the Senate has been due to the filibuster, a parliamentary rule that prevents the ending of debate on a proposal unless sixty senators vote to move to end the discussion. With Democrats having only a slight 51-to-49 margin in the nation's legislative upper chamber, Republicans threatened to use this legislative tool. Possibilities for reform worsened after the 2024 election Senate Republicans now in the majority 53-47. For now, the Freedom to Vote Act looms as little more than wishful thinking. Nevertheless, the legislative tool is available if Congress is pressured to do something about it.

Note that this proposed legislation concentrates on congressional districts only so as not to interfere with "states rights" in the management of state and local redistricting. Nevertheless, for states to create separate redistricting criteria and methodologies for congressional and state districts would be a pricey enterprise, and hopefully not likely. At least, legislators would have to think about it.

Ending the Filibuster

Still, the path to true representation is possible if Congress—or more accurately the Senate—is willing to take it. To do so would depend upon the upper chamber ridding itself of the filibuster, which is entirely legally doable. That's because the filibuster is not mandated by the Constitution or congressional statute. Rather, it is an invention of the Senate itself under the belief that the upper chamber should be an institution of unlimited debate wherever possible.[60] As such, it was officially adopted as Senate Rule 22 in 1917. Still, a scholar of the filibuster notes that "there is nothing to suggest that the right to filibuster was a feature of the original Senate."[61] In other words, there is nothing sacred about filibuster which, it turns out, is a creation of the Senate and nothing more.

To be fair, there seemed to be a bit of logic for a thoughtful Senate in the early going of the Republic. Unlike the larger House of Representatives, the Senate was a small body with six-year terms, overlapping elections, and whose members would be selected by state legislatures, not the voters. All this seemed to position the Senate as a deliberate body that would depend upon consensus to move legislation. As such, the Senate would be something of a counterweight to the House whose members could be prone to act impulsively because of a direct connection with the voters courtesy of two-year terms.

Some of the Senate's isolation from voter pressure ended with the Seventeeth Amendment, which provided for direct election of senators by the voters, just like elections of the House of Representatives. The body's six-year terms, however, still provided a kind of distance from sudden public sentiments that threatened members of the House of Representatives. With its relative isolation from the public still in place, the Senate became famous for dithering on proposed legislation to the consternation of its critics. Criticism of the Senate as an unresponsive institution continued.

Of note is that the filibuster has been changed at least three times, although the alterations have been modest. In 1917, senators established a two-thirds vote to end deliberations (technically called cloture) before proceeding with a vote on the bill. A second change occurred in 1975 when the Senate reduced the two-thirds cloture requirement of the members present to sixty votes, although there is disagreement on whether the rearrangement made it easier or harder to end debate. In 2013 and 2017, the Senate made a third change to the filibuster by excluding exercise of the rule from executive appointments and judicial nominations. These changes, notwithstanding, the filibuster remains an important vehicle for the minority in the upper chamber to prevent proposed legislation from becoming law. Nevertheless, the fact that the Senate has altered the filibuster on three occasions suggests that at least there is the precedent for additional reform.

Removing the filibuster as an obstacle to the legislative process would not only give the Senate an opportunity to end gerrymandering, but it would also make the Senate a body governed by simple majority rule, and as such a truly democratic body. In addition, it would make elections for senators all the more important with the realization that it would be easier for the upper chamber to move on countless policy proposals that have been held hostage by the minority. How do we solve this? By electing senators who advocate eliminating the filibuster as part of their campaign platform.

Eliminating Voter Suppression

From registration to election participation, in too many cases the right of an individual to vote has been made difficult or even denied by partisan opponents, officials abusing their authority, and suppression legislation. The task here is to eliminate these obstacles to democracy from Trumpists and others who have stifled citizen involvement for their own personal political gains.

Registration

Although states have responsibility for registering voters, the fact that they determine the rules pertaining to record-keeping makes it easier for individuals to register in some states than others. Yet, if we believe the Fourteenth Amendment's famous "equal protection of the laws" imperative, then that safeguard should be guaranteed to would-be voters for national elections in all states under the same terms. As with the gerrymandering issue, "states rights" proponents might argue that their governments wouldn't be subject to such registration terms for state and local elections, but they might be willing to do so in the name of simplicity. Happily, a prototype of this kind of guarantee is already in the books.

In the National Voter Registration Act of 1993, Congress established voter registration requirements for federal elections. In that legislation, states are required to make available a federal registration application for any citizen who wishes to register to vote by mail. Additional legislation, the Help America Vote Act of 2002 requires citizens who register by mail to provide additional information to assure eligibility. (Both of these laws require proof of citizenship in advance of voter registration which is why Congressional Republican demands for a citizenship requirement for their approval of a proposed immigration law are bogus.) But here's the most important point: Under the terms of the Help America Vote Act, any state receiving federal aid for myriad public assistance programs (e.g., Food Stamps, Unemployment, or Children's Health Insurance) was required to use the federal registration program. That meant almost everyone.

Using the ability of the federal government to establish conditions on voter registration in those states accepting federal funds, the conditions should be the same for voter registration. Inasmuch as there are examples of federal funds connecting state facilitation, Congress needs only to modernize the 1993 and 2002 laws by adding the category of voter registration consistency. By doing so, all states will operate registration programs under exactly the same terms for all applicants. The precedent is there; Congress needs to follow through. As with efforts to end the filibuster, it's up to the American people to see that the candidates dedicated to registration equality are elected.

Managing the Vote

The president serves all of the people. This office, and by extension the vice president, are the nation's only elected offices that govern everyone in the United States. Yet, the conditions of the voting processes, requirements, sites, and even tabulation of the votes vary with each state. There's no justification for such inconsistent differences other than the persistence of idiosyncratic local values. The rules for electing national officeholders should be the same in every state. By creating an even playing field for the voters, each citizen would be guaranteed the same rights, regardless of residency or political affiliation.

This idea carries more importance than simply streamlining rules. State autonomy on national matters must have limits, and there is no symbol more national than our presidential elections. Think about it—if we have the same rules regarding age and citizenship, it follows that those rules should be extended to the conditions under which the vote takes place.

A national system with the same voting rules and regulations would clearly provide the same opportunities for every American voter, regardless of residence. This symbolism would be an important unifying element for American society. Congress could certainly establish these conditions for the presidency, leaving it to states as to whether they would apply the same standards to their own elections or adopt a separate set. Or, Congress could legislate that the fifty secretaries of state put their heads together and devise a system that provides uniformity.

Beyond congressional activity, there is another possible route. The Electronic Registration Information Center (ERIC), a nonpartisan, nonprofit organization intended to gather and improve state registration and voting data could provide the same kind of service. Established by seven states in 2012, the organization's membership had swelled to thirty-three states by 2022. As a record-keeping body, ERIC keeps records on voter registration data, voter movements between states, and voter deaths. It also identifies for member states individuals qualified to vote but who have not registered. All of these activities guard against voter fraud.

In 2022, ERIC ascertained more than 4.4 million potentially eligible but unregistered voters. During the same year, the voter data organization uncovered 203,210 in-state voter duplicates and 65,437 deaths.[62] But most notably, ERIC's data management has prevented voter fraud. Clearly, ERIC has shown the capacity to assimilate and share data between its members. Given its framework, there's no reason why its responsibilities couldn't include the establishment of voting rules, again with the guidance of the fifty secretaries of state—and it would do so without any national involvement other than the assignment by Congress.

But there's one major hitch. Donald Trump's unfounded allegations of a rigged presidential election that began well before and lived on through the 2020 campaign continued long after his loss. The same rigged election claim became the foundation of his 2024 campaign as well. Along the way Trump argued that ERIC was part of the rigged election conspiracy, alleging that the organization was a left-wing organization that had shared sensitive voter information with the Democrats.[63] This, too, took a toll. Between 2022 and 2024, nine states—all led by Republicans—followed Trump's lead, contending without any evidence that ERIC had become a nefarious tool of the Democrats. With fewer members, it's become harder for ERIC to do its job of detecting voter registration fraud, which has long been a depository of Trumpist anger.

Making All Votes Truly Equal and Safe

In their effort to present a fundamental distinction between English aristocracy and would-be American democracy, the authors of the Declaration of Independence boldly asserted that "all men are created equal." It was a pretty brazen claim that didn't live up to its promise at the time, given that only wealthy White males were considered in the voter universe in the then-colonies, many of which relied heavily on Black slaves for economic success. In fact, when compared against today's potential American electorate the voting population in 1776 amounted to only 6 percent of today's voters. But at least in theory, the importance of equality in the future United States was established as a key benchmark for the soon-to-be nation. In many respects, the validity of that claim has grown with the elimination of wealth as a franchise inhibitor and the inclusion of people of color and women as equal members of the modern American polity. In theory, anyway.

Clearly, we still have a long way to go. Our evolving voter participation framework is shaky, given the obstacles that too often are placed in front of people of color, women, and poor citizens despite constitutional guarantees. Sometimes the obstacles are subtle, sometimes they are blatant, but either way they are obstacles nonetheless. Most of all, they are unacceptable in a democracy.

Which takes us to a central difference between Trumpists and democrats (with a small "d"). When considering elections, Trumpists work toward a particular outcome of the vote, regardless of the process that facilitates the outcome. It fits, therefore, that Trumpists perceive elections as "rigged" if they don't win. It's that simple and so unfortunate. Their only concern is outcome—*their* outcome.

Conversely, democrats support an open political process that gives everyone the same opportunity to weigh in on election matters. According to this simple yet fundamental principle, if one side loses an election, there's always the next time to try again.

In today's political climate, many Trumpists will do whatever it takes to win, regardless of any illegality connected with their efforts. Think of the "alternate" state election delegates organized to change the outcome of the 2020 presidential election and the numerous ways to intimidate voters and election officials alike. And given the horrific events of January 6, 2021, violence against Congress itself encouraged by Donald Trump was not out of bounds. Such malevolent behavior has the potential to upend the very concept of democracy altogether.

Our task is to do everything possible to provide for an even playing field on all matters related to the franchise from voter registration to vote tabulation and beyond. It's not a perfect system, but one that philosophically embraces the search for perfection, while denying the effort of anyone to interfere with that objective. Clearly, some national traditions and state laws need correction to reinforce equal voting opportunities and results. Addressing the issues outlined in this chapter would be a healthy start.

NOTES

1. Barbara F. Walter, *How Civil Wars Start* (New York: Crown Books, 2022), p. 206.
2. Anthony King, *The Founding Fathers v. People: Paradoxes of American Democracy* (Cambridge, MA: Harvard University Press, 2012), p. 11.
3. The exceptions are Maine and Nebraska. In those two states, whichever candidate wins the most votes in each congressional district is awarded an electoral vote. Whoever wins the state's overall vote wins the other two electors. In the 2024 presidential election, Donald Trump won the first and third congressional districts in Nebraska, while Kamala Harris won the second. Because Trump won the overall state vote, he also received the remaining two electoral votes. giving him four electoral votes, with one for Harris. In Maine, Harris won the first congressional district, with Trump winning the second district. However, because Harris received the most state overall, she won three of the state's four electoral votes.
4. John O. McGinnis, "Popular Sovereignty and the Electoral College," *Florida State University Law Review*, 29, no. 2 (Winter 2001), https://ir.law.fsu.edu/cgi/viewcontent.cgi?article=1622&context=lr,
5. "The Fake Electors Scheme, Explained," *The New York Times*, August 3, 2022, https://www.nytimes.com/2022/07/27/us/politics/fake-electors-explained-trump-jan-6.html.

6   Quoted in "In DC Rally Speech, Trump Urges Pence to Reject Electoral College Vote, Repeats Baseless Fraud Claims," *Spectrum News NY 1*, January 6, 2021, https://ny1.com/nyc/all-boroughs/politics/2021/01/06/in-dc-rally-speech--trump-urges-pence-to-reject-electoral-college-vote--repeats-baseless-fraud-claims.

7   Much of this section is derived from "The Essential Electoral College," The Heritage Foundation, https://www.heritage.org/the-essential-electoral-college/the-benefits.

8   For an in-depth discussion of this topic, see Larry N. Gerston, *American Federalism: A Concise Introduction* (Armonk, NY: M.E. Sharpe, 2007), pp. 117–40.

9   "About 8.2 Million People Moved Between States in 2022," U.S. Census Bureau, November 21, 2023, https://www.census.gov/library/stories/2023/11/state-to-state-migration.html#:~:text=This%20increase%20in,12.8%25%20to%2012.6%25.

10 "Where Do Immigrants Live?" United States Census Bureau, April 9, 2024, https://www.census.gov/library/stories/2024/04/where-do-immigrants-live.html.

11 "Majority of Americans Continue to Favor Moving Away from the Electoral College," Pew Research Center, September 25, 2024, https://www.pewresearch.org/short-reads/2024/09/25/majority-of-americans-continue-to-favor-moving-away-from-electoral-college/.

12 See "61% of Americans Support Abolishing the Electoral College," Gallup Poll, September 24, 2020, https://news.gallup.com/poll/320744/americans-support-abolishing-electoral-college.aspx and "The Electoral College: How It Works in Contemporary Presidential Elections, EveryCRSReport.com, May 17, 2017, https://www.everycrsreport.com/reports/RL32611.html#_Toc482718966.

13 "Gerrymandering Explained," The Brennan Center for Justice, June 9, 2023, https://brennancenter.org/our-work/research-reports/gerrymandering-explained.

14 For some examples, see "How Partisan Redistricting Divides and Harms Communities," *Democracy Docket*, June 24, 2022, https://www.democracydocket.com/analysis/how-partisan-redistricting-divides-and-harms-communities/.

15 The cases were *Shelby v. Holder* (2013), *Rucho v. Common Cause* (2019), and *Brnovich v. Democratic Committee* in 2021.

16 *Ibid.*

17 The four Democratic states and their extra seats were Illinois (3), New Jersey (2), New Mexico (1), and Oregon (1). The eleven Republican states and their extra seats were Florida (5), Georgia (2), Indiana (1), Iowa (2), North Carolina (2), Ohio (2), South Carolina (1), Tennessee (1), Texas (5), Utah (1), and Wisconsin (1). See "How Gerrymandering Tilts the 2024 Race for the House," The Brennan Center for Justice, September 24, 2024 https://www.brennancenter.org/our-work/research-reports/how-gerrymandering-tilts-2024-race-house.

18. See "How the Supreme Court Is Helping Bake Racism into Our Electoral Maps," Alliance for Justice, March 31, 2022, https://afj.org/article/how-the-supreme-court-is-helping-bake-racism-into-our-electoral-maps/.
19. "Block the Vote: How Politicians Are Trying to Block Voters from the Ballot Box," ACLU, August 18, 2021, https://www.aclu.org/news/civil-liberties/block-the-vote-voter-suppression-in-2020.
20. For a brief history of voter suppression, see "America's Long History of Black Voter Suppression," CNN Politics, May 2021, https://www.cnn.com/interactive/2021/05/politics/black-voting-rights-suppression-timeline/.
21. "Voting Laws Roundup: September 2024," The Brennan Center for Justice, September 26, 2024, https://www.brennancenter.org/our-work/research-reports/voting-laws-roundup-september-2024.
22. "Voter Registration—Method and Location," Florida Division of Elections, Florida Department of State, September 10, 2024, https://dos.fl.gov/elections/data-statistics/voter-registration-statistics/voter-registration-reports/voter-registration-method-and-location/.
23. "'The Restrictions Are Unbelievable': States Target Voter Registration Drives," The Center for Public Integrity, May 16, 2024, https://publicintegrity.org/politics/elections/who-counts/the-restrictions-are-unbelievable-states-target-voter-registration-drives/.
24. "Supreme Court Allows Virginia to Purge Possibly Ineligible Voters for Now," *The New York Times*, October 30, 2024, https://www.nytimes.com/2024/10/30/us/politics/supreme-court-virginia-purge-voter-registration.html.
25. Carol Anderson, *One Person, One Vote* (New York: Bloomsbury, 2018), p. 70. Anderson goes on to cite data showing a vast difference in minority turnouts between those states that require voter IDs and those that do not.
26. "Why There's a Long-Standing Voter Registration Gap for Latinos and Asian Americans," NPR, April 2, 2024, https://www.npr.org/2024/04/02/1238751749/voter-registration-gap-racial.
27. "DeSantis Announces 20 Voter Fraud Arrests of Floridians, Calls It an 'Opening Salvo,'" *Tampa Bay Times*, August 19, 2022, https://www.tampabay.com/news/florida-politics/elections/2022/08/18/desantis-announces-20-arrests-of-floridians-for-voter-fraud/.
28. "Cases against Arrested Voters on Shaky Legal Ground. Florida Issued Them Voter IDs," *Miami Herald*, August 31, 2022, https://www.miamiherald.com/news/politics-government/state-politics/article265138721.html.
29. "Ohio Sec. of State LaRose Wants to Fight Voter Fraud, but Pulling Out of ERIC Will Make That Harder," *Ohio Capital Journal*, September 28, 2023, https://ohiocapitaljournal.com/2023/09/28/ohio-sec-of-state-larose-wants-to-fight-voter-fraud-but-pulling-out-of-eric-will-make-that-harder/.
30. "Prosecutors Fire Back after LaRose Says Voter Fraud Cases Aren't Adequately Investigated," Cleveland.com, September 12, 2024, https://www.cleveland.com/news/2024/09/prosecutors-fire-back-after-larose-says-voter-fraud-cases-arent-adequately-investigated.html.

31 "Youngkin Stokes Fear of Vast Noncitizen Voting in Virginia. Records Don't Show It," *The Washington Post*, October 9, 2024, https://www.washingtonpost.com/dc-md-va/2024/10/09/youngkin-noncitizen-voters-virginia/.
32 "A GOP Operative Accused a Monastery of Voter Fraud. Nuns Fought Back," *The Washington Post*, October 23, 2024, https://www.washingtonpost.com/politics/2024/10/23/pennsylvania-republican-voting-nuns-erie/.
33 "Voting Laws Roundup: September 2024," The Brennan Center for Justice, September 26, 2024.
34 *FastDemocracy*, HB 538, https://fastdemocracy.com/bill-search/al/2021rs/bills/ALB00012780/.
35 "Iowa Governor Signs Sweeping Voter Suppression Legislation into Law," Democracy Docket, March 8, 2021, https://www.democracydocket.com/news-alerts/legislation-alert-iowa-governor-signs-sweeping-voter-suppression-legislation-into-law/.
36 The states are Arkansas, Georgia, Missouri, New Mexico, North Carolina, Ohio, South Carolina, New Mexico, and Texas. See "Amid New Ballot Drop Box Limits, Florida's Shorter Hours Cause Voting Rights Worry," *USA Today*, July 31, 2024, https://www.usatoday.com/story/news/politics/elections/2024/07/31/florida-absentee-ballots-drop-boxes/73624783007/.
37 "Ballot Drop Box Policies and Availability," Map Advancement Project, October 11, 2024, https://www.lgbtmap.org/democracy-maps/drop_box_policies.
38 "In Newark, 16-Year-Olds Win the Right to Vote in School Races," *The New York Times*, January 10, 2024, https://www.nytimes.com/2024/01/10/nyregion/newark-voting-age.html.
39 "What Bills Passed; What Didn't? 2024 Idaho Legislative Session Adjourns for the Year," *Idaho Capital Sun*, April 10, 2024, https://idahocapitalsun.com/2024/04/10/what-bills-passed-what-didnt-2024-idaho-legislative-session-adjourns-for-the-year/.
40 "Indiana Sends Bill Adding ID Requirements for Mail-in Voting to Governor," Democracy Docket, April 12, 2023, https://www.democracydocket.com/news-alerts/indiana-sends-bill-adding-id-requirements-for-mail-in-voting-to-governor/.
41 "5 Ways Texas Suppresses the Vote—and How to Make Your Vote Count," Texas ACLU, January 17, 2022, https://www.brennancenter.org/sites/default/files/2020-06/6_02_WaitingtoVote_FINAL.pdf. https://www.aclutx.org/en/news/5-ways-texas-suppresses-vote-and-how-make-your-vote-count.
42 "States Have Added Nearly 100 Restrictive Laws since SCOTUS Gutted the Voting Rights Act 10 Years Ago," The Brennan Center for Justice, June 23, 2023, https://www.brennancenter.org/our-work/analysis-opinion/states-have-added-nearly-100-restrictive-laws-scotus-gutted-voting-rights.
43 "Polling Place Consolidation: Negative Impacts on Turnout and Equity," Voting Rights Lab, January 2021, https://votingrightslab.org/wp-content/uploads/2021/01/Polling-Place-Consolidation-Negative-Impacts-on-Turnout-and-Equity.pdf.
44 "Waiting to Vote: Racial Disparities in Election Day Experiences," The Brennan Center or Justice, June 3, 2020, https://www.brennancenter.org/media/5927/download/6_02_WaitingtoVote_FINAL.pdf?inline=1.

45 See Enrico Cantoni, A Precinct too Far: Turnout and Voting Costs, *American Economic Journal: Applied Economics*, 12, no. 1 (2000), https://doi.org/10.1257/app.20180306.
46 "'Chaos and Confusion': The Campaign to Stamp Out Ballot Drop Boxes," *Stateline*, October 31, 2022, https://stateline.org/2022/10/31/chaos-and-confusion-the-campaign-to-stamp-out-ballot-drop-boxes/.
47 "Yes, Voter Fraud Happens. But It's Rare and There Are Safeguards to Catch It," *Los Angeles Times*, October 18, 2024, https://www.latimes.com/politics/story/2024-10-18/yes-voter-fraud-happens-but-its-rare-and-there-are-safeguards-to-catch-it.
48 "Ballot-Box Fires in Oregon, Washington Are Linked; Police Identify Suspect's Car," OregonLive, October 29, 2024, https://www.oregonlive.com/news/2024/10/3-ballot-box-fires-in-oregon-washington-are-linked-police-identify-suspects-car.html.
49 SB 202, Fulton County, https://www.fultoncountyga.gov/inside-fulton-county/fulton-county-departments/registration-and-elections/sb-202-changes.
50 "South Dakota Legislature Sends Bill Banning Drop Boxes to Governor," *Democracy Docket*, March 2, 2023, https://www.democracydocket.com/news-alerts/south-dakota-legislature-sends-bill-banning-drop-boxes-to-governor/.
51 For a list of the most prominent legislation, see "Federal Laws Protecting against Intimidation of Voters and Election Workers," The Brennan Center for Justice, October 28, 2022, https://www.brennancenter.org/our-work/research-reports/federal-laws-protecting-against-intimidation-voters-and-election-workers.
52 "Can You Bring Your Gun to Vote?" CNN, November 8, 2016, https://www.cnn.com/2016/11/07/politics/can-you-bring-your-gun-to-vote/index.html.
53 "Increasingly Normal: Guns Seen Outside Vote-Counting Centers," AP, November 7, 2020, https://apnews.com/article/protests-vote-count-safety-concerns-653dc8f0787c9258524078548d518992.
54 "Can You Carry Concealed on Election Day," United States Concealed Carry Association, September 19, 2024, https://www.usconcealedcarry.com/blog/guns-and-polling-places/.
55 These data come from "Americans' Fears Suppressing Participation in Democracy," Global Project against Hate and Extremism, August 4, 2022, https://globalextremism.org/post/fear-and-elections/.
56 "Remarks by President Trump on the Election," The White House, November 5, 2020, https://trumpwhitehouse.archives.gov/briefings-statements/remarks-president-trump-election/.
57 See "When Absentee/Mail Ballot Processing and Counting Can Begin," National Council of State Legislatures September 23, 2024, https://www.ncsl.org/elections-and-campaigns/table-16-when-absentee-mail-ballot-processing-and-counting-can-begin.
58 For a list, see "Absentee Ballot Deadlines," Vote.org, https://www.vote.org/absentee-ballot-deadlines/.
59 For the contents of the 2021 House version, see Congress.Gov, H.R. 5746, October 27, 2021, https://www.congress.gov/bill/117th-congress/house-bill/5746.

60 For a history of the filibuster, see Sarah A. Binder and Steven S. Smith, *Politics or Principle? Filibustering in the United States Senate* (Washington, DC: Brookings Institution
61 Ibid., p. 29.
62 "Access to Voter Registration Information," Electronic Registration Information Center, https://ericstates.org/statistics/.
63 "G.O.P. States Abandon Bipartisan Voting Integrity Group, Yielding to Conspiracy Theories," *The New York Times*, March 7, 2023, https://www.nytimes.com/2023/03/07/us/politics/gop-voter-registration-fraud-eric.html.

CHAPTER 11
ASSURING MEDIA INTEGRITY

Democracies thrive best with an informed public because, at least in theory, an informed public keeps tabs on issues and leaders. Democracies are more transparent than authoritarian regimes, which gives the people opportunities to learn about and respond to issues of the day. In addition to what they may learn from government leaders, people gather their knowledge from various sources, among them the news media, public education, family, friends, and the workplace, with some being much more accurate and reliable than others.

Public officials and the media have an uneasy relationship. On one hand, each needs the other; public officials need the media to circulate information that they want the public to know, while the media need to learn and share what public officials are doing. On the other hand, even the most open public officials sometimes don't want to share controversial or potentially embarrassing news with reporters, while reporters are all too happy to uncover that which public officials don't want known. The fact is these two forces prevail in a world of competing objectives as each side attempts to manage the other.[1]

Presidents and the press exemplify this tug and pull relationship where they simultaneously coexist while attempting to control the boundaries of communication. As one discussion of the presidency notes, "No matter who is in the White House or who does the reporting, presidents and the press always struggle for dominance."[2] That's true regardless of which political party controls the office and which news organizations report. Yet, whatever the differences or moments of tension, the two sides not only need each other but also (sometimes grudgingly) respect each other. And democracy is the better for it.

Authoritarians are particularly concerned with the news media. That's because authoritarian leaders often pursue objectives that may be harmful to the public interest, and they would rather keep the public in the dark about their activities. Inasmuch as the news media may accumulate and disseminate information that authoritarians wouldn't want made available to the public, they do everything possible to weaken the media's reporting capabilities, especially if the news is potentially embarrassing. Thus, for authoritarians, Ruth Ben-Ghiat writes, "discrediting the press is a kind of insurance policy. When journalists turn up evidence of the government's violence or corruption, the public will already be accustomed to seeing them as partisan."[3] Controlling the press through arrests, lawsuits, and various means of intimidation is essential to authoritarian rule. And too often, it works.

This chapter begins with a discussion that centers on the critical role of mainstream media in American politics and its often-contentious relationship with Donald Trump. The difficulty between the two not only stems from the mission of mainstream reporters clashing with Trump, but also from his authoritarian commitment to suppressing news he deems "unacceptable," which tends to be anything critical of the president.

Next, we'll focus on the growing dependence by the American public on social media as news sources. We'll also compare social media with mainstream media (sometimes called "legacy" media) for their accuracy, reliability, and accountability, as well as what can be done to protect Americans from misinformation routinely presented on social media platforms. Here, we'll give close attention to Section 230 of the Communications Decency Act of 1996, which has responsibility for dealing with social media. Lastly, we'll consider the future of social media in American society and the vital role the public must play as consumers of news.

The Mainstream Media and Donald Trump

Newspapers, television, and radio have the capabilities to transmit information that people might not know otherwise. They are called "mainstream media" for their legendary roles in conveying news to large swaths of the population. We depend on them to provide us with information that we wouldn't know otherwise. In doing so, the press focuses on developments and situations that impact the public, base their reports on information gathered from reputable sources, and in an ideal format, present information with as little bias as possible. That independent function of the mainstream media is critical to holding democratic leaders responsible to the public for their actions.[4]

Most important about the mainstream media is their accountability. If reporters or their media companies knowingly write or discuss false information, they can be held accountable in at least two ways. Companies or individuals who believe they have been wronged can sue. That's what happened when Dominion Voting System sued Fox Corporation after the media company falsely claimed that Dominion's vote-counting machines used in the 2020 presidential election were used to rig the election outcomes in several states. Dominion sued on the basis that Fox deliberately and knowledgeably spread false information about the vote tabulating company. Rather than go through the uncertainties of a jury trial, Fox settled with Dominion for a whopping $787.5 million, the largest settlement ever paid in an American media libel case.[5] In another instance, two election workers in Georgia sued Rudy Giuliani, the 2020 Trump presidential campaign member and the former mayor of New York City, for repeatedly lying that they were engaged in "surreptitious, illegal activity" that denied votes to Donald Trump. As a result, the plaintiffs complained, and they were harassed and threatened to the point that they couldn't leave their homes.[6] A jury awarded the election workers $148 million from Giulani.

A second opportunity for accountability of the mainstream media exists through the Federal Communications Commission's (FCC) ability to punish a radio or television entity for violations of the rules established by the government agency. One example occurred in 2020 when the FCC fined Sinclair Broadcast Company $48 million for repeated instances of misleading business practices.[7] More on the FCC later in this chapter. The point is that traditional media can be held accountable for abusing the public trust and/or violating laws.

Donald Trump has a long history of tangling with the mainstream media, no doubt because of occasionally unflattering reports that have come from these independent conveyors of information. For more than a decade, Trump has defined the traditional press as "the enemy of the people." More accurately, he views the mainstream media as *the enemy of Trump*, and as such, will do anything he can to intimidate the Fourth Estate and deny the public valuable information as a consequence. In 2023, Trump sued *The New York Times* over its investigation of his tax returns. He went after the newspaper for allegedly conspiring with his niece, Mary Trump, to illegally obtain the information, but a New York judge dismissed the case for having no basis and ordered Trump to pay $393,000 to the newspaper company for attorneys' costs.[8]

Even winning often isn't good enough for Trump. After his victory in the 2024 presidential election, Trump sued the *Des Moines Register* for "election interference" resulting from a Register-sponsored preelection statewide poll showing Trump losing the election in Iowa, a state where he actually won.[9] Most legal observers expected that case to die, and it did after Trump dropped the case well after his inauguration.

Occasionally, Trump has prevailed against the mainstream media, an effort that has produced particular success in the wake of his 2024 presidential election victory. In 2025, he sued the ABC television network after anchor George Stephanopoulos claimed several times that Trump had raped E. Jean Carroll rather than exert "sexual abuse" for which the former president was held liable by a New York jury.[10] The network settled with Trump out of court for $15 million.

Around the same time, Trump sued CBS for $10 billion (!) on the grounds that the network engaged in "deceptive doctoring" of a preelection interview with then-presidential nominee Kamala Harris. Despite the network's claim, and the near-universal beliefs among experts, that the suit was "without merit," Paramount, the owner of CBS, settled out of court for $16 million. And why? Several CBS executives believed that settling the suit would reduce the odds of the Trump administration blocking the network's planned merger with Paramount.[11] The head of CBS News was forced to resign because of what she opposed as excessive network pressure for reporters to discuss political issues in ways more favorable to Trump.[12]

On another front, shortly after the 2024 presidential election, Trump went after the press by demanding that Senate Republicans kill a bipartisan bill to strengthen the ability of reporters to protect confidential sources after the bill had passed unanimously in the House of Representatives. To no one's surprise, the bill died in the Senate.[13]

Attacking the mainstream media has also become a tool of Trump's allies. Prior to his appointment as Trump's new FBI Director in 2024, Kash Patel warned, "We're going to come after the people in the media who lied about American citizens who helped Joe Biden rig presidential elections."[14] On X, Elon Musk chastised the editors of *The New York Times*, *The Washington Post*, and *The Wall Street Journal* as the people who "decide what is newsworthy." Instead, he said, "the cumulative voice of the people should decide what is newsworthy."[15] That sounds more like a free-for-all, not news. In February 2025, new FCC Chair Brendan Carr announced that his agency was investigating a San Francisco radio station for announcing the locations of immigration officials in the midst of an attempted immigrant roundup.[16]

In a strange way, endless assaults on mainstream journalism have had long-term benefits for Trump. How can that be? By attacking the mainstream media, Trump lawsuits have often consumed "considerable time and resources and can threaten the survival of smaller news outlets that are already struggling to make ends meet," according to Anna Dunlin of the Knight First Amendment Institute. "Even the threat of legal action may lead some to self-censor, rather than risk retribution. This is no accident—it appears to be Trump's goal," she added.[17] And that seems to be the Trump plan: intimidate the mainstream media into submission and thereby eliminate independent sources of information. It may not be a coincidence that just before the 2024 presidential election, *The Washington Post* and *Los Angeles Times* decided not to offer endorsements for the first time in memory. One critic explained their actions as "anticipatory obedience," placating Trump in the hope that he'd leave the newspapers alone after his election.[18] Judging from Trump's litigious action after the election, that hasn't worked.

Trump's willingness to go after the press for its reporting is unprecedented. He has done much more than grumble. His lawsuits and threats to shut down various media sources underscore his intolerance for coverage that he views as an affront to his presidency.

Enter Social Media

Although mainstream news has received the bulk of Trump-supported criticism, members of the Trump team have occasionally directed their anger at social media when they have perceived threats. For example, shortly after receiving his appointment as Chair of the FCC in 2025, Brendan Carr publicly complained about *NewsGuard,* a nonpartisan organization that analyzed the quality of news put out by online publishers, calling the organization a "censorship cartel" of conservative news.[19] Carr's comments gave a good indication of the FCC's role in the second Trump administration as a disrupter of anything that might cause problems for Trump.

Were the post-2024 election interactions between Trump and the media extortion by Trump, deferential accommodation by the mainstream press, or both? Either way, the line between the two forces has become distinctly unhealthy. That angst has also intruded into the relationship between Trump and social media.

Originally designed as an online interaction source for sharing information among friends, social media has developed into a multifaceted transmissions network that includes a portal for business marketing, video sharing, chat groups, and interpersonal exchanges, as well as the dissemination of all kinds of information. The extensiveness of this twenty-first-century communications system is ubiquitous, to say the least. Statistics compiled by DataReportal in 2024 estimated that 239 million Americans (70.1 percent of the total US population) would use social media.[20] Among the most utilized social media sources, a 2023 review by the Pew Research Center found that 83 percent of Americans had used YouTube, followed by extensive use of Facebook (68 percent), Instagram (47 percent), Pinterest (35 percent), and TikTok (33 percent).[21]

Several other private social media platforms have smaller user populations. Some, such as 4chan, host exclusive member groups on topics ranging from adult cartoons to science and math, along with numerous alt-right hate groups.[22] For several years, Reddit, another closed social media company, hosted numerous hate groups, but after considerable pressure, the site banned them in 2020. Nowadays, the most controversial hate sites are on the "dark web," far removed from most social media users but nevertheless highly effective in arousing their members to action.

Some people consider social media sites as reliable depositories of news—about half of all Americans at various times, according to Pew Research.[23] As such, dependence on these sources has the potential to foster serious problems related to their accuracy. That's because the material sometimes described as "news" on social media platforms may be opinion, rumor, or exaggeration rather than fact. In other cases, "information" presented on social media sites may be whimsical concoctions without any truthful basis, but still with the perception of legitimacy by users because of the author or topic connected with them.

Of late, authoritarian leaders around the world have been adept at utilizing social media to their advantage, offering alleged "news" of events or controversial situations to convince the populations of their countries of their importance and power.[24] That's also the situation in the United States. Increasingly, Trumpists have been all too willing to disseminate false or misleading "information" eagerly consumed by people who lean on social media sites for their "news."[25] As a result, user dependence on outrageously false material has fertilized the potential for threatening the well-being of American democracy.

The Problems from Relying on Social Media as News Sources

To be fair, not all social media is informationally corrupt, or even incorrect; some of it can be quite helpful in facilitating and nurturing social relationships, promoting a sense of community, enabling professional development and

Assuring Media Integrity

networking, and providing people with useful information, to name a few benefits. People often rely on social media for many of these welcome benefits.

The advantages of social media notwithstanding, malevolent contributors can utilize social media for political purposes with potentially damaging outcomes for democracy. Sadly, social media consumers don't necessarily distinguish alleged news offered on social media platforms from the more reliable mainstream media. In particular, three social media properties—the intentional lack of media accuracy, manipulation of audiences, and corporate responsibility—harm American democracy by allowing inaccurate "news" to become part of the information environment. In fact, they embrace the "news" particularly when it reinforces their political values, thereby providing a sense of validation to their beliefs.

Intentional Inaccuracy

In the world of politics, some people intentionally share via social media platforms "information" with little resemblance to the truth. Donald Trump has long headed the list of false news distributors. The businessman-turned-reality TV star-turned politician owes much of his popularity to his "exploiting media's power to broadcast lies and conspiracy theories to the masses, starting with racist 'birther' attacks on President Barack Obama," according to one analysis.[26] Nowhere has this been easier than through the megaphone-like capabilities of social media, where the "facts" and truth can be far apart without anyone to show the differences.

How abusive of social media is Trump with the truth? According to Politifact, a nonpartisan fact-checking organization, between 2011 and 2024, 76 percent of one thousand statements made by Trump on social media were Mostly False, False, or "Pants on Fire," the category that Politifact describes as "not just false but ridiculous."[27] 76 percent! Most of these statements appeared on social media either through Twitter (now X) or Truth Social, Trump's own social media platform launched in 2022. With that kind of volume, it's hard for anyone to make people aware of their malice.

Trump's social media lies continued during his run-up to the 2024 presidential election, reaching a crescendo during the election year. Now fully engaged in Truth Social, Trump worked it to display his "grievance politics and anger."[28] He averaged more than twenty-four posts a day. A few examples: during the campaign, he lied about taking credit for lower insulin prices (that was Biden), that Democrats supported postbirth measures that kill babies (no history of such a claim), that the New York fraud judgment against him was a communist plot (no evidence provided), and that Democratic presidential nominee Kamala Harris was a communist (again, no evidence). In their totality, Trump's endless lies on social media paid off, especially among new voters. An independent exit poll of 2024 election voters found that 59 percent of new Trump voters relied on social media and podcasts for their news, considerably higher than 43 percent for the overall electorate.[29] In a close election, those numbers can mean the difference between victory and defeat.

His repeated falsehoods notwithstanding, Trump's deceitful behavior was exceeded during the 2024 presidential election campaign by billionaire and X social media platform owner Elon Musk. Data gathered by the Center for Countering Digital Hate tallied more than a billion views of Musk's false claims on X between January 1 and July 31, 2024. That's a lot of eyes. Some examples: Musk's posts falsely claimed that Democrats were importing illegal immigrant voters were viewed 747 million times; he falsely claimed about an abused voting process, which was viewed 288 million times; and a Musk-shared artificial intelligence (AI) voice clip of Vice President and Democratic presidential nominee Kamala Harris purportedly describing herself as the "ultimate diversity hire" that was viewed 133 million times.[30] Whether the posts have emerged from Trump, Musk, or other Trump acolytes, it's clear that they have repeatedly misled social media users.

This is not to make the Democrats and Kamala Harris social media angels. Several investigations have uncovered social media lies and misleading statements by the Harris presidential campaign. Among them, Trump said that neo-Nazis did nothing wrong in the 2017 Charlottesville riot (he said both sides had very fine people), Trump's Vice Presidential nominee JD Vance supported privatizing veterans care (he wanted veterans to have more choices), warned that Trump would end Head Start (Trump never said that), and that Project 2025, a very conservative plan for future policies, was a Trump initiative (Trump didn't participate, although more than 140 former Trump administration employees did).[31] Simply put, the Harris campaign also deceived the public through social media.

So, who abused social media more, Trump or Harris? That's a hard question to answer definitively, given the lack of any objective comparisons. But we do know this: according to independent research, between 2016 and 2021, Republicans lied about various issues 55 percent of the time, compared to Democrats who lied 31 percent of the time.[32] Further, a *Washington Post* fact-checking effort of the televised debate between Trump and Harris found that Trump made four times as many false statements as Harris.[33] That's quite a difference.

Manipulation of the Audience

Social media has the capability to persuade users in various ways, and not always positively. For example, with respect to youth mental health, the US surgeon general has found that the use of social media by young people contribute to feelings of body dissatisfaction, low self-esteem, and eating disorders.[34] Social media can also impact consumer behavior. One study found that 71 percent of social media users are more likely to purchase products and services after receiving online offers and referrals.[35] These examples beg the question, to what extent do social media influence behavioral changes in political attitudes? And if so whose, and how?

We have some answers. Research on President Donald Trump's hateful social media posts during the COVID-19 pandemic where he attributed the virus to malevolent Chinese behavior showed a powerful correlation with changing public opinion toward China and Asian Americans. An extensive investigation reviewed several dozen tweets by Trump between March 16 and March 20, 2020. During that period, Trump wrote damning messages alleging the disease that ultimately killed more than 1 million Americans was caused by "the onslaught of the Chinese virus." Beginning March 20, 2020, and for the next few days, the country experienced a "clear and dramatic spike in the number of Asian-American incidents." The authors of the study concluded that Trump's social media posts influenced "not only the beliefs of his supporters, but also their actions."[36] Over the next few months, anti-Chinese sentiment in the United States rose dramatically.[37]

Fast forward to the results of the 2024 presidential campaign between Trump and Democrat Kamala Harris for another example of Trump-related hate speech. In this situation, evidence suggests that Trump's persistent social media appeals to young men during the period between October 1 and November 6, 2024, relied on "a spike in [social media] misogynist content in late October just before the election." In addition, social media posts by the Trump campaign appeared, calling for repeal of the Nineteenth Amendment to the Constitution that empowered women with the right to vote in 1920. The research found that hate speech toward women at elevated levels continued after the election.[38] The point is that posts on social media can mold minds in ways that they may not have been otherwise, and that those sentiments can persist long after the "information" is consumed.

Overcoming Trumpism

Corporate Irresponsibility

Social media, of course, is a very open communications system that allows virtually anyone to publish almost anything online, at any time. That ability alone can make it difficult for the consumer to separate facts from fiction. Which brings us back to politics. The impact of social media on voter behavior can be substantial in several respects, including exposing end users to content that limits their support for democracy through messages about election fraud, voter suppression, foreign interference, and legitimacy of the election itself.[39] On this issue, social media companies are hardly neutral bystanders in hosting questionable, if not harmful, information on their platforms.

The fact is that to a great extent, the ability of people to present untrue social media messages depends on the management of the content by the companies and their platforms rules. Not so many years ago, the CEOs of social media companies took seriously the role of preventing unscrupulous statements and misinformation on their platforms with "content moderation" systems that use independent fact-checkers to prevent misuse. In 2017, then-Twitter CEO Jack Dorsey promised to prevent tweets dealing with unwanted sexual advances, nonconsensual nudity, hate symbols, violent groups, and tweets that glorify violence.[40] Similarly, at Facebook, after complaints about false material appearing on Facebook pages, CEO Mark Zuckerberg committed to fighting "fake news" as early as 2016.[41] Further, after the Trump-inspired January 6, 2021, insurrection against Congress, Zuckerberg wrote on his Facebook page that he could no longer tolerate Trump's "use of our platform to incite violent insurrection against a democratically elected government," and that Trump's Facebook and Instagram accounts would be suspended immediately.[42] By monitoring hateful speech and deceptive content, these companies appeared to take seriously their responsibility for protecting the public from abusers when necessary. But as they say, appearances can be deceiving, although in these cases, there was a delaying effect until their true colors came out.

Changing Social Media Cultures

Over time, major social media companies such as X, Meta (Facebook and Instagram), TikTok, and Google have abandoned any pretense of controlling the quality and accuracy of information placed on their platforms. Both

X and Meta replaced content monitoring by experts with "community notes," where contributors comment on the veracity of posts, a haphazard system of checks. That's considerably different than corporate responsibility for oversight. The result led to a dramatic increase of faulty, hateful, and often bigoted information that fit in well with the Trump campaign. We can't emphasize enough the relationship that ensued between cause and effect. Without the need to account for their statements on social media, contributors can present inaccurate information to their heart's desire without anyone with knowledge otherwise to step in and correct the record or remove the posts.

The Changing Culture at X

Soon after acquiring Twitter (renamed as X shortly thereafter) in October 2022, new owner Elon Musk dismissed an estimated three thousand content moderators. In easing restrictions on social media writers in the name of "free speech," Musk said that Twitter "should not show people content that they would find offensive."[43] He also pledged not to take sides in the 2024 presidential election.

Neither of those assurances lasted very long. Critics worried that hate speech on X would soar. Not so, said Musk, who reported in November 2022 that hate messages actually declined on X by 95 percent as a result of his new "free speech" policy.[44] However, independent research discovered otherwise.

Analysis of messages placed on X following Elon Musk's "free speech" policy change found slurs against Black Americans more than tripled; insults toward gay men increased by 50 percent, and anti-Semitic tirades went up by more than 60 percent within two weeks, according to the Center for Countering Digital Hate and other hate monitoring groups.[45] Many of the most disingenuous and hate-filled remarks on X were filed by Musk, himself; in doing so, he gave others license to do the same thing.[46] And license they took, adding to the numbers of increasing appearances of hate and conspiracy posts on the site.

As for his political neutrality, that promise disappeared almost as fast as Musk made it. As the 2024 election approached, Musk posted false claims that the Democrats were bringing in immigrants illegally to vote for presidential candidate Kamala Harris that the Biden administration failed to help hurricane victims, that Democrats are manipulating the weather, produced a manipulated video in which Harris described herself as "the ultimate diversity hire;" the endless list goes on.[47] Worse yet, X personnel repeatedly and systematically deleted pro-Democratic posts during the 2024 presidential campaign, at times labeling them as spam.[48] Musk basically used X as a pro-Trump election outlet.

Musk became the largest financial supporter of Donald Trump's 2024 presidential candidacy, contributing an unprecedented $277 million to Trump's campaign and affiliated pro-Trump groups.[49] Musk's contributions amounted to about one-quarter of all the money generated for the 2024 Trump presidential campaign. After committing to Trump, Musk used X as his "personal messaging machine," often focusing on election conspiracy theories, racist outbursts, and deceptive Democratic practices.[50] Let's remember that Elon Musk has 163 million followers on X, far more than anyone else. On the issue of promoting hate on social media, Musk and Trump were on the same page with continuous messages of hate and distortion typically without any merit.

The Changing Culture at Meta

Facebook—the social media platform of Meta and the largest social media entity with more than 3 billion users as of 2025—began its monitoring with the intent to do good. In his 2016 apology to users for fake news and conspiracy theories allowed by outsourced monitoring agencies, a contrite Mark Zuckerberg wrote, "The bottomline is this: we take misinformation seriously."[51] From there, Zuckerberg committed to defending truth on his social media platform.

Through most of 2020, Facebook scrutinized and removed hundreds of accounts linked to White supremacy groups, conspiracy theories, child pornography, and activities viewed by the organization's in-house content monitoring team as unacceptable.[52] The company was rather diligent in watching for hate speech and extremism on its platform by a large team and an independent panel of experts known as the Oversight Board.[53] But Facebook's attitude on misinformation was about to change. The first hint came on January 25, 2023, when Facebook (now Meta) ended Trump's suspension, promising "new guardrails to deter repeat offenses."

On April 29, 2024, Facebook, along with Instagram and Threads—Meta's other platforms— announced the end of its Oversight Board and a reduction in content moderation staff, thereby weakening standards and responses to questionable posts. In July 2024, Facebook removed all restrictions on Trump's participation. The company's 180-degree turnabout was completed in January 2025, when following Trump's reelection, Meta announced an end to fact checking entirely, relying instead on users to correct inaccuracies.[54] All this was in the context of what Zuckerberg proudly calls "free expression." Yet, Meta's "free expression" has not been for everyone. In January 2025, reports emerged that on several occasions beginning just after the November 2024 presidential election, Facebook and Instagram had blurred, blocked, or removed several posts from abortion providers.[55] A coincidence? According to the account, upon complaints by the providers, Meta restored some of the removed posts but not all. Moreover, this wasn't the first time abortion information was removed on Meta. In 2022, just after the *Dobbs v. Jackson Health* abortion case placing responsibility for the procedure on the states, posts about abortion access were also removed at Facebook.[56] Another coincidence?

Meta has made other changes that fit in with the second Trump presidency. In January 2025, days before Trump's inauguration, the social media company declared that it would end its Diversity, Equity, and Inclusion policy, previously criticized by Trump.[57] Those programs had been established as ways to offset discrimination against women and minorities. Zuckerberg also met with Trump at Mar-a-Lago and announced that he would contribute $1 million for Trump's inauguration along with the social media CEOs of Google, TikTok, and of course Elon Musk at X, Trump's recent benefactor courtesy of his $277 million in campaign contributions.

Meta completed its political rebirth in late January 2025 when the company settled a lawsuit with Trump that filed against it after suspension by the social media platform for his role in the January 6 insurrection. In announcing a $25 million payment to Trump, Zuckerberg added, "This is going to be a big year for redefining our relationships with governments."[58] Indeed.

How much of this was coincidental, and how much was Zuckerberg realigning with Trump intentionally? In the end it doesn't matter as much that these fundamental changes in Meta policy occurred, now leaving the social media platform open to unprecedented amounts of fake news and conspiracy theories.

Bye, Bye Self-Regulation

X and Meta today are social media platforms that operate with radically different values compared to a few years ago. Without apology, upon purchase of Twitter, Elon Musk quickly removed all semblances of social discourse and transformed his site into an unequalled political megaphone for Trumpism and the far right. Among those welcomed back to the X fold was Alex Jones, an Internet conspiracy broadcaster who had labeled the mass shooting at Sandy Hook Elementary School a lie, and who later was successfully sued for his malicious claim.

At Meta, Mark Zuckerberg did away with virtually all attempts to moderate content, turning the platform into a receptacle for just about anything. According to one analysis, Facebook's (and other Meta products') new policy now easily allows for attacks on women, gay people, transgender, and nonbinary persons.[59] Meta's conversion conveniently complemented DEI and other policy initiatives of the second Trump administration.[60]

Today, these two social media platforms have much more in common than not. They have removed the guardrails shielding society from falsehoods and hateful language. Most of all, they have shown that self-regulation is meaningless in the social media space, with discriminated elements of American society the victims.

The resurgence of hate on social media in the absence of self-regulation has been a boon to Donald Trump and his allies. Inasmuch as Trump depends on hate and bigotry for producing political division as well as support from the alt-right, conditions in the new social media environment became just what the doctor ordered. The beauty of it lay in the free-for-all setting where Trump and his allies could say almost anything, no matter how provocative, without any consequences.

Section 230 of the Communications Decency Act

Regulatory agencies are odd policymaking institutions of American government. Upon creation by Congress, they usually operate independently of the three major branches of government with fairly broad powers to investigate, deliberate, execute, and enforce decisions in relatively narrow areas of public policy.[61] By law, these organizations are typically governed collectively by several appointees (usually five) with overlapping terms and members of both political parties to reduce the ability of one political party to dominate membership. With this form of organization, regulatory agencies are designed to operate independently in an insulated environment that protects them from political influence whether it be from inside or outside of traditional political sources.[62] That's how they're supposed to conduct their work in theory, anyway.

Of the many contradictions in American governance, no regulatory commission is more confounding than the FCC. Established in 1934, the five-member agency of the national government was set up initially to regulate radio communications. Over the next fifty years, the FCC was given national oversight of television, satellite, and cable industries.[63] Then, through the Communications Decency Act of 1996, Congress added the burgeoning social media industry to the responsibilities of the FCC. In Section 230 of that legislation, the commission was given the obligation to protect social media *from* regulation. That designation was a rather odd task, considering that government regulatory agencies typically direct behavior of their industries in the name of the public good rather than turning away from it.

Let's remember that social media is a fairly new form of communications and information exchange. When Section 230 of the Communications Decency Act was passed in 1996, the idea at the time was to protect nascent social media sites attempting to connect people in novel ways from being overwhelmed by frivolous lawsuits. The most important part of the section reads, "No provider or user of an interactive computer service shall be treated as the publisher or speaker of any information provided by another information content provider." Those words absolved social media from anything untoward that appeared on their sites. However, the section allowed the social media companies to remove posts that were considered obscene or unacceptable.[64]

Early on, the federal courts put their stamp of approval of Section 230. In what most legal scholars view as the defining moment, a 1997 decision by a federal appeals court declared that the legislation barred lawsuits from seeking to hold a social media platform "liable for its exercise of a publisher's traditional editorial functions—such as deciding whether to publish, withdraw, postpone, or alter content."[65] Thus, the first sites were given room to grow, although all are long gone and have been replaced by next-generation platforms.

Nevertheless, the goal of allowing social media platforms to develop free of bothersome legal challenges worked. Steven Brill, a critic of Section 230, writes that without the legislation's regulation of social media in the early days of the industry, "the interactive internet and all the good that it brought by way of connecting people and spreading knowledge would have been strangled in the crib by an avalanche of litigation or self-censorship."[66] Thus, the protection provided by Section 230 seemed to be appropriate under the circumstances.

Now, a quarter of a century later, conditions in the social media space have dramatically changed, and not necessarily for the better. Brill points to a phenomenon that has rearranged assumptions regarding the industry's existence and value. Specifically, over time, advertising revenue for many social media companies has become far more important than the social engagement patterns thought to be the original basis for the innovations. There is great significance to this development. Brill writes, "The more time people spent on a platform, the more advertising [the social media companies] would see. Online, truth didn't pay. So, [social interaction] would be de-ranked" in importance to social media company core values.[67]

It turns out that the lies published by contributors to social media have been beneficial to the bottom lines of company revenues. An examination by several MIT professors of information circulated on Twitter between 2006 and 2017 confirms the point. Their research found that false news traveled faster and to more people than truthful information, as much as ten times faster in some cases.[68] Another investigation has found that a relatively small percentage of people sharing false information on social media produce a disproportionately large percentage of the information.[69] Worse yet, false information is disseminated on the Internet much more often than accurate information—up to 70 percent according to one study.[70]

There have been serious consequences from the loosening, and in some cases even ending, content guardrails. Without any guardrails, one assessment summarized, "disinformation, hate speech, revenge pornography, harassment, terrorism activity, and sex trafficking run rampant on social media sites."[71] This is the new reality with social media and American politics, and it fits in well with the Trumpist goals of dividing American society.

To summarize, a relatively small number of social media contributors spread false information that is gobbled up by large numbers of users. More users increase the capability of companies to charge more for advertising. Simply put, lies bring dollars! That's become the model for modern social media companies. Therefore, why should anyone who promotes social media platforms care about accuracy or the truth? Perhaps they don't. More importantly, perhaps they never did.

Assessing Section 230 in the Mature State of Social Media

Clearly, today's social media platforms operate much differently than in the early days. Without any serious intention of monitoring speech, social

Assuring Media Integrity

media platforms are now depositories and transmitters of information. Major platforms have stopped any serious attempts of self-regulation through fact-checking, leaving such "management" to user groups in the form of commentary. All of which implores the crucial question: Should we continue to permit unregulated use of social media, or should we find ways to regulate them much as government regulates other industries?

The Arguments for Keeping Section 230

Proponents of Section 230 view it as a beacon for protecting free speech, a key guarantee in the First Amendment in the Bill of Rights, found in the US Constitution. They see a slippery slope between content monitoring and censorship. As such, controversial thoughts that might not have a home anywhere else have a home on social media. The American Civil Liberties Union writes that rather than be some kind of a government gift to social media, Section 230 is a welcome asset to individuals. For example, the ACLU maintains, "Without this protection, important speech such as communication about abortion, especially in states where abortion is outlawed, could be silenced."[72] That ability to discuss anything on social media is just as important as talking to a crowd.

Then there's the question about the importance of neutrality online. For those who claim that the content on social media platforms should be neutral or impartial, Section 230 defenders counter that the sites are special for their roles as depositories for controversial topics. Section 230, they explain, is the Internet equivalent of a bookstore. Just as a bookstore has no responsibility for the contents of its books, social media platforms do not bear responsibility for the messages on their sites. Therefore, messages don't have to be sanitized to the point that controversy is removed. Social media platforms are safe places for anyone to comment on just about anything, and that ability exists because under Section 230, these companies have immunity from liability for content they host.

A third area centers on representation for those members of society who have difficulty being heard in traditional communication settings. Defenders of Section 230 contend that the absence of barriers on social media help those who have difficulty being heard elsewhere gain a sizable audience. Such unregulated access is particularly helpful to people of color, LGBTQIA+ communities, immigrant populations, religious or language minorities, activists, and political dissidents; in other words, groups who feel drowned out in the public square.[73] Section 230 proponents argue that

The Arguments for Deleting Section 230

In considering the arguments for removing Section 230 from the Community Decency Act, it's important to understand whether its intent matches up with the consequences. One analysis points to legislation replete with ambiguities. Law professor Alan Rozenshtein writes that Section 230 was the convoluted outcome of an attempt to simultaneously address the competing themes of freedom of speech and the prevention of "indecent" content online—all this within a voluntary content moderation framework. Because of these and other conflicting objectives, it's difficult to understand Congress's intent, and therefore hard for the courts to act. In fact, on the few occasions that Section 230-related issues have reached the US Supreme Court, the justices have punted and settled cases on other grounds.[74] Given this and other confusing language in the statute, Rozenshtein writes, Congress should clarify its intentions in the form of new legislation.

A second critique of Section 230 centers on the generational differences between the time it was written in 1996 and present-day conditions. Specifically, like so many changes in other industries, experts in social media Michael D. Smith and Marshall W. Van Alstyne describe the law as written "during a long-gone age of naive technological capabilities."[75] Since the enactment of the legislation, the authors write, serious questions of accountability have emerged on such tragedies as the conspiratorial discussions before and after the January 6 insurrection; terrorist recruiting; sexual exploitation of children; and illicit sales of pharmaceuticals, assault weapons, and endangered wildlife. To this the authors write, "When you grant platforms complete legal immunity for the content that their users post, you also reduce their incentives to proactively remove content causing social harm."[76]

This takes us to the third concern about Section 230, namely the exercise of free speech on social media platforms in almost any form, excepting terrorism, revolution, or any federal law. The First Amendment of the Constitution holds in part that Congress "shall make no law abridging the freedom of speech." That sounds pretty clear, but is it? Robert Jensen contends that there is no such thing as *absolute* free speech, noting that "every society distinguishes between permitted and prohibited speech." In drawing the line between the two, "we are valuing the value of the expression against the harm or potential harm that expression can cause."[77] Jensen is not alone. More than one hundred years ago, the US Supreme Court held that if language presents a "clear and present danger," that language may no longer be allowable.[78] In Section 230 of the Communications Decency Act of 1996, it was assumed that social media sites would moderate content so as to prevent harmful speech, and for a while that was the case. However, as discussed earlier, moderation is yesterday's news—social media companies no longer do it in fear of suppressing speech. But bearing in mind the "clear and present danger" of incendiary language, it can be argued that without content moderation, free speech is abused when its message spew hate and jeopardizes members of society.

A fourth concern centers on the lack of neutrality of social media with respect to influencing consumer behavior. Meta has become known for its ability to provide advertisers with pinpointed data for specific users through complex algorithms that create specific information. That tool enables the business clients to drive user engagement at phenomenal rates that they wouldn't have otherwise.[79] They show the consumer what they know the consumer likes. With respect to the political consumer, the "information" disseminated through advertiser-provided algorithms creates "echo chambers" where users are exposed only to specific values or products rather than the totality of information. The result, according to one study, is "an atmosphere of intellectual stagnation by restricting our exposure to varied opinions and challenging ideas."[80] Whether socially or politically driven, sophisticated algorithms shape a sense of "reality" that is anything but. As a result, the user lacks complete information and may well not even know it.

A Call for Reform

Unmoderated social media yields far more problems than benefits. Admittedly, there are solid arguments on both sides of the question, yet clearly the inflammatory language we have seen on these platforms over the past few years has made it clear that some form of content moderation is necessary to protect our democracy from falling victim to an authoritarian form of government. Yes, it's that bad.

Consider for a moment the role of social media in the January 6, 2021, insurrection against the US Capitol, the most serious threat to our democracy since the Civil War. A review of 280 assessments of communications before and during that period found a web of rebellious conversations. According to research, "Both mainstream and alternative platforms allowed domestic extremists and prominent figures on the right to accelerate the growth of alt-right terrorist movements like QAnon and Stop the Steal, contributing directly to the insurrection."[81] The entire event was well planned from beginning to end. Particularly in advance of the riot, Trump's followers discussed their intentions "with their friends and family, and especially with like-minded souls online, which led to more extreme and confidently held attitudes."[82] This underscores the multiplier effect of negative messages nurtured by Donald Trump and his acolytes and the damage that came as a result.

And President Donald Trump was right in the middle of it. One of those assessments tracked Trump's recurrent false statements via social media during the runup to the horrific event. Over and over again, his online messages trashed the mainstream press, reinforcing the beliefs of his followers that social media sites like Twitter were their only true sources of information. But, the research found, "Trump did not do this alone. Trump lit the spark, but the internet provided the oxygen."[83] There must be change.

By itself, social media can be beneficial to society, particularly as an agent that facilitates a sense of community. But if abused, social media can be a major contributor to tearing people apart. That capability must be minimized as much as possible. Below are some possible solutions to the problems connected with these communication platforms.

Modification of Section 230

Like other conveyors of information, social media must be held accountable in the ways that television, radio, and print media are held accountable. That obligation begins with Congress modifying Section 230 of the Communications Decency Act of 1996. Now that the social media industry has matured, companies must bear responsibility for the material they allow on their sites. Just like people can sue traditional communications sectors for libel and other misdeeds, so should those who feel victimized be able to sue social media for similar misdeeds. For those who scream about the Freedom of Speech component in the First Amendment to the Constitution, the courts have long held that "free speech" has its limits. That should also apply to social media.

This idea is not entirely new. For several years, Facebook, Twitter, and others hired independent fact-checkers to assure content moderation and the limits of free speech. Then, for several reasons, the platform companies stopped the moderation practice. Internal corporate disagreements about what constitutes questionable language were chief among the reasons for stopping overview of controversial material that appeared on these platforms.

But in the absence of any content moderation, threats, lies, and an abundance of hate have flourished in what could be called the "content vacuum." This abuse is harmful to democracy, particularly as it applies to conspiratorial theories that spread like wildfire. Unregulated social media has also been a primary concern of groups that focus on children, both in terms of contributing to low self-esteem and providing a haven for pedophiles. So, how can such oversight of social media content develop? One answer comes with tough federal oversight through regulation.

Regulation

This policymaking tool is a well-established mechanism to address conflicting objectives between two or more constituencies. When all is said and done, regulations control behaviors of individuals or groups. Key to the development of such rules is that bargaining often takes place between the parties en route to determining and enforcing a regulatory policy outcome.[84] This is standard in the American policymaking arena. That's because when agencies award approval or impose sanctions on clientele pursuing activities that fall within their purview, industry knowledge and input are part of the policy recipe that emerges.[85] In this case, the FCC is the government agency for managing social media per the Communications Decency Act. Its decisions must take into consideration those it regulates. "Consideration," however, does not mean capitulation.

With social media regulation, there are three categories of stakeholders: social media companies, the government (the FCC), and public interest entities interested in determining the boundaries of free speech. Given the events of recent years highlighted by, but not limited to, absolute free speech, the regulation argument can be that some limits are in order to protect the public good. Regarding what those limits might be, that answer should be the outcome of meaningful negotiations among the parties. As with most regulatory agency issues, those negotiations should include public hearings that would call for input from all the parties as well as individuals and organizations outside the loop but with strong interest in the process and its outcome. Public interest parties might include the Organization for Social Media Safety (children), Council for Responsible Social Media (democracy), the Center for Humane Technology (disinformation), NetChoice (free speech), the ACLU (free speech), and the Software and Information Industry Association (digital content), as well as many others. Government bodies such as the Department of Health and Human Services and the FBI also should be among the participants. The hope would be that out of these meetings and negotiations, the parties could reach agreement on the rules for rejecting questionable material posted online.

There's no guarantee that the FCC would adopt new regulations after holding hearings and meetings. But at least the issue would be socialized in such a way that government representatives, social media companies, and public interest groups outside the social media space all would be heard and considered. Then, with rules for social media content determined and firmly established, lawsuits would be permitted upon allegations of violations that the social media companies committed.

State Laws and Lawsuits

In recent years, several states have passed legislation to control abusive behavior by social media companies. In 2023, the Utah legislature passed legislation requiring parental consent for minors to open social media accounts. In 2024, the states of New York and California enacted similar laws prohibiting social media platforms from providing deliberately addictive feeds, content designed to take advantage of a child's profile, for children under the age of eighteen without parental permission. Also in 2024, the attorney general of New Mexico sued Snap Inc., the parent company of Snapchat, for "ignoring reports of sextortion, failing to implement age verification rules, and admitting to features that connect minors with adults."[86] Other states are now actively pursuing similar legislation.

Some states have confronted social media companies in court, particularly with concern about children's issues. In 2023, more than forty states sued Meta's Facebook and Instagram for allowing posts that have aggravated the mental health crisis sweeping America's youth. Meta representatives asked a judge to dismiss the case, but the judge refused, clearing the way for a possible trial.[87] In 2024, thirteen state attorneys general sued TikTok for violating state consumer protection laws, alleging that "TikTok exploits and harms young users and deceives the public" about the platform's threats to children's health.[88]

Social media companies have not remained idle over state challenges to their domination. Within weeks of the California law attempting to fight social media addiction among the state's youth, NetChoice—a social media industry group—sued California, claiming that the new law would be expensive. Moreover, NetChoice argued, the new law "risks all Californians' safety online, and it creates more opportunities for criminals and predators to target and compromise minors' information on covered services."[89] Ironically, many of those abuses were the basis of the California legislation in the first place!

Whether states can firmly puncture the Section 230 bubble that prevents lawsuits against social media companies remains to be seen. Thus far, the US Supreme Court, the final referee in these questions, has not ruled whether there are limits to social media impenetrability. For example, in 2024, the US Supreme Court remanded two cases in Texas and Florida prohibiting social media companies from censoring content based on viewpoint to lower courts for more information about the First Amendment and algorithms.[90] For now, however, states are becoming increasingly aggressive in challenging the power of these companies.

Social Media Controls in Other Countries

Interest in regulating social media content in countries outside the United States extends back to the original debate about the wisdom of Section 230. Meanwhile, other countries have been concerned with what they perceive as the lack of content moderation in areas such as child abuse, elections, and disinformation. On that score, American social media companies have found themselves under pressure abroad, where several nations have slapped controls on their behavior.

It's worth remembering that many democratic nations regulate social media to protect citizens from harm, especially children from hate language, sexual exploitation, and other potentially harmful material. Authoritarian rulers seek to limit social media in order to prevent the free flow of information that, in turn, can be a threat to those in power.

With respect to the first case, in 2023, the twenty-seven nation European Union passed the Digital Services Act in 2023. Under the terms of this unprecedented legislation, eight social media platforms, online marketing places, and mobile app stores were required to manage their platforms so as to protect European users from hate speech, disinformation, terrorism, child sexual abuse, and commercial scams. Failure to comply with the law could cost a violating company up to 6 percent of its annual revenue.[91]

Other approaches have been more targeted. For example, in 2024, Australia became the first nation that required "reasonable steps" by social media companies to prevent the presence of harmful posts to children through age sixteen.

Failure of a company to do so could bring fines of up to $32 million. Initially, at least, the new law was incredibly popular, with a public opinion poll showing 77 percent approval.[92] Finally, in 2024 and 2025, Brazil tangled with X and Meta over hate speech. Although both companies claimed to have adjusted their content, Brazilian authorities found their changes unacceptable. For now, that's a developing story.

In some instances, countries have regulated social media in such a way so as to prevent the transparency of information. China, Iran, Saudi Arabia, and Russia are particularly strict in controlling social media content, with fines and possible imprisonment if their policies are violated. In all of these circumstances, authoritarian governments work very hard to keep the lid on information that might cause problems for those who undemocratically hold power.[93]

Clearly, what social media companies and their allies allege can't be done in the United States can be done elsewhere. Increasingly, countries have shown the capability to force social media companies to moderate content in such a way so as to comply with local values. And given the alternatives of banishment or fines, the companies have managed to obey the laws.

Leveling the Social Media Playing Field

With few guardrails to intercept and prevent abuse, social media has fostered a new, robust means of communication. Evolving at lightning speed, it has reorganized the way we absorb and share information regardless of its accuracy. There's little doubt that social media still plays a major role in enabling users to learn matters they would not have known prior to its creation, and that's good. Commerce has soared, thanks to the growth of the social media industry.

However, over time, the capabilities of social media have expanded greatly, much of it hardly benign. What started out as a means to bring people together has morphed into a sophisticated system with the

Assuring Media Integrity

malevolent capability to shape people's mindsets, often through delivery of incomplete, or worse yet, intentionally distorted presentations. Often, there is no clarity of authorship. As a result, these days this unregulated system operates without transparency and is accountable to no one.

Social media has been a boon for Trump and his acolytes, who have thrived on the ability to publish "information" intentionally designed to deceive viewers. They have continuously employed social media to whip up distrust among users, dividing and angering some segments of society against others. At the same time, they have spent great amounts of energy persuading viewers that the mainstream media is their enemy. It's a terrible combination of manipulation that threatens the well-being of American democracy.

Trumpists aren't the only violators of public trust in their unscrupulous use of social media. Certainly others, even political opponents, have abused social media, but not nearly as successfully as Donald Trump and his followers. They are masters of deceit, unparalleled in their devious skills, who through their communication talents have successfully turned followers against others as well as the basic institutions of government.

This untenable situation takes us to a reconsideration of Section 230. Section 3 of the Findings portion of the act writes that "The internet and other interactive computer services offer a forum for a true diversity of political discourse." Clearly, with content moderation no longer used by social media platforms, Section 230 must be modified to firmly structure a set of rules that hold these companies responsible for published material that violates those rules. A starting point for establishing the rules should come from existing FCC regulations on radio and television, as well as precedents established by court decisions on the appropriate conditions for suing newspapers and magazines. For those who feel unfairly harmed by social media posts, lawsuits should be the mechanism through which offended people and organizations take the violators to task.

No doubt, reaching an agreement of those published pieces of information that fall outside the boundaries of proprietary will be difficult. But, if the conversation begins with the commitment to end untruths, discrimination, incendiary behavior, and other harmful conduct, American society will be the beneficiary.

Social media companies should be responsible for the posts they host the same way that mainstream media are responsible for the contents on their platforms. By being required to impose standards, these platforms will be forced to keep abusers in line or face punishment. That responsibility should be created through rigorous content management as per the rules established by policymakers in accordance with the input from various stakeholders. Such specifications have already been successfully established in other countries. There is no reason that they can't be similarly instituted in the United States.

There are those who argue that exposing social media companies to possible lawsuits will open the door for Trump and his allies to sue those companies that allow publication of posts that call attention to Trump abuses. That may well be the case, but the fact is that through the FCC and the Department of Justice, Trump can already intimidate and even punish social media platforms. At least with a revamped situation that allows lawsuits against social media companies, opponents of hate, disinformation, and authoritarianism will be able to level the playing field. The correction is imperative if we believe that those who manipulate social media should be held accountable.

NOTES

1 Aeron Davis, *Political Communication* (Medford, MA: Polity Press, 2019), p. 92.
2 George C. Edwards III, Kenneth R. Mayer, and Stephen J. Wayne, *Presidential Leadership*, 10th edition (Lanham, MD: Rowman & Littlefield, 2018), p. 172.
3 Ruth Ben-Ghiat, *Strongmen: Mussolini to the Present* (New York: W.W. Norton, 2021), p. 95.
4 Jan E. Leighley, *Mass Media and Politics* (New York: Houghton Mifflin, 2004), p. 143.
5 "Fox Settles Dominion Lawsuit for $787.5 Million over US Election Lies," Reuters, April 18, 2023, https://www.reuters.com/legal/dominions-defamation-case-against-fox-poised-trial-after-delay-2023-04-18/.
6 "Election Workers Describe 'Hateful' Threats after Trump's False Claims," *The Washington Post*, June 21, 2022, https://www.washingtonpost.com/national-security/2022/06/21/ruby-freeman-shaye-moss-jan6-testimony/.
7 "FCC Fines Sinclair Record $48 Million for Deceptive Bid for Tribune Stations," NPR, May 7, 2020, https://www.npr.org/2020/05/07/851783937/fcc-fines-sinclair-record-48-million-for-deceptive-bid-for-tribune-stations.
8 "Court Says Trump Owes *New York Times* Nearly $400,000 in Legal Fees," The Hill, January 12, 2024, https://thehill.com/regulation/court-battles/4405833-court-says-trump-owes-new-york-times-nearly-400k-in-legal-fees/.
9 "Trump Sues Pollster J. Ann Selzer, Claiming Iowa Poll Was 'Brazen Election Interference,'" weareiowa, December 18, 2024, https://www.weareiowa.com/article/news/politics/elections/trump-lawsuit-des-moines-register-selzer-iowa-poll-kamala-harris/524-34ecdb18-92a1-4795-b0c6-2fae7e465da6.

10 "ABC News Settles Defamation Suit with Trump for $15 Million," CNN, December 14, 2024, https://www.cnn.com/2024/12/14/politics/trump-abc-news-defamation-lawsuit-settle/index.html.
11 "Paramount in Settlement Talks with Trump over '60 Minutes' Lawsuit," *The New York Times*, January 30, 2025, https://www.nytimes.com/2025/01/30/business/media/paramount-trump-cbs-news-settlement.html.
12 "Wendy McMahon Pushed from Her CBS Post amid '60 Minutes Crisis,'" *Los Angeles Times*, May 5, 2025, https://www.latimes.com/entertainment-arts/business/story/2025-05-19/wendy-mcmahon-resigns-from-role-as-head-of-cbs-news-and-tv-stations-amid-60-minutes-crisis.
13 See "Trump Tells Republicans to 'Kill' Reporter Shield Bill Passed Unanimously by House," *The New York Times*, November 20, 2024, https://www.nytimes.com/2024/11/20/us/politics/trump-press-act-freedom-reporters.html, and "Senate GOP Blocks Bill to Protect Journalists after Trump Opposes It," CNN, December 10, 2024, https://www.cnn.com/2024/12/10/politics/senate-gop-blocks-press-protections-bill/index.html.
14 "Trump Sparks Fears over Retribution against Media with Patel FBI Pick," *The Hill*, December 11, 2024, https://thehill.com/media/5030896-threats-kash-patel-fbi-media/.
15 Elon Musk, post on X, October 18, 2024.
16 "Trump's Crackdown on Immigrants Includes People Who Share Information with Them," *San Francisco Chronicle*, February 14, 2025, https://www.sfchronicle.com/politics/article/trump-ice-media-information-20164081.php.
17 Quoted in "Trump and Allies Are Waging Campaign against Media to Stifle Dissent—Experts," *The Guardian*, December 21, 2024, https://www.theguardian.com/us-news/2024/dec/21/trump-media-assault-silence-criticism.
18 See "'Anticipatory Obedience': Newspapers' Refusal to Endorse Shines Light on Billionaire Owners' Motives," *The Guardian*, October 24, 2024, https://www.theguardian.com/us-news/2024/oct/26/anticipatory-obedience-newspapers-endorsement-refusal.
19 "This Company Rates News Sites' Credibility. The Right Wants It Stopped," *The Washington Post*, December 15, 2024, https://www.washingtonpost.com/technology/2024/12/24/newsguard-disinformation-censorship-free-speech/.
20 "Digital 2024: The United States of America," DataReportal, February 22, 2024, https://datareportal.com/reports/digital-2024-united-states-of-america.
21 "Americans' Social Media Use," Pew Research Center, January 31, 2024, https://www.pewresearch.org/internet/2024/01/31/americans-social-media-use/.
22 "Inside 4chan's Top-Secret Moderation Machine," Wired, June 5, 2023, https://www.wired.com/story/4chan-moderation-buffalo-shooting/.
23 "Social Media and News Fact Sheet," Pew Research Center, September 17, 2024, https://www.pewresearch.org/journalism/fact-sheet/social-media-and-news-fact-sheet/.
24 See P. W. Singer and Emerson T. Booking, *Like War: The Weaponization of Social Media* (New York: Houghton Mifflin Harcourt, 2018), p. 103.
25 For an overview, see "Trump's 'Big Lie' Fueled a New Generation of Social Media Influencers," *The Washington Post*, September 22, 2022, https://www.

washingtonpost.com/technology/2022/09/20/social-media-influencers-election-fraud/.
26 "Trump Is Drowning in the Misinformation Swamp He Helped Create," CNN, September 2024, https://www.cnn.com/2024/09/12/business/trump-misinformation-social-media-moderation/index.html.
27 "What Politifact Learned in 1,000 Fact-Checks of Donald Trump," Politifact, February 1, 2024, https://www.politifact.com/article/2024/feb/01/what-politifact-learned-in-1000-fact-checks-of-don/.
28 "Truth Social and Consequences," *Columbia Journalism Review*, November 25, 2024, https://www.cjr.org/business_of_news/truth-social-trump-media-how-important-stocks-shares-announcements.php.
29 "2024 Post-Election Survey: A Majority of New Trump Voters Used Social Media as Main News Source," Navigator, December 2, 2024, https://navigatorresearch.org/2024-post-election-survey-a-majority-of-new-trump-voters-used-social-media-as-main-news-source/.
30 "Musk Misleading Election Claims Viewed 1.2bn Times on X—with No Fact Checks," Center for Countering Digital Hate, August 8, 2024, https://counterhate.com/research/musk-misleading-election-claims-viewed-1-2bn-times-on-x-with-no-fact-checks/.
31 "Fact Check: Harris Campaign Social Media Account Has Repeatedly Deceived with Misleading Edits and Captions," CNN, September 14, 2024, https://www.cnn.com/2024/09/14/politics/fact-check-harris-campaign-social-media/index.html.
32 "Top Fact-Checker Finally Reveals Which Party Lies More: Democrats or Republicans," Independent, October 18, 2024, https://www.the-independent.com/news/world/americas/us-politics/republicans-democrats-lies-bill-adair-fact-check-politifact-trump-b2631493.html.
33 "Fact-Checking 55 Suspect Claims, Mostly Trump's, in Debate with Harris," *The Washington Post*, September 12, 2024, https://www.washingtonpost.com/politics/2024/09/11/fact-check-presidential-debate-harris-trump/.
34 US Surgeon General, "Social Media and Youth Mental Health," Washington, DC, June 5, 2023, https://www.hhs.gov/sites/default/files/sg-youth-mental-health-social-media-advisory.pdf.
35 "How Social Media Influences 71 Percent of Consumer Buying Decisions," SonicsSEO.com, November 20, 2020, https://www.sonicseo.com/social-media-influences/.
36 Andy Cao, Jason M. Lindo, and Jiee Zhong, "Can Social Media Rhetoric Incite Hate Incidents? Evidence from Trump's 'Chinese Virus' Tweets," National Bureau of Economic Research, October 2022, https://www.nber.org/system/files/working_papers/w30588/w30588.pdf.
37 "Trump's 'Chinese Virus' Slur Makes Some People Blame Chinese Americans. But Others Blame Trump," *The Washington Post*, September 16, 2020, https://www.washingtonpost.com/politics/2020/09/16/trumps-chinese-virus-slur-makes-some-people-blame-chinese-americans-others-blame-trump/.
38 "'Your Body, My Choice': Women Face New Surge of Hate Speech on X and TikTok following Trump's Election Victory," Fast Company, November 8, 2024,

https://www.fastcompany.com/91225746/your-body-my-choice-hate-speech-against-women-after-trump-election.

39 "The Effects of Facebook and Instagram on the 2020 Election: A Deactivation Experiment," National Library of Medicine, March 8, 2024, https://pmc.ncbi.nlm.nih.gov/articles/PMC11126999/pdf/pnas.202321584.pdf.

40 "Twitter's Dorsey: Site to Get 'More Aggressive' Policing Tweets," CNET, October 14, 2017, https://www.cnet.com/tech/services-and-software/twitter-jack-dorsey-ceo-women-boycott-harvey-weinstein/.

41 "Zuckerberg Says He'll Take Steps to Solve Facebook Fake News," Bloomberg Invest, November 19, 2016, https://www.bloomberg.com/news/articles/2016-11-19/zuckerberg-says-he-ll-take-steps-to-solve-facebook-fake-news?embedded-checkout=true.

42 Post on Facebook by Mark Zuckerberg, January 7, 2017.

43 Quoted in "Elon Musk-Twitter Deal Finalized after Months of Legal Drama," The Free Speech Project, January 25, 2023, https://freespeechproject.georgetown.edu/tracker-entries/employee-concerns-mount-as-elon-musk-twitter-deal-to-protect-free-speech-remains-uncertain/.

44 "Twitter Claims There's 95% Less Hate Speech on Twitter after Musk Took Over," BT Tech Today, November 10, 2022, https://www.businesstoday.in/tech-today/news/story/twitter-claims-theres-95-less-hate-speech-on-twitter-after-musk-took-over-352399-2022-11-10.

45 See "Hate Speech's Rise on Twitter Is Unprecedented, Researchers Find," The New York Times, December 2, 2022, https://www.nytimes.com/2022/12/02/technology/twitter-hate-speech.html.

46 For an example, see "Guess Who Just Brought back Pizzagate?" The New Republic, November 20, 2023, https://newrepublic.com/post/177055/guess-just-brought-back-pizzagate.

47 These messages and others are referenced in "2 Years in, Surrogate Elon Musk Has Remade X as a Conservative Megaphone," NPR, October 25, 2024, https://www.npr.org/2024/10/22/nx-s1-5156184/elon-musk-trump-election-x-twitter.

48 "Elon Musk's X Accused of Bias after Pro-Harris Accounts Labeled as 'Spam,'" The Washington Post, August 7, 2024, https://www.washingtonpost.com/technology/2024/08/07/musk-x-harris-bias/.

49 "Elon Musk Put $277 Million into the Election. He's $200 Billion Richer This Year," The Washington Post, December 15, 2024, https://www.washingtonpost.com/business/2024/12/15/elon-musk-trump-election-wealth/.

50 "How Elon Musk Has Turned X into a Pro-Trump Machine," CNN, August 13, 2024, https://www.cnn.com/2024/08/13/tech/elon-musk-donald-trump-x/index.html, and "Elon Musk's X App Ran Ads on #Whitepower and Other Hateful Hashtags," NBC News, June 6, 2024, https://www.nbcnews.com/tech/social-media/elon-musk-x-twitter-antisemitism-hashtags-trending-hate-rcna151945.

51 Quoted in "Mark Zuckerberg's Political Evolution, from Apologies to No More Apologies," The New York Times, January 7, 2025, https://www.nytimes.com/2025/01/07/technology/mark-zuckerberg-meta-free-speech.html.

52 "Facebook just Revealed Its Secret Strategy for Taking Down Hate Groups," Mother Jones, March 25, 2020, https://www.motherjones.com/politics/2020/03/facebook-just-revealed-its-secret-strategy-for-taking-down-hate-groups/.

53 "Facebook Expands Definition of Terrorist Organizations to Limit Extremism," *The New York Times*, September 18, 2019, https://www.nytimes.com/2019/09/17/technology/facebook-hate-speech-extremism.html.

54 "Meta Says It Will End Its Fact-Checking Program on Social Media Posts", *The New York Times*, January 9, 2025, https://www.nytimes.com/live/2025/01/07/business/meta-fact-checking.

55 "Instagram and Facebook Blocked and Hid Abortion Pill Providers' Posts," *The New York Times*, January 23, 2025, https://www.nytimes.com/2025/01/23/technology/instagram-facebook-abortion-pill-providers.html.

56 "Facebook Says 'Incorrect Enforcement' Removed Posts on Abortion Pill Access," The Hill, June 28, 2022, https://thehill.com/policy/technology/3540043-facebook-says-incorrect-enforcement-removed-posts-on-abortion-pill-access/.

57 "Meta Terminates Its DEI Programs Days before Trump Inauguration," *The Guardian*, January 10, 2025, https://www.theguardian.com/us-news/2025/jan/10/meta-ending-dei-program.

58 "Meta Agrees to Pay Trump $25 Million to Settle His Lawsuit," *The New York Times*, https://www.nytimes.com/2025/01/29/technology/meta-trump-lawsuit-settlement.html.

59 "Meta's New Policies Open Gate to Hate," Axios, January 9, 2024, https://www.axios.com/2025/01/09/meta-moderation-transgender-women-hate.

60 "Trump Curtails Protections around Diversity, LGBTQ Rights," Reuters, January 20, 2025, https://www.reuters.com/world/us/trump-sign-orders-ending-diversity-programs-proclaiming-there-are-only-two-sexes-2025-01-20/.

61 Larry N. Gerston, Cynthia Fraleigh, and Robert Schwab, *The Deregulated Society* (Pacific Grove, CA: Brooks/Cole, 1988), p. 4.

62 William D. Schreckhise, *Evaluating American Democracy and Public Policymaking* (Lanham, MD: Rowman & Littlefield, 2018), p. 27.

63 The Federal Communications Commission (FCC), https://www.ntia.gov/book-page/federal-communications-commission-fcc.

64 "What You Should Know about Section 230, the Rule That Shape Today's Internet," PBS, February 21, 2023, https://www.pbs.org/newshour/politics/what-you-should-know-about-section-230-the-rule-that-shaped-todays-internet.

65 The case was *Zeran v. America Online, Inc.* Quoted in "Section 230: An Overview," Congressional Review Service, January 4, 2024, https://crsreports.congress.gov/product/pdf/R/R46751.

66 Steven Brill, *The Death of Truth* (New York: Alfred A. Knopf, 2024), p. 19.

67 Ibid., p. 25.

68 Soroysh Vosoughi, Deb Roy, and Sian Aral, "The Spreads of True and False News Online," *Science*, March 9, 2018, https://www.science.org/doi/10.1126/science.aap9559.

69. Gizam Ceylan, Ian A. Anderson, and Wendy Wood, "Sharing of Misinformation Is Habitual, not just Lazy or Biased," *PNAS*, 120, no. 4, January 17, 2023, https://www.science.org/doi/10.1126/science.aap9559.
70. Katie Langin, "Fake News Spreads Faster Than True News on Twitter—Thanks to People, not Bots," *Science*, March 8, 2018, https://www.science.org/content/article/fake-news-spreads-faster-true-news-twitter-thanks-people-not-bots.
71. Karis Stephen, "The Social Responsibility of Social Media Platforms," *Regulatory Review*, December 21, 2021, https://www.theregreview.org/2021/12/21/stephen-social-responsibility-social-media-platforms/.
72. "Is This the End of the Internet as We Know It?" ACLU, February 22, 2023, https://www.aclu.org/news/free-speech/section-230-is-this-the-end-of-the-internet-as-we-know-it
73. Yanni Chen, Candace Clement, and Matt Wood, "What Is Section 230? Why Ending It Would Create Problems," Free Press, May 14, 2024, https://www.freepress.net/blog/what-is-section-230#:~:text=Without%20Section%20230%2C%20online%20platforms,or%20abandon%20content%20moderation%20altogether.
74. Alan Z. Rozenshtein, "Interpreting the Ambiguities of Section 230," Brookings Institution, October 26, 2023, https://www.brookings.edu/articles/interpreting-the-ambiguities-of-section-230/.
75. Michael D. Smith and Marshall W. Van Alstyne, "It's Time to Update Section 230," *Harvard Business Review*, August 12, 2021, https://hbr.org/2021/08/its-time-to-update-section-230.
76. Ibid.
77. Robert Jensen, "There Is No Such Thing as Free-Speech Absolutism," *3 Quarks Daily*, July 21, 2024, https://3quarksdaily.com/3quarksdaily/2024/07/there-is-no-such-thing-as-free-speech-absolutism.html.
78. The case was *Schenck v. U.S.* (1919).
79. "Decoding Meta's Algorithms: Maximizing Organic and Paid Outreach," Playcreative Design, June 20, 2024, https://www.playcreativedesign.com/meta-algorithms-business-growth/.
80. Salsa Della Guitara Putri, Eko Purnomo, and Tiara Khairunissa, "Echo Chambers and Algorithmic Bias: The Homogenization of Online Culture in a Smart Society," SHS Web of Conferences, 202 (2024), https://www.shs-conferences.org/articles/shsconf/pdf/2024/22/shsconf_icense2024_05001.pdf.
81. Dean Jackson, Justin Hendrix, and Tim Bernard, "The Science of Social Media's Role in January 6," *Tech Policy Press*, October 29, 2024, https://www.techpolicy.press/the-science-of-social-medias-role-in-january-6/.
82. Ibid.
83. Helen C. Harton, Matthew Gunderson, and Martin J. Bourgeois, "'I'll Be There with You': Social Influence and Cultural Emergence at the Capitol on January 6," *Group Dynamics: Theory, Research, and Practice*, 26, no. 3 (2022), https://psycnet.apa.org/doiLanding?doi=10.1037%2Fgdn0000185.
84. James E. Anderson, *Public Policymaking: An Introduction*, 7th edition (Boston, MA: Wadsworth, 2011), p. 233.

85 Larry N. Gerston, *Public Policy Making: Process and Principles*, 3rd edition (Armonk, NY: M.E. Sharpe, 2011), p. 96.
86 "Social Media Experts Are Skeptical about the Power of New State Laws," *Stateline*, January 24, 2025, https://stateline.org/2025/01/24/social-media-experts-are-skeptical-about-the-power-of-new-state-laws/.
87 "Meta Must Face US State Lawsuits over Teen Social Media Addiction," Reuters, October 15, 2023, https://www.reuters.com/legal/meta-must-face-us-state-lawsuits-over-teen-social-media-addiction-2024-10-15/.
88 "13 States Sue TikTok for Operating Like a 'Virtual Strip Club' for Kids," Cybernews, October 8, 2024, https://cybernews.com/news/us-states-sue-tiktok-addictive-features-harm-children/.
89 "A Tech Industry Group Is Once Again Suing California over a Social Media Law," The Sacramento Bee, November 13, 2024, https://www.sacbee.com/news/politics-government/capitol-alert/article295448059.html
90 See Robert Diab, "Has the US Supreme Court Made It Harder to Regulate Social Media—or the Opposite?" Center for International Governance Innovation, July 2024, https://www.cigionline.org/articles/has-the-us-supreme-court-made-it-harder-to-regulate-social-media-or-the-opposite/.
91 "EU Law Targets Big Tech over Hate Speech, Disinformation," AP, April 23, 2023, https://apnews.com/article/technology-business-police-social-media-reform-52744e1d0f5b93a426f966138f2ccb52.
92 "Tech Companies Put on Notice as Australia Passes World-First Social Media Ban for Under-16s," CNN, November 29, 2024, https://www.cnn.com/2024/11/28/australia/australia-passes-social-media-law-intl-hnk/index.html. The companies included Facebook, TikTok, X, YouTube, Instagram, Pinterest, Snapchat, Amazon, Booking.com, Alibaba AliExpress (China), Zalando (Germany), Google, and Apple.
93 "10 Countries Where Social Media Faces the Most Restrictions," *The Economic Times*, September 6, 2024, https://economictimes.indiatimes.com/nri/latest-updates/10-countries-where-social-media-faces-the-most-restrictions/logging-off/slideshow/113125384.cms.

CHAPTER 12
EDUCATING FOR DEMOCRACY

We often take K–12 public education for granted. Kids go to schools where teachers help them acquire knowledge about all sorts of subjects, some fun, some serious, some fascinating. While a relatively small percentage of students leave school early for a variety of reasons in the United States, about 90 percent graduate high school, after which they begin the next chapters of their lives, whether it's a job, military service, apprenticeship, trade school, or higher education.[1] For most students, however, the twelve years they spend in public education expose them to a body of information, ideas, and values that are often influential for the rest of their lives. Beyond facts and figures, much of their education centers on developing empathy for others, exchanging ideas in a safe setting, and cultivating an understanding between oneself and the community.

Being open to the multitude of ideas allows students to better appreciate themselves as well as the different people and ideas around them. The more that students absorb this aspect of education, the more they are prepared to fully embrace their roles as participants in the political world and citizens in our democracy, which itself has been designed to allow for the free expression of ideas and issues of the day. The delivery and absorption of such knowledge, Amy Guttmann writes, must not "restrict rational deliberation of competing conceptions of the good life and the good society."[2] To that end, the public education environment should be a haven for exchanging ideas and more.

The connection between public education and democracy can be powerful linkage for society. In a sense, American democracy is only as strong as our public education system. That's because as youngsters wend their ways through the public education experience, they should be socialized to the basic tenets of citizenship. In a 2022 national survey asking respondents to identify very important purposes of public education, 67 percent cited "teaching children about government and other civics topics," which cover the rights and responsibilities of citizens in society. Only "teaching children subjects like reading, writing and math" (86 percent) and the idea of a "free education" (70 percent) scored higher on the twelve-question survey.³ Growing that sense of citizenship from the earliest years on provides a major asset for future generations to promote and ensure a stable democracy. Behaviors that minimize, or worse yet, dismiss independent thought as well as the ideas of others are the enemy of democracy and must be treated as such in the schools, which have the capability of being social incubators for competing values and thoughts.

The authoritarian mindset directly contradicts the democratic approach to nurturing free expression and diversity in the schools. In an authoritarian environment, "incorrect" attitudes such as tolerance for different cultures and challenging conventional theories have no place, for they conflict with rigid preset values created and reinforced by those in power.⁴ Sadly, this condition is playing out in the current American political environment.

Within the first ten days of his second term, Donald Trump signed three executive orders directing the secretary of education to end what he referred to as indoctrination in the public schools.⁵ For Trump, "indoctrination" meant discussions of themes such as gender identity, systemic racism, equality, inclusion, and the notion of White privilege—concepts that he considered un-American, yet are in fact dynamic, real-world topics in twenty-first-century America.

Inasmuch as Trumpism approaches an American version of authoritarianism, it behooves Trumpists to control the education system as much as possible. Why? Because, as cultural critic Henry Giroux observes, the American public education enterprise is "one of the last remaining institutions or public goods capable of fostering critical thought, historical memory and civic responsibility."⁶ Independent public education is therefore a threat to Trumpists, who seek to steer it away from potentially controversial topics that are mined by sizable swaths of American society. But Trumpists know that if children are raised with values that ignore potentially divisive social, political, and economic issues, they're likely to be placid as adults in an authoritarian political environment. Under such circumstances, future generations of Trumpist educations become unwittingly complicit in the creation and continuation of an undemocratic political environment.

This chapter delves into the traditional role of public education in American society and the threat to its independence from Trumpism. Constructed on narrow-minded bigotry and White racial superiority otherwise presented as "American culture," Trumpism has little room for discussing diversity of races, gender, or other building blocks of a contemporary multicultural society. For Trumpists, the stakes are high; unfortunately, an unsuspecting public may not have the same appreciation of those concerns. Still, there is little doubt that part of overcoming Trumpism consists of saving public education from the authoritarian values promoted by Trump and his allies.

A Little History

In the United States, public education began as anything but "public." In fact, education in this country began in the colonies as a way of developing future leaders. Driven by religious convictions especially in New England's Puritan colonies, local leaders promoted education as the antidote to ignorance. They established taxes to support schools to teach boys who weren't slaves. As the colonies inched toward seeking independence, education and liberty became core elements of a free society. Democracy also emerged as a key theme related to liberty and independence.

Over time, education systems developed under the auspices of the states, not the federal government. "Public" schools didn't emerge in large numbers until the mid-1800s. Massachusetts became the first state to adopt compulsory public education in 1852, while Mississippi was the last to require public education in 1918. At various junctures along the way, states added young girls into the system. With the emergence of the Progressive Reform Movement early in the twentieth century, public schools gained esteem as valuable building blocks to prepare children for the adult world. During this period, influential education reformer John Dewey promoted education as a wellspring of individual social development and democracy.[7]

To this day, states remain responsible for developing major education initiatives, curricula, and policies. Other than Hawaii, which has only one school district for the entire state, individual school districts within the states are mandated to implement state policies with locally hired personnel. In most cases, on average, states and local school districts pay close to 90 percent of the cost of public education.

Enter the Federal Government

It's worth noting that unlike most countries, the US Constitution is devoid of any guarantees to a public education.[8] Further, the federal Department of Education wasn't even created until 1979. These facts may well explain the limited interest in the topic by some members of Congress and other government leaders. That relatively distant relationship has made it easier for the federal government to give public education less importance than perennial topics such as healthcare, social security, public safety, and national defense.

Still, over time, the federal government became at least tangentially involved in supporting public education. Heightened interest by the federal government was generated on October 4, 1957, with the launch of Sputnik I by what was the then-Soviet Union. That scientific breakthrough also had profound military implications. Caught flat-footed by the Soviet success, the relatively nascent National Science Foundation (NSF), originally created by Congress in 1950, was given a huge funding increase by Congress to develop a comprehensive curriculum for training future scientists and engineers.

At first, NSF's focus concentrated on America's universities. Over time, new curricula were developed for the public schools, eventually reaching all the way down to elementary education institutions.[9] Instructional materials expanded from the hard sciences to the social sciences, particularly focusing on human behavior, social organizations, and "how social, economic, political, cultural and environmental forces affect lives."[10] These areas included such diverse areas as public health, economic well-being, ethics, and national security. NSF's new outreach was coupled with the objectives of the National Defense Education Act of 1958 (NDEA) where Congress appropriated more than $1 billion over seven years to bolster education in science, mathematics, and foreign languages. With these two investments, the federal government was squarely in the public education business.

That level of participation was cemented with the passage of the Elementary and Secondary Education Act of 1965 (ESEA), part of which was intended to close skill gaps in reading, writing, and math between disadvantaged children and others. Congress has updated and broadened the act several times to include federal assistance for rural communities; English learners; after school instruction and care; and attention to unique populations such as indigenous Americans, Native Alaskans, and Native Hawaiians.[11]

Creation of the US Department of Education

Interest by the federal government in public education intensified with the creation of the US Department of Education, a cabinet-level agency in 1979. In the Department of Education Organization Act, Congress declared the federal commitment to ensure equal education opportunity for every individual; supplemented education efforts of the states; encouraged increased involvement of the public, parents, and students in federal education programs; sought to improve education quality through federally supported research, evaluation, and shared information; and increased accountability of federal education programs to the states.[12] Overall, they focus on supporting state education programs particularly in terms of research and financial assistance. The new department emphasized inclusion and cooperation, not heavy federal handedness condemned by President Trump.

Major education initiatives from that time to the present have clearly centered on the states as the organizers of education programs rather than the federal government. For example, under the No Child Left Behind Act legislated in 2001 during the George W. Bush presidency, the federal government provided funds for states to raise student test scores to "proficiency levels," which were determined by the individual states.[13] Similarly, in the Race to the Top education initiative created in 2009 under the Barack Obama presidency, states determined their own proficiency goals in their applications for federal awards for their academic successes.[14] Even the Common Core State Standards, a program designed to establish uniform standards in language, arts, and mathematics for all K-12 students, emerged from a state-led initiative at the National Governors' Conference in 2009.

As part of the federal government's support of state and local education programs, Congress has provided financial assistance for low-income families and retention assistance. Other federal agencies have also participated in the overall effort to improve public education, among them, the National School Lunch Program administered through the Department of Agriculture and Head Start preschool program under the auspices of the Department of Health and Human Services.

Because of differences in funding capabilities among school districts within the same states, the federal government has stepped in to improve the education opportunities in states and districts with fewer financial resources. Today, on average, the federal government contributes about 10 percent to various state public education programs. Depending upon the capacity of a state, however, the federal contribution can approach as much as 25 percent of an educational program,[15] a sizable chunk of the state's public education financing pot.

Trump Moves to Eliminate the Department of Education

When President Trump declared in a press conference that "we're going to move the Department of Education into the states so they can run their programs,"¹⁶ he ignored the fact that the states largely had already been running those programs! In fact, the Department of Education hasn't inserted itself into states' education policies for a simple reason: it can't. As public education expert Diane Ravich pointed out in 2014, "The U.S. Department of Education is legally prohibited from exercising any influence or control over curriculum or instruction at the schools, so it could not contribute any funding to the expensive task of creating national standards."¹⁷ The point is that despite all the Trumpist ballyhoo about out-of-control federal domination of state education, the federal role has been modest at best.

So, what is it that has led President Trump to shut down almost all the activities conducted by the Department of Education? Officially, Trump has offered little explanation. In fact, his concern is more about what the states have done than any federal interference with their programs. During the 2024 presidential campaign, Trump vowed to cut federal funding for any schools or programs that promoted "critical race theory," taught "gender ideology," supported what he referred to as "race-based discrimination," "weaponized" civics education, employed teacher tenure instead of merit pay, or relied on diversity, equity, and inclusion (DEI) programs. In addition, Trump promised to implement a credentialing program that certified teachers who embrace patriotic values, adopt direct election of principals by parents, and remove radicals who infiltrated the federal Department of Education.¹⁸ "Patriotic," "radicals," and "infiltrated" were terms left undefined and subject to confusion for those school administrators in charge of implementing the new rules.

Trump also criticized states for their dedication to Critical Race Theory (CRT) for twisting history into a discussion of "White privilege" that has discriminated against non-Whites.¹⁹ As discussed earlier, CRT focuses on systemic causes of racism and is rarely found in K–12 schools because of its intellectual complexity. More commonly, CRT is a theory discussed at the university level of education.

Regarding Trump's complaints that non-Whites and women are given unfair advantages over Whites, discrimination has long been outlawed by the federal courts. In addition, the federal courts also declared affirmative action unconstitutional. With respect to most of the other issues concerning Trump, they are about policies developed in the states by the states. Beyond that, Trump's rhetoric is hard to decipher. What does he mean by "weaponized" civics education? How does he define "patriotic values?" Trump has not answered these questions with any clarity.

For someone who routinely expresses the imperative of states having control of policy areas such as education, Trump seems poised to deny states administration of their own programs. If anything, and this is critically important, it appears that Trump seeks to inject federal control of state policies and initiatives he doesn't like. Moreover, rather than limit federal intervention into state programs, Trump hopes to use federal power to direct what states can or can't do. In other words, Trump's bravado about "states rights" can best be understood as states' rights under Trump's definition.

Case in point: within days of the second Trump administration ascending to power, one of Trump's executive orders required the Department of Education to end financial support for any state public education institution that employed any DEI initiatives because of their "illegal discrimination and wasteful spending."[20] Note the contradiction. The president who prides himself on eliminating national programs in the name of states' rights uses a national agency to dismantle state programs!

In fact, Trump would be the most satisfied if the Department of Education was dismantled altogether, which is his primary objective. While only Congress has the power to eliminate the Department of Education, or any cabinet department for that matter, Trump can virtually neuter the body through reducing the staff and funding. That's exactly what he did as part of the administration's plan to dramatically reduce the number of civil service employees and replace executives with political appointees. In the case of the Department of Education, the Trump administration nearly halved the staff of approximately 4,200 by 1,900 employees in March 2025, with 600 accepting buyouts and 1,300 terminated. In summarizing the impact of the reductions, Education secretary Linda McMahon declared, "This [reduction] is a significant step toward restoring the greatness of the United States education system." McMahon did not explain the relationship between a reduced Department of Education staff and the restoration of education greatness in the states, probably because there isn't any.[21] That effort, as with so many DEI initiatives, has been challenged and awaiting resolution by the US Supreme Court.

The US Department of Education has two major functions: to distribute funds to various categories of students and programs and to capture data about student needs and successes.

Regarding the first major area, the department's budget for FY 2025 was $102 billion, less than 2 percent of the national budget.[22] Of that amount, $47 billion was slated for different categories of student assistance including students with disabilities, the Head Start program for young children in poverty, civil rights protection for LGBTQ students, grants for school improvements, and student financial aid and loans.

Overcoming Trumpism

Since the second Trump administration has taken control, efforts have been made to eliminate funds for most of those categories. In July 2025, after the start of the public schools' fiscal year, OMB director Russell Vought announced that the administration would keep nearly $7 billion for after-school programs focusing on English learners, teacher training, and other programs set aside mostly for lower income students. Although the funds had been made available in earlier congressional legislation, Vought said that the administration would ask Congress to take the money back. Meanwhile, school administrators were in a tizzy because they had put the previously allocated funds into their budgets.[23] These kinds of erratic administrative moves had become a constant in the Trump administration, with schools expected to deal with the debris left in their wake.

Two points are of interest here. First, almost all the programs administered by the Department of Education have been authorized by congressional legislation. In normal times, congressional approval would be required to end the funding since the legislative branch is the funding source. Then again, these are not normal times, given that the Trump administration has not considered congressional action a necessity for the dismemberment of cabinet departments and other government agencies. Second, the states most dependent on Department of Education funding all voted for Donald Trump—the same Donald Trump who intends to end the Department of Education programs. Because of impoverished populations in many of these states, they have been receiving a disproportionate share of federal education funds. The irony is that the more those federal funds dry up, the more these states—largely the poorest in the nation—will suffer. That's because many of the Department of Education programs have been designed to ameliorate funding differences between the states.

With respect to the Department of Education's role in measurement and evaluation, the basic approach is to provide data that the states often are not able to generate due to their financial constraints. With that information, states are better equipped to address their particular needs, often with funds provided by the Department of Education. Again, the idea is much more to help the states rather than to guide them. In doing so, they will be able to push away any discussion regarding inequality of instruction or student performance.

What Trumpists Really Want

In reality, Trumpists are not against federal money for education as much as they oppose the way it is spent. Along those lines, Trump has said that as part of rearranging (if not eliminating outright) the Department of Education activities, he would support reconstituting federal spending through smaller block grants to the states. Under this approach, federal funds would not be distributed to states for specific programs; instead, each state would be able to spend a chunk of money allocated from the Department of Education as they see fit. For example, state education departments could direct block grants for religious instruction or revisionist history that plays down the importance of slavery; they could also decide to stop afterschool programs in working-class communities that need them, various subject matter specialists, or English learner programs for immigrants. Simply put, under Trump's block grant proposal, states could distribute funds for purposes far from the specific intentions of the original congressional legislation. Efforts toward providing programs to help those most in need of special assistance because of learning disabilities or physical incapacities could easily fall by the wayside.

As loose as the proposed block grant guideline seems, it's hard to believe that the Trump administration would put up with a state that spends block grant funds on a high school course dealing with "transgenderism and civil rights" or a middle school health program that discusses "pregnancy and contraception." From what we've seen of Trump's definition of education, those subjects would be strictly prohibited. So, what's the ideal version of public education along Trumpist lines? *Project 2025*, which has been responsible for the lion's share of initiatives emerging from the second Trump administration, provides a blueprint. It's a near certainty that the Trumpist version of block grants for education would be laden with conditions, such as no federal funds spent on DEI or funding provisions for school choice programs that benefit poor kids more than affluent kids.

Replacing Values

Proposed elimination of the Department of Education is only the starting point for Trumpists. The details as written in *Project 2025* extend way beyond the elimination or reconstitution of financial support, however. To begin with, schools should no longer emphasize civil rights, especially to the extent of discussing the subject in such a way that White students might feel "guilt" from historical or current events that focus on racial suffering. Instead, education should be free of such topics. In fact, Trumpists say, as a general principle, education should be centered on students and their families. After all, parents know what's best for their children, and that includes the content of their education as well as the credentials and methodologies used by the teachers.

Regarding the Trumpist approach to gender, educators should recognize males and females as the only true genders determined at birth. Any discussions of gender transitions or hormone treatments should be outside the purview of schools and left solely to the discretion of parents in the home environment. On January 29, 2025, President Trump stated as much as federal policy by issuing an executive order entitled "Ending Radical Indoctrination in K–12 Schooling." That new requirement stipulated a ban of federal funds for schools that dealt in any way with gender identity issues.[24] This could be particularly harmful to LGBTQ students or students considering gender transitions who view schools as a safe place for comfort from discrimination.[25]

Parents over Teachers

With respect to parents, Trump has emphasized their role in education as so fundamental that they should be responsible for selecting and monitoring school principals. In Trump's words, "More than anyone else, parents know what their children need. If any principal is not getting the job done, the parents should be able to vote to fire them and select someone who will."[26] In other words, parents—not trained teachers or principals—know best about how their children should be educated. Given that most parents have little training in education topics or policies or teaching methodologies, it's hard to imagine a faster way of dumbing down the educational enterprise, not to mention isolating their children from the real world.

Trump also endorses the "right" of parents to send children to the schools of their choice. This selection opportunity will allow students and their parents to feel comfortable about where students learn, Trumpists say. It's also a way for students to be cloistered in narrow environments that leave them unaware of the true conditions and circumstances of American society. That's because less affluent students have the same mobility as more affluent students, according to research.[27] Along those lines, to the extent that parents want to see religion discussed in the schools, Trumpists believe parents should be accommodated as long as they subscribe to America's Judeo-Christian values. Note the narrow view of religion. In fact, Trump has stated that daily prayers should be part of the public school experience,[28] an activity declared unconstitutional by the US Supreme Court in 1962 because, the justices contended, school prayer violated the separation between religion and the state.

Put it all together and the public education picture would look radically different under Trumpism than most present-day state education systems and policies. Students would likely have an unrealistic and ahistoric curriculum excluding the important aspects of life, teachers would be dramatically constrained as to what they could discuss with their students, and administrators would be under the thumb of parents, most of whom know next to nothing about education requirements and needs.

It's important to remember that eradication of the Department of Education wouldn't remove federal rules for the states; rather, it would replace current state rules with a new set of federal rules and conditions. Minimizing or, worse yet, eliminating the US Department of Education would represent a dramatic reduction of federal financial assistance to state education programs and their students, especially disadvantaged populations and residents in poor states. And considering what Trump himself describes as the overall poor education product coming from the states, removal of federal assistance would further jeopardize the futures of millions of young people along with the well-being of the nation. Nevertheless, new federal rules relative to subject matter, education personnel, and school choice would take their place.

Trump's negative view of the federal role in public education notwithstanding, the public is hardly in agreement. A national poll taken shortly after the President's announced intention to eliminate the Department of Education found likely voters against the idea by a margin of almost two-to-one. The same poll found that instead of curbing the abilities of states to provide well-rounded public educations for our students, the federal government should ensure that equal opportunities for education success exist throughout the nation.[29] Nevertheless, Trump has been adamant about imploding the department in the name of "states' rights," although his true intention is anything but.

The Perversion of Public Education

At its heart, the proposed evisceration of the Department of Education abolishes programs designed to promote equality of opportunity. This is not to say that all students complete their education the same way and under the same conditions, for surely some show more interest in taking full advantage of their opportunities than others. But without those opportunities in the first place, some students in states and communities that possess fewer resources unquestionably would risk being at a competitive disadvantage in adult life.

Overcoming Trumpism

The differences can be stark. Consider that according to the 2025 *Nation's Report Card* produced by the National Assessment of Educational Progress, students who live in high socioeconomic status (SES) environments score higher in math and reading.[30] Conversely, students who live in low SES environments tend to score below average in math and reading. Why is this important? During the decade when states received substantial federal financial assistance from the No Child Left Behind Program (2002–12), student performances excelled everywhere; once that program ended, student results plummeted in some states more than others.[31] The difference between academic success and retreat lies in the ability of the states and federal government in concert to target problems and provide quality programs to address those problems.

To that end, the federal government should focus on state test scores as necessary data for measuring, identifying, and addressing weaknesses in their public schools. The imperative of such protection stems from the Fourteenth Amendment to the Constitution, which holds that all people are guaranteed "equal protection under the laws." To take this one additional step, equal opportunity to education as any other basic right is a hallmark of democracy.

In abandoning this necessary research, the Trumpist brand of public education is a death knell to the concept of helping all students reach their potentials, regardless of their starting points in the educational experience. Fundamentally, it divides the affluent from the poor, the able from the other able, Whites from non-Whites, citizens from noncitizens, and potentially Christians from non-Christians. It also uses the education environment to impose divisive policies while redefining history. All this results from utilizing a perverted public education policy as a cudgel to promote division. Sound familiar? By reinforcing the "us" versus "them" chasms in a public education setting that should serve as a democratic building block for American society, Trumpists encourage an environment where society is at war with itself.

The Trumpist-inspired networks of division risk the "have nots" in American society being brought up to the conditions of the "haves." But that's less likely to happen with an education system that perpetuates separation. Then again, separation and division in American society are exactly what Trumpists want. As a result, under Trumpism, the few, namely Whites, could rule the many (non-Whites) who are basically denied a range of opportunities thanks to state public education policies with no desire, means, or both to do otherwise.

Finally, we must consider the pure financial component of considerably reduced (if not eliminated) federal aid to K–12 public education as it relates

Educating for Democracy

to the overall national budget and taxation picture. For the 2024-5 academic year, the federal government contributed more than $100 billion to the states, or 13.6 percent of the total K–12 education budget.[32] The much-ballyhooed Trump tax cut passed in 2025 amounts to a tax saving of $4.5 trillion over ten years. That comes to an average of $450 billion per year. Wiping out K–12 federal spending would represent a huge portion of the money desperately needed to offset the tax cut, and as a consequence, reduce the burdensome addition to the national debt. For many conservative Republican budget hawks, that "twofer" is too juicy to ignore. Moreover, it helps to provide the rationale for restructuring the federal commitment to public education as well as other recipients.

All of this gets to the bigger question of what we want from our government. For the federal government to deny the best education opportunities possible for all students as part of an effort to protect a federal tax cut falls into the "penny wise and pound foolish" idiom unbecoming of the most powerful nation in the world, especially if Americans hope to continue that historic standard.

The Road to Democracy through Civic Education

We pause here to consider the relationship between public education and democracy. We know that democracies depend on active citizen involvement for their existence. That engagement most commonly appears on a widespread basis through periodic participation in free elections of leaders. Democracy affords participation in other ways as well through activities such as public rallies, protests, letter writing to public officials, townhalls, or even personal meetings with public policymakers. But while these activities have the potential to connect citizens with their governments, they don't speak to the quality of citizen involvement. "Quality" refers to the extent to which citizens fully understand public issues as well as their abilities to knowledgably weigh in with their sentiments about them. The more that citizens are not only educated but also enthusiastic about expressing themselves, the more likely they are to help their democracy stay true.

Saving Democracy by Learning It

As discussed in Chapter 1, many Americans are dissatisfied with democracy; some would welcome a government where a "strongman" would solve our problems. For those who believe in democracy, these sentiments are disconcerting. Even more worrisome, however, is the disconnect from democracy found in so many young people. According to the results from a national poll of young people between the ages of eighteen and twenty-four, 46 percent are dissatisfied with American democracy.[33] That nearly half of this group is dissatisfied with democracy is chilling in itself for those of us who believe in the concept. Even more disturbing is the fact that so few people in this age group understand democracy. Of a four-question set of questions testing basic civic knowledge, the respondents answered an average of 1.6 questions correctly; only 4 percent answered all four questions correctly.[34] There was a bit of good news. Of those who scored high on civic knowledge, 66 percent planned to vote in the 2024 presidential election; only 44 percent of those with low civic knowledge planned to vote. Finally, those with high civic knowledge were more likely to participate in a civic activity in 2024 than those with low civic knowledge.

Much of the lack of student commitment to democracy stems from the lack of opportunity to discuss their thoughts about civics-related ideas in the classroom. Their knowledge gathering experiences also varied by race. In a 2020 poll of recent high-school graduates, two-thirds of White high-school graduates recall receiving encouragement to vote versus slightly more than half of Blacks.[35]

The Power of Civic Education

To the extent that citizens understand issues and realize their prospective roles in expressing opinions about them in a democracy, they stand a better chance of repelling attempts to derail it. Given the way that Trumpists have worked to eliminate neutral civil service along with the acquiescence of Republican majorities in Congress, institutional retardants against authoritarianism have been severely weakened. However, beyond the much discussed constitutionally designed roles of "checks and balances" of government institutions, there is another check: the people. Only when society is moved to exercise its power does the chance to rein in despotic government appear. That's because, in a democracy, the public has the potential to be the ultimate guardrail against despotism. To that end, a politically educated and efficacious society is critical as the last line of defense against those who would overturn democracy. For those capabilities, we focus on civic education and engagement. But how does this happen?

Unlike subject matters such as math or science, civic education teaches students how to become effective citizens. This area of learning includes understanding the important roles of citizens in democratic societies, the avenues of participation to express their concerns, and the ways they can impact the public policymaking process at all levels of governance. The benefit of civic education is that it functions as "a tool to combat the effects of propaganda and decrease human susceptibility to propagandistic/populistic efforts."[36] It is a powerful tool for promoting and protecting democracy.

In the absence of civic education, propaganda and lies dominate the public square often through government-controlled institutions and material presented through social media. Civic education leading to citizen action can break through these biases by providing methods to gain knowledge that can determine truth irrespective of the government's attempts to rewrite history by limiting what students learn.

Historically, states have been the innovators for civic education programs to the extent that they exist. For its part, the federal government has ignored interest in the topic. According to one study published prior to the near elimination of Department of Education spending, even then of every $54 the federal government invested in Science, Technology, Engineering, and Math (STEM), the federal government spent five cents on civic education.[37] But whereas the federal government's interest in civic education might have been unfortunate in the past, it's become an unforgivable tragedy with the onset of Trumpism. Given the unimportance of the topic at the federal level, states are the best hope for providing civic education to their students. More than ever, it's a critically needed tool as a means for young people to understand their role in fighting to preserve the nation's democracy.

Civic education shouldn't be viewed as something we might stumble upon as adults in town councils or public rallies, for it's less likely to surface later in life after K–12 students have left the learning environment. As such, it should begin early in the public education experience in ways that students can understand and act. It teaches us to think of our roles as citizens both in terms of rights and obligations. Democracies depend upon active citizens taking part in our governance through elections. But there are countless other ways that citizens can be involved in shaping governance between elections. When citizens see the holders of powerful government positions behaving in undemocratic ways, they need to speak and act in those moments, and not just at the time of a scheduled election. Their best opportunities to do so are when they are trained to recognize abuse and respond to it. That's the condition that Americans face today because of

Trumpism, and why civic education may be the only long-term means to save our democracy.

Educators in some states may declare that they already have civic education, but in many instances such a claim is likely to be misleading. That's because many states define civic education courses as lectures covering the branches of the federal government without getting into the how's and why's of the government's development as well as the roles of citizens with it. Such presentations tend to be devoid of analytical thinking and offer little discussion of the themes that undergird American political thought. Another point: to the extent that they have it, most states restrict civic education to a single twelfth-grade class as part of a discussion of American government. A detailed examination by the Fordham Institute found only four states "exemplary" in the teaching of civics (Alabama, California, Massachusetts, and Tennessee), with twenty falling in the "inadequate" category.[38] The rest don't even touch upon the subject.

The inadequate civics preparedness of America's students leaves them unaware of how and why governments function, as well as with a basic ignorance about the political system. Under this condition, students have a fuzzy understanding of government institutions often based more on myth than reality. The results aren't pretty. A national survey of young adults aged 18–34 in 2024 found that only 15 percent of 18–34-year-old Americans trusted the government.[39] Well, how can they trust the government if they know little about what it is? Perhaps that's one powerful reason why so few young people vote. Less educated people are more disposed to authoritarianism,[40] something no doubt appreciated by Trumpists who seek to govern without meaningful opposition. Clearly, there is work to do in preparing American students for adult citizenship.

Four conclusions emerge from these data: First, too many students don't know about democracy; second, interests in political participation depend upon the knowledge that students acquire; third, race is a factor in terms of exposure to civic learning; and fourth, clearly, there is work to be done.

How Civic Education Works

Let's be clear about what civic education is and what it is not. Civic education is not an ideology focused on a particular political viewpoint, nor is it a mechanism for overthrowing those in power. Rather, civic education helps students understand their roles as citizens in public policymaking and how to exercise them. Projects, investigations, and simulations often help students see just how they can be part of the political world. In a democracy, civic education is especially valuable because of the relative ease through which people can mobilize and be heard.

The more that students learn from civic education about their roles as citizens, the more likely they are to engage in politics as well as other forms of activity, whether in their local communities or larger political environments. Civic education gives students a sense of empowerment and the sense that they can make themselves heard. Civic education also gives students a sense of efficacy, the feeling that they can get things done. Most of all, whereas authoritarianism discourages independent thought and activity, civic engagement can serve as a healthy antidote against undemocratic activities by policymakers.

Just like students learn how to read or solve math problems, they can also learn the value of opportunities to politically engage through civic education. The key to engagement stems from the development of civic knowledge and civic disposition. Civic knowledge comes with an understanding of politics and institutions. A civic disposition emerges when students develop a concern for others, acquire trust for the political system, and seek to participate meaningfully in political life. These core elements are crucial to promoting and protecting a democratic system of governance.

In the schools, civic education programs are designed to facilitate student discussion of thorny issues in safe environments that accommodate different opinions, explore possible ways of solving public problems, determine appropriate public policymakers capable of managing those issues, and even learn strategies for approaching officials who can address and resolve the problems brought to them. Civic education enables civic engagement, and civic engagement simultaneously gives its users a sense of satisfaction while connecting them in productive ways with public policymakers. Simply put, students learn by doing, and the good news is that these programs work!

From Civic Education to Civic Engagement

Part of the beauty of civic education is that students can operationalize it at all levels of instruction.[41] The problem-solving process can unfold in several steps over time, with the trained teacher there to guide student discussion. On this note, it is vitally important that the classroom teacher has the civic engagement knowledge and capabilities to nurture the students on the civic engagement path. The teacher should work with students in nonpaternalistic ways so that students appreciate the power of independent discovery without judgment or arbitrary limits.⁴² That guidance notwithstanding, students gain not only knowledge about the political process but self-esteem through their ownership of managing their research and action.

There are several curricula designed to facilitate civic engagement in the classroom. *Project Citizen*, one example, is a program that provides "hands on" student involvement for problem solving in a democratic society on real issues. Developed by the Center for Civic Education, this step-by-step interactive curriculum begins with students learning how to research and determine a public policy issue; understand the problems associated with managing the issue, including costs and benefits; recommend possible solutions to the issue; and determine the appropriate policymakers to address the issue. *Project Citizen* has the potential for transforming the passive bystander into an active, engaged member of the polity. Along with teacher preparedness, *Project Citizen* provides instruction books at the elementary, middle, and high-school levels that guide the students on their civic engagement journey.⁴³

Among the areas covered in *Project Citizen* are civic knowledge (American government, democracy, and the public policy process), civic skills (policy issues, group problem solving, various government responsibilities and capabilities), civic engagement (willingness to become involved in problem solving), and social and emotional learning (self-management, relationship skills, and classroom behavior). The idea behind *Project Citizen* is that students will grow into and embrace their multifaceted roles as citizens, which will lead them to be involved members of their communities long after they have left their education.

Project Citizen can be used in classrooms of all ages, although it is more often applied in middle school and high-school environments. At all grades, trained teachers interact with their students typically during a semester, although the time periods can be lengthened or shortened depending upon class needs.

Young students in the early grades might initially focus on something like a broken water fountain for their "problem" in need of a solution. Upon agreeing on the broken water fountain as their issue for investigation, they could then discuss the problems stemming from the malfunctioning water source and the harm from not repairing the problem—perhaps something as serious as dehydration or simply unattended thirst. Next, students might try to determine the best person, organizations, or other sources to provide information and a possible solution. In the instance of a broken water fountain, the principal or a repair person who reports to the principal might most likely be the one to help. Then they might make an appointment to take their concern to the principal to gain the principal's buy-in. Should the principal address the water fountain issue, the policy issue will have been addressed. If for some reason the principal ignores the students, they might take their issue to their parents for redress through the local Board of Education. Note the extent to which they are active in the problem-solving process.

Middle school students might begin their search for a public policy problem with a survey of their peers. Upon assessing the results from their data gathering effort, they might focus on an issue such as unacceptable school cafeteria food (a favorite student complaint just about everywhere). Recognizing that the cafeteria operates on a fixed budget, the students could then look to alternative foods with costs that fit into the cafeteria financial framework—perhaps something like more salads instead of sandwiches. With data and proposals in hand, the students could take their recommendations to the cafeteria worker responsible for purchasing food supplies, with the intent to negotiate for a more favorable menu. If the food buyer balks at a reasonable request, the middle school students could then take their case up the policymaking ladder to the principal or other decision-maker up the "food chain."

After considering several issues, high-school students might turn to a nearby polluted creek for their policy problem. They might begin by ascertaining the types of contamination, the evidence for that decision, and most of all, the source. In doing their research, high-school students might turn to experts as well as government data on illnesses or even deaths of people who drink water from the polluted creek. They might also study pollution data at the water district or city environmental services office. After they reach conclusions on what or who is responsible for the polluted condition, students might try to build coalitions for action with environmental groups, fishing organizations, or nearby neighborhood associations that have been negatively impacted by the polluted creek. They will also have to determine the appropriate level of government with the potential to address the pollution problem. Empowered with research, alliances, and the knowledge of where to take their concerns, these high-school students would then have the tools to take their issue forward to appropriate policymakers.

The above examples show how students can become engaged in the public policymaking experience. The complexity of the selected problems and sophistication of the action steps would differ with age but the call to investigation and action is universal. Along the way, they use math, writing skills, analytical capabilities, and other learning blocks for their research and proposals. In the process, students also learn the benefits of working with one another, articulating, listening, and compromising to reach decisions on their various action steps to problem solving as a group. Research shows that students who go through *Project Citizen* compared to those who do not are more civically engaged, have more civic knowledge, and are more inclined to keep informed about the government and become active members of their communities.[44]

Even if their problem isn't solved or solved to their satisfaction, students realize the advantages of working together for their benefit as well as the benefit of the greater school community. Along the way, they can discover how issues emerge, are researched, and resolved, or perhaps why they haven't been addressed in the past. They also learn which policymakers are responsible for dealing with the problem. Most importantly, through civic engagement, students discover that they can have a role in identifying and solving problems. Upon reaching adulthood, they feel empowered with a set of participatory tools to make themselves heard in our democracy—tools developed from the earliest ages on. The end result is that civic engagement turns students into adult stakeholders, and that's good for our democracy.

Some civic engagement programs focus on placing college students in organizations. These curricula take students out of the university classroom and assign them to hands-on activities ranging from one-day programs such as tree planting to semester-long projects such as literacy programs. These activities can be valuable for providing students with the satisfaction of appreciating the results from doing good in a community.[45] While they are helpful in enabling students to give back to their communities, they are not as comprehensive as others in providing the pedagogy that goes along with engagement. Still, they do connect students with their communities and that is hardly a trivial matter.

The Benefits

Research confirms that students who develop the means to become civically engaged are more supportive of the rule of law, political discussions, community engagement, government service, faith in government, and trust in the media. In attaining these values, they become more interested in being active citizens in adulthood.[46] Students with high-quality civic education experiences are more likely to vote, to form political opinions, to learn about campaign issues, to have a sense of how the American political system works, and to appreciate their roles in it.[47] For students, these are the kinds of participatory building blocks to pursue democracy for all Americans, rather than a system that minimizes, if not excludes, anyone different from White Christian males.

There are other powerful benefits. Those who are civically engaged in their youth remain engaged in adulthood. One study of at-risk minority youth found that those who become involved during adolescence make it more likely that they will be more motivated to pursue education after high-school graduation. They also remain engaged during adulthood with fewer instances of violent behavior and substance abuse than their peers who don't participate civically as youngsters.[48]

Adoption of civic education in the schools doesn't guarantee elimination of Trumpism, nor is that the intent. But the engagement and participatory tools from civic education would enable development of students with a better understanding of how the system works as well as their potential roles in it. With an enhanced understanding of society's issues, students-turned-adults will be in a much better position to play their part in dealing with them head on. They will also be more likely to be active in their communities.

Education as a Powerful Guardrail against Dictatorship

Democracy depends upon a nation's population that is knowledgeable, thoughtful, and accepting of one another. Democracy also depends upon a population where equality of opportunity is not simply a slogan but an open road to a healthy, fulfilled existence for all citizens. Education provides the stepping stone to civic engagement, a trait that comes from the exercise of our knowledge and values that are nurtured by a thorough, open, and embracing pedagogy.

The Trumpist approach to education denies critical thinking, the discussion of competing ideas, and equal citizen opportunities to grow and participate in the political arena. Trumpism stifles truth and the diversity of thought, both cornerstones of civic education. By virtue of heavy-handed control of unacceptable conditions and curricula, Trumpism is the antithesis to a society powered by a public education system that fosters curiosity, free discussion, and a participatory society.

The inculcation of critical thinking tools and values in our children prepares them to become fully engaged adults who trust our institutions, respect the political system, and engage in it. They will know the difference between right and wrong, legal and illegal, while respecting the diversity of opinions and proposed solutions to society's problems. A muzzled press, a discriminated minority, revisionist history, and unconstitutional dismissal of laws all stand as undemocratic barriers to a civically engaged population that comprehends their significance as threats to democracy.

Will all American children utilize their civic education as adults? Of course not, but we need as many as possible to be given the opportunities to grow and thrive as thoughtful democrats with as many concerns for the general community as well as for themselves. People with these tools become the true guardians of democracy, and with Trumpism as the enemy of democracy, we need an army of civically engaged and educated people who are willing to challenge authoritarianism.

NOTES

1. "Education Attainment Statistics," Education Data Initiative, January 14, 2025, https://educationdata.org/education-attainment-statistics,
2. Amy Guttmann, *Democratic Education* (Princeton, NJ: Princeton University Press, 1987), p. 44.
3. "Searching for Common Ground," University of Southern California, Center for Applied Research and Education," April 2024, https://www.the74million.org/wp-content/uploads/2024/04/UAS_CARE_Searching_For_Common_Ground.pdf.
4. Karen Stenner, *The Authoritarian Dynamic* (New York: Cambridge University Press, 2005), p. 134.
5. "With Sweeping Orders, Trump Aims to Control Race Teaching, Boost School Choice," *The Washington Post*, January 29, 2025, https://www.washingtonpost.com/education/2025/01/29/trump-education-orders-indoctrination-school-choice-antisemitism/.
6. Henry A. Giroux, "Erasing History, Erasing Democracy: Trump's Authoritarian Assault on Education," Truthout, February 6, 2025, https://truthout.org/articles/erasing-history-erasing-democracy-trumps-authoritarian-assault-on-education/.
7. See John Dewey, *Democracy and Education* (Middlesex, England: Echo Library, 2007). Dewey's book was originally published in 1916.
8. "Constitutional Approaches to the Right to Education," World Policy Analysis Center, January 2020, https://www.worldpolicycenter.org/constitutional-approaches-to-the-right-to-education.
9. This history comes from David J. Hoff, "The Race to Space Rocketed NSF into Classrooms," Education Week, May 19, 1999, https://www.edweek.org/teaching-learning/the-race-to-space-rocketed-nsf-into-classrooms/1999/05.

10 "People and Society," National Science Foundation, https://www.nsf.gov/focus-areas/people-society.
11 "The Elementary and Secondary Education Act (ESEA), as Amended by the Every Student Succeeds Act (ESSA): A Primer," Congressional Research Service, February 12, 2024, https://www.congress.gov/crs-product/R45977.
12 "An Overview of the U.S. Department of Education," US Department of Education, January 15, 2025, https://www.ed.gov/about/ed-overview/an-overview-of-the-us-department-of-education--pg-1.
13 Linda Darling-Hammond, "Evaluating 'No Child Left Behind,'" The Nation, May 2, 2007, https://www.thenation.com/article/archive/evaluating-no-child-left-behind/.
14 "States Raise Proficiency Standards in Math and Reading?" *Education Next*, 15, no. 3 (April 2015), https://www.educationnext.org/states-raise-proficiency-standards-math-reading.
15 "Red States More Dependent on Federal Education Funding," *Forbes*, January 24, 2025, https://thehill.com/homenews/campaign/3833686-trump-calls-for-principals-to-be-elected-by-students-parents/.https://www.forbes.com/sites/petergreene/2025/01/24/are-red-states-more-dependent-on-federal-education-funding/.
16 Press conference, March 12, 2025.
17 Speech before the Modern Language Association on January 11, 2014, reprinted as "Everything You Need to Know about Common Core," *The Washington Post*, January 18, 2014, https://www.washingtonpost.com/news/answer-sheet/wp/2014/01/18/everything-you-need-to-know-about-common-core-ravitch/.
18 "President Trump's Plan to Save American Education and Give Power Back to the States," Trump campaign post on X, July 25, 2024.
19 "Trump Tells Agencies to End Race Trainings on 'White Privilege' And 'Critical Race Theory,'" NPR, September 5, 2020, https://www.npr.org/2020/09/05/910053496/trump-tells-agencies-to-end-trainings-on-white-privilege-and-critical-race-theor.
20 "U.S. Department of Education Takes Action to Eliminate DEI," US Department of Education, January 23, 2025, https://www.ed.gov/about/news/press-release/us-department-of-education-takes-action-eliminate-dei.
21 "U.S. Department of Education Initiates Reduction in Force," US Department of Education, March 11, 2025, https://www.ed.gov/about/news/press-release/us-department-of-education-initiates-reduction-force.
22 US Department of Education, January 30, 2025, https://www.usaspending.gov/agency/department-of-education?fy=2025.
23 "Trump Withholds Nearly $7 Billion for Schools, with Little Explanation," *The New York Times*, July 2, 2025, https://www.nytimes.com/2025/07/01/us/trump-education-funds.html.
24 "Ending Radical Indoctrination in K–12 Schooling," The White House, January 29, 2025, https://www.whitehouse.gov/presidential-actions/2025/01/ending-radical-indoctrination-in-k-12-schooling/.
25 "2022 National Survey on LGBTQ Youth Mental Health Florida," The Trevor Project, https://www.thetrevorproject.org/wp-content/uploads/2022/12/The-Trevor-Project-2022-National-Survey-on-LGBTQ-Youth-Mental-Health-by-State-Florida.pdf.

26 "Trump Calls for Principals to Be Elected by Students' Parents," The Hill, January 27, 2023, https://thehill.com/homenews/campaign/3833686-trump-calls-for-principals-to-be-elected-by-students-parents/.

27 Peter Iglinski, "Do the Benefits of School Choice Miss the Grade?" News Center, University of Rochester, August 11, 2023, https://www.rochester.edu/newscenter/what-is-school-choice-pros-and-cons-564712/.

28 "Trump Pledges to Bring Back Prayer in the Schools and Offer 'School Choice' Everywhere," Baptist News Global, November 11, 2024, https://baptistnews.com/article/trump-pledges-to-bring-back-prayer-in-schools/.

29 "Polling on Eliminating the Department of Education (January 2025)," Data for Progress, February 5, 2025, https://www.dataforprogress.org/datasets/polling-on-eliminating-the-department-of-education.

30 "Results from NAEP 2024 Mathematics and Reading at Grades 4 and 8 Are Here!" National Assessment of Educational Progress, January 24, 2025, https://nces.ed.gov/nationsreportcard/.

31 "Nearly 5 Years after Schools Closed, the Nation Gets a New Report Card," NPR, January 29, 2025, https://www.npr.org/2025/01/29/nx-s1-5270880/math-reading-covid-naep.

32 "U.S. Public Education Spending Statistics," Education Initiative, February 8, 2025, https://educationdata.org/public-education-spending-statistics.

33 "The Civic Outlook of Young Adults in America," Institute for Citizens and Scholars, September 2023, https://citizensandscholars.org/wp-content/uploads/2023/09/Citizens-Scholars-Civic-Outlook-of-Young-Adults-in-America-Executive-Summary.pdf.

34 The four multiple choice questions were: Who casts the tie-breaking vote in the US Senate? What's the primary purpose of the Electoral College? The First Amendment guarantees which freedoms? Which political parties currently hold majorities in the US Senate and House of Representatives?

35 "Youth Who Learned about Voting in High School More Likely to Become Informed and Engaged Voters," Center for Information and Research on Civic Learning and Engagement, August 31, 2020, https://circle.tufts.edu/latest-research/youth-who-learned-about-voting-high-school-more-likely-become-informed-and-engaged.

36 Tetyana Hoggan-Kloubert, "Civic Education and Indoctrination: Overlapping Areas and Demarcation Criteria," in Tetyana Hoggan-Kloubert, Paul E. Mabrey III, and Chad Hoggan, eds, *Transformative Civic Education in Democratic Societies* (East Lansing, MI: Michigan State University Press, 2023), p. 29.

37 "Civics Education," The Council of State Governments, 2022, https://web.csg.org/csghealthystates/wp-content/uploads/sites/23/2022/05/Healthy-States-National-Task-Force-Policy-Brief-Civics-Education.pdf.

38 "The State of State Standards for Civics and U.S. History in 2021," Thomas Fordham Institute, 2022, https://fordhaminstitute.org/sites/default/files/publication/pdfs/20210623-state-state-standards-civics-and-us-history-20210.pdf#page=15.

39 Nadzeya Shutava, "Let's Talk: Rebuilding Young Adults' Trust in Government through Authentic Communications," Partnership for Public Service, October

10, 2024, https://ourpublicservice.org/publications/lets-talk-rebuilding-young-adults-trust-in-government-through-authentic-communications/.
40 Stenner, *The Authoritarian Dynamic*, p. 154.
41 "History and Social Science Framework, Grades Pre-Kindergarten to 12," Massachusetts Curriculum Framework, 2018, https://www.doe.mass.edu/frameworks/hss/2018-12.pdf.
42 Bernadine Brady, Robert J. Chaskin, and Caroline McGregor, "Promoting Civic and Political Engagement among Marginalized Urban Youth in Three Cities: Strategies and Challenges," *Children and Youth Services Review*, 116 (September 2020), https://doi.org/10.1016/j.childyouth.2020.105184.
43 "What Is Project Citizen?" Center for Civic Education, https://www.civiced.org/program-project-citizen. For a step-by-step explanation of Project Citizen, see Larry N. Gerston, *Public Policymaking in a Democratic Society: A Guide for Civic Engagement*, 3rd edition (New York: Routledge, 2022), pp. 184–91.
44 See Diana Owen, "Project Citizen Research Program," *2024 Report*, Georgetown University.
45 "Center for Civic Engagement," Illinois State University, https://civicengagement.illinoisstate.edu/students/.
46 See Diana Owen, "Strengthening Democracy through History and Civics: Presidential and Congressional Academies 2019 and 2021," The Center for Civic Education, November 2021, https://files.civiced.org/pdfs/research/Academies_FinalReport_Georgetown_November2021.pdf.
47 "High School Civics Linked to Voting, Political Knowledge," Center for Information and Research on Civic Learning and Engagement (CIRCLE), Tufts University, January 17, 2013, https://circle.tufts.edu/latest-research/high-school-civics-linked-voting-political-knowledge, and "Youth Who Learned about Voting in High School More Likely to Become Informed and Engaged Voters," Center for Information and Research on Civic Learning and Engagement (CIRCLE), Tufts University, August 31, 2020, https://circle.tufts.edu/latest-research/youth-who-learned-about-voting-high-school-more-likely-become-informed-and-engaged.
48 WingYi Chan, Suh-Ruu Ou, and Arthur Reynolds, "Adolescent Civic Engagement and Adult Outcomes: An Examination among Urban Racial Minorities," *Journal of Youth and Adolescence*, 43 (May 31, 2014), pp. 1829–43, https://link.springer.com/article/10.1007/s10964-014-0136-5.

CHAPTER 13
REINFORCING DEMOCRACY FOR THE PEOPLE AND BY THE PEOPLE

The saying "Democracy is not a spectator sport" often appears as an unstated exhortation for citizens to become actively involved in the political process. Beyond the message, the source of that profound thought is equally important. This astute observation has been attributed to Lotte Scharfman, a Jewish refugee-turned-American immigrant who fled from Austria in 1938 with her parents during the Holocaust. In expanding upon the basis of her fervent commitment to democracy, Scharfman recounted her horrifying experience with "I know what can happen if citizens cease to be diligent."[1]

In her role as a new American citizen, Scharfman was anything but a spectator. In fact, she was elected president of the Massachusetts chapter League of Women Voters in 1969. Lotte Scharfman knew the value of political participation firsthand and seized it, offering a civics lesson to all of us. In comparing the words of immigrant Lotte Scharfman with Donald Trump's claim that immigrants "are poisoning the blood of our country,"[2] one can't help but wonder who is really poisoning our country.

An assessment of the current condition of American politics gives us our own need to be diligent. From the powerful position of his presidency, Donald Trump has been single-minded in his disdain for American democracy. Within the executive branch, he has ignored laws and democratic norms with long and cherished histories, politicizing once nonpolitical government entities in the process. Depending upon the issue in Trump's clashes with the judiciary, he has either minimized, misinterpreted, slow-walked, or in some cases, outright ignored decisions handed down by the federal courts. As for Congress, Trump has circumvented its key legislative tax and spending powers stipulated in the Constitution while intimidated members of the Republican majority have meekly looked the other way. Checks and balances guardrails have crumbled.

Beyond his corruption of government institutions, Trump has attempted to stifle the press and has succeeded to some extent through what judicial experts have described as frivolous lawsuits, making it even more difficult for society to understand the significance of his deceitful and often unconstitutional actions. He has politicized long-treasured educational bodies all the way from grades K–12 through higher learning institutions. Trump has gone so far so as to punish civil servants perceived as enemies and major law firms that have represented individuals and companies opposed to the president.[3] Meanwhile, more than two hundred thousand federal employees have left their posts through termination and intimidating buyouts. New applicants have been required to answer questions such as whether they support Trump's 2024 presidential candidacy and answer "What part of President Trump's campaign message is most appealing to you and why?"[4] Once-nonpolitical civil service has become an extension of the presidency.

To be sure, Donald Trump has had plenty of allies assisting his efforts, but as president he has the unequalled ability to destroy American democracy as we know it. With each day, Trump comes closer to achieving what political observer Arthur Schlessinger, Jr., once described as the "imperial presidency." His account of the abuses by then-president Richard Nixon during the Watergate crisis led Schlessinger to conclude that only "the vigilance of the nation" could ultimately stand up to Nixon.[5] Compared to Trump's abuses of our democracy, Nixon's crimes were little more than child's play.

At such a critical juncture in the nation's storied political history, it's tempting for Americans to throw our hands up in the air and whimsically hope that somehow, someone will find the means to topple the most serious threat to our democracy in the nation's history. But while waiting for "someone, somehow" to rescue us may spell a temporary escape from addressing the problem head on, avoidance only feeds the unappeasable authoritarian appetite of Trumpism. Our nation's vigilance is required not somehow, sometimes, but now.

Instead of watching American democracy crumble, we have an opportunity to save it. But let's not kid ourselves—the task will not be easy. Along the road to political repair, we must not ignore the painful reality of Trump's penetration of American politics. Overcoming Trumpism will come not from winning a single presidential election or even the political demise of Donald Trump, for the threat to American democracy has been years in the making. Moreover, there are plenty of would-be Trumpist demagogues ready to take his place if Trump disappeared.

The effort to rescue our democratic ethos must begin with a national commitment to reconstitute our sense of belonging in a manner that extends well beyond geography and political tribalism. The effort must give all Americans the feeling that they are part of the possible solution. A hint of that potential emerged with the "No Kings" anti-Trump rallies on June 14, 2025. On that day, approximately two thousand coordinated protests took place across the nation by between an estimated 4 million and 6 million people.[6] But it will take much more than a one-time spate of anger, or even a series of protests, to overtake Trumpism.

So, where do we begin? Civic education is certainly a necessary starting point for our renewal. However, education alone is hardly sufficient to restore democracy. Our national repair must include elements of proactive action that bond us. As Lotte Scharfman implied years ago, democracy depends upon our meaningful participation in ways that make us proud. She reminded us that democracy doesn't appear out of thin air, but it surely can disappear that way. Cloistered passive observers on the sidelines at this moment in time will only diminish the chances of defeating authoritarianism.

This is a moment when we should not look for others to save us; rather, we must take it upon ourselves. As Joseph Tussman has written, "The essential feature of a democratic polity is its concern for the participation of the member in the process by which the community is governed."[7] To that end, our ability to reclaim and solidify our democracy will grow with the numbers of American patriots who join the movement.

In the remaining pages of this chapter, we will consider several potential action steps for promoting connections between citizens, institutions, and a strengthened democracy, which has clearly become the enemy of Trumpism. The discussion will also focus on what everyday activities we can undertake individually and collectively to nurture and restore our political health. While the list is far from complete, it gives us a starting point to overcoming Trumpism.

The Value of National Attachment

Individual political ownership is an essential element of democracy. If people feel part of this precious form of government and appreciate its virtues, they are less likely to let it get away. But we need to connect with one another to move in sync. Linkages are found through universal participation in nation building, resurrecting the dignity of all Americans, constituting a sense of community, and embracing those who come here as valuable members of society. Universal participation in the franchise is a common practice through which Americans express their commitment to ownership, but is that enough to assure support for the political system and all that it provides? We need to do more as members of society for what again could become the world's leading democratic beacon.

Mandatory National Service

Part of belonging to a democracy comes with taking part in endeavors that promote the common good. Mandatory national service is an excellent example of community building regardless of whether it takes place at the national, state, or local levels of government. With this activity, everyone regardless of their socioeconomic status takes part in contributing to the well-being of the polity. That vibrant participation helps to promote a sense of collective purpose. Given the wide differences of opportunities, experiences, and exposure to the various aspects of life, mandatory national service can go a long way toward leveling the nation's uneven playing field. Out of different life experiences can come the satisfaction from working with others for the collective good.

Mandatory national service can facilitate an environment of individuals joining for the benefit of the entire nation. Adam Garfinkle writes that this enterprise can create a culture with "long-lasting benefits for civic participation that will frontload some equity for those young Americans who don't experience equality of opportunity and that, above all, will refurbish the country's stock of social capital."[8] There is another important benefit: for the millions of Americans who have felt isolated from society and now reside on the fringe of right-wing radicalism, participation with others in a common purpose can give them an extended family of sorts and an alternative to their otherwise lonely existences.

Around the world at least seventy-five countries require assorted forms of mandatory service. Some focus exclusively on military conscription, while others offer a broad variety of participation opportunities. The lengths of service also fluctuate from as little as four weeks to two years or more. The point is individual citizens are giving themselves to do good for the national community.

With respect to a potential template for the United States, one proposal could require individuals to sign up for eighteen months between the time of high-school graduation (or eighteen years of age) and twenty years of age. They would choose from a long list of possible organizations in which to serve and be paid a modest stipend while performing their service. Upon completion of their commitment, participants would receive a lump sum of money to be used for college, vocational training, or other uses. In doing so, everyone should contribute to benefit an aspect of American society. No doubt, mandatory service would include additional details but at least this rough blueprint could be a start.

The beauty of mandatory national service lies with its flexibility. Enlistment in the military is an option, but it's only one of innumerable possibilities. In fact, there are already several other ongoing programs in place, although many have been dealt serious blows by Donald Trump's efforts to eradicate voluntarism. At the national level, participation in the Peace Corps or AmeriCorps are obvious examples. Introduced by President John Kennedy in 1961, the Peace Corps accepts about fifteen thousand applicants annually for twenty-seven-month assignments in more than one hundred countries. As for AmeriCorps, this domestic service program created under the President Bill Clinton administration in 1993 had about two hundred thousand participants in 2024. These programs must be restored.

Beyond AmeriCorps and the Peace Corps, working for a forest agency, agricultural facility, national park, or almost any public institution in need of help is among possible opportunities. Endless prospects also exist at the state and local levels, including police cadet, firefighting aide, hospital attendant, veterinarian tech, and teacher's assistant. There could also be opportunities in the nonprofit sector such as a position with a food bank, local shelter, assisted living facility, local Habitat for Humanity chapter, the Salvation Army, or Goodwill Industries. Given so many unfilled needs throughout the nation, there is no shortage of places and vocations for people entering mandatory national service.

Research shows that national service is a powerful bonding agent for community building. In their post–national service lives, participants are more likely to pursue jobs in the public sector, more committed to community involvement, and more likely to obtain university educations. They could also continue volunteering in their communities after their assignments.[9] In other words, they are thinking beyond themselves.

Sadly, the Trump administration has turned its back on public service. In April 2025, Trump via Elon Musk's Department of Government Efficiency (DOGE) eliminated $400 million from the AmeriCorps budget, laying off 85 percent of the organization's paid staff and forcing tens of thousands of AmeriCorps members to stop work on more than one thousand community projects throughout the nation. As to the reason for reduction of the organization's activities, AmeriCorps participants were simply told that work "no longer effectuates agency priorities."[10] Sizable reductions in the numbers of Peace Corps paid staff members were also ordered, which not only removed Americans from public service, but also curtailed the spread of American goodwill in dozens of underserved nations around the world in areas such as education, health, and environmental deterioration throughout the world.

Trump's dismissal of public service programs shouldn't be surprising considering that he attempted to dismantle so many national agencies dedicated to humanity ranging from agricultural research to the study of potentially deadly viruses and other international commitments. Whereas national service promotes community, Trumpism thrives on division.

Instead of tearing down institutions and dividing society, we need to build up national community in ways that serve all Americans. Mandatory national service is one route to accomplish those connections and make our country a better place. It may sound corny to some, but it works.

Restoring Diversity, Equity, and Inclusion

The pursuit of equality is a longstanding attribute of American democracy. Diversity, Equity, and Inclusion (DEI) is the latest effort to guarantee that precious value. Beginning with the Civil Rights Act of 1964, the US government developed policies to correct the underrepresentation of racial minorities in employment and university admissions. Over time, DEI policies incorporated women, religious minorities, military veterans, and eventually members of the LGBTQ communities as members of society who may have suffered from underrepresentation because of their race, gender, compromised physical abilities, or religious beliefs. During the same period, diversity programs have served to educate employees about different cultures and discrimination that can emerge in public and private sectors. The idea behind the programs was to make certain that people were not denied employment opportunities and advancement because they fell into any of these minority categories. DEI programs also address pay differences by gender, such as women earning an average of 83.6 percent of men overall, and in some cases, much less than that.[11]

The DEI concept has expanded beyond employment discrimination. Realizing that their customers might be unhappy with staffing policies that failed to represent the actual composition of America's workforce, many companies eventually realized that it was in their self-interest to pursue their own DEI policies.[12] Some studies even showed that companies could be more profitable when they relied on DEI as part of their business model.[13] Other independent research found that DEI programs had the effect of reducing employee departures while increasing employee motivation and productivity.[14] DEI-produced profits and stable workforces have added additional benefits for society.

Despite the many benefits from DEI curricula in recent years, conservative critics have labeled DEI as disguised racist programs that cater only to certain groups, and not others. Left out but certainly implied is the accusation that DEI discriminates against White males. Some critics have gone so far as to declare DEI as anti-American. And then there are the unfounded claims that obliquely correlate disasters with DEI-hired personnel. For example, in the wake of the massive Los Angeles fires in 2025, some conservative critics pointed to the county's Black female fire chief as a DEI hire, and as such, lacked the capability to properly manage the crisis.[15] In another instance, critics attempted to connect employees hired through DEI programs with a collision between a military helicopter and a passenger jet at Washington, DC's Reagan Airport that led to sixty-seven deaths. Among them was President Donald Trump who implied that unqualified people hired by the Federal Aviation Administration through DEI efforts were responsible for the tragedy.[16] In both instances, there was no evidence of DEI-related employees being responsible for the calamity; nevertheless, the accusations were made and further circulated through the Trumpist network of sycophants and followers.

Trumpists have a certain political logic connected with their baseless accusations of DEI attributes. They know that conservative White males have been major supporters of Trump's voting coalition. By virtue of their political values, they are not part of the DEI movement. Assigning blame to women and non-Whites for their inability to secure good jobs in government or the private sector keeps Trump in good stead with this group. Given his history with women and non-Whites, Trump's criticism of DEI has certainly meshed with his lifelong pattern of blaming minorities for society's problems. And with the recent Supreme Court decisions declaring Affirmative Action unconstitutional for university student acceptance methods, Trump felt he was on solid ground to take on DEI. That being said, it's quite the leap from using rejected university acceptance programs to justifying elimination of all DEI programs.

The irony of all the DEI flak is that utilization of the concept hasn't had much of an impact on corporate diversity. An examination by *The Wall*

Street Journal of the workforce of the S&P five hundred companies between 2020 and 2023 found modest gains for Asian and Hispanic workers. The percentage of White women remained almost identical. Meanwhile, White males continued to dominate upper corporate ranks.[17] Equally modest gains have also been found in the public sector, with the largest gains coming with Hispanics.[18]

Nevertheless, Trump and his acolytes have viewed DEI as the most recent way to force division between Whites and non-Whites, straights and gays/trans, and males and females. And as noted throughout this volume, societal division breeds distrust, a condition that is highly favorable for authoritarians to control the population through their promises to bring order from the chaos they created.

Trump Moves in on DEI

Within days of assuming his second administration, Trump issued executive orders for all national government departments and agencies to disband their DEI programs and fire their employees. He threatened to end federal funding to state governments, K–12 schools, and universities that failed to comply with his order. He also went so far as to promise federal investigations of companies that continued to use DEI programs.[19] Some of the state and local public institutions reluctantly yielded to the pressure while others took to the federal courts for relief.

What's remarkable is the extent to which so many DEI-friendly companies rushed to erase their DEI policies to placate Trump, who had intimated action through some form of government investigation or other punishment if they failed to do so. In explaining the sudden turnaround, an advisor to several Fortune 500 companies explained, "There's a sense of, 'Oh gosh, the Trump administration or his allies could target us next and we need to be prepared for that.'"[20] Translation: they don't want to lose current government contracts or possible future contracts. One of the biggest DEI reversals came at Meta (formerly Facebook), which had set a goal in 2019 that by 2024 at least 50 percent of its workforce would be from diverse or underrepresented backgrounds. But in January 2025, Meta disbanded its DEI team as unnecessary while terminating a special program designed to purchase materials and goods from diverse suppliers.[21]

Not all businesses deserted their DEI programs. Stockholders at Apple and Costco were among the few companies that bucked the trend, but they stood out as exceptions to Trump's demands.

Why We Must Revive DEI

Contrary to Trump's claims that DEI policies are harmful to society, public opinion polls show that people support them. In a Pew Research poll taken in April 2025, two months after Trump's purge of DEI programs and employees from the federal government, a solid majority of Americans disapproved of the president's actions to end DEI policies;[22] moreover, these data are similar to findings before Trump took office.[23] And, in a surprise to some anti-DEI promoters, there's polling evidence showing that Whites are in fact *more* supportive than not of DEI programs. In an April 2025 public opinion survey that asked Americans about regulations that would require foreign companies to ban DEI programs to do business with the US government, 48 percent of Whites opposed the idea, compared with 34 percent who favored it.[24] Put it all together and we discover that Trump's signature representation of DEI as harmful to American society does not correspond with the sentiment of most Americans.

Experts may well argue over whether DEI programs are substantive or symbolic, that is, major forces of change or mere dents in the armor of White male supremacy. Regardless, if equality is a mainstay of democracy, then meaningful DEI programs must be revived as guarantors of equality. Even if their programs are slow to change the employment of minorities, DEI programs can play an important role in educating people about the history of underrepresentation as well as the benefits for a democratic society resulting from a diverse workforce truly reflective of its members. As noted above, a diverse workforce yields positive results ranging from increased productivity to employee satisfaction.

The point here is simple: Democracies should bring people together instead of separating them. That sense of belonging must extend to the public sector workspace, private sector workspace, education institutions, and any environment where people are judged for their capabilities rather than artificial criteria. By reaching out to those who may be unaware of employment opportunities, DEI policies assure that all people will have the same starting point regardless of their backgrounds. While males are not denied opportunities, rather women and non-Whites are made more aware of them.

Embracing Immigration

It goes without saying that Donald Trump views immigration as enemy number one of what he refers to as "American culture," which is implicitly the synonym for a White Christian culture. What Trump conveniently overlooks is that immigration is a historic component of American society.

The fact is, however, that Trump is not against immigration per se; rather he opposes immigrants of color and non-Christian religions, who he accuses of "poisoning our culture." Recall how Trump embraced White South Africans in response to unproven claims of genocide by Black leaders, while he paused admission of Afghani citizens who risked their lives while helping Americans root out Taliban terrorists. Trump hides his contempt for immigrants behind false data on immigrant crime and abuse of government benefits. He repeatedly describes undocumented immigrants as murderers, gang members, and lazy people feeding at the government trough. Yet, undocumented immigrants have lower crime rates than native-born Americans and contribute far more to American taxes than they collect in the form of benefits.[25] Those facts may not comport well with the Trump diatribe, but they are the facts, nonetheless. In this sense, the behavior of the most recent wave of immigrants, largely from Spanish-speaking countries and Asia, is no different than that of our predecessors.[26] They're searching for freedom and opportunity the same way our forebearers did.

The racial bigotry of Trump and his acolytes notwithstanding, undocumented immigrants account for significant portions of the workforce. According to a 2023 report, undocumented immigrants account for about 30 percent of the nation's plasterers and drywall installers, 30 percent of the nation's agricultural workers, 20 percent of the nation's maids and housekeepers, and about one-sixth of the nation's construction laborers. Moreover, these very areas have attracted decreasing numbers of native-born Americans.[27] It doesn't take a rocket scientist to realize that without undocumented immigrants in these and other jobs, there would be massive holes in the nation's economy, no doubt driving up expenses for related products and activities as a result.

Does this mean that the federal government should just accept every undocumented immigrant who comes into the United States? Of course not. Immigrants must obey US laws, but so must the president. Deporting undocumenteds without giving them due process and resisting Supreme Court orders to return those wrongly deported are violations of US laws. Revoking the Temporary Protected Status of refugees who were given that status by previous presidents for fleeing wars, gangs, and rampant disease violates previous federal authorizations, not to mention sacred norms. And deporting innocent undocumented residents in the midst of searching for suspected criminals is also wrong. At a different time in history, that same treatment might well have prevented our ancestors from settling here, leaving us, their descendants, in another country.

This list is long of immigrants who have provided the foundation for today's United States and people. Whether in science, education, the arts, sports, or so many other categories, immigrants have made the United States a pluralist nation that has attracted the world's envy—until now. We must resist this bigotry. Along the way, we must demand a new law that creates a way for the millions of law-abiding undocumented immigrants in the United States to gain citizenship. If we have benefitted from their labor, they should at a minimum benefit from our acceptance.

Making America Whole Again

Instead of finding ways to tear us apart, we need positive strategies that will bring us together. Creating mandatory national service, restoring DEI, and embracing the many talents of immigrants would be three major steps toward restoring the greatness of this country.

Building Communities through Political Participation

When we think about civic engagement in a political sense, most people point to voting. Presidential elections generally draw the highest turnout, compared to state and local events. In the 2024 bitterly contested campaign between Republican Donald Trump and Democrat Kamala Harris, 63.7 percent of eligible voters cast their votes. That means more than one-third of those eligible to vote—about 90 million Americans—refrained from doing so. Yes, there were some obstacles in selected areas of the country such as gerrymandering and burdensome voter registration requirements, but these in no way accounted for more than one-third of the eligible electorate refraining from the franchise. In fact, if anything, most states have moved in the other direction. Thirty-nine of the fifty states allowed people to vote by mail. Twenty-eight states set up their procedures for people to vote early. Of course, some nonvoters lived in the less voter-friendly states, but nowhere near 90 million.

So, why did so many people refrain from voting in the 2024 presidential election, the most critical election in recent memory? Most nonvoters just didn't have the motivation to participate. According to a Pew Research survey of nonvoters taken at the time of the election, 35 percent responded that their vote didn't matter, while another 31 percent added that they didn't like politics.[28] These explanations for not voting—apathy and an aversion to politics—smack of political alienation. Such behavior is fodder for Trumpist authoritarianism,[29] the antithesis of democracy.

Given the blase attitude toward Trumpism by the US Supreme Court and the willingness of the Congressional Republican majority to rubberstamp Trumpism, only an activist public can stop his tyranny. In her discussion of the antidemocratic climate created by authoritarians, *Strongmen* author Ruth Ben-Ghiat writes that people can respond to antidemocratic conditions by taking one of two distinctly different approaches: "They can dig their trenches deeper, or they can reach across the lines to stop a new cycle of destruction, knowing that solidarity, love, and dialogue are what the strong man most fears."[30] Even in these precarious times, we have a choice.

Which is why we turn to community building, defined as the process of forming and cultivating meaningful relationships among individuals who seek to improve conditions in their environment. With community building, people work on solving problems through forging bonds and trust from their shared interests. Out of these developments can come the hope that by working together, we can impact the policymaking process either by connecting with policymakers directly or becoming part of the policymaking network ourselves. Community building is not an instant cure for apathy and disinterest in politics. It's a step-by-step endeavor with risks for people who have dropped out of the political realm, but who are tentatively willing to become a bit more involved. Most important, community building can be a step to participatory democracy.[31] That step is critical to saving our republic.

Below are some suggestions for impacting the political process. The list is hardly complete, but rather a place to begin. You might ask, how can any of these recommendations rid us of Trumpism? The short answer is, they won't, but what they will do is serve as initial building blocks for local, state, and national political involvement. Over time, achieving success from modest starting points can lead to larger efforts toward restoring democracy in a depressed society where too many of us have relegated ourselves to the sidelines.

Write a Letter to a Public Official with Your Concern about an Issue

Letter writing is a direct way for someone to connect with a public official. It puts the official on notice to the extent that the official learns that a constituent is taking the time to express concern about an issue of importance. Letters should be respectful and concise; you don't want to give an elected official a reason to ignore you. They should be individually composed and not copies, for copies of the same letter dilute the value of an individual's outreach.

Individual letter writing has the potential of being much more influential than petitions and emails. Both can smell of slick organizational efforts that, again, diminish the value of the message. By contrast, individual letters draw attention because of the way they are put together.[32] They are original and time consuming for the writer. And if people collaborate with others to write individual letters on the same topic, the significance of letters builds exponentially.

There are a couple of important guidelines that will help your letter score with a public official. First, make sure that the official you are addressing has responsibility for dealing with your issue. Writing to your member of Congress about large class sizes in your kid's school will go nowhere; writing to your congressperson regarding your anguish over the potential harm such as larger classes caused from a defunded Department of Education program gets to an issue the member can address through looking into your complaint and voting on related legislation. Additionally, including published data about the problems associated with large class sizes is also valuable in that it shows your knowledge about the topic.

Don't be surprised if the elected official passes off your letter to a staff member for a response or, worse yet, ignores your effort altogether. An informed staffer on your subject could be potentially helpful as an ally. However, if your letter doesn't generate a sufficient reply to your issue or the official to whom it has been written responds with a kind of wishy-washy, generic reply, you need to go back and ask why the official has not answered you in a sincere way.

That said, letters can be important drivers for political change. Especially if the public official is elected, has a tight reelection race looming, and is uncertain on which way to manage the issue you've broached, a letter-writing campaign may have a powerful effect on moving the person not only in the form of a response to you but acting on the issue. Since the most important task of an elected official is to get reelected, even the most ideologically rigid or inattentive elected official can bend on a vote if it will help to keep them in office. That may sound crass, but it's real politics.

Join Political Postcard Teams

Sometimes, the best way to obtain favorable results on an important topic is through teams of people reaching out to the voters in a state or district where that issue looms large as an election matter. For this tactic, political postcards can be effective tools for helping voters understand the significance of an issue brought to their attention. Political party organizations make available political postcard campaigns for interested individuals who want to work with others to achieve positive election results.

Political postcards are important in two respects. First, they educate voters with vital election information they may not have known initially and show them the value of their participation in solving a particular problem or set of problems through their vote in the election. In other words, they help to motivate voters, some who may not have previously seen a reason to take part in the election. Second, political postcards serve as political instruments for bringing activists together and empowering them to promote an important cause that they might not have been interested in working on individually, but they would be interested in as part of a group. In other words, they build community.

One example of a political postcards group is Postcards to Swing States, a program of the Progressive States Project that focuses on congressional and state legislative elections in highly competitive states. Sometimes, the outcome of a single race can change the leadership of a legislative chamber or even the majority in a congressional chamber. Upon request, organizers of the project send a package of materials to participants that includes postcards, likely or persuadable voter names and addresses, and writing instructions with tested campaign messages. All the postcard writer must do is purchase stamps, write the message, and mail the postcards on a predetermined schedule.

Studies show that political postcards can work both in increasing voter registration and turnout and in support for the issue advocated by the postcard writers. The difference may be only a percentage or less, but in a close election, that difference can separate victory from defeat. It's hardly a niche activity.[33] In the 2022 midterm elections, thousands of postcard volunteers reached more than 5 million voters.[34]

Attend Campaign Rallies for Political Issues and Candidates Important to You

Political candidates have long used political campaign rallies as a means for mobilizing support and generating voter enthusiasm. Donald Trump has been a master in his ability to attract large audiences. One study about the 2016 presidential campaign determined that Trump rallies were responsible for increasing his voter support over opponent Democrat Hillary Clinton by 4.5 percentage points, which is significant in any election. Trump's campaigns have also been a magnet for political campaign contributions.[35] Future candidates for elected office could take a lesson from Trump on this campaign technique.

In addition to campaign rallies serving as mobilizing tools for candidates, they are equally treasured by those in attendance. That's because rallies provide a special sense of candidate "personalization" for attendees who may not connect as intimately through social media, legacy television, or print.[36] Through the information they learn first-hand at campaign rallies, rally attendees are more likely to feel more connected than they might have been otherwise, and therefore more likely to participate in elections.

The wonderful point about political candidate campaign rallies is that they require minimal investment from attendees. Unlike a designated fundraising event, usually there is no charge to attend. But the commitment of attendee time in exchange for the information and campaign enthusiasm provided by the organizers makes the experience well worth the investment. Moreover, the experience may well draw you to future involvement in the campaign.

Join a Political Group That Reflects Your Values

For some people, campaign rallies have too much pageantry and too little substance. Other than over-the-top applause from the attendees, there is precious little interaction between the candidate or rally organizers and the audience.

Political groups meet in a more intimate setting. Whereas campaign events focus on quantity, these clusters can emphasize quality discussions by their members. For these people, joining a political group such as a Democratic Club or a local chapter of a proactive organization such as an equal rights group can provide information plus the sense of "hands on" involvement.

Compared to rallies, political groups are relatively intimate bodies, especially at the local chapter level. To begin with, working with people who agree on political positions offers a combination of comradery, gravitas, and a reinforced sense of purpose. Sometimes friends join political groups, and on other occasions, friendships are developed in political groups.

Working at the local level, political groups can organize activities of their choosing such as candidate fundraisers, meetings with local elected officials or candidates, lectures on important issues, information on upcoming events, and even meetings with similar groups. Depending upon their size and interest, they may have several events going on at the same time.

Participants have a stake in the group and are routinely valued for their thoughts. Along with participation, small political groups or chapters of larger organizations tend to be internally democratic. They are led by dedicated volunteers who are committed to the cause. As a result, group members have a sense of worth that is not likely to be nurtured in a large setting.

Political groups have great flexibility regarding the activities they undertake. To that end, whereas the campaign rally concentrates on promoting the candidate or the issue, small groups lean on their own members to promote their issues. There's an important benefit here. Given the nature of their organization, small groups offer attendees a sense of validation that is not seen in a large, more formal setting. Participating outside of the general parameters connected with a cause or campaign, small groups often march to their own beat.

Some political groups exist by virtue of their members. Unions, chapters of conservationists, and education organizations are by definition political groups. They exist not only to advocate for their members, but also to pressure elected officials and those seeking election. These groups can be influential in helping candidates see the importance of their issues.

Create Your Own Political Organization

Sometimes individuals feel the need to create their own organization, especially when their passion doesn't seem to fit with the current discussions or political movements. Rather than pout on the sidelines, they begin their own organization from scratch. Such undertakings require extraordinary commitment. But for people determined to form new political groups in the name of issue advocacy, passion is the fuel for their success, and the extraordinary commitment is a given.

Teresa Shook is hardly a household name. Yet, the Hawaii resident became a national symbol of resistance to Trumpism. Up to the moment of the 2016 presidential election between Hillary Clinton and Donald Trump, Shook was by her own definition an apolitical retired grandmother: Shaken by Trump's unexpected triumph over Clinton, Shook became a first-time activist. She felt provoked by what she perceived as Trump's pejorative attitude toward women. By the end of the election night, Shook created a Facebook page that asked whether anyone would accompany her to a march on Washington in protest of Trump's victory.[37] In her words, "I was thinking about my granddaughters, and I didn't want them to grow up in a world full of hate speech and bigotry."[38] By the time she retired for the evening, forty friends had signed up. But she touched a political nerve. When Shook awakened the next morning, more than ten thousand people had signed up to be part of the event. Mobilization exploded over the next two months. On January 17, 2017, the day of the protest, 470,000 people joined her on the march on Washington. Since Shook's original effort, she has remained active on women's issues in Hawaii.

Cause and dedication are key to creating a political protest group. But as noted with the Women's March, the energy can be contagious when the issue touches a political nerve, or in this case 470,000 political nerves. The Women's March spawned a new generation of anti-Trump political activists.[39] It may have also been at least partly responsible for the record election of women to the House of Representatives in 2018, the year following the march.

Contribute Money to Candidates and/or Political Organizations That Reflect Your Interest

Fifty years ago, Jess Unruh, a powerful Democratic politician in California, said "Money is the mother's milk of politics." Unruh's comment might have been a bit tactless, but it was on the mark. The better-funded candidate in a campaign doesn't always win the election, but the better-funded candidate wins more times than not.

We can spend endless hours airing our grievances about money in politics. Nevertheless, the nature of our political system and its election rules make money more necessary than ever thanks to the *Citizens United* case, where the US Supreme Court removed virtually all limits on election spending.[40] In the words of one examination of the case, "The result has been torrents of political spending from a small group of the very wealthiest megadonors via super PACs, as well as steadily increasing amounts of untraceable money."[41] Big Money is a reality in American politics. Its distribution to political campaigns is often lopsided with respect to its recipients. In an examination by *Open Secrets* of the twenty-five largest campaign contributions for the 2024 presidential election, eighteen were awarded to Republicans and only seven to Democrats.[42] The only way to counter that distribution is through large numbers of small donors. The silver lining with this approach comes with the recognition that the "large number" of small donors augers a large number of voters.

Election contributions can be directed to two major categories of recipients. One source centers on candidates and their party organizations, which will use the funds for various campaign needs, including personnel, office supplies, polling research, and commercials. The other source spotlights organized political groups with missions that comport with your values. With respect to the latter, possible recipients include groups that focus on civil rights, conservation, immigration, free speech, gun safety, LGBTQ+, and reproductive rights, as well any other of the many organizations that oppose antidemocratic candidates and policies.

Small amounts of monetary contributions by millions of donors can go a long way toward offsetting the huge Republican advantage. By making contributions to these groups monthly, quarterly, or another time period, people stay involved and satisfied that their donations are going to the right cause.

For those who are jaundiced about money "buying" an elected office, money alone is not necessarily enough to win. In the 2024 presidential election, the campaign of Democratic nominee Kamala Harris outraised the Trump campaign by a three-to-two margin. Still, campaigns can always use donations and seemingly never have enough.

Running for Office

There's nothing wrong with doing what we expect others to do. Running for political office directly connects the individual with governance. It's the essence of assuming responsibility for getting things done rather than leaving the task to others. There are lots of positions in government that exist as first steps in elective office. Running for school boards or town councils are great places to begin. From there, who knows where you might go?

If pursuing elected office is too great a leap, think about getting appointed to a policymaking position. City planning commissions are instrumental in constructing the footprint of their cities. A town's historical preservation committee or senior citizens council appointment are among the positions that are vital to the well-being of a local community. Getting appointed could be a vital first step to seeking higher elected office. It's a valuable form of political participation that is so important in democracy. By doing so, you step up to take a role in serving your community and caring for the collective good. From there, the sky's the limit both for you and your constituents.

Serving in a local government position is often just the beginning for those who seek to participate in governing. State and federal offices are filled with elected officials who began their careers as elected or appointed local officials. Some begin later in life while others get the political "bug" early in their lives. For example, in 2024, two people in their teens were elected to state legislatures, one of whom assumed office on her eighteenth birthday! At the national level, in 2022, Maxwell Frost of Florida was elected to the US House of Representatives at the age of twenty-five, the youngest age to legally assume office for that chamber. For those who cynically contend that politics is a closed system left only to elite individuals and families, there are plenty of examples to prove otherwise.

A Nation of Sheep or a Nation of Lions?

In 1961, William J. Lederer published *A Nation of Sheep*. In the book, he lamented that Americans were thoughtlessly accepting suspicious government explanations of American foreign policy disasters with little question or concern. Lederer wrote that government leaders needed to be more honest and transparent, while the press needed to be more inquisitive about the government's actions and explanations. Equally important, he continued, was the fundamental obligation for people to actively participate in the nation's political well-being: "The average man or woman can have a powerful effect on the national scene once the realization strikes home that no voice goes unnoticed, particularly if it is raised in intelligent question, objection or praise,"[43] he wrote. In other words, our voices can make a difference if we speak up. We can't afford to become a nation of sheep, at least, not if we want to save our democracy.

Today's circumstances are a bit different than Lederer's time in that our concern is not about the government's disastrous foreign policy, but rather how Donald Trump and his allies are abusing the powers of government to take away our democracy. There is great similarity, however, to the extent to which many of today's Americans resemble Lederer's sheep. Trump's callous approach to divide Americans for the purpose of achieving and maintaining power is not conducive to democracy. In fact, it is the antithesis to democracy. His weaponization of government offices, punishment of political opponents, attempts to silence an independent press, and outright dismissal of the otherwise empowered branches of government are all self-serving of a narcissistic leader who can't get enough of everything. All these actions and more have been carried out to consolidate power for himself and his allies. Trump's actions reek of authoritarian behavior, and as we know now more than ever, authoritarianism is the enemy of democracy.

Overcoming Trumpism

Like in Lederer's day, Trumpists are counting on an acquiescent public for success. They think that because few, if any, people speak out against Trump, members of the public are either satisfied with the Trumpist's management of current affairs or don't care one way or another. It may be unintended, but an acquiescent public is a tacit endorsement of the status quo, and the status quo these days is Trumpist through and through.

Rather than passively accept what happens around us, we must show through our voices, activities, dollars, and unity that we care deeply about the illegitimate goings on in government and the very real threat to our democracy. Those who understand the dark outcomes of Trumpism need to help others less aware become conscious of the movement's significance and its cost to American society. More than ever, we need an active, independent press to resist government threats and muzzling efforts to help us comprehend the evil doings of Trumpism. We need elected officials with the capability to stop Trump to do so or be replaced in the next election if they don't. The cost of remaining on the sidelines at this critical point in time is simply too great to ignore or, worse yet, wait for someone else to fight for what should be paramount to us all: democracy.

Our call to action should not be viewed as a once-every-four years political engagement. We need to be vigilant not only at election time but also every day between the last election and the next, as well as many more days and elections to come. As for elections, victories don't come by accident; they come as the result of hard work. And while that simple formula alone does not assure victory over the authoritarian threat, victory certainly won't come without it.

None of this guarantees the disappearance of Trumpism, but without our concern and involvement, Trumpism will have little opposition. That's a condition we cannot afford if we have any hope of keeping our democracy. The threats to our democracy are that real. To the extent that we ignore them, it will be on our conscience to explain to future generations why we let them down.

Finally, we're reminded of Lotte Sharfman's observation, which we should take as a stern warning: "Democracy is not a spectator sport." Perhaps the June 14, 2025, "No Kings" national protest against Trumpism is a start to the public's awakening. But to cast Lotte Sharfman's remark in baseball parlance, you can't get a hit if you don't swing the bat. It's long past time for us to get into the game. We need to get into the game of democracy now. And striking out is not an option.

NOTES

1. Quoted in *Congressional Record—House*, January 20, 1970, p. 282, https://www.congress.gov/91/crecb/1970/01/20/GPO-CRECB-1970-pt1-2-1.pdf.
2. "Trump Says Immigrants Are 'Poisoning the Blood of Our Country.' Biden Campaign Likens Comments to Hitler," NBC News, December 17, 2023, https://www.nbcnews.com/politics/2024-election/trump-says-immigrants-are-poisoning-blood-country-biden-campaign-liken-rcna130141.
3. "Trump Signs Order Targeting Law Firm behind $787.5m Fox Defamation Suit," *The Guardian*, April 9, 2025, https://www.theguardian.com/us-news/2025/apr/09/trump-executive-order-fox-news-law-firm.
4. "Loyalty Tests and MAGA Checks: Inside the Trump White House's Intense Screening of Job Seekers," U.S. News, January 25, 2025, https://www.usnews.com/news/politics/articles/2025-01-25/loyalty-tests-and-maga-checks-inside-the-trump-white-houses-intense-screening-of-job-seekers.
5. Arthur M. Schlessinger, Jr., *The Imperial Presidency* (Boston, MA: Houghton Mifflin, 1973), p. 418.
6. "'No Kings' Was the Biggest Protest in U.S. History," Daily Beast, June 15, 2025, https://www.yahoo.com/news/no-kings-biggest-protest-u-172552711.html.
7. Joseph Tussman, *Obligation and the Body Politic* (New York: Oxford University Press, 1960), p. 105.
8. Adam Garfinkle, "Bonds of Citizenship," *Washington Monthly* (May 2, 2013), https://washingtonmonthly.com/2013/05/02/bonds-of-citizenship/.
9. "Americorps: Changing Lives, Changing America," Corporation for National Community Service, Washington, DC, 2007, https://dph.illinois.gov/content/dam/soi/en/web/idph/files/publications/americorps-lives-america-041816.pdf.
10. "DOGE Orders Major Cut to AmeriCorps Funding, Imperiling Agency's Work," *The Washington Post*, April 25, 2025, https://www.washingtonpost.com/nation/2025/04/25/americorps-grant-cuts-doge/.
11. "New Report: Women Earn Less Than Men in All Occupations, Even Ones Commonly Held by Women," Institute for Women's Policy Research, March 7, 2024, https://iwpr.org/new-report-women-earn-less-than-men-in-all-occupations-even-ones-commonly-held-by-women/.
12. Barron Witherspoon, Sr., Here's the Real Reason DEI Makes Many White Men Uncomfortable," Fortune, April 19, 2024, https://fortune.com/2024/04/19/dei-under-attack-real-reason-it-makes-white-men-uncomfortable-careers-leadership-diversity/.
13. "Diversity, Equity and Inclusion 4.0," World Economic Forum, June 2020, https://www3.weforum.org/docs/WEF_NES_DEI4.0_Toolkit_2020.pdf. Also see "Diversity Matters Even More: The Case for Holistic Impact," McKinsey and Company, December 5, 2023, https://www.mckinsey.com/featured-insights/diversity-and-inclusion/diversity-matters-even-more-the-case-for-holistic-impact.
14. "An Inclusive Workplace Is Good for Business," Boston Consulting Group, June 27, 2024, https://www.bcg.com/publications/2024/an-inclusive-workplace-is-good-for-business.

15 "What Is DEI, and Why Is It Dividing America?" CNN, January 23, 2025, https://www.cnn.com/2025/01/22/us/dei-diversity-equity-inclusion-explained/index.html.
16 "Trump Blames D.E.I. and Biden for Crash under His Watch," *The New York Times*, February 1, 2025, https://www.nytimes.com/2025/01/30/us/politics/trump-plane-crash-dei-faa-diversity.html.
17 "DEI Didn't Change the Workforce All That Much. A Look at 13 Million Jobs," *The Wall Street Journal*, February 7, 2025, https://www.wsj.com/business/dei-impact-us-company-workforce-charts-2e6a6bb7.
18 "Diversity, Equity, and Inclusion in the Public Service Workforce," MissionSquare Research Institute, Washington, DC, September 30, 2021, https://research.missionsq.org/content/media/document/2021/09/deireport_092421.pdf.
19 "The Trump Administration Has a New Way to Pressure Companies to Ditch DEI," CNN, March 26, 2025, https://www.cnn.com/2025/03/26/business/dei-fcc-media/index.html
20 Quoted in "'Lifting' Becomes 'Leveling': Companies Reframe DEI amid Trump Upheaval," *The Washington Post*, February 24, 2024, https://www.washingtonpost.com/business/2025/02/21/trump-business-dei-policy-rebrand-representation-goals/.
21 "Mark Zuckerberg Says Hello to Joe Rogan, Goodbye to DEI," *The San Francisco Standard*, January 10, 2025, https://sfstandard.com/2025/01/10/meta-zuckerberg-rogan-dei-censorship/.
22 "Tariffs, DEI and Cuts to Government: Views of Trump's Key Actions," Pew Research Center, April 23, 2025, https://www.pewresearch.org/politics/2025/04/23/tariffs-dei-and-cuts-to-government-views-of-trumps-key-actions/.
23 "Diversity, Equity and Inclusion in the Workplace," Pew Research Center, May 17, 2023, https://www.pewresearch.org/social-trends/2023/05/17/diversity-equity-and-inclusion-in-the-workplace/.
24 "YouGov Survey: Policy Support," YouGov, April 22–25, 2025, https://d3nkl3psvxxpe9.cloudfront.net/documents/Policy_Support_poll_results_ZJyLq1A.pdf.
25 See Larry N. Gerston, *Trumpism, Bigotry, and the Threat to American Democracy* (Lanham, MD: Lexington Books, 2024).
26 "Immigrants and Crime in the United States," Migration Policy Institute, October 2024, https://www.migrationpolicy.org/sites/default/files/publications/mpi-explainer-immigration-crime-2024_final.pdf.
27 "Illegal Immigration and the U.S. Labor Market," Testimony by Steven A. Camarota, Center for Immigration Studies, before the House of Representatives Subcommittee on Health, Employment, Labor, and Pensions, of the Education and Workforce Committee, September 13, 2023, https://edworkforce.house.gov/uploadedfiles/9.13.23_camarota_testimony_help_subcommittee_hearing_on_open_borders_and_workforce.pdf.
28 "Voters' and Nonvoters' Experiences with the 2024 Election," Pew Research Center, December 4, 2024, https://www.pewresearch.org/politics/2024/12/04/voters-and-nonvoters-experiences-with-the-2024-election/.

29 Marc J. Hetherington and Jonathan D. Weiler, *Authoritarianism and Polarization in American Politics* (New York: Cambridge University Press, 2009), p. 140.
30 Ruth Ben-Ghiat, *Strongmen* (New York: W.W. Norton, 2020), p. 260.
31 Craig A. Rimmerman, *The New Citizenship*, 3rd edition (Boulder, CO: Westview Press), p. 23.
32 See "Emails vs Letters. What Works, When and Why," BehaviourWorks, March 13, 2023, https://www.behaviourworksaustralia.org/blog/emails-versus-letters-what-works-when-and-why.
33 "Postcards to Voters: How Much Does Handwriting Matter?" Sister District Project, December 15, 2022, https://sisterdistrict.com/b/research/handwritten-postcards-to-voters/, and "Postcards That Work," Blue Wave, https://shop.bluewavepostcards.org/pages/why-postcards?srsltid=AfmBOoq-_zOhPJYV_hLCcqIhOswtiObq7_sM7IlbI5_GH3kYYl6j0ILE.
34 "Neighbor to Neighbor GOTV Letters in 7 States," A Progressive Turnout Project, https://turnoutpac.org/wp-content/uploads/2023/08/2022-PTP-TMC-Neighbor-GOTV-Letters-Results.pdf.
35 James M. Snyder and Hasin Yousaf, "Making Rallies Great Again: The Effects of Presidential Campaign Rallies on Voter Behavior, 2008–2016," National Bureau of Economic Research, Working Paper 28043, October 2020, https://www.nber.org/system/files/working_papers/w28043/w28043.pdf.
36 James B. Ang and Dian Gu, "Democracy in Action: The Impact of Political Rallies on Voter Engagement," Social Science Research Network, November 29, 2024, https://papers.ssrn.com/sol3/papers.cfm?abstract_id=5038603.
37 "It Started with a Retiree. Now the Women's March Could Be the Biggest Inauguration Demonstration," *The Washington Post*, January 3, 2017, https://www.washingtonpost.com/national/it-started-with-a-grandmother-in-hawaii-now-the-womens-march-on-washington-is-poised-to-be-the-biggest-inauguration-demonstration/2017/01/03/8af61686-c6e2-11e6-bf4b-2c064d32a4bf_story.html.
38 "Grandmother Who Organized Washington March 'Felt Women Needed to Stand Up,'" "Good Morning America," ABC News, January 17, 2017, https://abcnews.go.com/US/grandmother-organized-washington-march-felt-women-needed-stand/story?id=44814367.
39 Dorothee Benz, "The Women's March: Protest and Resistance," Southern Poverty Law Center, March 20, 2023, https://www.learningforjustice.org/magazine/the-womens-march-protest-and-resistance.
40 The case was *Citizens United v. Federal Election Commission* (2010).
41 Marina Pino and Julia Fishman, "Fifteen Years Later, Citizens United Defined the 2024 Election," The Brennan Center, January 14, 2025, https://www.brennancenter.org/our-work/research-reports/fifteen-years-later-citizens-united-defined-2024-election.
42 "Who Are the Biggest Donors?" Open Secrets, February 6, 2025, https://www.opensecrets.org/elections-overview/biggest-donors.
43 Wiliam J. Lederer, *A Nation of Sheep* (Greenwich, CN: Fawcett, 1961), p. 127.

ABOUT THE AUTHOR

Larry N. Gerston, political science professor emeritus at San Jose State University, is a prolific academic researcher and author. In addition to *Overcoming Trumpism: How to Save American Democracy*, he has written *Making Public Policy: From Conflict to Resolution*; *Politics in the Golden State: The California Connection*; *The Deregulated Society*; *California Politics and Government: A Practical Approach*; *American Government: Politics, Process and Policies*; *Recall: California's Political Earthquake*; *American Federalism: A Concise Introduction*; *Confronting Reality: Ten Issues Threatening to Implode American Society (and How We Can Fix It)*; *Public Policymaking: Process and Policies*; *Not So Golden After All: The Rise and Fall of California*; *Reviving Citizen Engagement: Policies to Renew National Community*; *Public Policy Making in a Democratic Society: A Guide to Civic Engagement*; *California's Recall Election of Gavin Newsom: The Politics of Political Reform in the Era of COVID*; and *Trumpism, Bigotry, and the Threat to American Democracy*.

Along with his academic work, Larry Gerston serves as the on-air political analyst for NBC Bay Area television and KCBS radio. He has appeared on NBC Nightly News, CBS Evening News, CNN, PBS, and BBC, and has been quoted in numerous newspapers and online news sites. He speaks often about the intersection of civic engagement, political empowerment, and democracy. In his "spare" time, he has also authored four children's books.

INDEX

Note: Endnotes are indicated by the page number followed by "n" and the endnote number e.g., 20 n.1 refers to endnote 1 on page 20

ABC television network 44, 64, 278
abortion 17, 18, 143, 192, 196–7, 287, 291
ACLU (free speech) 296
Adams, John Quincy 248
Affordable Care Act 111, 182
African Americans 45, 60, 61, 69, 96, 158–9, 197
  discrimination of 159
Africans 56
Afrikaner 56
Alabama 96, 158, 259, 322
Alaska 33
Alien Enemies Act of 1798 209, 210
al-Qaeda, a terrorist group 33, 57, 246
Amazon 225
America First Legal 179
America First 34, 214, 221, 222
American Bar Association 231
American Civil Liberties Union 255, 291
American culture" 308, 341–3
American democracy 5, 46, 84, 91, 105, 106, 206, 245, 257, 268, 280, 281, 299, 307, 320, 333–4, 338
  beliefs 16–22
  on democratic values 5
  essentials of 7
  federalism 12–13
  fragile 20–1
  freedom of expression 13–14
  inclusivity 16–17
  law-based governance 8–9
  political culture 16–22
  power from the people to the government 14–15
  regularly scheduled elections 9–10
  separation of powers 10–12
  support for clashing principles 17–19
  toward perfect union 19–20
  values, restructuring 5, 16–22, 43–4
  on the wane 21–2
American electoral system 246
American First Policy Institute 179
American government 3, 5, 8, 95, 107, 111, 144, 146, 160, 220, 227, 288, 322, 324
  executive branches 3, 11, 12, 107, 110, 111, 157, 186, 205, 206–8, 219, 226, 229–31, 333
  judicial branches 107
  legislative branches 106, 107, 111, 179, 233, 314
American Muslims 31
American Populist movement 29
American Revolution in 1776 15
AmeriCorps 337–8
anarchy 20, 165, 263
Anderson, Carol 257
Animal Farm (Orwell, George) 166
antidemocratic combination 28
authoritarianism 34–6

Index

isolationism 32–4
populism 28–30
racism 30–2
Trumpism 36
anti-Semitism (Jews) 29, 55, 58
anti-transgender laws 161
Apple 212, 340
Applebaum, Anne 56
The Apprentice (television show) 122, 205
Arizona Republic 113
Arizona 84, 113, 118, 121, 196
    stuffed ballot boxes in 82
artificial intelligence (AI) 282
Asian Americans 30, 283
asylum seekers 42
Atkinson, Michael 108
Atlanta, Georgia 125, 180
Australia 298
authoritarian 1, 2, 3, 5, 6, 7, 15, 19, 22, 35, 36, 92, 105, 131, 143, 146, 147, 170, 180, 210, 223, 275–6, 280, 297, 298, 308–9, 334, 351, 352
authoritarianism 5, 6, 7, 28, 34–6, 44, 47, 56, 131, 132, 147, 153, 320, 322, 328, 335, 344, 351
    American version of 308
    democracy over 5
    examples of 35
autocracy 3, 6, 7, 36, 55, 59, 105, 226, 246

Babbitt, Ashli 91
Baker, Peter 183
Barr, Bill 79, 109
Bash, Dana 61
beliefs 16–22
Ben-Ghiat, Ruth 122, 187, 276, 344
Berman, Geoffrey 108
Bessent, Scott 221

biased state actions
    gerrymandering 95–6
    state voting laws 97–8
Bible 157
Biden, Hunter 108, 114
Biden, Joe 27, 28, 34, 35, 66, 70, 77, 82, 84, 86, 88, 89, 96, 97, 108, 109, 110, 119, 123, 124, 141, 142, 145, 177–81, 183, 184, 188, 190, 191, 192, 194–5, 209, 220, 222, 249, 278, 285
Biggs, Andy 62
bigotry 213, 288, 308, 342–3, 349
    definition of 68
    explosion of 55
Bill of Rights 13, 14, 17, 194, 291
birtherism 30–1, 124
Black Lives Matter 31, 57
Blacks 30, 57, 97, 168, 257, 320
the blue wall" 82
Bobb, Christina 121
Bolton, John 110
Bongino, Dan 230
book bans 164–6, 168
BookLooks.org 165
Booth, John Wilkes 66
Boston Globe 253
Bove, Emil 218
Bowling Alone 135
Bragg, Alvin 77
Branch Davidians 59–60
Brazil 19, 298
Brennan Center for Justice 65, 97, 118, 254, 256, 258
Brill, Steven 289, 290
Brown people 30
Brown v. Board Education 18, 154
Budapest Memorandum 222
Bush George H. W. 115, 178, 190, 248, 251, 311

Index

Bush, Cori 61
Butler, Laphonza 195

California 32, 210, 247–8, 252, 259, 296, 297, 322, 349
Canada 12, 223, 234
Cannon, Aileen 94, 117
Carlson, Tucker 144
Carnegie Endowment for International Peace 67
Carr, Brendan 278, 279
Carroll, E. Jean 77, 116, 278
Carter, Jimmy 115
CBS News 278
censorship 167, 279, 291
Center for Countering Digital Hate 282, 285
Center for Humane Technology (disinformation) 296
Centers for Disease Control (CDC) 37, 38, 39, 182, 206, 215
Central America 194
Central Intelligence Agency (CIA) 185, 206, 219
Chao, Elaine 60
Charlottesville, Virginia 31, 64, 282
Cheney, Liz 83, 120
Chesebro, Kenneth 90
Chicago Board of Commissioners 81
China 21, 31, 33, 34, 36, 182, 214, 252, 283, 298
Chinese Communist Party 62
Christian Nationalism 56, 60
Christians 43, 224, 342
  clashing principles 17–19
  nationalists 56
  and non-Christians 43, 187, 318
  Whites 56, 58
Chu, Judy 61
Chutkan, Tanya 94, 116

Citizens Defending Freedom 165
Citizens United case 349
civic education 156, 319, 320
  to civic engagement 323–6
  power of 320–2
  working of 322–3
civic engagement 135, 323–4, 326, 327
Civil Rights Act of 1964 338
Civil War 28, 43, 55, 60, 91, 105, 153, 164, 177, 294
Cleveland, Grover 248
Clinton, Bill 178, 337
Clinton, Hillary 30, 81, 85, 108, 122, 142, 182, 197, 248, 251, 347
Clyde, Andrew 91
CNN 61, 69, 357
Cobb, Ty 230
Coca-Cola 212
Cohen, Michael 85
collective good" 135
The Color Purple (Walker, Alice) 166
Comey, James 35, 107, 109, 218
common core" 155, 157, 311
Communications Decency Act,
  Section 230 124, 276, 288–90, 293, 194, 295
  arguments for deleting 292–4
  arguments for keeping 291–2
  modification of 294–5
communism 165
community building 344
Comstock Act 164
Congress 11–12, 14, 20, 28, 35, 37, 38, 42, 45, 46, 56, 61, 88, 89, 90, 95–6, 106, 109, 111, 113–14, 116, 118, 120, 123, 141, 145, 146, 164, 181, 184, 188, 192, 193, 198, 214, 226–8, 231, 233, 246, 247, 249, 264, 266, 284, 288, 289, 292, 309, 310, 313, 333, 345

Index

Consent by the people 15
Constitution of United States *see* US Constitution
Consumer Financial Protection Bureau (CFPB) 216, 219, 220
Conway, Kellyanne 182
Cook, Jesselyn 137
Coronavirus Aid, Relief, and Economic Security Act (CARES) 184
Costco 212, 340
costs of censorship 167–8
Cotton, Tom 61
Council for Responsible Social Media 296
COVID-19 pandemic 31, 34, 39, 42, 59, 64, 119, 136, 144, 169, 178, 179, 181, 183, 184, 185, 188, 191, 192, 205, 215, 260, 283
  alternative facts" about 182
Crimea 222
crime-infested" cities 110
critical race theory (CRT) 156, 158–9, 167, 312
Cruz, Ted 38
Cuba 33, 209
cultural integration 251

Daniels, Stormy 77, 85
DataReportal 280
De Lauro, Rosa 215
de Toqueville, Alexis 153
deceptive doctoring" 278
Declaration of Independence 17
deep state" bureaucrats 1, 37, 39, 40, 63, 144, 183, 185–6
  and radical press 185
Deferred Action for Childhood Arrivals (DACA) program 115
DEI, abolishing programs of 211–13
democracy 1, 5, 13, 14, 20–3, 27, 44, 46

vs. authoritarianism 6
deterioration of 22–3
educating for 307
essential elements of 335
and freedom 192
lost faith in 46–7
meaning of 2, 5
restoring power of vote in 245
vs. Trumpism 6–7
Democratic party 20, 27, 180
Democrats 5, 13, 41, 43, 58
  on abortion constituency 194–6
  democracy and freedom theme goes flat 192–4
  about racism 196–7
  and Republicans 194
  2024 elections, campaign failure reasons 190–2
  view on misogyny 196–7
  views on immigrants 69
Denmark 187, 223
Department of Agriculture 215, 311
Department of Defense 215
Department of Education Organization Act 310
Department of Education 39, 111, 154, 156, 160, 206, 212, 215, 231, 309, 310–11, 312, 313, 314, 315, 317, 321, 345
  Trump moves to eliminate 312–14
Department of Energy 215–16
Department of Government Efficiency (DOGE) 219–20, 230, 337
Department of Health and Human Service 137, 206, 215, 216, 296, 311
Department of Homeland Security (DHS) 63, 109, 206, 210, 216
Department of Housing and Urban Development 215

Index

Department of Justice 38, 63, 79, 91, 93, 125, 144, 145, 168, 206, 208, 218, 253–4, 300
   desegregation 18
Department of State 206
Department of the Treasury 215
Department of Transportation 217
Department of Veterans Affairs 206, 217
deporting undocumented immigrants 209–11
Des Moines Register 277
DeSantis, Ron 60, 144, 158, 169, 257
Dewey, John 153, 309
DeWine, Mike 189
Diamond, Larry 19
dictatorships 105
Digital media 132
Digital Services Act in 2023 297
direct democracy 9
discrimination 18
disease prevention 38–40
disenfranchisement 77
dismembering federal employment 214–17
Disney 212
distrust of government 37
diversity 19, 43, 47
Diversity, Equity, and Inclusion (DEI) 208, 338
   programs 312
   revive 341
   Trump moves in 340
Divided America 36–7
   American values, restructuring of 43–4
   democracy, lost faith in 46–7
   disease prevention 38–40
   distrust of elites 40–1
   distrust of government 37

federal law enforcement 38
   immigration, renewed controversy over 41–3
   military 37–8
   tolerance, hate over 44–5
   Trumpism on the ascent 47–8
Dobbs v. Jackson Women's Health Organization 18, 195, 287
Dominion Voting Systems 124, 277
$Trump 225
Dorsey, Jack 284
Douglass, Frederick 167
Dunlin, Anna 279
Dye, Thomas 8, 47

Economist Democracy Index 22
education 16, 47, 132, 137, 153–7, 170, 309, 310–11, 312–15
   against dictatorship 327–8
Edwards, Griffin 44
egalitarianism 17
Egypt 213
Egyptian Revolution in 2011 15
El Salvador 42, 232
election deniers" 80
election fraud 80
Election Integrity Network 179
election interference 7, 77, 78, 80, 83, 85, 207, 277
   attempt to falsify Georgia presidential vote 86
   campaign contributions 78–9
   corrupt voting machines 86–8
   hush-money payments 85–6
   insurrection against the capitol 90–2
   late tallies 82–4
   missing ballots accusation 81–2
   phony state electors 88–9
   stuffed ballot boxes 82
   Trumpism style 85

Index

of 2020 presidential election 79
election management
  voting process 258–9
  voting requirements 259–60
  voting sites 260–1
elections, regularly scheduled 9–10
electoral college 28, 88, 89, 90, 105, 106, 246, 247–8, 249–50, 251, 252, 254, 255
  arguments against 251–2
  arguments for 250–1
  assessing 249–50
  election management 258–61
  eliminating voter suppression 265–6
  ending gerrymandering 263
  ending the filibuster 264–5
  gerrymandering, unrepresentativeness of 253–5
  impairment to equal representation 252–3
  road to repair 263
  voter suppression 255
  voters and election officials 261–3
  votes truly equal and safe 268–9
electoral vote 269 n.3
electors 67, 78, 85, 87, 88, 89, 90, 92, 98, 247–8, 249, 250, 269 n.3
Electronic Registration Information Center (ERIC) 267–8
Elementary and Secondary Education Act of 1965 (ESEA) 310
Eliot, T. S. 194
elites 28–9, 37, 43, 47, 57
  distrust for government 40–1
  meaning of 40
el-Sisi, Abdel Fattah 36
Emhoff, Doug 57
Engle v. Vitale 162
enter authoritarians and trumpism 143

casting doubt about government 144–6
vulnerable society 146–8
Environmental Protection Agency (EPA) 208
equality 18, 246
equity 158
Erdogan, Recep 36
ethnic minorities 22
Europe 33, 34
evangelical Christian Whites 56
evangelicals 56, 157, 160, 162–4, 165, 224
executive branch, of US 3, 11, 12
  reformulating 206–8
Executive Order on Preventing Censorship" 124
executive order 56
expanded power of the Trump presidency 208
extremism 143
extremist violence 147

Face the Nation 113
Facebook (Meta) 67, 125, 140, 141, 280, 284, 286–7, 288, 295, 296, 340, 348
  far-right groups 67
Facebook Oversight Board 286
fake news" 122
far-right conspiracy theories 56
far-right groups 62
  violence 67
Fauci, Anthony Dr. 39, 144
Faulkner, William 166
Federal Aviation Administration (FAA) 216, 339
federal budget 214, 217, 227
Federal Bureau of Investigation (FBI) 35, 37, 38, 44, 64, 107, 108, 109,

Index

125, 144, 161, 179, 185, 206, 218, 221, 230, 231, 278, 296
  special trump retribution for 218
federal bureaucracy
  expertise gaps in 217–18
Federal Communications Commission (FCC) 111, 124, 186, 277, 300
Federal Emergency Management Agency (FEMA) 216
federal employment, dismembering 214–17
federal government 309–10
federal indictments to dismissals
  investigation and federal charges against trump 92–3
  sometimes, being right is not enough 94
  Trump's defense 93–4
federal judicial system 117–18
federal judiciary 229–32
federal law enforcement 38
Federal Reserve Board 185
Federal Trade Commission 111, 185
federalism 8, 12–13, 153, 206, 250
filibuster 264–5, 266
Finland 22
First Amendment in the Bill of Rights 291
First Amendment of the Constitution 124
First World War 33
Florida 82, 158, 163, 165, 169, 297
  League of Women Voters in 256–7
Food and Drug Administration (FDA) 185, 217
Food and Drug Agency 215
foreign aid program 114, 213–14, 231
  ending, effects in US 213–14
Forest Service 215
formal institutions

abusing the presidency 107
formal political institutions 106–7
Fortune 500 companies 340
Fourteenth Amendment 246, 266
Fox Corporation 124, 277
Fox News 124, 144
France 33
free press 13
freedom of expression 13–14
freedom of speech" 124
Freedom to Vote Act 263, 264
Frost, Maxwell 351
Fulton County 78

Gab 141
Gallup poll data 5, 46, 132, 189, 194
Garcia, Kilmar Abrego 232
Garfinkle, Adam 336
Garland, Merrick 93
gay/transgender 55, 340
gender 160–2, 189
  minorities 22
Georgia presidential vote 86, 87
Georgia 78, 84, 87, 89, 116, 177, 261, 277
  stuffed ballot boxes in 82
Germany 12, 33
Gerry, Elbridge 95, 253
gerrymandering 95–6, 253–5, 263, 265, 266, 343
Giffords, Gabby 66
Giroux, Henry 308
Giuliani, Rudy 108, 277
Glasser, Susan B. 183
Golding, William 166
Gooden, Lances 61
Google 284, 287
Gore, Al 248, 251
Gosar, Paul 45
government programs, cutting 217

Index

Graham, Lindsey 113, 114
The Grapes of Wrath (Steinbeck, John) 166
Great American Tragedy 1
Great Awakening Christian faith movement (1740s) 27
Great Britain 33, 55, 222
Great Depression 11, 208
Great Replacement Theory" 60
Greene, Marjorie Taylor 61, 144
Greenland 223, 233–4
Grisham, Stephanie 182
Gruber, Jonathan 132
guardrails 46, 105, 106, 109, 286, 288, 290, 298, 333
gun rights 17, 39, 90, 143
Guttmann, Amy 307

Haiti 42, 56, 61, 188, 189, 209
Haitians 56
Haley, Nikki "Nimarata" 32, 60
happiness and politics 131
Harding, Warren 115
Harris, Kamala 27, 31–2, 59–60, 61, 142, 181, 185, 189, 190, 191, 194, 195, 227, 269 n.3, 278, 282, 283
  abortion issue 194–6
  Biden's presidential performance impact on 191
  democracy and freedom theme goes flat 192–4
  misogyny 196–7
  popularity 194–5
  racism 196–7
  2024 elections, campaign failure reasons 190–2
Harrison, Benjamin 248
hate
  crimes 44, 68–9, 161, 168–9
  as fuel for violence 62–5

  after Trump's political entry 70
  hate-filled allies 66
Hawaii 309, 348
Hayes, Rutherford B. 248
Hegseth, Pete 221
Help America Vote Act of 2002 266
Heraclitus 133
Heritage Foundation 84, 156, 179, 207
Hitler, Adolf 32
Hoffman, Jake 121
Homan, Tom 210
Houdini, Harry 98
House of Representatives 45, 115
House Select Committee investigating January 6 Attack on the United States 83, 94
Houthis 224
How Fascism Works 185
Hudson, William 153
Hungary 19, 36
hush money payments 85–6, 123
Hutchinson, Cassidy 83

Illegal Immigration Reform and Immigrant Act of 1996 259
illegal immigration 31, 188, 209
immigrant
  deporting undocumented 209
immigration 16, 19, 28, 29, 37, 41, 187–9
  embracing 341–3
  pro-immigration and anti-immigration contingents 42–3
  renewed controversy over 41–3
Immigration and Customs Enforcement (ICE) 209–10, 232
impeachment 92, 108, 114, 230
Impoundment Control Act 233
Inauguration Day 205
inclusion 158, 268, 287, 308, 338
inclusivity 16–17, 193

Index

independents 41, 59, 69, 183, 262, 263
India 12, 19, 252
indictments 80, 89, 92, 93, 178, 193, 205, 218, 229
indigenous Americans 30, 310
individualism 17, 19
inflation rate
   during Biden administration 184
   during Trump administration 184
informal political institutions 106–7, 118
independent media 121–5
   Republican Party National Committee (RNC) 119–21
Instagram 140, 141, 280, 284, 286, 287, 296
Insurrection Act of 1807 110
Insurrection against the Capitol 21, 35, 38, 41, 45, 62, 63, 90, 98, 112, 178, 249
insurrectionists 45, 67, 89, 91, 92, 109
Internal Revenue Service (IRS) 39, 63, 108, 185, 206, 215, 217
International Emergency Economic Powers Act (IEEPA) 228
Internet 138, 143
Iowa 165, 278
Ipsos public opinion poll 69, 86
Iran 7, 34, 223, 224, 298
Ireland 12
ISIS, an international terrorist organization 31
Islamophobia 55
isolationism 32–4, 221–4
   Trumpist Twist to 221
Israel 58, 112, 213
   and Hamas 223

Jackson, Andrew 116
James, Letitia 78
The January 6th Report 84, 94
January 6, 2021 1, 3, 6, 20, 21, 28, 35, 38, 41, 45, 46, 62, 63, 65, 67, 83, 84, 85, 89, 90, 93, 96, 109, 116, 120, 125, 141, 153, 178, 192, 218, 229, 249, 269, 284, 293–4
insurrection against the Capitol 1, 3, 20, 21, 35, 38, 41, 45, 62, 125, 153, 249, 284
Japan 12, 33
   attack on Pearl Harbor 33
Jensen, Robert 292–3
Jews 31, 32, 45 55, 58, 64, 142, 168
Jinping, Xi 36
Johnson, Lyndon 160
Johnson, Mike 113, 114, 227
Jones, Alex 288
Judicial branch, of US constitution 11
Judiciary Act of 1789 11

K-12 public education 154, 158, 160, 162, 167, 169, 212, 307, 316, 319, 321, 334, 340
Kansas
   voter-initiated pro-abortion laws in 196
Kelly, John 108
Kennedy, John F. 66, 160, 337
Kentucky 165
Kenya 31
To Kill a Mockingbird (Lee, Harper) 166
King Charles II 55
King, Anthony 147
Kitzinger, Adam 120
Knight First Amendment Institute 279
Krebs, Christopher 108
Ku Klux Klan 60
Kupchan, Charles 34

LaCivita, Chris 121
Lake, Kari 145

Index

Lankford, James 112–13
Las Vegas 113
late tallies 82–4
Latin America 31
Latinos 45, 96, 197, 257
law-based governance 8–9
Lederer, William J. 351
Lee, Harper 166
Lee, Mike 231
legacy" media *see* mainstream media
Legislative branch, US 11
letter writing 344
Levitsky, Steven 35
LGBTQ 157, 160, 161, 165, 166, 314, 316, 338, 350
   management of 160
liberty" and "freedom" 165
Lincoln, Abraham 66
loneliness 131, 137, 143, 146, 147
   in American adults 136
   in American society 132
Lord of the Flies (Golding, William) 166
Los Angeles Times 279
Los Angeles, California 21, 211, 339
Louisiana 154, 158, 163
Lyons, Alyssa 168

magazines 138–9. 299
Maine 88, 269 n.3
mainstream media 59, 123, 124, 147, 185, 186, 276, 277, 278, 279, 281, 299
   and Donald Trump 276–9
   vs. social media 276
"Make America Great Again" 34
making America whole again 343
Manafort, Paul 116
mandatory national service 336–8, 343
Manhattan 77, 125
Marbury v. Madison (1803) 11, 226–7

Marriott 212
Maryland 259
mass democracy" 134
mass media 58–9, 132, 139
Massachusetts League of Women Voters 333
Massachusetts 55, 164, 253, 309, 322
Mature State of Social Media 290–1
McCabe, Andrew 108
McCain, John 37–8
McCarthy, Kevin 38, 83, 109–10
McCarthyism (1950s) 27
McConnell, Mitch 60, 114
McDaniel, Ronna 120
McDonnell, Jim 210
McGahn, Donald 109
McMahon, Linda 313
Meadows, Mark 79, 83
media integrity, assuring 275
media 121–5
mental illness 64–5
Meta (Facebook) 141, 284–5, 286–7, 288, 293, 296, 298, 340
   changing culture at 286
Mexico 19, 31, 65, 209, 223, 252
Miami, Florida 78
Michigan 64, 82, 84, 89
Middle East 225
military 37–8
Miller, Chad 109
minimizing foreign aid 213–14
Minnesota 58, 122
misogyny 155, 166, 192, 196–7
missing ballots 81–2, 98
Mississippi 309
Missouri 196
Moms for Liberty 165
Mongolia 22
Monmouth University poll 86
Montini, E. J. 113

Index

Morgan, J.P. 212
Mubarak, Hosni 15
Mueller Report 109, 109, 142
Murkowski, Lisa 228
Murthy, Vivek 141
Musk Factor 218–20
Musk, Elon 125, 141, 144, 213, 218, 220,
 231, 278, 282, 285, 286, 287, 337
 and DOGE team 219–20
 "free speech" policy 285
Muslims 31, 45, 55, 57, 64, 69, 187

A Nation of Sheep 351
Nation's Report Card 318
National Archives 38, 78, 93, 117, 177
national attachment 335
 Diversity, Equity, and Inclusion
 (DEI), restoring 338–40
 immigration, embracing 341–3
 Making America Whole Again 343
 mandatory national service 336–8
National Border Patrol Council 113
National Defense Education Act of 1958
 (NDEA) 310
national Gallup poll, 2024 5
National Governors Association 155
National Governors' Conference 311
National Guard 21, 109–10, 210
National Labor Relations Board 111
National Nuclear Security
 Administration 216
National Science Foundation (NSF) 310
National Security Agency 144
National Security Council 108
National Voter Registration Act of 1993
 259, 266
Native Americans 96
NBC poll 69
Nebraska 88, 269 n.3
Nehls, Troy 61

neo-Nazi organizations 66
NetChoice (free speech) 296, 297
Neustadt, Richard 111–12
Nevada 84, 89, 196
New Jersey 259
New York Times v. Sullivan 124
New York Times 81, 139, 220, 277, 278
New York 78, 296
New Zealand 22
news media 275
News, abandoning 138
NewsGuard 279
Newsom, Gavin 210
newspapers 138
 and print media 124
Nicaragua 209
Nixon, Richard 20, 160, 334
No Child Left Behind Act 311, 318
No Kings" 335, 352
non-Christians religions 2, 30, 43, 57,
 58, 67, 147, 153, 157, 187, 318, 342
non-Hispanic Whites 68
nonviolent Black Lives Matter
 movement 57
non-Whites 43, 56, 57, 96, 97, 155, 187,
 189, 312, 318–19, 339, 340, 341
 and non-Christians 187
normalization of hate 57–62
North Atlantic Treaty Organization
 (NATO) 33–4, 223
North Carolina 79
Norway 22, 42, 56, 187
Nye, Joseph Jr. 213

O'Connor, Maureen 118
O'Neill, Tip 139
Oath Keepers 66, 90
Obama, Barack 31, 57, 111, 160,
 189, 197
Obergefell v. Hodges 18

Index

obstruction of justice 109
Office of Management and Budget (OMB) 208, 216, 230
Ohio 61, 257
　voter-initiated pro-abortion laws in 196
Oklahoma 112, 154
Omar, Ilhan 58, 61
One Person, No Vote 257
Orban, Viktor 36
Oregon 261
Organization for Social Media Safety 296
organized institutions 106
Orwell, George 166

Panama Canal 234
pardons 91
parents over teachers 316–17
Paris Climate Accord 34
Paris Climate Agreement 221
Parkland, Florida 146
Parler 140, 141
Patel, Kash 221, 278
Patrick, Tammy 260–1
Patriot Front 66
Peace Corps 337–8
Pelosi, Nancy 63
PEN America 165, 186
Pence, Mike 63, 89, 192, 249
Pennsylvania 84, 145, 258
　stuffed ballot boxes in 82
perfect union, importance of 19–20
Pew Research Center 40, 139, 167, 193, 195, 280, 341, 343
Pharmaceutical Research and Manufacturers of America (PhRMa) 134
Philippines 19, 252
phony state electors 88–9

Pinterest 280
Pittsburgh, Pennsylvania 64
political culture 16–22
political group that reflects your values 347–8
political issues and candidates
　attend campaign rallies for 346–7
political organizations 349–50
　create your own 348–9
political participation
　building communities through 343–4
　contribute money to candidates and/or political organizations 349–50
　create your own political organization 348–9
　join a political group 347–8
　letter writing with public official 344–5
　political campaign rallies 346–7
　political office 350–1
　political postcard teams 345–6
political postcards 345–6
Politifact 281
popular vote
　and electoral vote 248
populism 28–30, 47
post-2024 presidential election 56
Postcards to Swing States 346
power from the people to the government 14–15
presidency 3, 6–7, 27, 30, 32, 34
presidential election 3, 6, 21, 27, 28, 30, 31, 35, 41, 44, 46, 48, 77, 78, 79–82, 83, 84, 85, 86, 89, 90, 91, 92, 93, 94, 95, 97, 108, 109, 116, 117, 119, 121, 123, 124, 125, 142, 145, 162, 177, 178, 179, 181, 183, 187, 189, 192, 194, 196, 197, 198, 205–6, 209, 229, 247, 248, 249, 250, 251, 253, 256, 257, 258, 259, 260, 261, 262,

267–8, 269 n.3, 277–8, 279, 281, 282, 285, 287, 320, 334, 343, 348, 349, 350
  of 2012 30–1
  of 2016 6, 29, 31, 35, 38, 43, 44, 68
  of 2020 3, 6, 7, 20, 21, 22, 28, 31–2, 35, 36, 39, 41, 45–6, 68
  of 2024 27, 31, 32, 34, 36, 39, 41, 45, 46
PRESS act 186
Pressley, Ayanna 60
print media 294
Proctor and Gamble 212
Progressive Party 29
Progressive Reform Movement 309
Progressive States Project 346
Project 2025 207–8, 220, 282, 315
Project 2025 220, 315
Project 2025: Mandate for Leadership 156
Project Citizen 324, 326
Proud Boys 62, 66, 90, 92, 146, 179
public education 3, 13, 18, 153, 195, 275, 307–9
  costs of censorship 167–8
  and democracy 319
  destabilizing 153
  gender 160–2
  perversion of 317–19
  race 157–60
  redefining "public" in 170–1
  religion 162–4
  restricted curriculum 157
  restructured classroom 164
  school book bans 164–6
  teachers on the run 169–70
  Trump's Approach to 155–7
  Trumpist weapon for the future 170–1
Public Hate, growth of 68

public schools
  anti-LGBTQ hate crimes 161
public spiritedness" 135
Public" schools 309
puncturing formal institutions
  abusing the presidency 107–11
  challenging the courts 114–18
  taking on congress 111–14
Putin, Vladimir 36, 143, 192, 224
Putnam, Robert 135

QAnon 67, 137, 294
Qatar 225
Quill, Lawrence 134
Quinnipiac University Poll 69

race 157–60, 165, 189
racial discrimination 22, 63, 95, 96, 253, 254
racism 29, 30, 31, 47, 55, 196–7
radio 138–9, 277, 294
Raffensperger, Brad 86, 87
Ramaswamy, Vivek 60, 219
Rand Research 167, 169
Ravich, Diane 312
Red Sea 223, 224
Reddit 280
refugees 42
reinforcing democracy
  mandatory national service 336–7
  for the people and by the people 333–5
  restoring diversity, equity, and inclusion 338–40
  value of national attachment 335–6
religion 162–4
religious minorities 22
remote work 135–6
replacing values 315
representative democracy 9

371

Index

Republican Convention 35
Republican Party 3
Republican Party National Committee (RNC) 119–21
   Election Integrity Team 121
Republican political party 225
Republicans 5, 13, 39, 41, 43, 46, 58–9, 67, 69–70, 80, 82, 84, 95, 96, 97–8, 111–14, 119–20, 123, 186, 188, 194, 196, 226–8, 254, 258, 263, 268, 278, 282, 349
restricted curriculum 157
   gender 160–2
   race 157–60
   religion 162–4
restructured classroom 164
   costs of censorship 167–8
   school book bans 164–6
   teachers on the run 169–70
Reuters 62, 69, 140
rigged elections 80, 185
Right to Privacy 18
right-wing authoritarianism 131
Right-wing White supremacy groups 145
rioters 45, 90, 91, 125
Robart, James 117
Roe v. Wade 18, 195
Romania 12
Roosevelt, Franklin D. 11–12, 208
Roosevelt, Theodore 11
Rosenstein, Rod 108, 109
Roy, Chip 61
Rozenshtein, Alan 292
Rubio, Marco 221
Rumble 140, 141
Rushin, Stephen 44
Russia 7, 21, 33, 34, 35, 36, 38, 107, 108, 113, 142, 143, 180, 191, 192, 218, 222–3, 224, 298

   beyond employment discrimination 338–9
   immigration, embracing 341–3
   Making America Whole Again 343
   restoring 338–40
   violation of Budapest Memorandum 222

Salvadorians 56
Samoa 22
San Antonio, Texas 64
San Francisco 259
Sanders, Bernie 29–30
satanic rituals 165
Saudi Arabia 298
Save America 120
Scalise, Steve 67
Scharfman, Lottes 333, 335
Schlessinger, Arthur Jr. 334
school book bans 164–6
Schumpeter, Joseph 6
science, technology, engineering, and math (STEM) 321
Second World War 6, 42, 208
Security and Exchange Commission (SEC) 220
segmented democracy" 134
separation of powers 8, 10, 11, 12–13, 20, 116, 226, 230
   checks and balances 11
   presidential power and executive branch 11
September 11, 2001, Twin Tower attack 57
Sessions, Jeff 108, 109
sexuality 165
Sharfman, Lotte 352
Shelby v. Holder 96, 97, 260
Shook, Teresa 348
Shou Chew 61–2

Index

Sierra Club 134
Sinclair Broadcast Company 277
Smith, Jack 93, 94, 117, 125
Smith, Jason 112
Smith, Michael D. 292
social change in America 133
   abandoning news 138
   bye, bye traditional media 138–40
   fewer group attachments 134–5
   hello, social media 140–3
   loneliness 136–7
   working at home 135–6
social media 14, 35, 61, 64–5, 124, 140–3, 279–80, 294
   Chinese interference with 62
   companies 299–300
   controls in other countries 297–8
   corporate irresponsibility 284
   Cultures 284–5
   intentional inaccuracy 281–2
   vs. mainstream media 276
   manipulation of the audience 283
   as news sources 280–1
   problems from relying on 280–1
   vs. traditional media 140–1
Social Security Administration 215, 217
socioeconomic status (SES) environments 318
Software and Information Industry Association (digital content) 296
The Sound and the Fury (Faulkner, William) 166
South Africa 56
South Carolina 79
Southern Poverty Law Center 62
Soviet Union 33
Spain 33
Spanish American War 33
Spencer, Richard 64
Springfield
   immigrants in 188
Stanley, Jason 185
Stanley, Richard 207
State Laws and Lawsuits 296
state voting laws 95, 97
Stefanik, Elise 63
Steinbeck, John 166
Stephanopoulos, George 278
Stone, Roger 115
Stop the Steal 67, 88–9, 249, 294
Strongmen 344
stuffed ballot boxes (also called drop boxes) 82
Supreme Court 339
Switzerland 187

Taiwan 112
teachers on the run 169–70
Telecommunications Act (1996) 14
television 138–9, 277, 294
Temporary Protected Status (TPS) 209
Tennessee 322
Texas 84, 154, 163, 165, 220, 248, 297
theocratic nation 7
Three Percenters 66
TikTok 62, 140, 141, 143, 280, 284, 287, 296–7
Tilden, Samuel J. 248
Title IX 160
tolerance, hate over 44–5
traditional media 138–40
   vs. social media 140–1
Transgender 55, 156, 160, 161–2, 168, 288, 315
Trans-Pacific Partnership 34, 221–2
Truman, Harry S. 183
Trump v. United States 94, 229
Trump vs. Biden presidency
   economy 183–5
   illegal immigration 184

Index

inflation 183-4
manufacturing jobs 183-4
unemployment 183-4
Trump, Donald 6, 111, 208, 248, 251, 256, 282, 339
  abusing presidency 107
  anger-fueled bigotry 57
  approach to public education 155-7
  Article of Impeachment against 114
  attacks on the rule of law 118
  and bigotry 31
  charges against 77
  concept's violation by 12
  COVID-19, mismanagement of 38-9, 181-3
  deep state" bureaucrats, neutralizing 185-6
  defense against prosecution 93-4
  DEI, abolishing programs of 211-13
  deporting undocumented immigrants 209-11
  dismembering federal employment 214-17
  doing away with DEI 211-13
  domination of the Republican party 70-1
  drain the swamp", failure of 224-6
  on election results 6-7
  executive branch, reformulating 206-7
  fallout from the cuts 217-18
  foreign aid program 213-14
  immigrant, deporting undocumented 209
  on immigration 187-9
  indoctrination" 308
  investigation and federal charges against 92-3
  isolationist foreign policy approach 223-4
  mainstream media, neutralizing 186-7
  master puppeteer of American political organizations 125
  minimizing foreign aid 213-14
  mismanagement of COVID-19 pandemic 205
  Musk factor 218-21
  opponents 27
  Presidency, Expanded Power of 208
  puncturing formal institutions 107-18
  racial bigotry of 342
  social media attacks on judges 118
  special Trump retribution for the FBI 218
  Stand on Ukraine issue 222-3
  supporters 22, 27
  taking over informal political institutions 119-25
  treatment of undocumented immigration 211
  Trumpist Twist to Isolationism 221
  2018 executive orders 35
  "us" versus "them" approach 30, 36-7, 43, 79, 155, 168
  victory in the presidential election of 2016 6
  views on African Americans 69
  views on Mexicans 69
  views on Muslims 69
  "weaponization" of government agencies 206-7
Trump, Donald Jr. 225
Trump, Eric 225
Trump, Lara 121
Trump, Mary 277
Trump, Melania 225
  Judges, selection 115
  2016 as president

Index

Trumpism 70, 165
  antidemocratic combination 28
  on the ascent 47–8
  attempt to falsify the georgia presidential vote 86
  authoritarianism 34–6
  bigotry in 56
  corrupt voting machines 86–8
  disease prevention 38–40
  distrust of elites 40–1
  distrust of government 37
  divided America 36–7
  election Interference 85–9
  federal law enforcement 38
  hate and violence through 68
  hate over tolerance 44–5
  hush-money payments to conceal information from the voters 85–6
  insurrection against the capitol 90–2
  isolationism 32–4
  lost faith in democracy 46–7
  military 37–8
  phony state electors 88–9
  populism 28–30
  and public bigotry 68–9
  racism 30–2
  renewed controversy over immigration 41–3
  restructuring of American values 43–4
  rise of 27
  threat to democracy 36
  as "Total control" 105
  Trumpism 2.0 205
  us" against "them" 56, 58
Trumpists 1, 39, 42, 44, 47, 70, 147, 299
  intention of 315
  legal efforts for 2024 election victory 179–81
  separating fact from fiction 98
Truth Social 35, 116, 124, 125, 140, 144, 163, 281
Tuberville, Tommy 60, 62
Turkey 19
Tussman, Joseph 335
Twitter (rebranded as X) 125, 144, 281, 285, 287, 295
2000 Mules" 82
2012 presidential election 30–1, 197
2016 presidential election 6, 29, 31, 35, 38, 43, 44, 262
  campaign 109
  hush-money case 85
  Russian interference in 142
2020 election grievances 80–1
  late tallies 82–4
  missing ballots accusation 81–2
  stuffed ballot boxes 82
2020 presidential election 3, 6, 7, 20, 21, 22, 28, 31–2, 35, 36, 39, 41, 45–6, 77, 78, 97, 124
  election grievances 80–1
  election interference 79
  Gallup Poll 132
  Harris, Kamala, campaign failure reasons 190–7
  hush-money payments 85–6
  hush-money" trial 123
  late tallies 82–4
  missing ballots accusation 81–2
  stuffed ballot boxes 82
  Trump returns to the presidency 177
  winning formula of campaign 183
2024 presidential campaign 27, 31, 32, 34, 36, 39, 41, 45, 46, 77, 142, 156, 189, 196, 205, 277, 350
  Musk Factor in 218–19

375

Index

racial, ethnic, and religious undesirables in 57

Ukraine 33, 108, 112, 113–14, 180, 191, 195, 222–3, 224
Un, Kim Jong 36
unAmerican propaganda" 159
undermined institutions 105
undocumented immigrants 7, 15, 21, 31, 32, 45, 56, 57, 178, 182, 188, 208, 209, 210, 342–3
undocumenteds 113, 188, 209, 210, 342
unitary executive theory 110, 230
unitary system of authority 12
Unite the Right 64
United Nation 222
United Nations Educational, Scientific, and Cultural Organization 221–2
United States 1, 12, 8, 33, 34, 65, 153
   flawed democracy 22
   history of bigotry in 55
   immigrants 252
   Trumpism-like movements 27
   violation of Budapest Memorandum 222–3
United States Capitol Police (USCP) 63–4
United States intelligence community 144
universal participation 335–6
University of Arizona College Republicans 62
Unruh, Jess 349
US Agency for International Development (USAID) programs 208, 213–14
US Census 88, 95, 96, 247–8, 253, 254
US Congress 3, 111
US Constitution 6–7, 11, 12, 13, 17, 20, 35, 116, 194, 226, 309

Article I 13, 107, 110, 226, 228
Article I, Section 8 13, 228
Article I, Section 9 226
Article II 107, 110, 233
Fifteenth Amendment 17
Fifth Amendment 210
First Amendment 13, 14, 121, 124, 162, 163, 212, 279, 291, 292, 294, 297
Fourteenth Amendment of 18, 246, 252, 256, 256, 318
Fourth Amendment 63
Nineteenth Amendments 17, 256, 259, 283
Seventeeth Amendment 265
Tenth Amendment 12, 13, 17
Thirteenth Amendment 17
Twelfth Amendment 248
Twenty-Sixth Amendments 256, 259
Twenty-Third Amendment 88, 247
US Cybersecurity and Infrastructure Security Agency 108, 216
US Department of Education 111, 212, 310
   Trump moves to eliminate 312–14
US Department of Justice 144, 168
US Government Accountability Office in 2022 18
US Immigration and Customs Enforcement (ICE) 232
US Marshalls Service 117
US military 144
US News and World Report 187
US population 247–8
US Postal Service 81–2
US Senate 45, 190, 247
US Supreme Court 3, 11, 14, 18, 20, 46, 66, 95, 160, 162, 210, 226, 349
   on abortion 18

376

Index

US Surgeon General 137, 141, 283
USA Today 139
Utah 158

vaccination 18
values 16–22
Van Alstyne, Marshall W. 292
Van Buren, Martin 190
Vance, J. D. 61, 116, 145, 188, 230, 282
Venezuela 19, 209
Verba, Sidney 137
Vermont 259
video games 64–5
Vietnam War 37, 42
Vindman, Alexander 108
violence 57
Virginia 31, 257
voter
  and election officials 261–3
  fraud 79, 84, 257, 258, 267
  registration 96, 97, 255, 256–8, 266, 268, 269, 343, 346
  suppression 96, 255, 265, 284
  suppression, eliminating 265–6
  turnout 97
votes truly equal and safe 268–9
voting 18
  machines 35
  process 258–9
  requirements 259–60
  rights 95–6, 97, 253, 256, 260, 261
  sites 260–1
Voting Rights Act of 1965 95–6, 253, 256, 260
Vought, Russell 208, 216, 314
vulnerable Society 146–8

Waco, Texas 59–60
Walker, Alice 166

The Wall Street Journal 278, 339–40
Wallace, Chris 145
Walter, Barbara 246
Walton, Reggie 118
Washington Post 123, 139, 165, 168, 169, 182, 278, 279, 282
Washington, DC 64, 78, 79, 94, 116, 117, 229, 261, 339, 349
Watergate 20
weakened sociopolitical fabric 131
weaponization" of government agencies 206–7
Whatley, Michael 120–1
White Christian society 165
White Christians 30, 42, 47, 170, 187
White House 21
White Nationalist 66
White Separatist movement (1880s) 27
White South Africans 56
White supremacist groups 66
Whites and non-Whites 97
Whitmer, Gretchen 64
Willis, Fani 78, 87, 116
Wisconsin 84, 95, 165
  stuffed ballot boxes in 82
World Health Organization 34, 222
Wray, Christopher 218
Wyoming 247, 252

X 125, 140, 141, 142, 144, 145, 213, 219, 220, 230, 258, 278, 281, 282, 284–7, 298
  changing culture at 285–6
  and Meta 287–8
xenophobia 131

Yahoo 136
Yemen
  Houthi rebels in 223–4

Index

YouGov national poll 181, 197
YouGov 136, 181, 189, 192, 197
Youngkin, Glenn 257
YouTube 125, 140, 280

Zeigler, Harmon 8, 47
Zelenskyy, Volodymyr 108, 114
Ziblatt, Daniel 35
Zuckerberg, Mark 284, 286–8